Out of Context

Modernist Literature & Culture

Kevin J. H. Dettmar & Mark Wollaeger, Series Editors

Out of Context

The Uses of Modernist Fiction

Michaela Bronstein

OXFORD
UNIVERSITY PRESS

Oxford University Press is a department of the University of Oxford. It furthers
the University's objective of excellence in research, scholarship, and education
by publishing worldwide. Oxford is a registered trade mark of Oxford University
Press in the UK and certain other countries.

Published in the United States of America by Oxford University Press
198 Madison Avenue, New York, NY 10016, United States of America.

© Oxford University Press 2018

First issued as an Oxford University Press paperback, 2020

Library of Congress Cataloging-in-Publication Data
Names: Bronstein, Michaela, author.
Title: Out of context : the uses of modernist fiction / Michaela Bronstein.
Description: New York, NY : Oxford University Press, [2018] |
Series: Modernist literature and culture | Includes bibliographical references and index.
Identifiers: LCCN 2017038161 | ISBN 9780190655396 (hardback) | ISBN 9780197527009 (paperback)
ISBN 9780190655419 (epub)
Subjects: LCSH: Modernism (Literature) | Fiction—20th century—History and criticism. |
Time in literature. | Narration (Rhetoric) | Discourse analysis, Literary.
Classification: LCC PN56.M54 B75 2018 | DDC 809/.9112—dc23
LC record available at https://lccn.loc.gov/2017038161

To accept one's past—one's history—is not the same as drowning in it; it is learning how to use it.

—James Baldwin, *The Fire Next Time*

How can we "prey" on the rich humanist and democratic heritage in the struggles of other peoples in other times and places to enrich our own?

—Ngũgĩ wa Thiong'o, *Decolonising the Mind*

A shiny new ax, taking a swing at somebody's next year's split-level pinewood pad, bites all the way to the Civil War.

—Ken Kesey, *Sometimes a Great Notion*

Contents

Series Editors' Foreword

"Literature," Ezra Pound remarks in *ABC of Reading*, is "news that stays news." A few decades later his friend William Carlos Williams responded in "Asphodel, That Greeny Flower":

> It is difficult
> to get the news from poems
> yet men die miserably every day
> for lack
> of what is found there.

Late in life, Williams invokes Pound's characteristically blithe assertion in order to acknowledge the space of reading—an often difficult space—in which literature may or may not endure, may or may not translate from one context to another. Locating what poems have to offer in the moment of their reception, Williams anticipates a key aspect of Michaela Bronstein's *Out of Context*, a study of modernist and midcentury fiction that explores the forms writers project into the future and how later writers-as-readers receive and rework them. Bronstein asks, how did Henry James, Joseph Conrad, and William Faulkner solicit the attention of future readers through their formal innovations, and how did James Baldwin, Ngũgĩ wa Thiong'o, and Ken Kesey, respectively, respond to their appeals?

But this account, accurate though it is, does not really get at the radical nature of Bronstein's interventions in modernist studies and contemporary theory. Take the following remark on Conrad, James, and Faulkner: "For these authors, their revolutionary literary forms, the new ways they decide to write novels, are attempts to preserve older epistemologies for the future." Accustomed as modernist scholars are to aligning disruptive formal inventions with instability, skepticism, and critique, Bronstein's claim for the writers' literal conservatism—"conservative in the sense of desiring to find something worth conserving, not in the sense of indiscriminate hostility to change," Bronstein is careful to note—seems almost like a bid to get pushed out of the modernist treehouse. Or what about a claim that "characters with clear individual identities" are not necessarily outmoded conventions but have served, in James and Baldwin and Kesey, as vehicles for asserting a "universalist individualism" that "becomes a way of highlighting a paradoxically shared capacity of individuals to dissent from norms"? Or a call, grounded in modernist fiction, for greater attention to forms of continuity and—dare I say it?—the "transhistorical" element of literature?

Here we arrive at the heart of Bronstein's provocation: the New Modernist Studies has been, like most criticism over the last few decades, resolutely historicist, and Bronstein, finding a sympathetic context in Rita Felski's playful animadversions upon context (it stinks) and Eve Sedgwick's call for reparative reading, questions why the political relevance of art must derive from the context of its production. The transhistorical, Bronstein argues, has too often come to mean timeless and thus withdrawn from pressures of history and politics; but in her usage the "trans" in "transhistorical" signals not "outside of" or "beyond" but "across, through, over, to or on the other side of," as in "transport" (in temporal, aesthetic, and material senses at once), not "transcend." And so the question becomes not how do Conrad's narrative anachronies mimetically reproduce in the reader a sense of modernity's bewildering dislocations ("I can't find my way out of this mall!"), but how do narrative discontinuities afford what Ian Watt called thematic appositions that speak to the future readers Conrad addresses in his preface to *The Nigger of the "Narcissus"*: he wants to make "you" see, and the pronoun carries the force of the transhistorical as a moving across time to encounter an endless (writers always hope) succession of future readers. Conrad's texts found their way to Ngũgĩ in Kenya, who took what he needed from *Heart of Darkness*, *Nostromo*, and *Under Western Eyes* and left the rest (including the now unspeakable title of the novel cited a moment ago) in order to use Conrad's techniques to address Kenyan independence and its prospects for long-term decolonization. What travels, then, is not content but forms, forms that, anticipating the evaporation of their contents, "do not direct our attention toward an absence but toward the variety of possible substances the container might hold."

The skeptical or suspicious reader who currently dominates the profession could pounce here on what may seem a clear embrace of empty formalism. But Bronstein is not herself letting politics evaporate along with the contents of her modernist trio's forms: the paired structure of her argument, in which the midcentury writers repurpose modernist forms for new progressive ends, traces an arc from authors situated securely as elites to those "who are marked by their lack of or opposition to social privilege." Baldwin, for instance, finds the notion of individualism in James useful for countering racial prejudice. So the point here is not to eliminate the kind of political work performed by critique, in which exposure of ideological blind spots makes possible, one hopes, a more inclusive future. The task is rather to think more carefully about the ways in which texts, in this case modernist novels, open themselves to the future, and how the present looks to the past in the process of imagining new futures. As Bronstein acutely remarks, "We have more theories about the relation between past and present than we do about the relation between present and future." Indeed, politics is not possible without commitment: to the values one hopes to see embraced in the future, to the shape of a new future. Demoting the hermeneutics of suspicion need not amount to adopting a more "modest" approach to the project of criticism.

One of Bronstein's ambitious aims is to rescue influence study from the shadows of backwardness and to redeploy it, rethought, as alternative to critique. Countering common criticisms of influence, Bronstein argues effectively for its methodological value: influence study grasps the unexpected, idiosyncratic response of one author to another (and Bronstein's ear for stylistic nuance is extraordinary); it understands authors as both agents and objects of the agency of others; and it grasps texts as they are read, and reading itself as at once passive and transformative. The transhistorical, the universal, and influence study: the new sexy.

This is the last book in the Modernist Literature and Culture series. We founded the series a decade ago in part because no series in modernism existed at the time. We also wanted to provide a forum for rethinking the literary within the broader spectrum of aesthetic and historical experiences demanded by the New Modernist Studies. The aesthetic experience of reading, of paying close attention to shifting resonances and jostling codes, what Roland Barthes called the rustle of language, while also letting the affordances of theory generalize such experiences in order to speak across disciplines—this has always been part of what we sought. For this reason, among many others, we are truly delighted to seal the series with this book, and this foreword, nearly, with Bronstein's words:

> Seeking aesthetic contact with the future . . . is not a way of evading the messy issues of one's own time, but of attempting to discern within one's present that which is potentially relevant to other times. . . . By gaining distance on events, by replacing the chaotic flux of experience with right names and larger patterns, they become potentially shared – not just with others, but with the unknowable readers and peoples of the future.

Yes.

MARK WOLLAEGER
KEVIN DETTMAR

Acknowledgments

Despite my desire to trouble the reflexive appeal to "context" in literary studies, I want only to highlight, rather than to efface, the contexts in which this book took shape. Scientists sometimes publish papers with thousands of listed authors; this acknowledgments page stands in for the many acts of collaborative work concealed by the single name on the cover of this book.

This began to be something like a book during my years at Yale. My two indefatigable advisors helped me on the long and often pathless road from early ideas to real arguments. Ruth Yeazell never hesitated to ask, "Do you really mean that?" when I had chosen the wrong words, and usually had a pretty good idea of the right ones. Pericles Lewis helped me find my way into the broader world of modernist studies. As my third reader, Paul Grimstad brought both a sharp critical eye and excitement about some of my ideas that often preceded my own ability to see what was exciting about them. I'm also grateful for the comments made by my external readers Langdon Hammer, Stefanie Markovitz, and Margaret Homans, which propelled me into the first of many rounds of revision. Conversations and emails with Paul Fry and Anthony Reed helped me through crucial moments of confusion. Fred Strebeigh taught me how to teach others to write, and in the process taught me again how to read.

The members of my graduate cohort made me the scholar I am today; but they also show how, in the happiest possible sense, the boundaries between friends and colleagues can disappear. Sam Alexander, Nathan Suhr-Sytsma, and Dave Gorin are the best of both. Jeanne-Marie Jackson and I hammered out our opinions together on narrative form and more over lunches, dinners, and drinks for years. All books are the products of institutions as well as individuals; but all institutions are made up of individuals: the Modernist Dissertation Working Group was the first audience for these ideas and always a wise one; its members included Sam Cross, Tony Domestico, Colin Gillis, Elyse Graham, Jesse Schotter, and Emily Setina. The Yale Twentieth- and Twenty-First Century Colloquium, which during my own time at Yale gained that second, awkward century, always provided a rich environment for the nurturing (and the pruning) of ideas.

At Harvard and the Society of Fellows I owe particular thanks to Elaine Scarry, who read the entire manuscript and without whom I might never have figured out what the first chapter of this book would be. Conversations with Bill Todd helped me think outside the confines of anglophone culture. Marta Figlerowicz and Len Gutkin read the manuscript and generally constituted the scholarly texture of my life for years. Michael Weinstein and Daniel Williams not only helped work out ideas as the brilliant people they are, but also found me audiences for my work at various Harvard colloquia; thanks to them, the colloquium members, and the members of the Mahindra Humanities Center Modernism Seminar. I can't begin to sort out the myriad ways in which my fellow Fellows, in literature and beyond, helped me sort out these ideas, but I'm pretty sure all of the following people were part of it: Julien Ayroles, Yvonne Chen, Will Cheng, Clay Cordova, Stephanie Dick, Ben Golub, Kevin Holden, Daniel Juette, Abhishek Kaicker, Florian Klinger, Scott Kominers, and Maura Smyth. I talked out parts of this book and everything else in life with Patrick Pritchett on I-90 between Boston and Amherst on a weekly basis.

Thank you to all my colleagues at Stanford. Particular thanks to Alex Woloch, whose guidance helped make my first year at a new institution a time when I actually could accomplish things like finishing this book. Mark McGurl read parts of the manuscript in the final stages. I have been saved from numerous embarrassments by my research assistant Casey Patterson, who found my misquotations and errors, as well as offering some wise last-minute suggestions. I also benefitted from the friendship and thoughts of Angèle Christin, Rowan Dorin, Marci Kwon, and David Pedulla.

In the most immediate sense, this book would not appear without Kevin Dettmar and Mark Wollaeger: thanks to them for inviting me to be part of this eminent series and for guiding me through this process. Thanks, also, to the anonymous readers at Oxford University Press for their thoughtful responses, as well as the editors and copy-editors who helped turn manuscript into physical object.

Thanks to *Modern Language Quarterly*, the *Journal of Modern Literature*, and *Essays in Criticism* for permission to reprint pieces of analysis I've published with them—and to the editors and readers of these journals for improving my ideas immeasurably. I'd also like to express my gratitude to Tiana M. Taliep at the

Schomburg Center for Research in Black Culture for helping me arrange access at the last minute to the newly acquired James Baldwin archives. In addition, some of the archival research in this book was generously supported by Harvard's Milton Fund.

Rhiannon Bronstein read many of these chapters, and always reminded me not just to keep an audience outside academia in mind, but also occasionally to get outside and go hiking, which almost certainly made this book better in untraceable ways.

I owe Elliott Bronstein and Gitte Folz not just life, but books: I would never have been in grad school had they not, throughout my youth, been willing not just to suggest the next book to devour but to talk through all my wonderings and opinions on reading, and every other subject, and to send me off to study English.

Chris Grobe gave me some of the best lines in this book, as well as most of the best things in my life for the last almost-a-decade. This book is for him.

Out of Context

Introduction

Works for Other Times

"What for do we nail down the dead?"
     The boy barely paused, tapping out each head with two neat strokes. "It's so the horrible old buggers don't spring out and chase us."
     He knows different now. It's the living that turn and chase the dead. The long bones and skulls are tumbled from their shrouds, and words like stones thrust into their rattling mouths: we edit their writings, we rewrite their lives.

—Hilary Mantel, *Wolf Hall*

What power does the past hold over the present? And what, conversely, can the present do to the past? We're haunted by fears of a zombie canon, popping the nails out of its coffin and unnaturally shuffling forward into a future that is not its own, swarming over and stifling the vitality of the present.[1] The villains of today's fantasy novels seek immortality; the heroes accept death.[2] The past is another country; we, as critics, dutifully acknowledge our objects of study as its citizens and seek to understand the differences of its culture. Fearfully, we historicize our novels: we confine them and their meanings to their moments of production; we nail them down.

And yet the past, also, can do nothing. It's the living that turn and chase the dead, thinks the protagonist of Hilary Mantel's novel, implicitly commenting on her work as the author of historical fiction. The past's power is limited to the ways it is re-enacted, reused, repurposed, and reimagined by the present. The literary past has power only as it is read and thought through today, or permeates ongoing cultural practices. And so we as critics also resurrect these foreign entities; we shake their dead hands and pose smiling with them for our students.

So: on one side, the literary past has a sinister power; on the other side, it is helpless. The literary aspiration to produce lasting works of art, the dream of a novel that belongs to the future as well as its present, means that novels need us as readers. In turn we invite them into our minds: we seek their works as symbols of historical distance, or as transhistorically timeless, or relevant in some way to our particular present, or perhaps just as sources of exciting emotional and intellectual experiences. This book is a study of these shifting relations—the ways authors strategize to enlist the unknowable readers of the future as their audience; the ways those future readers turn the past to suit new purposes.

As critics, and as readers, we have no choice but to turn and chase the dead. Yet the dead are chasing us too. Sometimes we collide in a lover's embrace; sometimes we settle for wary distance or a staid handshake. At other times the chase becomes that of predator and prey. But it is harder than it seems to tell one from another.

Forms of the Transhistorical

This book is about the encounter between texts and readers across time—and the ways that encounter shapes the ongoing production and life of literature. The prospect of future audiences, not only present ones, drives the development of literary forms. Writing for the future is building a bridge aimed directly into an impenetrable fog: the future forces writers both to confront the possibility of radical difference from the present and to theorize what kinds of continuities might nevertheless persist. The case study before me is literary modernism—a field at one time stigmatized as disregarding history in favor of self-contained art objects, and more recently lauded on the grounds of its engagement with the complex political discourses of its own time. Yet, this book will show, many key examples of modernism's apparent turns away from history are not a deflection of politics in favor of art, but instead an openness to the unknowable, a vulnerability before the unpredictable politics of the future.

To begin: when we make use of the literary past, we often waver silently between seeing it as bound in its time and as aimed at us as its future. Is the literary past the object of our critique and correction? Or is it a tool for our use?

One example: in 2005, Cynthia Ozick published a brief short story entitled "An (Unfortunate) Interview with Henry James." In it, a twenty-first-century woman interviews James in the afterlife. Ozick's pastiche of his style is merciless, as is the interviewer's interrogation:

> JAMES (*seating himself before a finely tiled fireplace, and motioning for the visitor to join him there*): I must beg your pardon. I discover myself increasingly perplexed by the ever-accelerating extrusions of advanced women—
>
> INTERVIEWER (*interrupting*): You don't like us. You were opinionated enough about all that in *The Bostonians*. (16)

Or let's look at it the other way: five years later, Ozick offered the novel *Foreign Bodies*, an updating of James's *The Ambassadors*, set in 1950s Paris and New York. The style, now, is Jamesian, but not cruelly so. Here the protagonist approaches a door and contemplates the doorbell:

> Noiselessness behind the door, a ferocity of expectation—herself caught in a fixity, a movie-still excised from a scene of crisis, the frozen moment of her finger lifted, approaching the button, the button that was about to violate the silence behind the door (Iris's lifted finger seconds before it fell blindly on a violated key). (52)

There are many familiar Jamesian elements in this sentence. Ozick's language is a hair more abstract than we might expect ("Noiselessness" over *silence*; "a ferocity of expectation" rather than *fiercely* or *expecting*; "caught in a fixity" over *fixed*). There is, most obviously, a disproportionate emphasis on the violation of private space—the thought of ringing a doorbell or striking a piano key becomes an act of callous violence.

Yet this is not satire, not the voice of the short story with its comical alliteration ("ever-accelerating extrusions"). It is also much less obviously identifiable as Jamesian, though the plot itself is evident to any reader of *The Ambassadors* as James's.[3] Ozick's short story highlights the impossible gaps and frictions between eras: the stylistic contrast between the interviewer's abrupt colloquialisms and James's absurdly elevated involutions neatly aligns with the historical changes the characters discuss. The novel, on the other hand, blurs all these: Jamesian elevation and abstraction no longer stand out as absurd; the plot of *The Ambassadors* becomes as portable as any of the elements of folklore. As in the short story, on some level the politics have changed—rather than nineteenth-century French gender norms and American class dynamics, Ozick's characters confront mid-twentieth-century American Jewish identity and the plight of postwar refugees in Europe. The literary forms, however, no longer align with specific eras; the softer pastiche seems to suggest that the style of James might equally address both historical moments.

If the short story uses the conceit of a transhistorical space—the afterlife—to set historical periods against one another, the novel is less explicit about how the literary past is called into play. One could, after all, read *Foreign Bodies* without any knowledge of *The Ambassadors*. "An (Unfortunate) Interview" relies on its readers having at least a vague sense of James as a canonical Dead White Man who wrote in an old-fashioned style; *Foreign Bodies* does not. One way of describing the difference is that the short story relies on keeping James fixed in his historical moment, on seeing him as a reflection of it. The novel, by contrast, strips that away, leaving echoes of James for those who might recognize them, but treating his work as a source for particular literary effects that are not especially tied to his own era. In one piece, Ozick implies an irreducible gulf across periods that is reflected in contrasting literary styles; in the other, she implies that literary style and form are the elements of the literary past that seamlessly and tacitly become part of new contexts.

Modernist literature and criticism have a particularly complex relationship with accounts of dramatic rupture in both the literary and the historical sphere. On the one hand modernist writers famously asserted the uniqueness of their own present moment, glorying in its rupture from the past—insisting both that "human character changed," in Virginia Woolf's famous formulation (*Essays* III.421), and that literature, too, would rebel against its own norms in the service of a new openness to the diverse realities of modern life. The texts and the times move in lockstep. Criticism valorizes this modernism as a period of disrupted expectations, of frustration of norms, and of literary responsiveness and respect for rapidly changing history. Ozick's short story obviously trades on these paradigms—James's style and his ideas are equally out of date. The new style of the past becomes today's archaism.

On the other hand, as Rod Rosenquist puts it, "Modernist literature aimed to be new, but also to *stay* new" (2). Modernism is also a period of literary innovation turned, paradoxically, to assertions of continuity between past, present, and future; of insistence on enduring meaning and pattern underlying the apparently chaotic surface of reality; and of concentrated efforts to affirm long-held values and worldviews. From Eliot's "Tradition and the Individual Talent" through Joseph Frank's "Spatial Form" in 1945, where modernist literature transforms "the time-world of history into the timeless world of myth" (653), and onward, modernist form seems to reject time: it awakens from the nightmare of history; it gathers the fragments of many times and places to get beyond all of their local particulars.[4]

These two conceptions primarily disagree about the role of art in relation to history—the rejection of time, after all, is also an acknowledgment that, on the surface, the world appears to be rapidly changing, and an aesthetic intervention is needed in order to make sense of it. Apparent historical rupture is the crisis to which modernist art responds in all its diverse forms.[5] The different artistic responses to it, however, have cycled in and out of critical interest over time. The transhistorical theme generally holds less excitement in modernist studies today, which for the most part is as normatively historicist a field as any in English literary studies. When critics valorize modernism, they tend to do so by portraying it as an aesthetic response to the singularity of historical moments.

Just as integral to modernism, however, is a perspective we can glean from Ozick's novel, in which timelessness isn't quite the right term for what it means for art to be transhistorical. After all, Ozick seems deeply invested in historical particulars—in American Jewish identity, in the aftermath of World War II that provides crucial aspects of the novel's plot. James's form may swing free from its original context, but only in order to engage with a different historical moment. Her style and plot point to continuities in history and identity not to escape history but to illuminate it.

Critics have recently been calling for renewed attention to the transhistorical element of literary art. As Rita Felski puts it, "We cannot close our eyes to the historicity of art works, and yet we sorely need alternatives to seeing them as transcendentally timeless on the one hand and imprisoned in their moment of origin on the other" (*Limits* 154). Paul Armstrong similarly diagnoses a "contextualist consensus" due to which "the phenomenology of reception is still widely regarded as old-fashioned and passé" ("In Defense" 87). As these defenders of the transhistorical suggest, the problem is at least in part a kind of guilt by association, a feeling that transhistorical art had its day, and that its day was blind to important excluded contexts and social realities. To attend to the transhistorical seems to risk negating the historical.

Modernist criticism provides ample evidence for this: all those figures of art as an escape from time, art as autonomously ahistorical. Frank suggested that for the modernist author, "past and present are seen spatially, locked in a timeless unity which . . . eliminates any feeling of historical sequence by the very act of juxtaposition" (653). In other words, erasing the temporality of reading—imagining readers able to hold the whole work in their minds at once—is also a way of erasing the temporal process of history. This is the vision of modernism that the New Modernist Studies has persistently critiqued, as Brian Glavey notes: "Critics have tended to divide early-twentieth-century aesthetic production into good and bad modernisms: on the one hand a movement wholly devoted to subversion and provocation, on the other an elitist set piece of well-wrought urns" (750). Frank's spatial form, with its "timeless unity," looks like the kind of apolitical, ahistorical modernism Glavey is describing. Numerous critics—Glavey among them—have recently begun the work of recuperating the idea of the autonomous art object as politically useful.[6] Ozick's short story, for instance, deploys the afterlife—which is a kind of autonomous transhistorical space—precisely in order to comment on and highlight historical difference.

Despite critics and writers like Ozick, modernism's tendency to emphasize the importance of art lasting beyond its own time has become a troubled legacy today. We reflexively assume that the political dimensions of a work are in the way it is embedded in its moment of production; most famously, we *always historicize!* Continued critical interest in canonical modernism is both a habit and a source of anxiety. Take the conclusion to Jed Esty's *Unseasonable Youth*, which is not explicitly about the question of literary persistence, but turns to the subject at the end:

> The novels of Wilde, Conrad, Woolf, and Joyce constitute a somewhat domesticated modernism of the North American curriculum—the books many of us continue, rather unexperimentally, to read, love, and teach. But they are, however familiar now, still stunning narrative experiments. . . . To my view, that is the source of their ongoing relevance and resonance as historical artifacts marked by a certain moment in the history of forms and social formations, but also as irreducible narrative works in their own right, unexhausted by analysis and allegorization. (213)

The reflexively self-deprecating hedging ("somewhat domesticated," "rather unexperimentally," "however familiar") that opens this passage suggests the discomfort with which we view the transtemporal persistence of artworks. The reasons for this may be glimpsed in the two alternatives he presents at the end, which might be summed up, or perhaps caricatured, as historicism and aesthetic autonomy. What is missing is the notion that the transhistorical life of modernist works is a series of connections to later histories and later literary moments and movements.

Looking at these moments—Ozick is one of them—allows us to re-evaluate modernism's transhistorical aspirations—their successes, and their consequences. Scholars of modernism already have a model in front of us: the well-known transnational turn in the New Modernist Studies, which invigorated a paradigm—the transnational—by extricating it from a maligned older version—cosmopolitanism. Previous ideas of the cosmopolitan in literary studies seemed to emphasize the way an individual might transcend national limits.[7] New transnational critics attend closely to the locally embedded contexts of their writers' and readers' international circuits.[8] Similarly, the transhistorical need not be identified as a transcendence of time and history. A work's journey across national and temporal boundaries does not mark it as a cosmopolitan citizen of no era and every era at once. Doug Mao and Rebecca Walkowitz wrote in "The New Modernist Studies" for *PMLA* that while "temporal expansion has certainly been important in the study of literary modernism . . . the spatial and vertical expansions have been more momentous" (738). This is still true a decade later: even where critics press across temporal boundaries, we lack theories of the crossing to compare with those we have for transnational work. Isabel Hofmeyr's study of John Bunyan's reception and circulation in Africa from the seventeenth century to the twentieth, for instance, tells a compelling transhistorical history. But Hofmeyr consistently frames her analysis in terms of national borders wherever she can rather than temporal ones: time is the unexamined frame for a process of global "migration" that just happens to span three centuries (1). This points to a missing paradigm in critical methodologies: after all, if the past is another country, it is not one to which we can expatriate ourselves; equally, we are all, inevitably, immigrants to the future— or refugees from the past. Temporal boundaries interact with, but are not metaphorically captured by, spatialized imagery. David James and Urmila Seshagiri have recently called for reinvigorating the old mid-century period boundary of modernism, precisely in order to grasp the sense of modernism as being *in the past*, and exerting influence in the same way that events of history still do on the present (88).

Transnational comparisons often already have temporal dimensions. Paul Saint-Amour, for instance, demonstrates that the violence of imperial rule in the interwar period foreshadowed the violence of World War II: "Note how space and time lace up here, with the colony knotted into an active violence of the continuous present, the metropolis into a future or future-conditional violence" (53). Looking across national borders is looking across time periods: the colonial present is London's future. For Saint-Amour, interwar modernist narrative forms reflect a state of *anticipation*—they look not toward their own present, but to the advent of imprecisely known futures. Literature, in other words, always implies not only its past but a variety of possible futures.

To read transhistorically is neither to read ahistorically nor to suggest that art is in some way "universal." The transhistorical, in this sense, does not merely oppose the historical; it is its own form of history. This book is a study of literature's gestures toward the past and future not as a flight from historical relevance, but as an invitation to interaction with multiple historical moments. Literature is embedded in history, but not always and only the history of its moment of production. It makes an aesthetic appeal to the future, but an appeal that has political uses. And sometimes, in order to see the transhistorical uses of a text, it's necessary to allow it to break free of its context, so that a new context can take shape. Toni Morrison, whose long history of grappling with and repurposing Faulkner is well known, was asked in 1994 how she as a young reader had responded to "racial stereotypes in the classics of American literature."[9] She said simply, "I skipped that part. Read over it. Because I loved those books. I loved them" (*Conversations* 100–101). To make these novels her own, for a time, she had not to restore the ugly contexts their stereotypes point to, but to erase them. And she had to rewrite them, to take from them what she loved and skip what she rejected. A sense of the *pastness* of Faulkner, of his being, on some level, at the mercy of the future readers who disaggregate the different features of his works and read them for whatever is most useful, is precisely what makes him available in the future represented by Morrison.

Caroline Levine's emphasis on the "portable" (7) qualities of literary forms is useful here: to talk about literary forms sometimes requires displacing them from history, but only in order to see what new places they make for themselves—or are made for them. In order to understand the diverse uses texts find after their moment of production, we need to see what their forms look like outside that moment: forms, in other words, need a little bit of room to breathe as their abstract selves before we fix them down into new political contexts and meanings. Literary forms, stripped of their political contexts and "original" meanings, are often precisely the most useful things about the texts of the past for the readers of the future, whether or not those readers are other authors. Ozick's "(Unfortunate) Interview" ends with James imperiously ordering his visitor out: "You and I are not, cannot, shall never be, on the same page!" (17)—of history, it seems. Calling James to account for what he thought about (and how he behaved) with women leads only to the breakdown of communication, to the estrangement between eras and literary styles. Yet in *Foreign Bodies*, Ozick takes Jamesian semantic and syntactical habits, plot patterns, and more as empty vessels for a thematics and political commentary all her own that is not dependent on James for its meaning.

Wolfgang Iser wrote the history of the English novel as a sequence of formal developments surrounding the idea of the *gap*—blank spaces in the text that readers are scripted, with greater or lesser degrees of freedom, to fill in (*Implied*). The uses made of their predecessors by authors like Ozick and Morrison suggest that the act of reading is also a process by which readers *make* gaps—scouring from texts the detritus of the past in order to expose underlying contours. What they expose, in this book, are literary forms. Forms are transhistorical: the feel of texts opening up to a broad vision of society is more persistent—and more useful—than any particular vision. The gaps are not *merely* formal, not merely algorithms that every reader will follow in an identical way, but, like the text of a play, deliberately open to new interpretations and uses in new times and places.[10] To borrow Wai Chee Dimock's phrasing: the forms that constitute the deep time of literary history are forms of readership.[11]

Recuperative Modernism

Morrison and Ozick see the literary forms of the past as extractable. If they want, they can make a work bear only the history they find useful. One of the arguments of this book is that many aspects of modernist aesthetic innovation were designed precisely for this purpose.

As Conrad famously put it in the preface to *The Nigger of the "Narcissus"*, "The changing wisdom of successive generations discards ideas, questions facts, demolishes theories. But the artist appeals to that part of our being which is . . . more permanently enduring" (viii). The now-unspeakable title of the novella, of course, testifies to the precariousness of any effort to anticipate what will or won't endure; but the preface testifies to the seriousness with which theorizing the novel as art during this period required theorizing what, exactly, was persistent about human existence—what was likely to last, rather than what would be discarded, questioned, demolished by the future. The preface takes the ruptures of history for granted; but it suggests that the work of the artist is about what might remain on the other side of the shock. The modernist novel's bid to be taken seriously as an art form, in other words, requires both a confrontation with the changes of history and a commitment to think beyond the present. To theorize art as enduring requires theorizing what exactly will endure about the present and what will not, requires seeing the continuities as well as the divisions of history.[12]

The particular modernist authors I examine in this book are ones whose works seem to anticipate the evaporation of their contexts. Their literary forms are empty vessels—but they direct our attention not toward an absence but toward the variety of possible substances the container might hold. In the authors I study here, their bids to write lasting art often take the form of dramatizing the conversion of historical detail into abstraction or generalization. James worries incessantly about the artist's responsibility to give a scene "its right name, its formula, for convenient use" (*The American Scene* 579). Faulkner and Conrad always seem to begin their sentences with a character's specific situation and end with the mortality of mankind.

In some ways, this looks like that ugly older conception of modernism, with its timelessness and refusal of the historical. The presupposition that the politically valuable "aesthetic effects" are those that produce "destabilization, defamiliarization, and disruption" (Glavey 750) still has a strong hold in modernist studies, and part of the reason, I will argue in this book, is that those effects are the ones that bind our critical attention ever more tightly to context. By emphasizing a process of rupture and reversal, these effects are predicated on a sharp distinction between before and after, on the uniqueness of the moment at which the work of art appears and the irrevocability of the transformation represented by that moment. Aesthetic destabilization comes to seem an inevitable reflection of historical rupture.

As the defenders of spatiality and autonomy point out, disruption certainly isn't the only way of engaging with historical context. Nevertheless, I'm going to question instead the underlying principle: why is the context of production the source of the political relevance of art? There's another path toward the transhistorical that does not require autonomy and the erasure of time at all. The transhistorical dimension of art need not be timelessness, but instead can negotiate connections and relationships across the barriers of time: rather than fleeing the present, we can see authors as chasing the future. And rather than seek spatial form as an emblem of the erasure of the temporality of reading, these novels revel in the temporal dimension of reading as a microcosm of the drawn-out temporality of reception. They do not imagine masterly analytical readers, like Joyce's "professors" kept "busy for centuries" by the mysteries of *Ulysses* (qtd. in Ellmann 521). Instead, they make use of the immersive, irreversibly temporal process of experiencing a novel to find—and create—similarities between present and future.

Seeing modernism's orientation toward the future as responsive, as calculated vulnerability to repurposing, rather than static and domineering, also requires alternatives to the rupture model of modernism's relationship with the past.[13] Woolf's suggestion that "on or about December 1910 human character changed" sees a direct line between character and literature: she goes on to declare, "All human relations have shifted—those between masters and servants, husbands and wives, parents and children. And when human relations change there is at the same time a change in religion, conduct, politics and literature" (*Essays* III.421–422). James, Conrad, and Faulkner, the three authors I highlight here, have long been assimilated to an analysis of the modernist novel that privileges Woolf's formulation of shocking distance from the past: ideas of instability, of character as incoherent and life as incomprehensible, come to seem the most important and exciting aspects of their work. In this reading, their formal innovations become ways of reflecting a new vision of the world by which old conventions—of an authoritative narrator, of characters with clear individual identities—have become untenable. But this assimilation obscures the real nature of the formal devices with which they address their dilemmas: these authors all suggest alternatives to the critical commonplace that associates formal innovation and social change. Their literary experiments are acts of preservation, searching examinations of what ought to be preserved and repaired from the present and the past. These literary techniques are exciting; they are different; yet they are also conservative in the sense of desiring to find something worth conserving, not in the sense of indiscriminate hostility to change.

Like the other modernists, James, Conrad, and Faulkner do feel a rupture with the past: the world seems different, but the difference may not, they suggest, be as significant as it seems. Rather than accepting the state of the new world, they scrutinize and question it, seeking to sort out something beyond the mere "changing wisdom" that the next revolution will overturn. Their modernism is *recuperative*: they develop their techniques to avoid what they see as both a false sense of difference between modern life and that which has preceded it (human nature has changed), and an equally false idea that the old outlooks were never true and new ones have exposed their lies (we now understand human nature better and differently than we used to). These writers aren't certain that the present understands more than the past, and anticipate yet more change to come. They recuperate the past in order to access the future, to look to and beyond the next bends and forks of history. In other words, shoring fragments against ruins, in Eliot's famous phrase, is not an intrinsically conservative position—particularly not if the ruined status of the present is not taken as an index to some ideal past.

If it might seem merely a truism to describe modernism as yearning for an apparently impossible certainty, as anxious about social change, and as deeply invested in the production of transhistorical art, the rest of this book will testify that these traits all have politically progressive and occasionally radical uses that are only visible when the novels are removed from, rather than enmeshed in, their context of production. Even a few years later, the readers of James and Conrad did not see them as prophets of destabilizing skepticism. Woolf, for instance, constructs both Conrad and James as defenders of an old order, though always with praise. More recently, however, critics have tended to see both writers as stepping stones on the path to Woolf and Joyce, emphasizing what seems disruptive while acknowledging and dismissing their recuperative elements as backward artifacts of their time. Yet their recuperative outlooks are, I will show, integral to the parts of their projects that seem most forward-looking and have been most susceptible to radical appropriations. The same is true of Faulkner—though the critical problem is somewhat different.[14] Faulkner demonstrates that such recuperative impulses persist even after the revolution wrought by Joyce, and in the presence of Joycean influence. Recuperation is not limited to "early modernism," and the phenomena I will analyze in James and Conrad neither end there nor are cast aside by the modernism of the 1920s and 1930s.[15] The mid-century and contemporary repurposers of modernism testify to the persistence of recuperation on both sides of the Atlantic and beyond the changes wrought by the 1920s.

The chronological gaps between these authors also reveal the way attitudes toward the novel as art became naturalized over time. James set himself to making the case that the novel *ought* to be aimed at the future, that it could be a lasting art form. Conrad articulated what, in particular, he thought was lasting across historical moments, to devise a pathway the novelist could count on. And Faulkner, looking back two decades after his own high modernist experiments, talks about the dramas of failure and sacrifice of the artist as themselves his route to immortality.

For these authors, their revolutionary literary forms, the new ways they decide to write novels, are attempts to preserve older epistemologies for the future. In chapter 1, for instance, I'll show how the phrase "everything is relative" turns into a claim for why some things are less relative than others. The central chapters of the book show how formal experimentation works to recuperate possible forms of knowledge and commitment: James restricts the novel to the point of view of characters not to decry the assumption of authorial omniscience, but because by doing so he can show how characters' searching minds can eventually replace an omniscient narratorial perspective; Conrad scrambles time not to represent the confusions of life but because he can replace chronology with a more meaningful order. And Faulkner disrupts narrative conventions in order to represent both the inevitability and the positive value of imposing an interpretation on the raw material of experience.

All these authors *are* experimentalists—they all write works that seem strange, at odds with the way we might expect stories to be told. Whereas, for instance, E. M. Forster reacts to modernity by holding on to a relatively traditional style of narration and frustrating the traditions of plotting, James, Conrad, and Faulkner choose to make their writing alien in form and style. With few exceptions every work I treat at length in this book is formally challenging in an ostentatious and difficult way, is the kind of novel where even the best students will worry about not understanding enough, or missing something crucial. The difficulties of these books are conventionally read as compelling readerly awareness of the way the novels resist understanding and question familiar epistemologies. I argue instead that difficulty is a way of forcing readers to confront what their investments are and forming new commitments: of isolating what they are reading for, deprived of the stable content in which these investments might normally be embodied.

Critics tend to be skeptical of the artistic impulses of recuperative modernism today. These authors seem to look backward: James loves to believe in an ideal of whole, vivid, essential character; Conrad yearns toward abstractions and grandiose evocations of the possibility of human heroism; and Faulkner evokes the way people desire to find (or create) abstract meanings and patterns in their lives. This all sounds like what Greg Barnhisel describes as "Cold War modernism," a particular mid-century reception history for modernist art: "Art should be autonomous from the practice of daily life, not subject to evaluation by social or political criteria . . . with a celebration of the virtues of freedom and the assertion that the individual is sovereign" (3). This, he says was a view that made modernist works "safe for consumption by American middle-class audiences" (4). In this light, recuperative modernism's uses and reception seems intensely unpromising—even reactionary.

But the modernists' erasure of their own "social and political" context looks different when we see it as openness to the future, as part of the process by which Morrison, for instance, reimagines the past as useful to her. And if we want to talk about the lasting impact of Faulkner, we need to see what uses the turns toward the abstract and apolitical have, not just what they hide; removing context makes room for the future to pour in. The chapters of this book pair canonical modernists with mid-century authors who affiliated with them. All of the later authors are more politically radical, and none of them are what the phrase "American middle-class audiences" calls to mind. The uses they make of these forms shows that the well-trodden critical passageways between literary form and politics need some rearranging. James Baldwin's adaptation of Jamesian characterization, for instance, celebrates both "freedom" and "the individual" in order to demand recognition of the diversity of black American identities; those who are struggling to assert an identity aren't always moved to deconstruct the category.[16] Political commitment and action often requires some degree of epistemological stability. Recuperative modernism doesn't last because it questions the reality of character, or the possibility of knowing anything; its skepticism certainly isn't the appeal for those radical and countercultural authors who found it generative. Destabilizing old commitments feels urgent in some moments; in others, forging new ones feels more crucial. Later writers turn toward recuperative modernism because, even after skepticism, ideals and forms of commitment have uses and moments where critique does not. As Lauren Berlant says, "Any action of making a claim on the present involves bruising processes of detachment from anchors in the world, along with optimistic projections of a world that is worth our attachment to it" (*Cruel Optimism* 263).

This book is a study of such strategies of recuperation and commitment, and their later repurposings. In various ways, the recuperative modernists, like other writers from many periods, resisted their own time—innovated not in order to bring literature into closer contact with the teeming realities of modern experience, but in order to assert that however different they may look, the present and the past shared features. And continuity between past and present suggested the possibility of continuity between present and future—suggested the ways that art might outlast its own time.

Recuperation and Critique

We have more theories about the relation between past and present than we do about the relation between present and future. More positive connections between past and present seem to be on the rise in critical discourse lately. How literary critics feel about our objects of study has become ever more central to the debates of the profession in the last few decades. Eve Sedgwick called in 1995 for "reparative reading" to replace "paranoid reading"; Michael Warner demanded in 2004 that awareness of "uncritical reading" expose the hidden norms of "critical reading." 2009 saw the advent of "surface reading": Sharon Marcus and Stephen Best contrasted the "hermeneutics of suspicion" with the more "modest" posture of critics who "take texts at face value" (Best and Marcus 11). Most recently, Rita Felski explicitly called for an end to the dominance of "critique" as a critical "mood" (*Limits* 20). Suspicion, paranoia, and critique face off against the reparative, the modest, and the uncritical.[17]

These battle lines suggest two contrasting observations: on the one hand, there is—and has been for some time—widespread exhaustion with what Felski diagnoses as the normative habits of literary criticism today. Yet the range of negative affects these critics declare themselves against is far more focused than those they offer as substitutes: Sedgwick's reparative reading is akin to but different from the anthropological attention to alternative reading communities that

Warner advocates; *surface reading* as a term can scarcely contain the diversity of approaches harbored by the collection of essays it introduces. Everyone is dissatisfied; no alternative yet has the status of a paradigm shift. Critique, it's needless to say, remains hegemonically central.

Or does it? Felski writes as though the spirit of critique dwells in an antagonistic relationship between critic and text, but in fact many of the most common critical moves still privilege critique while shifting the target: rather than the text as passive medium of the blind norms of its age, the text becomes an ally in the act of critique. We're informed of the critical "pleasures" to be found in the way novels "urge on their readers committed scrutiny of their own forms of distinction and cultural commitment" (Blair, *Henry James* 14): aesthetic pleasure residing in the discovery of a novel's own suspicious affects. Or we're informed that novels "mount bohemian, queer, non-white, and feminist challenges to the stale dictates of bourgeois socialization" (Esty, *Unseasonable* 2). This might suggest, on the one hand, that critique has already lost: we've returned to comfortable, affectionate relationships with our objects of study.

On the other hand, it also suggests that the critique of critique doesn't go far enough: if we no longer consistently mobilize critique's power against the literary texts, critique remains the most familiar ideological priority claim of the profession. Only its location has shifted: we no longer critique texts; we affiliate with texts on the grounds that *they* critique, whether the object of critique is their world, the reader, or something else entirely.[18] This latter form of critique is the one I will decenter in the pages that follow: looking into the more diverse set of relationships texts have with their future readers doesn't just point away from the hermeneutics of suspicion; it asks us to recognize the limitations of the *politics* of suspicion. In other words, not only must we consider what various critics have described as the agency of texts, their political potential; we need to learn to value expressions of that agency—of literature's political consequences—that take forms other than unmasking, demystifying, and disillusioning. The dominance of critique is not just in scholars' affective relationship between critics or readers and texts, but in the range of political affects and tools the field assumes to be valuable.

Modernism might seem like a strange moment in literary history to look for forms of political commitment. Modernism, we've been told, taught us how to be critical readers:

> That we have learned to read between the lines has everything to do with the devices deployed in modern works of art: unreliable narrators, conflicting viewpoints, fragmented narratives, and metafictional devices that alert

> readers to the ways in which words conceal rather than reveal. . . . Indeed,
> much of what has counted as theory in recent decades riffs off, revises,
> and extends the classic themes of literary and artistic modernism. (Felski,
> *Limits* 42)[19]

This reading of modernism anticipates the transformation of critique's object: if the texts teach us to read skeptically, it's hard to argue that our posture toward them is itself skeptical. They are the teachers of suspicion, not suspects.

These remain the primary terms in which modernist studies celebrates its objects of study today. The New Modernist Studies was in part a response to the hermeneutics of suspicion—a turn to seeing modernist works as our allies in suspicious critiques of a broader society, rather than our recalcitrant opponents. But suspicion has remained the primary engine of political energy in criticism, even as novels now share in the critic's work of unmasking and undermining. In Mao and Walkowitz's foundational introduction to the anthology *Bad Modernisms*, they welcome the New Modernist Studies: "Across fields, 'modernism' seems again to be naming something that can surprise and challenge, if not indeed profoundly unsettle" (6). If we are now "after suspicion," it is time for us not just to cultivate more reparative practices ourselves, but to re-examine the unsuspicious aspects visible within the works themselves, literary affects that affirm rather than unsettle. As we'll see in chapter 1, modernists themselves—even early modernists—were, in some ways, after suspicion, were grappling with a skepticism they perceived as widespread. Particularly at political moments in which a society's malignancies are palpable and obvious, it's worth looking not for literature's ability to *unsettle* but for literature's strategies for committed response and for the construction of alternatives.

In criticism, then, the oppositional relationship between a text and its world replaces the oppositional relationship between critic and text. The association between such a stance and modernist literature is persistent, even when the word *modernism* no longer refers to its traditional late nineteenth- through mid-twentieth-century canon. Eric Hayot, for instance, building a claim that we need transtemporal modes of analysis, uses "Modernism" as the term for a work (of any time and place) that "assert[s] a total ontological rejection of the normative worldview of its era" (132). Modernism is the ultimate negative affect, in our critical narratives, wherever we might choose to locate it, and whatever positive affects we ourselves hold toward its negativity.

Recuperative modernism suggests a different line of development, whereby the most generative gestures of some of these texts are precisely their attempts to provide a counteracting force to the destabilization and uncertainty they perceive. And these attempts reside in precisely the techniques Felski lists as the origins of critique: "unreliable narrators, conflicting viewpoints, fragmented narratives, and metafictional devices." As numerous critics have pointed out, political action is often predicated not on destabilization and critique but decision and commitment: in many circumstances action requires not merely an unmasking of what is but a positive claim about alternatives.[20] This is what, I'll argue, the formal innovations of recuperative modernism provide: models for working through critique and coming to the value of commitment on the other side.

In an unpublished sketch, James Baldwin reads the titular protagonist of James's *Daisy Miller* as an example of a limited vision of what it means to experience the world.

> Penetrating nothing, penetrated by nothing, she moves about over the surface of human life like a fly on an infinite sheet of glass; and it is this absolute detachment, this absolute freedom to "see" everything and be contaminated by nothing, that constitutes her moral honor. (James Baldwin Papers, Folder 42.17, p. 4)

Baldwin condemns Daisy—and with her, a particular strand of American culture—for failing to recognize that the world she encounters might change her. In the language of Baldwin's critique of Daisy, it's easy to discern the language of Felski, or Best and Marcus, or even Sedgwick, anatomizing the suspicious critic's desire not to be fooled or made complicit by the text. But if on the one hand Daisy holds herself too aloof from the world, she also fails to accept that she has a perspective of her own: she "is unaware not just of social forms, but of 'form' itself"—the form of her own personality (p. 2). Baldwin, we might say, prescribes an immodest relationship with the world—neither holding oneself apart nor subordinating oneself to it.

Baldwin's description of what Daisy fails to do, in other words, can help remind us that "modesty" is not the only alternative to critique, and can be a misleading heading in describing the wide array of alternative affective positions critics can take with respect to our objects of study—or that literary objects can take with respect to the world.[21] Baldwin, always valorizing a complex form of "love," is one alternative; and the ancestor of so many of the anticritique polemics, Sontag's "Against Interpretation," famously called for an "erotics of art" (14). Daisy, in Baldwin's reading, "penetrating nothing, penetrated by nothing," lives a life without the erotic.

The effects of literary forms on their readers—and the uses readers make of literary experience—cannot be theorized by metaphors of distance and separation, not even so thin a separation as a sheet of glass. It is possible to have an intense—an *immodest*—relation to our objects of study without moving directly to the antagonisms of critique. Literary works do things to us; we do things to them, too, and neither action is ever uninflected by the other. The same is true of novels' relationships with the political worlds in which they are read: they can intervene in the world using modes of literary experience that solicit assent, affiliation, and judgment as much as negation and doubt.

Influence and Reception

Gayatri Spivak's famous discussion of strategic essentialism and the sacrifice of "theoretical purity" has familiarized the idea that members of marginalized groups might need to claim a shared identity that is itself a fiction.[22] We're very familiar with the idea that forms of political action sometimes require a distillation of more complex realities. Yet this is not necessarily a contest between efficacy and truth, but rather one of emphasis: which truths are more important to say in a given moment? In other words: critique and suspicion are just as strategic as commitment.

Literary forms, too, are tactical: they accomplish different things in different hands. Literary study has done a good deal of soul-searching recently about the ways in which our theoretical paradigms have been co-opted by reactionary political formations. Most notably, Bruno Latour, in "Why Has Critique Run Out of Steam?," calls for new theories "whose import then will no longer be to debunk but to protect and to care" (232). He declares that "history changes quickly and . . . there is no greater intellectual crime than to address with the equipment of an older period the challenges of the present one" (231). But literary history is nothing if not a vast and various body of testimony to the transformation of abstract ideas and forms from one political purpose to another. Pieces of conceptual architecture built to reactionary specifications have been as useful to various radical causes as the edifice of critique has become to conservative politics and the "merchants of doubt." We need to see beyond the purity politics of formalism, with its suspicions of ideas tainted by ugly origins. Critique is no vice, but it is not inherently virtuous; the same is true of commitment. Literary forms and the structures of literary experiences they create do not have an inherent politics. That does not make form irrelevant to the political uses of literature.

Changing times, in other words, do not obviate the literary forms of the past but open up new possibilities for them. What happens when the apparently backward-looking techniques of recuperative modernism actually meet their futures and find new contexts? The three central chapters of this study each frame a modernist novelist through the uses made of him by a mid-century writer. The modernist novels are out of context in two related senses. First, they are written in defiance of historical context, constantly redirecting the reader's attention away from historical facts and social detail toward abstract literary forms or statements of universal import. The world being represented in the novels—the aspect of fiction that reflects the world around it—is often secondary to the manipulation of the reader's experience and epistemological commitments. Second, as the epigraphs of this book suggest, I am analyzing them in the light of how later authors use them—how Ngũgĩ wa Thiong'o, for instance, pulls Conrad's novels away from the context of their writing and examines what uses he can make of them in his own time. My contention is that these are novels designed for such displacement, that their formal features are strategies for future-proofing their work, and that these antihistoricist strategies in particular have enabled a wide array of later political uses. Seeking aesthetic contact with the future, in other words, is not a way of evading the messy issues of one's own time, but of attempting to discern within one's present that which is potentially relevant to other times. Just as they see continuities between past and present, they see potential continuities between present and future. By gaining distance on events, by replacing the chaotic flux of experience with right names and larger patterns, they become potentially shared—not just with others, but with the unknowable readers and peoples of the future.

In the case studies I offer, it's clear that formal innovation, rather than producing skepticism and uncertainty, provides a pathway to greater authority. In adapting their modernist predecessors, later authors make the structures of fiction more complex, more apparently distant from the great tradition of the Victorian realist novel—and in doing so, make them *more* epistemologically secure, not less so. Techniques long read as creating doubt about what happened in a modernist novel become techniques for resolving doubt in later novelists. In Ngũgĩ's *Grain of Wheat*, for instance, he increases the temporal dislocations of the Conrad novel *Under Western Eyes* in order to increase the decisiveness of the conclusion. Ken Kesey's *Sometimes a Great Notion* uses even more various and elaborately interwoven forms of narration than *Absalom, Absalom!*—and it makes the reader more certain about the events described, not less so.

These later writers also find recuperative modernism's appeals to human nature and other abstract generalizations especially generative. Kwame Anthony Appiah claims that abstract universalism makes possible "respect for persons. . . . The encumbered self, laden with all the specificity of its manifold allegiances, is not something we can, as a rule, be bound to respect" (xv). These authors create "respect for persons" not only through the much-analyzed forms of empathy encouraged by the novel, but through explicit statements of universalist ideals—of a sacrosanct individual identity, through fascination that persists even when a character seems strange. Both Baldwin and Kesey, in particular, adopt a stance of universalist in-dividualism, where the appearance of sharp differences between people—one character's tremendous strength of will; another's magnetic liveliness—becomes a way of highlighting a paradoxically shared capacity of individuals to dissent from norms.

It is not happenstance that in moving to the authors who were influenced by the recuperative modernists, I am moving from authors marked by their elite so-cial positions (or performance of elite status, in the case of Faulkner) to authors who are marked by their lack of or opposition to social privilege. James Baldwin constructs his prophetic voice with the authority of one speaking as an outsider; Ngũgĩ wa Thiong'o writes from an explicitly Marxist perspective full of sympathy toward revolutionaries everywhere; Ken Kesey enjoyed playing the backwoods Oregonian ("Who the hell was ever from Oregon?" Tom Wolfe asked rhetori-cally in *The Electric Kool-Aid Acid Test* [31]) next to sophisticated New York Beats. And it is this sense of their outsider status that then becomes an ideological foun-dation for their attempts to speak generally. Ralph Ellison famously responded to Irving Howe in the essay "The World and the Jug" by claiming the right for African American writers to speak generally, not just from the perspective of oppressed, suffering victims: "If we are in a jug it is transparent, not opaque, and one is allowed not only to see outside but to read what is going on out there, and to make identifications as to values and human quality" (164).[23] For him oppression forms a basis for authorial authority, for a power of generalization and a claim to objectivity. Ellison imagines African American authors are particularly capable of making broad pronouncements on society precisely because they are excluded from it.

James wrote of Hawthorne in an 1896 essay, describing the vocation of the artist: "He is outside of everything, and an alien everywhere. He is an aesthetic solitary" (*Literary Criticism* I.467).[24] In a sense, then, Ellison's jug is not so far from one familiar notion of the modernist artist's position. James's evocation of the artist as "alien everywhere" contrasts with Woolf, declaring that the artist should represent faithfully, without mixing in the "alien and external" (*Essays* IV.160–161), James thinks that the artist's alienness—the difference, rather than the identifica-tion, between the self and the subject—qualifies him to see and perceive.[25]

Modernist studies has recently turned toward formulations of the field that focus on modernism as an inheritance.[26] There seems, in other words, a growing sense that modernism is now in the past. But the metaphors of legacy and inheritance will only take us so far. Some of these authors arrive not as heirs to the literary past but as the disinherited and dispossessed.[27] Images of inheritance naturalize the transmission from one generation to another—a gesture that fits Kesey's relationship with American literature well, as I'll discuss in chapter 4, with his connections to power brokers like Malcolm Cowley and his preference for metaphors of trees and other forms of organic growth to describe the relationships among generations. But the gesture that seems more central to Baldwin and to Ngũgĩ—and to more recent writers like Ozick, with her feminist confrontations—is an act of dislocation. Baldwin builds a major rhetorical turn in his essay "Stranger in the Village" around precisely this question. Early in the essay, speaking of the residents of a tiny Swiss village, Baldwin says, "The most illiterate among them is related, in a way that I am not, to Dante, Shakespeare, Michelangelo, Aeschylus, Da Vinci, Rembrandt, and Racine; the cathedral at Chartres says something to them which it cannot say to me" (121). At the climax of the essay appears the reversal for which we all hold our breath: "The cathedral at Chartres, I have said, says something to the people of this village which it cannot say to me; but it is important to understand that this cathedral says something to me which it cannot say to them" (128). Baldwin, in other words, claims Chartres—but it's a claim he has to make. For European art to become a usable past to him, he has to foreground his distance from it—to see his affiliation as a conscious choice, a declaration of the outsider's voice entering into the conversation.

Baldwin positions himself as outside of the preexisting conversation between Chartres and its Swiss inheritors—but as the voice the conversation needs to hear. Learning how to "use" history is learning to speak to it. Where Conrad, James, and Faulkner seem regularly to move beyond the local political realities of their works—sentences swerve unexpectedly from being about particular characters to being about the human condition in general—their successors view local history and the universally human as best addressed together. Baldwin, Ngũgĩ, and Kesey leverage their historical specificity to claim the authority to comment on human experience in universal tones. For them, evoking "human nature" has an immediate social and political use.

These kinds of readings unsettle our sense, less of what a modernist novel looks like, than of what kinds of readings critics reflexively celebrate, and why. It's often an unstated premise that Conrad's skepticism about moral codes, for instance, is more politically progressive than his yearning to affirm some kind of moral value;

we assume that James's excavations of the way character is shaped by the people and cultures that surround the individual might be more relevant to us than his insistence that individuals have their own identities. But, as David James points out, "The rupturing of generic or linguistic conventions has not always guaranteed or aspired to politically progressive ends."[28] The reason one has seemed more exciting than the other has very little to do with the political consequences the novels have had over their century-long readership, and much to do with current intellectual habits. And the real history of novels' uses and receptions often does not conform to today's cherished premises. It might, instead, rewrite them.

The transhistorical, in other words, challenges the locally historical, looking beyond the singular contexts of literary past and critical present alike. The study of literary influence, like the study of the transhistorical more generally, has an aura of backwardness about it. Between T. S. Eliot and Harold Bloom, it's been difficult to shake the implication that a vision of literary history that places influence at its center highlights the hegemonic power of the past, whether we speak in terms of Eliot's "sense of the timeless" (*Selected Prose* 38) or Bloom's emphasis on authors' contest for originality. Influence study, in this view, privileges the agency of the influencer at the expense of the later author.[29] This line of thinking tends to fear that discussing influence will make later authors somehow secondary artists, their achievement minimized as unoriginal next to their predecessors, playing into long-standing historical narratives whereby postcolonial culture and history are described as a belated afterthought to European and American phenomena. There's no shortage of history to justify this fear: one 1976 critic of Ngũgĩ's connection with Conrad asks rhetorically, "What else is there that makes Ngũgĩ's work worthy of independent assessment?"[30] The essay doesn't cite Harold Bloom, but it's easy to see it emerging from the same premises as his theory, whereby the driving anxiety of authorship is being too like a predecessor. But while the paradigm of originality still has some popular power, it seems virtually absent from authors' own discourse. Ozick never worries about her belatedness next to James; Ngũgĩ hardly seems to fear that critics will fail to recognize that he is doing something different from Conrad. Literary history as a history of originality is historiography that, we all know, comes in and out of fashion at various times.[31] When Dipesh Chakrabarty describes the dangers of a "'first in Europe and then elsewhere' structure of time" (8), we might also recall that part of the danger is the priority we give as historians of literature to *being* first.[32]

When originality vanishes from the equation, the power relations of literary influence reverse: rather than placing later authors at the mercy of their predecessors, as suppliants before the weight of history, we can see them as claiming the power to rewrite history. This book does not presume that reading James changes how we read Baldwin; it does, however, demand that we allow reading Baldwin to change how we read James.[33] Influence, in this book, is not a form of context for later authors but evidence of reception for earlier ones. Later authors, in this account, are exemplary readers of the literary past, producers of a form of criticism that, in its presentist focus on what they can make out of the past, has never been fully taken into account. Conrad did not know Ngũgĩ and has little to tell us about him; Ngũgĩ has everything to tell us about Conrad.

An alternate critique of influence comes from the opposite direction, suggesting that rather than undervaluing the agency of an influenced author, examining influence overvalues his or her conscious intentions and misses the dominating force of the cultural surround of the writer in which literary predecessors are merely one element.[34] Yet influence is in fact an excellent way of *reaching* precisely that surround, suggesting a broader history of readership than the individual author. Most readers don't leave behind convenient marginalia, and scholarly readings are often out of sync with the experiences of broader reading cultures. Later authors leave behind a great deal of evidence; they might be more thoughtful than ordinary readers, but their professional biases differ from those of scholars.

Influence study though, does tend to resist examinations of reception in which works' afterlives are determined primarily by the institutions in which they are read. Looking at authors opens up stranger, more surprising possible responses that are often invisible when we highlight the larger social forces that predetermine a work's reception.[35] I am, in other words, most interested in the way works escape the hegemonic institutions that propagate them.[36] Our archives are full of evidence for how particular cultural contexts created readings of texts. Yet even institutions can have surprisingly contradictory roles: Peter Kalliney, for instance, demonstrates that "midcentury cultural institutions . . . often served imperialist and anti-imperialist agendas at the same time."[37] The exciting thing about literary objects is that their uses are often counter to the contexts that present them— especially when read transnationally and transhistorically. Ngũgĩ writes about his college encounters with Conrad that "the formalistic close readings of texts and the Leavisite moral scheme of 'high' versus 'low' culture that were prevalent in the Makerere English Department were not adequate to study" Conrad's representation of colonial resource-extraction (*Birth* 185). But if we focus on the inadequacies of mid-century formalism, we'll miss the statements, in Ngũgĩ's fiction and nonfiction alike, testifying to the diverse uses he discerned for Conradian form when he rejected the institutional norms of Makerere. Conrad's novels interested him precisely because of this mismatch between what he saw in them and their cultural context—in Conrad's day and his own.[38] Influence studies do not exhaust reception—but they offer something new, and the methodology is particularly responsive to those who seek alternatives to critique, which so far have struggled to offer a consistent methodology to accompany their broad polemical diagnoses of the field.

The two opposing critiques—one fearful that later authors' originality will be disparaged; the other worried lest authors be seen as sovereigns over their own work in the style of Fielding—illuminate precisely what, for me, is so beguiling about influence: it contains within itself both the author as agent and the author as object of others' agency; it imagines reading both as a passive experience of being manipulated and as an active experience of response and recreation. It allows us to think about works as they are *read*, not merely as they are produced, and it captures the tension between authorship as control over the work and authorship as a conduit between the work and the various social forces that flow into it. Influence study fills out the missing middle ground between timely context and timeless theory.[39] It shows how the present can make the past it needs—sometimes easily, sometimes with tremendous effort. Influence is not the only potential methodology that can respond to the critique of critique, but it usefully evades both the limitations of the individual critic's phenomenological experience and the reduction of literary works into local historical forms of hegemonic reading.[40]

Paul Saint-Amour observes that "modernist studies has become a strong field . . . in proportion as its immanent theory of modernism has weakened" (41). The broadness of the field has led critics in diverse directions: some call for an expanded theory of modernism; others for a contracted one. The most expansive vision is Susan Stanford Friedman's claim that to place any geographic or temporal limits around modernism (beyond the association she considers central between modernism and rupture from the past) is an ethically dubious task, excluding voices who deserve to be heard.[41] Like Saint-Amour, I believe modernist studies is strongest when it does not insist too forcefully on the definitions delimiting its objects of study. Yet much of the argument that follows will depend on the specific ways in which later authors configure their predecessors as *belonging to the past*, or at least distant on some level from themselves. Therefore I do not tend to refer to Ngũgĩ, or Baldwin, or Kesey as themselves "modernist" but rather as readers and users of modernism. My point is not to exclude them from an elite group but rather to respect the ways in which membership in that group may not be especially desirous after all.[42] Whether or not Ngũgĩ *is* a modernist (or was at one time), modernist studies needs to take his existence, his analysis, and his achievement into account. For modernist studies to declare the world of rupture writ large as its domain strikes me as presumptuous. But we can consider ourselves responsible *to* a broader history without declaring ourselves responsible *for* it. Modernist studies will probably (hopefully!) not be the most important venue of interpretations of James Baldwin; to imagine otherwise is to erase the many other institutional homes and uses Baldwin already has. But James Baldwin needs to be important within modernist studies—not necessarily *as* a "late modernist" but as someone who found modernism useful in part because of its distance from him.

Modernist studies, in other words, must be a broader field than the particular works it labels as its objects of study—however various and diverse those may become. And to some extent the field regularly does this already: Baldwin, Ngũgĩ, and Kesey are all well within the institutional boundaries of modernist studies by now. We have theories of "late modernism" for mid-century works just as we have theories of "early modernism" for fin de siècle authors.[43] But all these frameworks tend to undervalue the transhistorical dimensions of literary reception—they expand the boundaries of a period in order to reduce the distance between its various moments. The limitations of this paradigm for understanding questions of reception and afterlives become clearer the greater the distance between authors. Few clamor for Cynthia Ozick to be labeled a modernist, perhaps because she is more clearly associated with contemporary American neorealism. Similarly, we only rarely apply the labels of earlier periods across centuries: T. S. Eliot's deep reading and complex engagement with the metaphysical poets does not usually lead to him being counted among their number.

What is obvious looking at transhistorical methodologies across such larger timescales is still important when the distances between authors are smaller. Ngũgĩ and Conrad may, on one level, be part of the same "singular modernity"; but Ngũgĩ very clearly perceives Conrad as part of history—as one of a list of available models stretching from Defoe to Faulkner (*Decolonising* 75). The periodization of reading and of literary history works by smaller increments than the periodization of history implied by words like "modernity."[44] Conrad at mid-century wasn't being read as contemporary by anyone. This sense of the *pastness* of modernism for these writers was essential to what made them useful: since they did not seem to be writing for the same world, their forms could be adapted more flexibly. The later authors would not necessarily have considered themselves modernists; and although they would all have been affected by the particular terms in which Anglo-American institutions valorized modernist form at mid-century, all of them conceived the work of writing as part of their own time, not as the production of aesthetically autonomous works apart from history. Mid-century was a moment in which the particular literary effects of recuperative modernism became useful for a diverse array of causes—a moment that, it may be, has some parallels to our own, as my last chapter on contemporary authors will suggest.

The later authors in this book are not, of course, the only ones I might have written about. They have representative qualities—in the case of Baldwin, later authors follow his lead in using Jamesian tools; in the case of Ngũgĩ, he fits into a surprisingly lengthy tradition of readings of Conrad. Kesey has elements in common with the much more widely studied uses of Faulkner by African American writers like Morrison and Ellison. But all three are outstanding in how central to their own work they made precisely the formal features of the earlier authors that I wanted to evaluate; as an archive of evidence of readership of these forms, their works are unusually rich. And it is the *forms* they have in common first, before the themes or tropes. The list of authors who allude to the idea of a "heart of darkness" is innumerable;[45] the list of writers who manipulate perspectives and chronology like Conrad is even longer, but it is far rarer to find one where it is inarguable that Conrad is a crucial source. Baldwin, Ngũgĩ, and Kesey all explicitly allude to their predecessors in interviews. In other words, they affiliated rather than sought to distance themselves.

At the same time, these forms are not meant to be visibly allusive; they are not allusions designed to build a conversation across time. Initial reviewers of Ngũgĩ's *Grain of Wheat* never saw its close resemblance to Conrad's novels, and the novel does not require knowledge of Conrad. The literary forms of recuperative modernism are all forms of decontextualization: they carry not references to the past but uses for the future. In this sense, they have much in common with Faulkner's absolutist claim to the neutrality of formal devices: at the end of a list of authors (the last of them Thomas Beer) he read deeply, he starts to speak generally about what he finds in past writers' works:

> [Thomas Beer] was to me a good tool, a good method, a good usage of words, approach to incident. I think the writer, as I said before, is completely amoral. He takes whatever he needs, wherever he needs, and he does that openly and honestly because he himself hopes that what he does will be good enough so that after him people will take from him. (Gwynn and Blotner 20–21)

Faulkner sees writing for the future not as a selfish claim to personal immortality but as a form of provisioning to that future. Writing is "good enough" when it is *useful*. Literature lasts not as a monument to the past but as a resource for future presents. The audience of the future, here, becomes a measure of what it means to be "good enough." Faulkner's imagery holds tensions in suspension, struggling to convey a relationship between present and future that is generous but also potentially full of tension. The author is "amoral" because he "takes," as in theft; but he is open and honest about it, and besides the literary past is designed to be taken up. He registers the struggle we have in coming up with language for the relationship between literature and its future audiences that does not fall back upon either antagonism or models of distance and objectivity.[46]

The epigraphs to this book, from the three later authors whose readings of modernism I foreground, suggest three metaphors for the relationship between past texts and present readers. If the past is at the mercy of the future, consumed or cut to pieces, it is also the material the future has to work with. Baldwin fears history might be a drowning flood but advocates instead "learning how to use it," transforming the past from liquid threat to solid tool; Ngũgĩ sees European literature as "prey" to nourish African national traditions; and Kesey sees the past as a natural resource, the concentric rings of a tree's history exposed in the process of converting it into tomorrow's house.

To examine what modernism is today is to examine how art negotiates both the changing and the unchanging aspects of its transhistorical audiences. These novels are not just consequences of history but causes of it, providing tools to shape debates and discourses far removed from their original purpose. When we turn to interpret them, their afterlives are not ghostly hauntings to be exorcized, or poor attempts at restoration to be stripped away in search of an originary past, but integral parts of a work's life.

The later writers show the generative capacities of modes of reading, revision, and repurposing that efface original historical contexts. But they also demonstrate that the future has always been part of modernism's bid to create lasting art. In committing to literary futurity, novelists confront the inevitability of change—and, in turn, must begin to theorize both what is and what isn't enduring about their worlds.

This is a book about the influence the future has on the past.

1. Rescue Work

Innovation and Continuity in Modernist Fiction

Action in its essence, the creative art of a writer of fiction, may be compared to rescue work carried out in darkness against cross gusts of wind swaying the action of a great multitude. It is rescue-work this snatching of vanishing phases of turbulence disguised in fair words, out of its native obscurity into a light where the struggling forms may be seen, seized upon, endowed with the only possible form of permanence in this world of relative values—the permanence of memory.

—Joseph Conrad, *Notes on Life and Letters* (16)

When Conrad describes art as "rescue work," the time frame of the action is deliberately a little paradoxical. Art rescues what is "vanishing" by offering it "the permanence of memory"—"snatching" things that are already on their way out and working them into a new form that can last into the future. The recuperative modernists' attempts to write for the future are inextricable from their refusal to reject the past. "In speaking of the future of the novel," says James, "we must of course, therefore, be taken as limiting the inquiry to those types that have, for criticism, a present and a past" (*Literary Criticism* I.104).

The promise of a future, in other words, depends on the relationship between past and present. We're used to thinking of Conrad and James as belonging to the moment of the invention of the anglophone art novel. Rightly, critics often analyze this shift as a history of excluding particular audiences, of seeking elite rather than popular appeal.[1] But the idea of the novel as art is also about the sudden inclusion of the most diverse and illimitable audience imaginable: the art novel consciously seeks the audiences of the future rather than simply the present.

Thinking of the novel as aimed at the future requires theorizing continuities across historical boundaries. Hence, the "rescue"—the emphasis on older ideas and faiths that these authors perceive as under threat. Note the slipperiness of Conrad's phrasing, "the only possible form of permanence in this world of relative values": he acknowledges the force of relativism and its potentially corrosive effects while still implying permanence might be possible. This move—to search for permanence and certainty while acknowledging its limits—shapes many formal features of these modernists' novels. In successive chapters I'll sketch out James's worry that identity might lose its meaning, dissolving in a sea of social influences; Conrad's sense that communication between people might, finally, be impossible; and Faulkner's sense that human activity might be meaningless. Yet in each case, these writers look for what *does* persist or have an impact, despite these long odds.

The "permanence of memory" bridges individual and collective memory—in context, it refers to art's ability to create new images in the memories of others; it also suggests the process, dramatized over and over again in Conrad's novels, by which characters come to grips through narration with the events of the past. They look at the past for the sake of the future. We can take into account not only their futurity—the futures the texts found—but also their futurism—their attempts to think on behalf of the future. The thought of writing for the future is often shadowed by a vision of writing as selfishness: one writes for the future in order to gain the literary version of immortality.[2] But as Faulkner's image of the amoral artist suggests, hoping to be read in the future is also hoping to be *useful* to the future. One writes for the future, in other words, as much for the future's sake as for oneself.

In this chapter, I will look at how the gesture of rescue connects the three authors at the center of this book: they acknowledge the tenuousness of an idea even as they commit to it. James, Conrad, and Faulkner share both recuperative gestures and real historical connections. James and Conrad knew each other, were, for a time "almost . . . neighbour[s]," as Conrad put it (*Collected Letters* II.189).[3] Conrad was a regular reader of James, and James eventually reciprocated, writing a generous letter to Conrad about *Lord Jim*; Faulkner alludes to and adapts Conrad again and again in his work. Yet there is only a small body of work comparing them.[4] In addition, Conrad's essay on James (quoted above) was famously parodied by Faulkner in his Nobel acceptance speech (a connection I'll discuss shortly). Yet even beyond the actual connections between them, these authors shared an attitude toward the relation between historical change and the role of art that differs from some of the more canonical ways scholars habitually characterize modernism.

When two of these authors both appear in the same critical work, it is usually in the context of a modernist march from James to Joyce or Woolf and beyond; critics tell a story about the genesis and genealogy of high modernism and seldom connect either author to Faulkner.[5] In broad stories of the modernist period, James and Conrad tend to appear as evolutionary midpoints between Victorian and modernist fiction. The deliberation with which they perform their balancing acts between past and present is sometimes lost when they are seen as stepping stones to modernism, as medial figures who, thanks to a misfortune of chronology, make only partial strides toward a new way of looking at the world. For instance, Jameson describes Conrad as practicing "nascent modernism" that he opposes to the "more fully achieved and institutionalized modernisms of the canon" (*Political Unconscious* 210). Michael H. Levenson writes of the preface to *The Nigger of the "Narcissus"* that it is "an entrance . . . into the general situation of early modernism; . . . the tensions in the preface point to certain widespread and fundamental literary tensions."[6] James and Conrad become conduits of these tensions, of imprecisely anticipated and imperfectly realized visions.

My goal in this chapter is to complicate this magisterial teleology by showing what unites these three authors with each other, rather than what they all share with the authors of the 1920s. These novels elicit from their readers mental acts of selection, exclusion, and pattern-making. Furthermore, they associate this order with older ideas of a coherent world—of whole identities and meaningful action, as well as the possibility of meaningful communication. Though none except perhaps James are realists, all carry a little of the pessimism implied in Lukács's famous epigram, "The novel is the epic of a world that has been abandoned by God" (*Theory* 88). This is a modernism that is more concerned with recuperating—or rescuing—forms of knowledge and communication than with disrupting them or representing their fallibility. In the Conrad quote already presented, the first half of the long sentence is as messy as the action described, unpunctuated and crowded with modifiers: "rescue work, this snatching of vanishing phases of turbulence disguised in fair words, out of its native obscurity . . . " Then, a tricolon crescendo sets it into order: "into a light where the struggling forms may be seen, seized upon, endowed with the only possible form of permanence in this world of relative values—the permanence of memory." This is a miniature of the transformation of reality into art, of life into memory, of the ephemeral into the enduring.

In this light the uniqueness of individual historical epochs looks less central. If Woolf described a lockstep connection between social changes and the literary forms that follow them, recuperative modernism sees literary forms as needing instead to be applicable in multiple times and places, to pare off the limitations of their own moment. Modernism has often been critiqued for its excitement about the idea of erasing the particular in favor of the general. Yet while the goals of the earliest critics of modernism might have been to exclude politics from the rarefied realm of art, this is not necessarily the purpose of the authors' own strategies of dehistoricization—nor was it necessarily the principal *use* of these authors among the actual readers they found.

The turn away from context is hardly endemic in all modernists; indeed, many of the features I will describe in James, Conrad, and Faulkner stand out most clearly in contrast to the kinds of stream of consciousness practiced by Joyce and Woolf, with their vividly particular masses of urban detail. But there is connection as well as contrast: Woolf's artist-figures are also rescuers—Lily Briscoe of *To the Lighthouse*, Bernard of *The Waves*—perpetually seeking order and meaning in apparent disorder, however temporary it might be. Recuperation, particularly when it is understood not as providing a final, stable order but instead as an orientation or process, is not only everywhere in modernism but, I will show in my studies of influence, far less politically retrograde than it might appear to be. Searching for understanding and knowledge is useful, even when particular conclusions are not.

The artist's ability to reorganize reality—and, moreover, to show reality in the process of coming into an organized state—is the foundation for recuperative modernism's address to the future. Even as these authors delineate all the pitfalls of the mind's shaping power—the mistaken impressions, the false shapes one character's imagination can force upon another—they show how the inevitable impulse to order can be undertaken responsibly, dramatizing the ethical imperative to do so. James's defense of the vivid autonomous individual arises out of a sense that human choices and experience lack significance if they do not, on some level, express an intrinsic self as well as social circumstances (discussed in chapter 2); Conrad is committed to the author's power to make broad, universalist claims about the world (chapter 3); Faulkner asserts that seeing order in reality, deducing general laws underlying experience, is inevitable and even can be useful (chapter 4). Yet ultimately it is the process—the expressing, the claiming, the deducing; the *rescuing*—that matters.

"Everything Is Relative": A Rescue with No Object

> Flaubert's letters, indeed, bring up with singular intensity the whole question of the rights and duties, the decencies and discretions of the

insurmountable desire to *know*. To lay down a general code is perhaps as yet impossible, for there is no doubt that to know is good, or to want to know, at any rate, supremely natural. Some day or other surely we shall all agree that everything is relative, that facts themselves are often falsifying, and that we pay more for some kinds of knowledge than those particular kinds are worth.

—James, *Literary Criticism* II.297

And the multitude feels it obscurely too; since the demand of the individual to the artist is, in effect, the cry "take me out of myself!" meaning really out of my perishable activity into the light of imperishable consciousness. But everything is relative and the light of consciousness is only enduring, merely the most enduring of the things of this earth, imperishable only as against the short lived work of our industrious hands. When the last aqueduct has crumbled to pieces, the last air-ship fallen to the ground, the last blade of grass has died upon a dying earth, man indomitable by his training in his resistance to misery and pain shall set this undiminished light of his eyes against the feeble glow of the sun. The artistic faculty of which each of us has a minute grain may find its voice in some individual of that last group, gifted with a power of expression and courageous enough to interpret the ultimate experience of mankind in terms of his temperament, in terms of art. I do not mean to say that he would attempt to beguile the last moments of humanity by an ingenious tale. It would be too much to expect—from humanity. I doubt the heroism of the hearers.

—Conrad, *Notes on Life and Letters* 16–17

The central nexus of these themes—the point at which all three of my authors meet—is the Conrad essay in which the above passage appears. James is the subject of the essay; Faulkner is its most famous respondent. Not only are the topics on which the essay dwells the key traits of recuperative modernism, but the history of the essay—its status looking backward and its repurposing half a century later—contains in miniature the dilemmas of aesthetic endurance in a changing world.

The centrality of recuperative approaches in these authors is a consequence of how completely they perceive disruptive work to have already taken place. In other words, rather than seeing them as undoing norms, we have to understand that they take for granted that certain norms are already untenable in their received forms. Take "everything is relative" in both passages above—they are not announcing it as a revelation, but alluding to it as a familiar truism. Then they turn it around to license new ideas of what truth might be. Bruno Latour, inquiring into the ends of critique as scholarly method, asks, "Is it really our duty to add fresh ruins to fields of ruins?" (225). Some of this spirit animates these quotations: the work of iconoclasm has occurred already; the icons are shattered on the ground; Conrad, like Latour, invokes the landscape after a catastrophe. Now, they imply, it's time to build again.

The doubts they raise about relativism are pragmatic as well as epistemological. They intertwine an idea that falsity is useful or tempting with the idea that their departures from facts or reality are ways to a truer form of truth, to alternative forms of knowledge. "Facts themselves are often falsifying," says James; Conrad slyly refuses to say that the "interpretation" the artist offers is merely the beguilement of "an ingenious tale"—or to deny it. "Everything is relative" becomes a fact that seems limited to both of them, a fact that may stand in the way of what is actually true.[7]

Both emphasize the limitations of the facts of the physical world, enacting a shift from the particular and temporally bounded to the abstract and enduring: Conrad elevates the "light of consciousness" above visible light; James bemoans detailed information about Flaubert's personal habits and interactions. For James, the desire to know details of an author's life obscures the more important things to know about the work, and this case—responding to the publication of Flaubert's letters—is merely one instance of the general tendency, evinced throughout his work, to value the knowledge produced by obscurity. At a moment of high drama in *The Golden Bowl*, the protagonist Maggie feels about her husband a "wish not to see his face again till he should have had a minute to arrange it" (XXIV.181). James wants to grant Flaubert a similar opportunity for deliberate self-presentation. These acts of arrangement, of suppressing certain facts and disclosures (of embarrassing emotion, for instance) in order to create others, are central both to the plots of James's novels and to James's conception of what is "true" in life.

And since the danger is that facts are *falsifying*, James is not discarding the usefulness of concerning oneself with truth—he is arguing for a different standard. His point that the "natural" human "desire to *know*" must be suppressed does not mean that people should not want to know things, but that "knowledge" must be liberated from a raw accumulation of facts. "Everything is relative" eventually starts to suggest that everything must be arranged, put into relation with other things. Not only does James represent the desire to know in his characters; he seeks to channel the similar desire of his readers, to create responsible ways of knowing.

Conrad's point is similar. When he says, "It would be too much to expect—from humanity," he may appear to express pessimism about the human audience of art, but he is also making a bid for the reader's desire to succeed and be better than the depicted audience. For him, "everything is relative" can separate the fruitful from the futile among human endeavors—and his phrasing is designed to galvanize his audience to try.[8] The following sentence seems to upset the absolute distinction between "imperishable consciousness" and fleeting physical activity:

> But everything is relative and the light of consciousness is only enduring, merely the most enduring of the things of this earth, imperishable only as against the short lived work of our industrious hands.

In this sentence, the imperishable really may not be much greater than the perishable; the previous sentence is revised or even reversed, and the reader's demand that the artist take him or her into the light of "imperishable consciousness" seems an impossible dream. Consciousness becomes only lasting rather than truly immortal, placed on the same scale as perishable goods.

The sentence ends, however, by emphasizing the ephemerality not of consciousness but of material goods, which effectively reinvigorates the value of the relatively lasting consciousness. "The short lived work of our industrious hands" is an unforgiving hysteron proteron, the rhetorical device that reverses the temporal order of events in order to emphasize the later event: the works are in ruin before they are built. Conrad dwells over short-lived work to prepare for the lead-in to the next sentence, which continues the emphasis on ruin but turns around and reasserts the power of consciousness. A catalog of the dying physical world ("When the last aqueduct . . .") gives way next to the "undiminished light" of the imperishable consciousness behind human eyes. This sentence offers an unremittingly heroic image, to which the reader is made to give his assent: after clause upon clause ("when the last . . .") opening in the same tone of desolation, it begins to seem inevitable that with the main subject and verb will arrive a contrast, as it eventually does: "man . . . shall set this undiminished light of his eyes against the feeble glow of the sun."

Thus, in his sentence of relativism Conrad holds open hopeful possibilities, and he follows it by a sentence of heroic absolutes ("last," "undiminished"), in which his meaning remains potentially (but very subtly) relative: the light of man's eyes is greater now *because* everything else has diminished. This is a crucial strategy throughout Conrad's work: while keeping up multiple possibilities, he throws the rhetorical weight behind some form of optimism about art or people that he impels the reader to imagine before it is offered on the page.

As with James, "everything is relative" becomes the basis for separating out more lasting or truthful human endeavors from those that are false or limited. Relativity becomes the basis for making choices among and privileging certain human endeavors.

One distinction between these two passages demonstrates an aspect of recuperative modernism more prominent in Conrad and Faulkner than in James. Compare the ways I read these authors: for James I glossed meanings and ambiguities in the words as they rest there on the page; for Conrad I followed the track of meanings thrown off, clause by clause, as I preceded down the length of a sentence. James creates the impression of having come to every conclusion beforehand: "Some day or other surely we shall all agree," he says, deliberately idiomatic and casual, before a tricolon of not-at-all-obvious statements. He deliberately compresses the sequential experience of prose, trying, as much as possible, to make it seem as though every statement is coextensive with every other, each implicit in all the others and all happening at the same time. By contrast, the Conrad sentence is a rollercoaster experience, flipping dramatically between meanings as it unfolds in time. As I discussed in the introduction, one of our most common paradigms for the transhistorical dimensions of literary art derives from Joseph Frank's spatial form, whereby the reader's ability to survey the entirety of a work of art at once metonymically stands in for the aesthetic as occupying a position outside of the time-world of history, looking instead toward the timeless.[9] Frank's alignment between spatial reading and timelessness points to the potential value of temporal reading by contrast, as a model for immersion in the flow of the historical time as well as literary experience. Between these two styles of close reading—not entirely distinct, but differing significantly in emphasis—occurs not a turn *against* representation, but a choice to supplement representation with other, more rhetorical strategies for creating literary meaning.[10]

Two major anxieties motivate this shift: first, that the most important features of life are irreducibly complex and shifting, and that to "represent" them in specific forms will inevitably mutilate that complexity; and second, that even if the thing to be represented were simple, the process of representational communication is doomed to failure, through the inevitable limitations of language. The first concern generally looms larger with James, the second with Conrad, and both anxieties are the specifically literary incarnations of broader philosophical and scientific questions alive at the time. As Christopher Herbert points out, tracing the philosophical waves sent out by Darwinian theory in the Victorian period, "The paradigm of all-encompassing interrelatedness brings with it . . . a threat of extreme epistemological disorder" (62). This threat reappears in literary contexts for both James and Conrad, as well as Faulkner. James makes his famous claim that "relations stop nowhere" (discussed below). Conrad describes in a letter an equally famous vision of a knitting machine, where human existence is tied together in hideous senselessness: "It evolved itself (I am severely scientific) out of a chaos of scraps of iron and behold!—it knits. . . . It knits us in and it knits us out. It has knitted time space, pain, death, corruption, despair and all the illusions—and nothing matters" (I.425). For Conrad, the vision is of a horrible sameness, in which everything is connected and therefore indistinguishable. The image of a hyperconnected order turning into disorder appears later too, in Faulkner, who may have been drawing on Conrad: Judith Sutpen, in *Absalom, Absalom!*, calls the human condition "five or six people all trying to make a rug on the same loom" (105).[11] Faulkner's view turns toward the more obvious modern sense of relativism: the problem of differing perspectives. Recuperative modernism answers by attempting to sort them out.

We often think of modernism through what it *includes*—the scatological joy of Joyce, the emphasis on the apparently trivial details of experience as Mrs. Dalloway walks up Bond Street, the sexual frankness of D. H. Lawrence. But modernism does not abandon the project of selection and exclusion; as James says, "Call a novel a picture of life as much as we will; . . . it has had to be selected, selected under some sense for something" (*Literary Criticism* I.798). "Some sense for something"—the process of selection matters more than any particular outcome. This opposition between a "picture of life"—defined by the threat of teeming inclusiveness—and the sense of the novel as having a particular purpose and necessary limits to its representativeness—is central to many of the aesthetic dilemmas faced and decisions made by the modernists. Recuperative modernism exists in moments where the decisions fall ostentatiously on the side of artistic selection over realistic inclusion. If, as we saw in chapter 1, "facts themselves can often falsify," the right facts can yet be true.

Representation and Interpretation

Two very famous passages illuminate the distinction between a modernism of expansive inclusion and one of high-stakes selection. In 1925 Woolf describes "life," in a context ambiguously poised between a description of Joyce's method and a prescription for the proper stuff of modern fiction: "Let us record the atoms as they fall upon the mind in the order in which they fall, let us trace the pattern, however disconnected and incoherent in appearance, which each sight or incident scores upon the consciousness" (*Essays* IV.161). This passage offers a contrasting image to the often-quoted passage in James's preface to *Roderick Hudson*: "Relations stop nowhere," James begins by saying, but the metaphor quickly turns to the writer as "embroiderer of the canvas of life" who "began to work in terror, fairly, of the vast expanse of that surface, of the boundless number of its distinct perforations for the needle. . . . The development of the flower, of the figure, involved thus an immense counting of holes and a careful selection among them" (I.vii). Woolf's particulate atoms are a perfect negative of James's surface with holes. Both represent reality untransfigured—for James a frightening prospect and for Woolf a freeing one. The divergence of the metaphors reflects divergent configurations of the relation between the mind and life: for James, the author actively creates the pattern by picking and choosing among multiple options, which are blank spaces until the pattern is drawn through them; for Woolf, the author is tracing after a pattern the atoms themselves create. The mind is the source of pattern in James, a passive recipient of it in Woolf. In James, reality is the surface and the author works upon it; in Woolf, the mind is the surface that atomized reality affects and the author records afterward.

In these passages, Woolf sees chronology as representational, as following the atoms, and James sees chronology as interpretive, tracking the author's slow apprehension of a pattern. Woolf's aims are ultimately realist.[12] For James, writing fiction involves numerous pragmatic questions—forming the diffuse material of a tale into the shape of novel—that impinge upon epistemological and ethical ones. He has to draw a boundary around the relationships that stop nowhere because the novel can't literally be unending; he also believes that the aesthetic merits of a well-formed novel are not just a matter of entertainment. The novel's artificiality—its quality as a constructed object, the product of a human mind—is the source of its capacity to evoke reactions in the reader's mind. Because the novel makes no pretense to reality—unlike rhetoric outside fiction, it does not claim to be true—it does not falsify.[13] If the novelist is "outside of everything and alien everywhere," in James's phrase, that does not make him or her *uninvolved*—the author is separate but complicit and responsible for all the interpretive choices of art-making.

Woolf's novels, of course, are full of aesthetic patterns—linguistic motifs, rhythmic effects, intricately developed metaphors. But she also valorizes the transitory, fleeting nature of such patterns. Lily Briscoe thinks, "I have had my vision" (*To the Lighthouse* 211): the vision of order is always already gone. If James's image suggests the stakes of committing to a particular selection of details in life, Woolf suggests that the most important patterns are those that come upon you unbidden—similar to Joycean epiphany.

Recuperative modernism stands not for modernism as a whole, but for a strong impulse that appears in some authors and at some moments. The suspicion that so many critics discern in modernist literary form—the reluctance to interpose an authorial vision upon the fractured realities of ordinary experience—is one use of modernist experimental form. But only one use. At various points in the chapters that follow, Woolf and Joyce will both furnish contrasting examples: modernists who emphasize the unstable, the fleeting, the moment of rupture (Woolf); or whose rendering of the idea of a comprehensive vision is resolutely spatial, distant both from the experience of reading and from a vision of the transhistorical focusing on engagement and change (Joyce). This is not to say that their visionary moments aren't also in some respects recuperative, but to acknowledge that there are real differences about how the canonical modernists approached these questions.

Faulkner, like James and Conrad, turns to the issue of sorting out different kinds of truth.

> Because listen. What was it the old dame . . . told you about how there are some things that just have to be whether they are or not, have to be a damn sight more than some other things that maybe are and it dont matter a damn whether they are or not? That was it. (Shreve, *Absalom, Absalom!* 266)

Things that just have to be whether they are or not: "have to be" means either "have to happen" or "have to be true." In context, *happen* makes more sense, but in the whole of the novel the question about what "has to be" the truth looms larger. Shreve and Quentin reconstruct the story of Thomas Sutpen from the fragmentary stories of multiple other narrators. Their work connects the imperative to coherent character—people have to behave in a certain way—with the imperative to ordering narration—the meaning of the tale demands that this be true; therefore it must be true. Thus relativity—the indeterminacy of facts lost in a multitude of perspectives—becomes both the motivation and the means of interpreting reality, of selecting and excluding among the range of impressions and data the mind receives. Rather than highlighting the individual's perspective as compromised, biased, always partial, Shreve and Quentin show how the limitations, biases, and partial visions of the human mind can be combined with other perspectives to reveal truth.

The endpoint of this line of development occurs in the work of one of Faulkner's disciples, in the words of the narrator of Ken Kesey's *One Flew Over the Cuckoo's*

Nest: "It's the truth even if it didn't happen" (8).[14] Truth appears even when there is nothing to represent.

Empty Vessels

Yet if the recuperative modernists defend the value of seeking general facts, they never alight with any stability on general conclusions. The form of their fiction is of constant search, delineating the shape of a conclusion while denying the conclusion itself. These works are empty vessels—by which I mean not that they are purposelessly hollow, but that they are open to many possible uses. This combination of decisive shape and open use is one of the points at which close connections between the recuperative modernists become visible. Take, for example, the following plot:

> Convinced all his life that he will find some extraordinary destiny, John—or is it Jim?—holds himself aloof from those around him. But his life seems to become the opposite of his anticipated adventures, a series of aborted gestures and incomplete possibilities. In the end, his heroic dream comes true, but in a catastrophic way: "at the call of his exalted egoism," he "goes away from a living woman." The extraordinary destiny has been achieved— but not in any form he had expected or desired.

This is a plot summary both of Joseph Conrad's *Lord Jim* (1900) and of Henry James's *The Beast in the Jungle* (1903).[15] The quotations are from *Lord Jim* (313), but they well describe the plot of the James story, in which John Marcher lives a life empty of emotion and event while waiting for his destined moment of crisis—the "beast" of the title. We all know, by now, that there's a great deal of consonance between Conrad's and James's works: as shared practitioners of literary impressionism, as authors poised between Victorian and modernist ways of writing.[16] Yet most criticism sketches the line of influence as Conrad following James, or focuses on consonance between their work without relying on influence.[17] *The Beast in the Jungle* is a case where the influence is direct—and in the opposite direction.

Understanding these works as directly related to one another rather than part of a larger set of modernist symptoms changes the meaning of what they are doing. The lineaments of shared story I have just noted seem to evoke some obvious modernist tropes: the self-aggrandizing dreams of egotists who disdain ordinary life are undermined and frustrated; such dreams have the overtones of suspect genre tropes (adventure literature in *Lord Jim*, an abstracted notion of romance destiny in *The Beast in the Jungle*). Both these works have been read as modernist extensions of nineteenth-century tropes of realist disillusionment. Leon Edel points to a Maupassant short story, "Promenade," as one potential model for James, in which an old man commits suicide upon sudden awareness of the empty tedium of his life (Edel V.134). Lyndall Gordon highlights a sketch in the notebooks of Constance Fenimore Woolson describing "a man spending his life looking for and waiting for his 'splendid moment'" (Benedict 144). In Woolson's version, the moment at last happens to the man's neighbor.[18] Flaubert's *L'Éducation sentimentale*, perhaps the closest alternative source for James, features a romantic ideal that the protagonist pursues at a distance until he experiences a deflation of the dream—like Marcher, after some years of travel abroad. But where Marcher realizes that the beast has already sprung in a form he failed to anticipate, Frédéric Moreau, Flaubert's protagonist, realizes that his dream has merely faded away and become empty.[19]

These models all eschew the possibilities of catastrophic fruition that Conrad and James highlight; in these other predecessors, the main emphasis of the tale is on the ironic deflation of the protagonist's dreams and aspirations. Yet Jim gets his romantic hero's end, and Marcher's beast springs—twice, even. The problem, of course, is that the cost of their climactic moment seems too high, and the ideal that had given rise to the dream has ceased to carry meaning.

Reading these stories in the light of influence, rather than as merely part of a broader modernist zeitgeist of disillusionment, shows us a different way of reading both Conrad and James. In the light of what James takes away from it, the second half of *Lord Jim* is not a retreat to romance, as it is often described, but an examination of the improbable, incredible appearance of romantic triumph where none might have been expected—and an anatomy of its catastrophic consequences. By contrast, in the light of James's use of Conrad over all those other alternatives, James's story seems less about the failure of human aspiration to the extraordinary than about the unexpected terror of the extraordinary when it does appear. In both stories, it is not that refusing a humdrum existence turns out to be a delusion, along the lines of Woolson or Flaubert—it is instead fearsomely, frighteningly *possible*.

We have one substantial piece of evidence regarding James's reading of *Lord Jim*: on November 12, 1900, only a few months after he had finished the novel, Conrad wrote to Edward Garnett, forwarding a letter from James that was apparently full of effusive praise: "A draught from the Fountain of Eternal Youth! Wouldn't you think a boy had written it? Such enthusiasm! Wonderful old man, with his record of wonderful work!" (II.303).[20] Less than a year later, in August 1901, James recorded in his notebook the idea that would become *Beast in the Jungle*; in 1902, he wrote the story. "*That* was what might have happened, and what *has* happened is that it didn't," says the notebook entry (199). This sketch sounds very little like Maupassant, Woolson, or Flaubert. None of the other predecessors, for instance, luxuriate in the paradoxes of the climax the way James does in the notebook, and none emphasize the self-fulfilling prophecy element of the story: James says that "his liabilities and exposures (as a *result* of the fear) [are] a good deal curtailed and cut down" (*Notebooks* 199). Where Maupassant and Woolson focus on the moment of a protagonist's revelation about life, James focuses on the ways in which the protagonist's psychological investment in his dreams has shaped his life over the whole course of the story, leading to a moment uniting irony and paradox.

The Beast in the Jungle is, of course, a title that sounds like Conrad rather than James, and the register of light-literature adventure sounds more than once in the story. When Marcher meets May Bartram, the woman who will spend the story awaiting the Beast with him and who eventually sees it more clearly than he, she reminds him that they had met previously in Naples. James writes: "Marcher could only feel he ought to have rendered her some service—saved her from a capsized boat in the Bay or at least recovered her dressing-bag, filched from her cab in the streets of Naples by a lazzarone with a stiletto" (XVII.66). Marcher's retrospective imagination strikingly resembles the youthful Jim's imagination of his future: "He saw himself saving people from sinking ships, cutting away masts in a hurricane, swimming through a surf with a line" (11). The heroism of rescuing someone seems absurdly distant to Marcher, and will be devastatingly immediate to Jim. Marcher, in effect, dreams of being Jim—of being faced with the crises that Jim confronts repeatedly. Where Conrad's world has a surplus of romantic excitement that turns bitter, James's seems to have a deficit, until that very absence is transmuted into the missing thrill.

Both works are about a search for danger in which to test oneself, and both figure the search as a desire to see one's life as having a decisive narrative shape. In 1906 James wrote to Conrad: "No one has *known*—for intellectual use—the things you know, and you have, as the artist of the whole matter, an authority that no one has approached" (*Letters* IV.419). In *Beast in the Jungle*, James experiments with making the realm of adventure usable to his literature—with the way the ideal of heroic, adventurous action shadows and teases the world of his dramas of renunciation and desire. James's discussion of romance in the preface to *The American* reflects this yearning: "The panting pursuit of danger is the pursuit of life itself, in which danger awaits us possibly at every step and faces us at every turn"

(II.xvi); this phrasing ought to point us toward a greater sympathy with Marcher than critics usually have. James's interest in Conrad's work, and his use of it in *The Beast in the Jungle*, feeds into his long-running campaign to see the intensity of danger in romance as usable in realistic genres of literature.

Lord Jim is a catalog of failures brought on by its protagonist's romantic dreams of heroism at sea. But Jim's first failure is not a catastrophic action, but a prosaic inaction that anticipates Marcher's habits. While on a training ship, he and his fellow trainees are suddenly afforded an opportunity to aid a foundering ship in a storm, and Jim finds himself struck still as his fellow trainees race to help: "There was a fierce purpose in the gale, a furious earnestness in the screech of the wind, in the brutal tumult of earth and sky, that seemed directed at him and made him hold his breath in awe" (12). Jim, like Marcher, does not act because of the very vividness with which he can imagine the dangerous stakes.

Even his most deluded imagination has an unexpected potential to turn toward the grandeur of bleak despair rather than heroic action: in the passage mentioned above, when Jim sees himself saving people, the list takes a sharp turn: "swimming through a surf with a line; or as a lonely castaway, barefooted and half naked, walking on uncovered reefs in search of shellfish to stave off starvation" (11). The reversal here from saving drowning souls to life reduced to bare self-interested essentials is, in a way, a twitch of the same rug James pulls out from under us at the end of *Beast in the Jungle*, whereby Marcher's extraordinary test becomes his lonely failure to experience anything.

It is telling that critics want to see Flaubert, Maupassant, and Woolson as models: their versions all are remorseless in mowing down their protagonists' ambitions, and in their rejection of standard forms of plotting. They can thus be assimilated very easily to understandings of modernism as being antiplot or invested in the ordinary rather than the extraordinary. But James is, on some level, backtracking from the harsh visions of these models; he remains invested in the possibility of romance as much as in its limits. In a letter to Edith Wharton in 1914, he disparages Conrad's fiction between *Lord Jim* and *Chance* (a period including *Nostromo, The Secret Agent*, and *Under Western Eyes*) as "wastes of desolation" (*Letters* IV.703). When he read Conrad's work, its preservation of romance thrill, rather than its fearsome existential doubts, appealed to him.[21]

Lord Jim, of course, is not actually a pure sea romance or adventure story; it is not difficult to distinguish the Jim of Stevenson's *Treasure Island*, tested and maturing in his adventures on the *Hispaniola*, from the Jim who is frozen in a kind of perpetual youth after his moment of cowardice on the *Patna* (Esty, *Unseasonable* 88). Conrad cloaks the idea of heroic fruition in irony and incomprehensibility: Jim's "extraordinary success" is a "pitiless wedding with a shadowy ideal of conduct" (312, 313). In typical Conradian fashion, words that seem to carry one connotation are modified or juxtaposed with those that seem to imply their opposite. The ideal is not shining but shadowy; the wedding can only be pitiless. But the shadows and the pitilessness are, in Conrad, ultimately what ratifies and creates the possibility of heroism; like relativism in the "Henry James" essay, a gesture of negation creates space for an affirmation.

James's work often moves in dimensions of paradox or at the very least incongruity: something is both nothing and everything; a silence speaks; lying to someone is lying for them. What has happened is that something didn't happen. In *The Beast in the Jungle*, James applies Conrad's approach to the dream of romance—balancing the dream against a negative shadow upon it—to his own language of paradox. Conrad, in essence, helps James solve a problem that haunted the fiction he was writing right before *The Beast in the Jungle*. In *The Sacred Fount* (1901) and *In the Cage* (1898), James also features protagonists who seem to project grandiose narratives where none may exist. Both are unnamed and voyeuristic: the protagonist of *The Sacred Fount* sees himself as uncovering a network of affairs marked by a quasi-vampiric transfer of life-force at a country house weekend; the protagonist of *In the Cage* becomes invested in an affair arranged through her telegraph office and injects herself into the parties' interactions. Leon Edel describes James's fiction between "The Figure in the Carpet" (1896) and *The Sacred Fount* as a "studies in the 'phantasmagoric,' in the ways in which the mind and the emotions, coping with realities, tend to invest them with beauty, terror, and mystery" (IV.339). *The Sacred Fount* was completed in the summer of 1900. James would have finished *Lord Jim* sometime between October 1900, when it was first published as a complete book, and November 12, when Conrad wrote to Garnett about James's praise. (The last serial chapter appeared in the November issue of *Blackwoods*.) Edel does not link *Beast in the Jungle* to these tales, despite their similarities: Marcher, like these protagonists, seeks a plot of high drama to give meaning to his life. But Edel's instinct is right: something does change fundamentally in *Beast in the Jungle*, and that something is the influence of Conrad.[22]

Both earlier works conclude with a relapse into the ordinary. After describing the imaginary constructions of the protagonists, then ironizing them, the novels return their protagonists to the familiar world in which they must go on nevertheless, slightly chastened. Yet the works also give the fantasies some real significance. In *In the Cage*, the telegraphist must return to her prosaic Mr. Mudge, but she genuinely played a crucial role in the affair she was following. Like Marcher, she sees fateful excitement in Everard, the hero of her chosen narrative: "He was at any rate in the strong grip of a splendid dizzy fate; the wild wind of his life blew him straight before it" (XI.419). At the same time, she sees herself as superior: "What I 'like' is just to loathe them," she says of the wealthy people whose messages she conveys (XI.408). In *The Sacred Fount*, the same verb—"like"—reappears, again contrasted with a weightier negative word ("horrors," now, instead of "loathe"): the irony against the narrator turns out to be the fact that he doesn't see the stories in serious enough terms: "Don't you sometimes see horrors?" asks his confidante Mrs. Brissenden, continuing, "It isn't, perhaps, so much that you see them . . . but . . . you like them" (181). The word *like* suggests both that he doesn't adequately morally condemn the vampiric affairs he claims to be detecting, and that he enjoys the thrill of discovery more than he cares about the fates of the people involved. These stories seem to end with the limitation of their protagonists' attempts to get beyond the prosaic surface of their lives—yet at the same time, they hold out the possibility that something extraordinary was somehow only just beyond their grasp, and that it is precisely the distance they preserve that walls them off from it.

In *The Beast in the Jungle*, the irony against Marcher is harsher than either of the other stories, but Marcher himself performs none of the same distancing moves that the earlier characters do. Marcher's tale turns at its conclusion in the opposite direction from *In the Cage* and *The Sacred Fount*—away from the ordinary toward the heightened register of melodrama. Marcher realizes that "the fate he had been marked for" is to be "*the* man, to whom nothing on earth was to have happened" (XVII.125). The moment mingles a grotesque irony with a delicious satisfaction: precisely the opposite of the destiny he imagined, it nevertheless is something extraordinary, fulfilling the scale of his premonition, and despite the fact that Marcher's fate is a self-fulfilling prophecy, the word *fate* does not really read as ironic.

Marcher displaces reality with fantasy: he wants a fate of such greatness that it will set him apart from a common existence he stigmatizes. His premonition may seem overwrought, but it is also the basis for why we read fiction: the expectation that something will happen. We read stories on trust that something extraordinary will be presented to us—even if the extraordinary thing is, in the end, only how high a character's delusional aspirations reach before they are crushed. In this instance, however, there is a bizarre fulfillment. Recalling after May's death the moment when she stood before him and attempted to convey her knowledge of his fate, Marcher thinks that his fate, his premonition, the titular Beast "had sprung as he didn't guess; it had sprung as she hopelessly turned from him, and the mark, by the time he had left her, had fallen where it *was* to fall. He had justified his fear and achieved his fate; he had failed, with the last exactitude, of all he was to fail of" (XVII.126). The statements stand equally as free indirect discourse—Marcher's realizations—and as a narrator commenting from outside. Marcher senses a waste and empty life, full of bitter irony and of failure, in which his destiny had none of the particular excitement he viewed as its earthly coordinates. Yet at the same time, the narrator records the absolute fulfillment of that premonition: he maps the spring of the Beast onto both a few seconds of Marcher's life and the inevitable-seeming rhythms of anaphora ("It had sprung as . . ."), circular repetitions ("fallen . . . *was* to fall"; "failed . . . was to fail"), and other parallelisms ("justified his fear and achieved his fate"). The point of the sentence is ostensibly that Marcher could have saved himself had he recognized in that moment what he was giving up (clearly, in context, some kind of love—whether of the woman speaking to him or his own repressed homosexual desires); yet each of these clauses could not end in any way other than they do. Punishing yet grandiose, the sentences make a serious claim that his fear and fate were just as he had imagined. Even as Marcher appears, in all his disappointment, to recover in part from his belief in his own extraordinary status, the narrator takes it over.[23]

The delight of this moment is the substitution of structural, narrative satisfaction for satisfaction in content. As narrative without content the premonition has been fulfilled: Marcher gets an extraordinary destiny, and we readers get every bit of melodramatic rhetoric due to the extraordinary. James has successfully established for us over the course of reading the novella terms of aesthetic encounter that dictate readerly reactions—like that jolt of pleasure in the fulfillment of the premonition—having nothing to do with any referential quality of the story.[24]

Those sentences also look more like Conrad than they do James; their rhetorical effects depend entirely on their sequential unfolding in time. "The pieces fitted and fitted" (XVII.125), Marcher thinks: the word is repeated in order to map the temporality of reading onto the character's moment of discovery. Like Conrad, reading this conclusion requires following the line of the sentence clause by clause and attending to the way the structures manipulate each moment of readerly expectation and response. James's syntax for a moment does not try to happen all at once; it no longer seeks to become a spatial form, but luxuriates in its unfurling in time. This might not be James's usual style—but it provides, in this moment, a crucial way of responding to the possibility that dreams of a significant life are only absurd. They may be empty, damaging, and cost more than they're worth: but you can have your significance, if you want it.

Signifying Everything: Faulkner's Response to Conrad

Faulkner responds to Conrad very differently than James, but his goal is the same: whereas James sees in Conrad a way to preserve romance by attributing significance to events that might seem prosaic, Faulkner constructs a vision of

Conrad in which the earlier author represents a threat to various forms of faith and belief. Faulkner's writing revises Conrad's forms and phrases in order to reply to and repair their sense of skepticism.

Faulkner always acknowledged that Conrad stood prominently among his inspirations, including Conrad on a list of authors he read every year and as an answer to a request for his favorite books.[25] Yet the connections between his work and Conrad's are discomfiting ones: even as he takes from Conrad, he reacts against him as well, presenting Conrad's aesthetic and philosophical positions as dangerously nihilistic.

The famous allusion to which I referred above, the quotation from Conrad's essay on James, is a clear example. Here's the Conrad sentence again:

> When the last aqueduct has crumbled to pieces, the last air-ship fallen to the ground, the last blade of grass has died upon a dying earth, man, indomitable by his training in his resistance to misery and pain, shall set this undiminished light of his eyes against the feeble glow of the sun.[26]

This is sincere rhetoric, with elaborate parallelisms, weighty modifiers, and periodicity designed to attribute emphatic significance to the action described—both the apocalyptic scene and the "undiminished light," which here refers to an artist's "imperishable consciousness" (13). There is no irony in the repetition "died upon a dying earth," only intensification. Conrad is staring down anyone who might doubt his claims.

Faulkner, in his Nobel oration in 1950, offers a rewrite:

> It is easy enough to say that man is immortal simply because he will endure: that when the last ding-dong of doom has clanged and faded from the last worthless rock hanging tideless in the last red and dying evening, that even then there will still be one more sound: that of his puny inexhaustible voice, still talking. I refuse to accept this. (*Essays, Speeches, and Public Letters* 120)

Conrad's summoning of a hypothetical apocalypse to demonstrate the dominion of the artist seems to Faulkner the indulgent dream of another age, next to the real fear of the atomic apocalypse. Yet even across decades of history dense with two world wars, and an ocean of national difference, there is a fundamental similarity to the Conrad essay: both authors imagine the artist as a heroic figure offering hope against a catastrophe that can be dispelled by acts of perceptive imagination.

Faulkner's response to Conrad has not met with much critical praise. "In this speech, a notable example of negative influence, Conradian rhetoric is

transformed into Faulknerian bombast" (Meyers 191). Bombast, perhaps, but skill-
fully deployed: this is not incompetent imitation but deliberate refusal of the grandeur of Conrad's rhetoric. Conrad's light of perception becomes Faulkner's "puny
inexhaustible voice"; Conrad's unrelentingly high register gives way to Faulkner's
comically alliterative "ding-dong of doom." Faulkner, however, is not writing
parody to undermine Conrad's possibility of hope, but claiming that his possibility is too limited.

The allusion here is a way of mapping out an ideological difference that does not
rely on recognition of the original: the wide audience to which Faulkner pitched
his Nobel address could not be counted on to recognize a particular Conrad
essay, but they could certainly recognize the generalized use of an opposing voice
to make an ethical claim. "It is easy enough to say . . ." creates the possibility of
present-tense speakers saying such things. Faulkner is making a past statement
into a contemporary one. By not demanding recognition of the original statement,
he paradoxically makes Conrad more immediate, makes him into a source of ideas
the weakness of which is not due to temporal distance. Conrad becomes a way of
expressing a present-day worldview.[27]

The sharp disagreement Faulkner creates tends to vanish when our understanding of allusion focuses too much on either form or ideas, on either aesthetic
gratitude and rebellion or a political revision to which the aesthetics are secondary.[28] The close formal parallels between their novels have led to critical comparison of the two authors that is widespread but thin, dominated by references in
which Faulkner is seen as bringing Conrad's methods to their logical conclusion.[29]
The vision of Faulkner as simply an even more elaborate version of Conrad—what
Conrad would have done, had he lived a few years later—obscures both real tech-
nical differences and the purposes and effects of many of the choices Faulkner
does make.

Most analyses of Faulkner's forms see them as signs of an ever more sophisticated skepticism about man's ability to know and understand events. Philip
Weinstein, for instance, in *Unknowing*, describes *Absalom, Absalom!*:

> It stages unknowing as an assault on the known. Faulkner's modernist
> style—his restless syntax and discontinuous sequences—registers time's
> disorienting power. . . . Faulkner's style lets him (and his fiction) not know
> and not judge, lets the fiction set up, by way of gathering juxtapositions and
> differed/deferred information, emergent patterns of dysfunction whose
> repercussions and permutations he sees—and lets us see—but does not
> pretend to see beyond.[30]

Yet it is precisely through what Faulkner does with form—specifically, what he does with forms adapted from Conrad—that Faulkner's defense of knowing takes place. The more Faulkner disorients and disrupts a linear flow of time and the more narrators interpose between an event and its interpretation, the more he defends the validity and importance of an attempt to see beyond the "juxtapositions" and "dysfunctions."

The Nobel oration's optimism has long been seen as a little embarrassing, one of the many examples critics like to cite of later Faulkner saying things about art that seem at odds with the bleak visions of the great novels of the 1930s. Ian Watt, for instance, claims that in his eagerness to affirm the triumph of man Faulkner "protests too much" (*Essays on Conrad* 17).[31] To Mark Greif, the speech is "hortatory boilerplate, junk," an example of Faulkner "recasting" his earlier work (120, 119). It is often a piece of evidence in readings of Faulkner's work that focus on the way his reputation was shaped by Cold War politics that postdate the prewar novels.[32]

Yet the distinction between Conrad and himself that Faulkner makes in the Nobel oration is built into Faulkner's use of Conradian techniques and rhetoric in his earlier novels. Rather than adding complexity in order to undermine knowledge, Faulkner was from the start reversing Conrad's skepticism—was, in fact, more epistemologically confident than his predecessor. Rather than positioning himself as a later author bringing his benighted predecessor up to speed with the times, Faulkner stands up for his "old verities" (*Essays* 120) against what he sees as Conrad's attacks on them. Conrad, the author of a previous age, becomes a voice symptomatic of the invidious perils of modernity.

Faulkner's sense that Conradian pessimism and its philosophical underpinnings go too far is central to the character conflicts of *The Sound and the Fury* and *Absalom, Absalom!* Conradian rhetoric and allusions occur in both novels, always with the implication that the beliefs they indicate are to be shunned. For instance, Razumov in Conrad's *Under Western Eyes* thinks to himself:

> In this world of men nothing can be changed—neither happiness nor misery. They can only be displaced at the cost of corrupted consciences and broken lives—a futile game for arrogant philosophers and sanguinary triflers. (201)

Quentin Compson in *The Sound and the Fury* recalls the voice of his father:

> Because no battle is ever won he said. They are not even fought. The field only reveals to man his own folly and despair, and victory is an illusion of philosophers and fools. (935)

Faulkner picks up several superficial characteristics of Conrad's style here—paired words and alliteration. More importantly, he also echoes with extraordinary precision the structure and content of the thought expressed. Both Razumov and Quentin's father start out with a point about futility so abstract and extreme as to be slightly obscure in significance:

> In this world of men nothing can be changed—
> No battle is ever won he said.

They then proceed to amplify and emphasize the absoluteness of the original negative statements without clearing their obscurity:

> neither happiness nor misery.
> They are not even fought.

Then new sentences explain the meanings of the original statements, in terms of sardonic dismissal ("only"), using paired phrases:

> They can only be displaced at the cost of corrupted consciences and
>   broken lives
> The field only reveals to man his own folly and despair,

They finish by denigrating the efforts of "philosophers" who believe in the utility or meaningfulness of human action:

> —a futile game for arrogant philosophers and sanguinary triflers.
> and victory is an illusion of philosophers and fools.

This revision has all the markings of parody—stylistic imitation, exaggeration of the original claim. Razumov sees action playing out as the tragic inverse of its intention; the elder Compson sees action play out only to reveal that the intended result is itself meaningless. By rendering the idea more extreme, Faulkner also makes it more estranged from human experience and easier to attack: Razumov's vision of the world as a zero-sum game at least suggests that this state of affairs is a tragic one, whereas Compson's "They are not even fought" contemptuously dismisses the apparent experience of people struggling in life—denigrating not just an attempt to act but the belief that action is meaningful. The victims of the delusion become broader as well: "arrogant philosophers and sanguinary triflers" is a narrower, more specific range of types of people than "philosophers and fools."

In context, the plot suggests that Compson's view is one of the causes of his family's disasters. This passage occurs at the beginning of the second part of *The Sound and the Fury*, which traces the thoughts of Quentin Compson over the course of the day on which he kills himself. Memories of his cynical, disillusioning father bracket the chapter, from the instance above to a long conversation immediately preceding the end. Conradian rhetoric is partially responsible for his death. Quentin is unable to offer a rhetorical counterpoint—unable to meet his father's words with any answering force of his own. The "puny inexhaustible voice, still talking" is not only insufficient—it is dangerous.

Faulkner engages even more fully with Conradian narrative structures in *Absalom, Absalom!* The novel is his most Conradian in technique, resembling *Lord Jim*, with its embedded narrators and the enigmatic object of their narration.[33] Faulkner is not merely developing Conrad's pessimistic skepticism further than Conrad was willing to go. Instead, his greater syntactic complexity and proliferation of narrators are ways of trying to defend some possibility of knowledge. In *Absalom, Absalom!*, as in *The Sound and the Fury*, Quentin is a paradigmatic instance of the way others' words and outlook burrow into and become part of one's mind. But whereas in *The Sound and the Fury*, he was unable to manipulate them and ultimately dies for it, in *Absalom, Absalom!* Faulkner demonstrates a productive response to the threat of mental takeover—and further develops his use of Conradian forms to refute Conradian ideas.

Here Quentin's grandfather anticipates the terms of the Nobel address, in a parenthesis on "language":

> that meagre and fragile thread, Grandfather said, by which the little surface corners and edges of men's secret and solitary lives may be joined for an instant now and then before sinking back into the darkness where the spirit cried for the first time and was not heard and will cry for the last time and will not be heard then either (208)

This "meager and fragile thread" will become the "puny inexhaustible voice" that Faulkner repudiates. Again paired words ("corners and edges"; "secret and solitary lives") occur in additive syntax through which one or two extra blows fall ("cried . . . and was not heard and will cry . . . and will not be heard"). The terms in which pessimism is presented here are crucial to why Faulkner thought Conrad's stance especially invidious: Faulkner wants men to hear the cry and respond with their revision. *Absalom, Absalom!*, where words echo in ears far removed from any original audience, repudiates the idea that the cries of men will go unheard.

Faulkner's insistence on the receptivity of an audience stands in opposition to Conrad's "doubt[ing] the heroism of the hearers." Faulkner's deliberate emphasis on the human audience of art in opposition to the devaluation of it he perceives in Conrad appears in the differing roles of the audiences in each novel. Marlow's listeners are undeveloped, scarcely differentiated voices, who hear without implications of permanent change. By contrast, Quentin in *Absalom, Absalom!* is both audience and confident recreator of the story.[34] Faulkner's desire to represent the possibility of truth leads to its endless deferral down the chain of storytelling: truth can exist only as an absent object—the missing contents of an empty vessel—but the contagious effects of the search for it testify to its possibility.

Although Marlow is an audience as well as a storyteller—he hears parts of Jim's story from many others—only his narration is synthetic, attempting to encompass multiple views and versions. Telling of Jim's childhood, he says, "Ever since he had been 'so high'—'quite a little chap,' he had been preparing himself" (76). Marlow breaks the words of others into fragments and rearranges them. By contrast, in *Absalom, Absalom!* quotation-fragments are more than mere marshaled evidence; they become part of the stylized language of the retelling, antagonistic and corrective. Rather than being granted meaning by being absorbed into a single style, sudden stylistic contrasts open up glimpses of significance.

These moments have an oppositional, destabilizing quality to which Marlow is seldom subject; but in destabilizing a specific moment in narration Faulkner suggests the possibility of a consensus interpretation. By presenting all the narrators as flawed, Faulkner makes the process of communication between them become the potential source of meaning. Take Faulkner's version of Conrad's interrupting quotations in *Absalom*:

> *It seems that this demon—his name was Sutpen—(Colonel Sutpen)—Colonel Sutpen. Who came out of nowhere and without warning upon the land with a band of strange niggers and built a plantation—(Tore violently a plantation, Miss Rosa Coldfield says)—tore violently. And married her sister Ellen and begot a son and a daughter which—(Without gentleness begot, Miss Rosa Coldfield says)—without gentleness. Which should have been the jewels of his pride and the shield and comfort of his old age, only—(Only they destroyed him or something or he destroyed them or something. And died)—and died. Without regret, Miss Rosa Coldfield says—(Save by her) Yes, save by her. (And by Quentin Compson) Yes. And by Quentin Compson.* (6–7)

This represents Quentin's internal dialogue, and, like Quentin and Shreve mentally and verbally unified near the end of the novel, the multiple voices seem to switch places constantly: the correction, from Rosa's voice, crosses in and out of parentheses; the parentheses start preceding the extraparenthetical versions; sometimes the parentheses seem to step in where the first voice fails. In all cases the voices are able to come to agreement; the interruption and correction of perspectives makes the narrative ultimately more stable.

Faulkner's formal distinctions from Conrad extend to the local, syntactic level. Both authors use style as another form of empty vessel. Their syntax is built out of some similar elements: lengthy sentences with complex subordination, phrases laden with adjectives, and ostentatious rhetorical patterns. But there are differences: language in Faulkner exists to be heard and strains toward some kind of universal human connection, while Conrad's language takes its shape because speech itself, an individual's interpretation, is the action that gives meaning to life, regardless of whether it is ever perceived. Faulkner's syntax is predicated on the illusion that the sentence is about to happen on a great truth, and surely would if it could just continue for another few clauses; Conrad's on an excess of apparent conclusiveness that conceals his horror at the idea of ceasing to speak:

> The artist in his calling of interpreter creates . . . because he must. He is so much of a voice that, for him, silence is like death; and the postulate was, that there is a group alive, clustered on his threshold to watch the last flicker of light on a black sky, to hear the last word uttered in the stilled workshop of the earth. (*Notes on Life and Letters* 14)

The artist ceasing to speak becomes here a sign of the end of the world. Interpretation ends only when creation does. Conrad's syntax is additive in structure. His sentences tend to swerve in meaning between the two poles of skepticism and moral idealism, ending without decisive resolution between them. They are not periodic: multiple points for grammatically acceptable conclusions appear before rhetorical satisfaction does. In the instance above, the second sentence could end at many points (e.g., *death, alive, threshold, light, sky, uttered,* and *workshop*). These points subtly tack back and forth between optimism and pessimism: end at *death* and the artist is a helpless pawn of his own gift; end at *alive* and the image is mankind persisting against all odds as the world crumbles around him; end at *threshold* and the artist is the powerful figuring presiding over this persistence; end at *light* or *sky* and the apocalypse reasserts its force; end with *uttered* or *workshop* and the artist once again rises dominant; with *of the earth* we realize that the workshop here is that of the universe, not the artist, and the end is inevitable. Conclusiveness in a Conrad sentence is purely rhetorical, an aesthetic satisfaction rather than a resolution of all the meanings and implications raised along the length of the sentence. We end with the artist still speaking, the apocalypse predicted but open to interpretation.

If Conrad's syntax puts off the end by offering an overabundance of potential ends in advance, Faulkner's syntax works by undersupplying conclusiveness. His periodic sentences, flaunting the distance to be crossed before they can be concluded, are miniatures of the endless transmission of knowledge and understanding down the chain of narrators and audiences. Conclusion is always imminent and never present. Whereas Conrad's syntax is full of parallels given irregular rhythms by additional clauses, Faulkner's is built on branching subordinate clauses punctuated by parallels. Even when writing his parody of Conrad he follows this pattern: "the last aqueduct . . . the last air-ship . . . the last blade . . ." becomes "the last ding-dong . . . *from* the last worthless rock . . . *in* the last red and dying evening" (emphasis added). Whereas Conrad offers flourishes of possible meaning that are undermined and then revised and re-established, Faulkner insists that communication between minds can be established even while the meaning to be communicated can be continually deferred.

The key syntactical element that Faulkner exploits in *Absalom, Absalom!* is a sentence arranged so that some crucial bit of syntax or logic is obviously missing. Movement forward in a sentence retroactively clarifies the relations between parts of the sentence that have already passed—it clarifies a phrase, for instance, by repeating it with further referents attached. The novel is always in the process of ordering itself, but as previous confusions are resolved, new ones are introduced. In the last few pages, just before the brief dialogue between Henry Sutpen and Quentin Compson, Quentin, in his room at Harvard, thinks back to his wakeful state upon returning home from Sutpen's Hundred, and remembers how at the time he could not escape the memory of the climactic encounter with Henry Sutpen at the house:

> then he was lying on the bed, naked, swabbing his body steadily with the discarded shirt, sweating still, panting: so that when, his eye-muscles aching and straining into the darkness and the almost dried shirt still clutched in his hand, he said "I have been asleep" it was all the same, there was no difference: waking or sleeping he walked down that upper hall between the scaling walls and beneath the cracked ceiling. . . ; waking or sleeping it was the same: the bed, the yellow sheets and pillow, the wasted yellow face with closed, almost transparent eyelids on the pillow, the wasted hands crossed on the breast as if he were already a corpse; waking or sleeping it was the same and would be the same forever as long as he lived (306)

The sentence sets up the reader to anticipate clarity that is exceptionally long-delayed: "so that when" sets up a requirement for two subordinate clauses (when x, y), both of which are delayed by the long clause about his eye-muscles and shirt;

and when the completing clause is provided, it is itself another mystery: "it was all the same." Immediately after the clause completes, we need to provide a referent for the "it"—and the colon prompts us to look ahead again. The most prominent device in what follows is lexical and syntactical repetition punctuated by varying lengths and types of intervening phrases. The anaphoric "waking or sleeping" ties the separate clauses and time periods together. The final sections of the sentence prepare for the break into spare, symmetrical dialogue by an increasing density of repetition: "yellow," "pillow," and "wasted" each occur twice, the adjectives attached to different nouns. Literally, the scene is becoming "the same": hands as well as face are wasted, the face as well as the sheets and pillow are yellow; Quentin on his bed at home is merging with Henry the near-corpse on his bed at Sutpen's Hundred, and two versions of his own past self and the other man are both resurgent in his mind many miles and months away at Harvard. The whole sentence culminates in the unification of the key phrases "waking or sleeping" and "it was all the same": the past has finally burst into the present in the form of the physical presence (within the memory) of Henry Sutpen, emissary of the Old South.

Even then Faulkner opens up a further avenue, anticipating the future ("forever"). "It" (as in, "it was all the same") receives a referent only after the end of the sentence at last with the conversation, which has, in a sense, been delayed for the whole novel; it is the scene that generated the inquiry Quentin and Shreve undertake. Still, even this encounter is another deferral: the dialogue we are given does not, in the end, tell us how Quentin found out answers to any of the mysteries of the plot. There is never an answer, to this or most of the other questions the novel poses; Quentin's final answer to Shreve ("*I dont hate it*" [311]) famously fails to offer the whole truth, and instead what remains is the process of continual reframing of increasing understanding rather than any final sense of certainty. The dominant idiom of *Absalom, Absalom!*, those massive sentences rolling on toward ever-deferred conclusions, is in this sense a direct denial of Conradian style, offering continual communication with continually deferred meaning to be communicated rather than aborted communication overfull of potential things to be communicated.

It seems unlikely Faulkner would have been able to leap forward technically the way he did without his predecessors; it is not merely a matter of ideological difference that allows for his narrative devices to be so much more intricate and elaborated than Conrad. The intervening revolution of Joyce's *Ulysses*, the influence of which is so obvious in *The Sound and the Fury*, clearly does some work in catalyzing his more baroque experimentations. But the genuine teleology of increasing narrative complication over the development of high modernist fiction does not map neatly onto a similar teleology of increasing skepticism and emphasis on subjectivity. Increasing stylistic complexity is not an index of the disappearance of Faulkner's faiths—in humanity, in art—but a bristling leap to their defense.

The two examples of influence in this chapter are not the same form of influence I will explore in the rest of this book. James's use of Conrad is that of a contemporary; Faulkner's use of Conrad is transhistorical, but Faulkner, strangely, treats Conrad as though he is a contemporary—makes him stand in for the onslaught of modern skepticism. It is closer to the classic form of influence for which we already have theories—Conrad is made to stand in as a voice distinct from his successor, representing a set of ideas Faulkner implies are present today. In Baldwin, Ngũgĩ, and Kesey, by contrast, recognizable allusions to James, Conrad, and Faulkner appear only sparsely (although in all cases there is ample evidence for conscious engagement with their predecessors); in them, the literary past becomes something like the neutral tool Faulkner claimed Conrad was for him.

Recuperation's Various Forms

One of the rhetorical powers of critique in literary discourse has been its status as an apparent teleological inevitability, the inevitable future to which all our ideas will fall prey, demolished by the "changing wisdom of successive generations," in Conrad's phrase. The past is the source of complacent certainty, the future of disruptive doubt. Faulkner's syntax does the opposite, rendering the future—the immediate future of the reader making his or her way through the novel—as the locus of a commitment and a moment of clarity that is always just around the corner. Faulkner's career arc follows the same pattern on a larger scale, which has discomfited critics: the Nobel oration is but one example of the way later Faulkner writings reflect confidence in value systems that the earlier novels put under pressure. (In chapter 4, I will discuss other examples, including Faulkner's rewriting of his own novel in the appendix to *The Sound and the Fury*.) The future awaiting him after *The Sound and the Fury* and *Absalom, Absalom!* was not skepticism but renewed knowledge—and the syntax pointed in that direction from the beginning. Recuperative modernism's empty vessels are suggestions that the resources literature might offer the future are habits of thinking that foster not critique but commitment.[35]

The word *rescue* usefully conveys the kinds of mental movements and commitments that the literary forms of recuperative modernism script for their

readers: against long odds, with no idea taken for granted or received complacently and passively. Critics didn't stop looking for "recognition" and "knowledge" in James or Faulkner because it became incontrovertibly true that these
experiences were absent from reading the text.[36] Critics stopped looking for them
because it became unclear what was important, interesting, or politically useful
about those experiences. The pathways between literary forms (say, multiple
perspectives), the structures of literary experience they create (say, creating uncertainty about truth), and the political valences we attribute to those structures
(say, destabilizing received and normative ways of viewing the world) sometimes
seem clear, with no forks or alternative possibilities. This is the " 'tacit,' allegorizing
leap" that Eli Park Sorensen decries: "the uncritical *assumption* that a set of politically subversive concepts corresponds to formal disruption, meta-fictive strategies
and labyrinths of narrative structures" (10). Those pathways, in fact, are not
a cathedral floor labyrinth but a networked maze: we might see the same form
(multiple perspectives, again) creating different experiences (say instead, forcing
readers to come to conclusions within complex situations), and as a result developing different political valences (say instead, modeling ideological commitment).
Critique tends to value the first political endpoint—destabilization—over the
second—commitment. As a result, much of the work on these authors attributes a
limited range of literary experience to the forms of the texts.

    And this is where the transhistorical is necessary to force us outside the well-
mapped intellectual landscape of today. Postcolonial studies, for instance, has for
some time questioned the value of the modernist affects of uncertainty and destabilization, defending realism's power to produce recognition and knowledge
as, under some circumstances, more politically valuable.[37] This book takes the
same starting point as many others on modernism—those experimental literary
forms—while tracing the structures of literary experience they create in precisely
the direction the forms are often assumed to undo. Looking at the transhistorical reach of modernist forms allows us to take into account these other ways of
valuing form. Modernist experiments, just like the forms that precede them, can
ask their readers to come to a conclusive understanding of events and to make
commitments; and their doing so enables, rather than disables, their political uses.

    Forms, then, can startle us into different understandings of politics and are,
as a result, worth placing at the endpoint of our analysis rather than merely as a
path through which we can gaze at the cultures that produce them.[38] Recuperative
modernism's abstraction confronts the reality that there is no intrinsic alignment
between a rhetorical or narrative structure and a particular political cause. These

authors furnish tools to the future and know full well they have no control over their use.

The next three chapters of this book will examine three classic elements of literary form: characterization, in Henry James and James Baldwin; nonchronological narration, in Joseph Conrad and Ngũgĩ wa Thiong'o; and perspective, in William Faulkner and Ken Kesey. In all three cases, what seem to be modernist gestures of negation become instead forms of recuperation. James, in chapter 2, defends the charismatic individual character of romance against a realist insistence on the way context shapes identity. In this form, characterization provides James Baldwin a template for resisting society's construction of individual subjects. In chapter 3, Conrad challenges his readers with nonchronological narrative structures that obscure plots and characters. These structures, however, don't allow the reader to rest in uncertainty: instead they train us in putting together partial knowledge. And when Ngũgĩ adapts them, he uses them to force a diverse audience to take a particular view on historical events, rather than letting them rest in unknowability or ambiguity. Chronological fragmentation produces the authoritative visions of realism. The following chapter, on Faulkner, looks at the ways shifting perspectives in Faulkner and Kesey create ever stronger stability in the reader's understanding of the plot, and how both authors use these complex structures to license universal statements about human activity.

In the last chapter, I examine contemporary literature—specifically, the brand-new genre of the novel about a nonfictional novelist, in which today's writers turn and chase the dead. These works always both critique their predecessors from the perspective of the future and reanimate them, recreating their styles and forms for a new audience. They represent, in this regard, a Möbius strip between today's suspicious and recuperative impulses toward the past, in which one perpetually transforms into the other.

2. Character and Identity

What makes a fictional character charismatic? Why is Henry James fascinated by vividly defined, startlingly individual characters—those innocent yet high-minded American girls, or their foils, the thrilling, chilling mistresses of social manipulation? By referring to a protagonist as "vividly defined," I have, of course, slightly stacked the deck—describing a character perhaps closer to what we think of as Victorian than modernist, one given certain broad traits that persist in his or her personality throughout the story, and which form a key part of the unfolding of the plot: for instance, Kate Croy's ambition and social skill in *The Wings of the Dove*, or Isabel Archer's independence in *Portrait of a Lady*. Within the worlds of the novels they stand out as unusual or exceptional to everyone around them. Perhaps the best instance in James's work is Isabel's arrival in *Portrait of a Lady*. Greeted with the question, "Who is that strange woman?" (13), she quickly finds herself an object of fascination, romantic and otherwise, for everyone around her. In other words, one way to make fictional characters charismatic to the reader is to present them as charismatic to other characters.

Yet James's striking protagonists—extraordinary within the worlds of their novels, and perceived as such by the characters around them—also have strong individual identities: they seem to have particularly vivid traits that originate from some internal source. And it is between these two ways of defining character—between a distinct self and a relational process of perception—that James's work of characterization and plotting takes place. James always claimed that fictive characters needed to be worth the readers' attention; this became his main criticism of Flaubert, whose novels, he says, are "a revelation of what the imagination may accomplish under a powerful impulse to mirror the unmitigated realities of life. . . . The fatal charmlessness of each and all of them is an eloquent plea for the ideal" (II.290).[1] More fundamentally, development of character is a crucial aspect of the plots of James's novels: the crises often turn on what kind of a person a given character will turn out to be. Characters agonize over choosing elements from American or European culture, personality traits from one acquaintance or another, over being open to or closed to influences. Character, in this sense, is the process of foreclosing alternatives, of choosing one possibility for identity over another.

James's complaint that Flaubert merely "mirrors" life was a repeating theme in his criticism: writing about Trollope, he detects the same failing: "Into this mirror the public, at first especially, grew very fond of looking." Trollope's "great, his inestimable merit was a complete appreciation of the usual. . . . his imagination [had] no light of its own" (I.1333–1334). Trollope is all mirror, not enough lamp. Mirrors show up again and again in James's aesthetic theory, but not as unambiguous gestures toward the value of realism: they are equally often signals of the perniciousness of *mere* representation. The distance between James's charismatic characters and those around them is also the distance between James's fictional worlds and the "unmitigated realities of life" he sought to modify or exclude from them. James's plots, then, are stories in which characters learn, under desperate pressure, how to be out of context: both their happiness and their formal roles as protagonists in the novels depend on gaining some sense of separation from what surrounds them.

The balancing of mirroring representation and the transformative light of art is one of the preoccupations of James's fiction. Those two character types—the vividly individual, yet strangely blank and innocent girl; the knowing woman who has perfectly mastered the currents and norms of a social order—represent opposing ways of negotiating the relationship between identity and the world. In *Portrait of a Lady*, the counterpart to Isabel, the "strange woman," is Madame Merle, who is "too perfectly the social animal that man and woman are supposed to have been intended to be" (185): Madame Merle is a conscious and calculated mirror of society. Isabel and Madame Merle both draw the attention of everyone in their novels—positively and negatively—and the plot plays out as an interaction between their contrasting relationships between self and society.

People and art alike in James are both at risk when they too closely mirror the world around them, and for some of the same reasons. An "eloquent plea for the ideal" might also describe a demand that art offer a vision of the world that doesn't merely conform to the norms of today's reality. The mirror, in other words, can become the trap of the present, and one of James's successors returns to the same image to make a similar point. In James Baldwin's "Everybody's Protest Novel," the protest novel fails because it is only "a mirror of our confusion, dishonesty, panic, trapped and immobilized in the sunlit prison of the American dream" (16). The novel, for Baldwin, is supposed to offer more—to illuminate the confusion and break the "cage of reality" (16). Mirrors multiply across Baldwin's creative and critical writing, but they consistently stand for the ways people attempt to see themselves as images of social norms—straight white American masculinity in *Giovanni's Room*; the ways white Americans attempt to limit the possibilities of black identity in his essays.

Jamesian strategies of characterization, in other words, become, for Baldwin, a way of confronting one of the great dilemmas of African American writers at mid-century: is the task of literature portraying what society does to the individual, or what individuals can do within and against the confines of society? Does the charismatically exceptional figure tell a more important story than the bleakly typical one? James's art, I'll argue, provided for Baldwin a model of the relationship between integral personal identity and the influence of social contexts that could articulate these tensions—both the brutal force of society's shaping power and the necessity of recognizing one's status as an individual out of harmony with it.

In James novels, characters learn where their limited forms of identity and agency lie: they learn to choose whether and how to make themselves into reflections of their various social contexts. The novels are case studies in the value of perceiving people as strongly individuated beings with their own persistent personalities, rather than naturalist nodes through which social forces flow. Julian Murphet suggests one analysis of modernist character, arguing that the major distinction between twentieth-century characterization techniques and those of the nineteenth century is the tendency of later authors to destabilize the presumed unity of the singular character by "the multiple"—multiplicity of interior psychological states, as well as multiplicity of the exterior world. "Modernism has been unjustly misconstrued as a movement concerned with the representation of individual subjectivity. Its sublime peaks are, however, . . . moments of linguistic intensity at which any conventional notion of the subject is displaced and evacuated by the multiple" (265–266).[2] In this chapter, I will suggest an alternate track for modernist character. James is fascinated by precisely the exterior multiple that

Murphet foregrounds, and by its effect on the individual character. He uses this multiplicity, however, not to destabilize the place of the protagonist or the solidity of individual identity but to reinforce it, to argue for the value of the individual as against the multiple. It is not that James insists that the individual can stand against and resist absorption in the outside world, but that he shows how, over time, individuality reveals itself through the capacity to choose one's own relations to other people and the outside world.

It is this reinforcement that Baldwin finds useful. Baldwin presents the individual as needing to express an identity *against* the invidious influence of social contexts; what seems to be most Victorian—and, criticism sometimes implies, politically retrograde—about James is precisely what Baldwin strengthens. If James's imagery occasionally valorizes the idea of mirror-like characters who perfectly reflect the world around them, seeing such reflection as an essential stage of self-development, Baldwin almost always uses the mirror as a metaphor for a personal, political, and aesthetic failure to see beyond the limited outlooks of normative society.

If we want to find out what the significance of James's art is for fraught political topics like race and sexual identity, we must look less at the context in which these works appeared and more at the meandering paths they have charted since—at, in short, the ways they have actually been used. More broadly, this argument questions the implicit priority claims undergirding many of the common ways of connecting authors to fraught political topics. Historicism and theory provide apparently different pathways, but in their most common instantiations neither attends very consistently to the history of reading experiences produced by works of art. Historicism sees literature as more the consequence of its context than as having its own consequences; theory tends to imply political consequences without necessarily determining whether such consequences have actually followed the works of art in question. These methods are often combined in order to produce a covert kind of presentism: take, for example, Sara Blair's treatment of James's "writing of race and nation." She argues, primarily using placement in historical context for her evidence, that "James's texts work contextually both to preserve and to exploit the inherent instability of racial identity in the era of modernity" (5). "The era of modernity" slides between James's time and our own; it's also hard to argue that the subtext here is anything other than a whole host of today's theories about identity as performed or constructed by social factors outside the self, drawn from Judith Butler and others. This isn't necessarily wrong, but it is limited, and it particularly leads to neglect of the far more various and surprising uses James's works have had over their history that seem less amenable to our current theories. It also tends to gloss over the transhistorical aspirations and afterlives of these works.

Baldwin's use of James offers a more overt presentism. Rather than discerning the use of racialized discourse within literature where it might have been repressed, he transfers Jamesian discourse on a wide array of topics, unified by more abstract themes, to the realm of race: think, for instance, of *The Princess Casamassima* making the list of Baldwin's important books. It's there because its treatment of class dispossession and the identity struggles attendant upon it has *analogies* with the racial dilemmas of Baldwin's period.[3] Criticism has been less attentive to those politicized uses of James that take shape by way of analogy and abstraction rather than history and specificity—perhaps because of the long history of criticism taking abstraction and generality as an escape from political relevance: abstraction from history tends to become erasure of the marginalized. Toni Morrison makes this point most influentially, in excavating the "Africanist" discourse of nineteenth-century American literature and exposing the limitations of a "criticism that needs to insist that literature is not only 'universal' but also 'race-free'" (*Playing* 6, 12)—which she takes to be the dominant modes of criticism at least at the moment of her writing in 1992. Baldwin sees the matter differently: he chooses to see as useful those abstractions that may not come from discourse about race or sexuality, but have something to say to it nevertheless. Like Faulkner's description of the "amoral" writer, Baldwin takes from the past and makes of it what he needs.

In this context, it is not instability that offers Baldwin racial empowerment but a promise of stable identity belonging to oneself rather than society. In order to see what James offers Baldwin we have to look beyond actual racial moments in James's texts; thematically, the international theme and the evocations of queer sexualities were far more generative to Baldwin. And while both themes are addressed by and expressed through the techniques I will be discussing in these chapters, the techniques themselves shape a reading experience with broader implications than the shared themes. The relation between a reader and a novel is, after all, also a relation between an individual and a world. The persistence and expansive use of James's theories and forms of characterization demonstrate that asserting continuity between past, present, and future on formal grounds can strengthen, rather than erase, politicized contexts and historical realities. The charismatic character, in the end, offers a template for resisting the ways societies construct individual subjects.

"An Old Story": How to Be Yourself in Henry James

> Emma Woodhouse, handsome, clever, and rich . . .
>
> —Jane Austen, *Emma* (1815)

> Her flexible figure turned itself easily this way and that, in sympathy with
> the alertness with which she evidently caught impressions. Her impressions
> were numerous, and they were all reflected in a clear, still smile.
>
> —Henry James, *The Portrait of a Lady* (1881)

> To her it was absolutely absorbing; all this; the cabs passing; and she would
> not say of Peter, she would not say of herself, I am this, I am that.
>
> —Virginia Woolf, *Mrs. Dalloway* (1925)[4]

The 110 years between Austen and Woolf drastically altered literary habits of characterization. From her very first sentence, Austen delineates her heroine's personal qualities (handsomeness, cleverness), with the same assuredness as she lists those granted by society (wealth). Despite the ironies that collect around these qualities over the course of the novel, this authorial bestowal of identity and importance stands. James's Isabel Archer is just as clearly an exceptional being, but rather than gaining her identity by authorial fiat on the opening page, she walks into the gaze of other characters in the second chapter. James appears to grant Isabel her importance through neither her social situation nor even her vivid personal qualities. Instead, her source of interest is in the other characters' perception of her. In particular, what they perceive is her own perceptive capacity: the way she connects the variousness of an outside world—those numerous impressions that cause her to turn "this way and that"—with a unified inner being represented by a smile that, unlike her figure, is "still." James's Isabel lives in a world where social place and experience are not directly connected with internal qualities, but instead impinge and press in upon the character, who must struggle to distill the impressions to a clear self.

By the time Virginia Woolf wrote *Mrs. Dalloway*, the refusal to bestow specific summations of identity had become one of her central artistic tenets. Woolf locates the material of fiction in the urban equivalent of Isabel's various impressions. Yet where Isabel catches impressions, Clarissa is absorbed by them. My point is not to read James as the partially developed evolutionary forebear of Woolf, but to show that James is grappling with many of the same problems as Woolf. Fully conscious of the way individual identities can become diffuse under the pressure of outside influence, he mounts an elaborate defense of the vividly singular character's place in fiction. James is committed to an idea of identity more coherent and less various than Woolf's; his fiction may usually refuse to say that people are "this" or "that," but his fictive project is defined by the attempt to convey to the reader whole identities.[5] Isabel Archer's smile both reflects the outside world and, Mona Lisa–like, points to an elusive yet unmoving interiority. Her smile reflects impressions as much in the sense of reflecting *on* them as mirroring their changes.

James, then, speaks well to our current critical moment, as studies in character begin to proliferate once more after fallow years when, as Rita Felski has recently described it, the idea of character as a "conception of a core selfhood imbued with a moral and social typology had been dissolved in the acid bath of critical theory, or superseded by linguistic and performative theories of identity" ("Introduction" v). As character re-emerges from the acid bath, we should consider how earlier novelists negotiated pressures upon character and characterization strategy that are cognate with those of modern critical theory, especially when, like James, their novels have been such touchstones for that theory. As various as the new character studies are, they share a common interest in examining how whole character functions as an element within large systems—whether market economies, the distribution of attention in character-systems, or the cognitive mechanisms that make us interested in one type of character over another.[6] But character is complicated enough on its own to need some attention: Omri Moses declares, "I insist on repsychologizing character" (57) and suggests that complexity and adaptive changeability of character is precisely what modernism can contribute to recent character studies, so far dominated by scholars of eighteenth- and nineteenth-century novels. Rather than taking characters' wholeness for granted and looking at the ways characters interact with such systems, I will argue in this chapter that for James individual characters are constituted through the interactions between exterior and interior sources of identity. James puts his characters through their own acid baths, and they come out transformed but still whole.

Isabel Archer's identity and her vividness take shape in the novel through the complex negotiations between her mind, the minds of those who observe her and whom she observes, and the outside world that she takes in through "impressions." A comparable phenomenon occurs in *The Ambassadors*, when Lambert Strether comes across Madame de Vionnet in Notre Dame. Before he recognizes her, she reminds him of "some fine, firm, concentrated heroine of an old story, something he had heard, read, something that, had he a hand for drama, he might himself have written, renewing her courage, renewing her clearness, in splendidly protected meditation" (185). Firm, concentrated—the heroine of "an old story" is defined by her solid and distilled identity. It is fragile and subject to strain but it is fundamentally *hers*—not only is she responsible for renewing her own clearness and courage, but the very word "renew" marks these qualities as traits she already possesses. The shadow of a grammatical ambiguity, however, falls upon Strether's mental phrasing, which points to one of the most important sources of the assault on the firmness of character in James: *renewing her courage* is evidently supposed to refer to her action in the church at this moment, but it is separated from the clause about Strether as author only by the light force of a comma (*something that he might have written, renewing her courage*). The identity Strether is so delighted to see as distinctively her own is also, oddly, potentially authored by him. The fact of its aesthetic satisfaction seems to undermine the very thing that makes it aesthetically satisfying: it seems from literature because of its self-created solidity, but suggesting that it is of literature renders it the creation of someone else.

This interplay between character as intrinsic to a person and as something constructed by other people appears throughout James's plots and theories of the novel. Again and again James shows characters both constructed by others and still recognizably themselves. While the outside world can present a threat, it also presents a valuable source of material for self-construction; in Strether's vision, Madame de Vionnet's individual existence can coincide easily with her having an author. James's fiction strives not to oppose but to connect the concentration of something grasped at a distance, without complexity, with the complications of the forces pressing upon the self in that same moment. In Strether's vision, characters possess consciousness of the forces pressing upon them, and therefore have the capacity to "renew" themselves within them. Being a heroine requires both a strong self and an involvement in outside forces that do not leave the self unchanged.

The idea of Madame de Vionnet renewing her identity, with no clear distinction between her own agency and Strether's authoring view, resembles familiar modern theories of an intersubjective, culturally constructed self. James stands out in consistently emphasizing human agency in the performance. Judith Butler, for example, has gone back and forth over precisely this point: in 1993 she insisted that identity "is not performed *by* a subject" (*Bodies That Matter* 95), forestalling readings of her own earlier work that might imply agency in the construction of gender.[7] James's fiction is about characters who learn how to be responsible for performing their own emergent identities. The 1990s saw an outpouring of James criticism that demonstrated the way his fiction responded to and reflected social phenomena and anxieties, a critical paradigm still dominant today. The major readings of this era tended to focus on flexibility and open-mindedness—in other words, how context shape characters—and consequently on the way James undermines naturalized notions of identity or refuses moral or epistemological absolutes.[8] While a valuable corrective to older readings that privileged the drama of individual characters' decisive moral choices, this trend has led to misapprehension of the way James's strategic flexuousness works. F. O. Matthiessen wrote back in 1944 that the use of Strether as a focalizing consciousness "serves greatly to reinforce such concentration, since if every detail must be observed and analysed by Strether, we obtain a heightened singleness of vision" (22). Concentration and singleness of vision still have an important place in these novels, emerging precisely out of the ways, as the more recent critics have shown, singleness is disrupted and concentration diffused. Strether must *learn* the importance of excluding irrelevant detail over the course of the novel; James was defending not a particular single vision but instead the *pursuit* of singular vision as a goal, maintained with sensitive specificity to particular situations. The philosopher Robert Pippin asks, "Why isn't James a moral skeptic?" (7). I wish to extend the tone of his question from ethics to characterization. As complexly aware of the challenges and ruptures of modernity as we can show James to be, how and why does he maintain ideals of design and coherence? What—for James, for Baldwin, and ultimately for us today—is the continuing appeal of the concentrated heroine of an old story in a world full of forces diffusing and mixing her identity?

Rather than demonstrating the artificiality of identity, James examines the uses of such artifice, the ways perceiving others and oneself as having coherent identities can be helpful rather than invidious. James's fiction is a laboratory for examining the ways in which readerly desires and experiences—the love of vividly distinct characters, for instance—both are and are not useful models for living. All of those strategic ambiguities about the sources of identity—James's unwillingness to confirm either a naturalized notion of an intrinsic self or a view of the self as entirely composed by exterior forces—represent a commitment to agency, to the idea that identity is granted entirely by neither nature nor culture. This agency resides not in the content of the personality but the faculty for *choosing* content by sifting outside influences. Rather than the solidity of Austen's Emma or the fluidity of Woolf's Clarissa, characters' changeability becomes the material with which they build something solid. James's characters learn to use others' personalities as the building blocks for their own. Character, for James, is constantly being produced by individuals' efforts of perception and agency.

Mirror of Miraculous Silver: The Structure of Character in James

The most familiar expression in James of character as a production of exterior forces is the "envelope of circumstances" (193) that the socially adept, morally ambiguous Madame Merle stresses in *Portrait of a Lady*: physical trappings such as clothes and houses, associated with wealth and the inherited traditions of Europe.

Madame Merle, who can afford to own no house of her own, declares that the self is expressed in "one's house, one's furniture, one's garments, the books one reads, the company one keeps—these things are all expressive."[9] This list is a mixture of the things she has (good company, culture) and the things she desires but lacks (a house, furniture). Her catalog of exteriority conceals the expression of her own desires. What seems to be a statement of a mediated, socially-contingent self turns out to register instead the individuality and will of a particular character.

Madame Merle is an example of the way social phenomena become the building blocks of personalities: by encountering them in the forms of others' personalities. Characters can both become the object of others' projections of personality and also change their personalities to incorporate others'. Sometimes these overlap—in *Portrait*, Madame Merle constructs a vision of Isabel's character that melds with Isabel's own desire to emulate Madame Merle. Sometimes, however, they diverge—in *The Golden Bowl*, Charlotte Stant constructs a particular idea of Maggie's character as virtually the opposite of her own, while over the course of the novel Maggie slowly changes her own character to be more like Charlotte's.

Personality, in James's fiction, can be transferred from one character to another—depending on context, to the peril of either party. This transference drives the plot of *The Ambassadors*, from the initial transformation of Chad Newsome— the American become a Parisian under the influence of Madame de Vionnet—to the changes in Strether's habits of perception over the course of the novel. Maria Gostrey, Strether's expatriate companion and advisor, says of Madame de Vionnet's relation with Chad: "Don't consider her, don't judge her at all in herself. Consider her and judge her only in *him*" (106). Similarly, Strether arrives in England the editor of the *Woollett Review*, saying in one breath, "My name's on the cover," and in the next that Mrs. Newsome, a formidable Woollett matriarch, is "behind the whole thing" (39).[10] Strether spends the novel first possessed by the personality of Mrs. Newsome, then by those of Maria and Madame de Vionnet. This susceptibility to influence, to a fluid intermingling and imposition of personality, is not a peculiar state of affairs, but an inevitable one in James's fiction.[11] The plots of the novels turn on how to cope with it. This action goes beyond the process of imaginative envisioning alluded to above; it results in actual changes in characters' personalities.[12] From being either unwittingly or uncritically open to influence, his characters must become manipulators of the process of influence and transference, consciously considering what they want their personalities to be, and capable of using others' personalities as building blocks. They must both recognize the material in the world around them and become critical and self-conscious about how they make it part of themselves. Character exists in these choices: identity is both constituted by and apart from context.

Like so many features of James's fiction, this dynamic becomes more pronounced but less explicit over the course of his career. The two major types of relationship to others' personalities are represented most clearly by Strether and Maggie Verver. Strether is a case study, for most of his novel, in excessive openness to others' personalities and a refusal to make a choice between them. The plot of *The Ambassadors* is simple: Strether travels to Europe on instructions from his wealthy patroness Mrs. Newsome to retrieve her son Chad; rumor has it that he has fallen into an affair with some scandalous woman. Strether arrives in Paris and promptly finds himself thrilled by the culture and complexity of the city and its people, including Madame de Vionnet, the woman with whom Chad is involved. He only belatedly realizes that their relationship is sexual, and this realization does not disrupt his affection for them; eventually, he departs back to America, although he has lost all his credibility with Mrs. Newsome. At first his name stands in for Mrs. Newsome; for much of the novel he instead stands in for Madame de Vionnet; only at the end does he begin to develop an identity of his own. Strether's state of indiscriminate absorption of others is unsustainable; like Isabel, he must choose.

Maggie Verver, while not arriving on the scene as quite so perfect an example of an absorbent personality as Strether, forms a much more fully developed example of the process of controlling and making use of those absorptions—a process only just begun for Strether as *The Ambassadors* concludes. In the second half of *The Golden Bowl*, once she has discovered her husband's infidelity and is scheming to regain him, Maggie feels like an actress who, "engaged for a minor part in the play and having mastered her cues with anxious effort, should find herself suddenly promoted to leading lady" (XXIV.208). This sense of taking over the part of another is closely aligned to her growing inquiries into events.

In both novels, characters' attitudes toward the construction of their own personalities correspond closely with their approaches to understanding their own perceptions of the world. Construction of character is dependent upon a developing epistemology. Maggie and Strether correspond to a major formal tension in James's theory of focalized narration, and to two classic forms of Jamesian thought process: the passive reception of impressions and the analytical arrangement of them. This is the tension of Isabel's passage over the lawn at Gardencourt, where she both "reflects" the outside world and seems to be reflecting upon and synthesizing it.

Mirrors come up specifically in one of James's most famous passages on his fictive method: in the preface to *The Princess Casamassima*, he states his intention of

> placing right in the middle of the light . . . the most polished of possible mirrors of the subject. Rowland Mallet, in "Roderick Hudson," is exactly such a mirror, . . . and I might exemplify the case through a long list, . . . down to such unmistakeable examples as . . . that of Lambert Strether in "The Ambassadors" (*he* a mirror verily of miraculous silver and quite pre-eminent, I think, for the connexion) and that of the Prince in the first half and that of the Princess in the second half of "The Golden Bowl." I should note the extent to which these persons are, so far as their other passions permit, intense *perceivers*, all, of their respective predicaments. (V.xv–xvi)

Representation does require an act of mirroring—a sensitive consciousness open to take into itself the people and objects of the outside world. But the confident sweep of James's list gives way to a more strained phrase: "so far as their other passions permit, intense *perceivers*, all." Not only is there a tension allowed between one's own passions and the ability to perceive accurately, but the emphasis on *perceivers* (along with the need for the word "intense") suggests that James recognizes that it is relatively weak as a climactic word, that *perception* risks implying a passivity that isn't exactly what he means. The most polished of possible mirrors is precisely what Isabel refuses to be. Her predatory husband Osmond *wants* her to have a mind that "reflected one's thought on a scintillating surface" (*Portrait* 339): such pure passivity has an invidious quality. The perception James exalts here requires some form of synthesis and evaluative insight. These characters are qualified for their narrative status not by their passive absorption, but by what they do with the material they absorb.

Mirroring, in other words, is not the whole story of James's point-of-view characters, and the implied conflict between passion and perception ("so far as their other passions permit, intense *perceivers*") fades away in the novels themselves. Isabel is most perceptive when least reflective of those around her, and in *The Golden Bowl* the responsibility of the viewpoint character is given to the Prince and Princess precisely when each is most passionately engaged in the plot: the Prince moving toward and consummating his affair with Charlotte, Maggie actively scheming to reclaim her husband. Having passions, gaining possession of one's own character, far from hindering characters' capacity to be viewpoint characters, actually enables it. Point of view has a double nature in Henry James: it both transmits and alters what it takes in. The "mirror of miraculous silver" is itself miraculously transformative, not just a miracle of faithful reproduction.

This is a development of the distinction from chapter 1 between leaving the atoms in the order in which they fall and embroidering a pattern out of the endless relations of life. Here, it applies not just to James's characters—using their relationships with others' personalities to develop a solid identity of their own—but to the experiences and plot being represented. The theory of centers of consciousness is not a capitulation to illimitable subjectivity. Rather, it is a way of building authority, of finding a new pattern, on more stable grounds. This is clear in one of the origin myths James tells for the center of consciousness, in the address "The Novel in *The Ring and the Book*" (1912), where he speaks of the necessity of a "lucid reflector" (I.806) in any attempt to transform Browning's poem into a novel. In another form of rescue work, the center of consciousness here "saves everything":

> The first thing we do is to cast about for some centre in our field; . . . I find that centre in the embracing consciousness of Caponsacchi, which, coming to the rescue of our question of treatment, of our search for a point of control, practically saves everything, and shows itself moreover the only thing that *can* save. (I.798)

The ideas of consciousness as "embracing" and of consciousness as a "point of control" appear not in competition but symbiosis.[13] For consciousness to take in everything, here, is not to be overwritten by the world but to control it. James's comment that novels must be "selected under some sense for something" occurs only a few lines before this. Facts proliferate, stretch away without any selective principle; and the novel must not. Behind the language of workmanlike inevitability James uses here is a commitment to the high stakes of the choice of center and to the selection that ensues. The "reflector" is necessary "to give [the subject] dignity by extracting its finest importance, causing its parts to flower together into some splendid special sense" (I.806)—an image connected to the embroidered flower of the "relations stop nowhere" passage. The images here are all ambiguous or even contradictory in their attempts to hold together the ideals of the selection and variousness. The dignity is given to, but also extracted from, the subject, rather like Strether imagining himself authoring Madame de Vionnet's own act of self-renewal in the church. The next image plays with the distinction between unity and variety: the subject is unitary, but has many "parts"; they "flower together . . . *into*" another singular noun ("some . . . sense"). The image hovers between describing many flowers and one, between a unity that exists beforehand (the subject) and one that only comes into being under the beneficent light of the reflector. "Lucid" itself is a word that for centuries could mean either *shining* or *transparent*: like "reflection," it can imply either faithful transmission or transformation. Yet James is less committed to any particular consequence of the selection or transformation: "some sense for something" deliberately leaves the end result of selection open; the phrase is an empty vessel, like the conclusions of *Beast in the Jungle* and *Lord Jim*, suggesting that aspiration toward a coherent vision is more important than the vision itself.

The Genres of Identity

In *The American Scene*, James suggests that it is "the prime business and the high honour of the painter of life always to *make* a sense" out of the "many-coloured picture of things" (579). Once again, the singular sense comes from the many—like the "parts" that become "some sense"; like Isabel Archer's "numerous" impressions becoming a "still smile." In *The American Scene*, this capacity becomes a matter of "honour"—suggesting that all this language is closely adjacent to James's theorization of the distinction between romance and realism. The act of unifying impressions, in some sense, has the stakes of romantic heroism.

Characters become heroes and heroines in James's fiction under the shadow of an anxiety that all the potential sources of heroism are exhausted. Long after Austen, by the middle of the nineteenth century, David Copperfield wondered whether he would be the hero of his own life: his protagonist's place is delicately balanced on his status as a first-person narrator. James's fiction responds to Dickens's anxiety: the machinery of his fiction is, on one level, an effort to substantiate his protagonists' claims to the status of the heroic, and to exploring sources for character that could replace those of the old stories—the divine favor, royal blood, and inborn virtue of romance.

James views romance as the primary source of ideas of the heroic, of exceptional and fascinating character. His sense of a dichotomy between character as vividly individual and character as constructed by outside influence corresponds to his dichotomy between romance and realism. The free capacity of choice James associates with an inner core of character is also an aspect of romance, while the continuous impingements of social condition and others' wills and personalities are connected to the realist vision of experience under "the conditions that we usually know to attach to it and, if we wish so to put the matter, drag upon it" (II.xvii).

This image—from the preface to *The American*—suggests one of the most important aspects of James's idea of romance: he dissociates the idea of romantic character—which retains its association with an inner core of essential being—from what might ordinarily be thought of as romantic social conditions. Rather than a perfect match between social status and soul, James opposes the interior and the exterior. In *The Wings of the Dove*, Kate Croy says to Milly Theale, American heiress of a deceased family: "You can do anything—you can do, I mean, lots that *we* can't. You're an outsider, independent and standing by yourself; you're not hideously relative to tiers and tiers of others" (XIX.281). Milly's wealth enables her romantic freedom, but only because she does not have any other social connections. Economic freedom (the shadow which always haunts more abstract discussions of freedom and its romance in James) is only romantic if it is *not* connected to family and social class.

In the preface to *The American* he goes on to discuss the "conditions" that "drag" down romance: "the inconvenience of a *related*, a measurable state, a state subject to all our vulgar communities" (II.xvii). James's self-appointed task is to place the romantic in relation to the real without making it "vulgar," to achieve a balancing act similar to what an audience member sees in the actress Miriam Rooth's triumphant appearance on stage in *The Tragic Muse*: "Miriam was a beautiful actual fictive impossible young woman of a past age, . . . who was exalted and heroic beyond all human convenience and who yet was irresistibly real and related to one's own affairs" (VIII.327). The alliance of the actual with the fictive and the impossible, the connection between the exalted and heroic and one's own affairs, of distance and relatedness—this is a fusion of romance and realism. Making such romantic heroism emerge from defensible reality is one of James's central artistic projects.

Romance, for James, has a much clearer definition than realism, as "experience liberated, so to speak; experience disengaged, disembroiled, disencumbered, exempt from the conditions that we usually know to attach to it" (II.xvii). Romance is an ideal of action and of identity free from the invidious taint of outside circumstances. As Philip Horne points out, James's image for this—a hot air balloon, its cord to the earth cut—directly contrasts with an earlier description of a Flaubert novel as "a huge balloon . . . that absolutely refuses to leave the ground" (*Literary Criticism* II.328). Horne argues that James's reservations about Flaubert particularly centered around character—Flaubert's protagonists, especially in *L'Éducation sentimentale*, simply aren't worthy of the reader's attention (156). This, then, is the risk of realism for James: its characters, defined by their restrictions, cannot justify the work of art.

In *Portrait of a Lady*, the sources of Isabel's character are a subject of debate and crucial to the plot of the novel. Her cousin Ralph and aunt Mrs. Touchett are each careful in their terminology about it.

> "If it's dry," said his mother with a laugh, "you can leave Isabel alone to water it! She is as good as a summer rain, any day."
>
> "Do you mean that she is a gifted being?"
>
> "I don't know whether she is a gifted being, but she's a clever girl, with a strong will and a high temper." (38–39)

Mrs. Touchett objects to Ralph's use of a fairly standard idiom—"gifted"—because it implies that Isabel's qualities are owed to someone outside herself. There is a quasi-mystical implication in "gifted," but in James's novel the implied source is not God, whom the idiom might traditionally have implicated. Mrs. Touchett sees that the very language Ralph uses to assert the absoluteness of individual defini-tion suggests an absent source of authority and identity. It is in the context of this change from a romance notion of character as gifted from birth to a realist idea of character invading from other people and society that "gifted" becomes potentially threatening. Mrs. Touchett makes Isabel into the god of her own experience, the source of rain, and wants to insist on her being only herself—"a clever girl."

Ralph is a romanticist through and through, speaking in allusions to Shakespearean romance and seeing no danger in the use of those old idioms de-prived of their referents. When Isabel's American friend Henrietta Stackpole asks Ralph to help Isabel by reversing changes in her, he responds:

> "Ah," said Ralph, "I am only Caliban; I am not Prospero."
>
> "You were Prospero enough to make her what she has become. You have acted on Isabel Archer since she came here, Mr. Touchett."
>
> "I, my dear Miss Stackpole? Never in the world. Isabel Archer has acted on me—yes; she acts on every one. But I've been absolutely passive."
>
> "You are too passive, then. You had better stir yourself and be careful. Isabel is changing every day; she is drifting away—right out to sea." (114)

Beneath a tone of playful fluidity is Ralph's belief that bedrock identity can't be altered. Thus, he refuses to believe Isabel can have been "acted upon" by Europe and Europeans, resolute in his belief in her romantic agency. Henrietta's image of Isabel "drifting away" will have an echo in Ralph's desire, when he asks his father to leave Isabel an inheritance, to "put a little wind in her sails" (175). Henrietta's image implies a fear in any departure from the stability of land; Ralph, meanwhile envisions an outward voyage as the expression of character, rather than its dissolution: Isabel is to be unchanged, merely made one of those "able to gratify their imagination" (176) in a specifically monetary sense. Ralph sees Isabel's imagination as a projection of her own personality, moving outward into the world; Henrietta sees it as receptive, as a way into her personality to change it. In the novel, it turns out that both perspectives are limited: Isabel is more susceptible to the influence of others' personalities than Ralph imagines; changes in personality cannot be entirely halted, as Henrietta desires.

Romance, of course, relies on some sense of external pressure on personality; in the preface to *The American*, James figures the distinction of romance in terms of the quality of dangers faced by the protagonist:

> There are immense and flagrant dangers that are but sordid and squalid ones, as we feel, tainting with their quality the very defiances they provoke; while there are common and covert ones, that "look like nothing" and that can be but inwardly and occultly dealt with, which involve the sharpest hazards to life and honour and the highest instant decisions and intrepidities of action. It is an arbitrary stamp that keeps these latter prosaic and makes the former heroic. (II.xvi–xvii)

The "sordid" stands against "honour," the "prosaic" against the "heroic." Tellingly, the words slant in the opposing directions of circumstances and character: "sordid" and "prosaic" describe the entangling circumstances; "honour" and "heroic" refer inevitably back to the human character caught in them. Danger is a constant in both genres; but whereas romance has to do with the belief in the potential heroic stature of mankind, realism has to do with the way circumstances conspire, not to make a character fail in the face of danger, but to keep him or her from a test that would offer a chance to shape his or her identity.

James's characters—especially characters without as much money as they would like—are always looking for such chances. Christina Light, in *Roderick Hudson*, asks Rowland if ending her affair with Roderick would be "something magnanimous, heroic, sublime, something with a fine name like that" (I.288). The concept has become a little less explicit by the time, thirty years later, that Kate Croy in *The Wings of the Dove* mourns for her family's "failure of fortune and of honour" (XIX.4) and determines that "the broken sentence, if she was the last word, *would* end with a sort of meaning" (XIX.6). James's form of romance has to do with making meaning—making a sense—rather than assuming it, and as such it relies on humans acting with some variety of freedom, when they reach the point of the test. Realism implies that circumstances will never give one the opportunity to express heroic dimensions, in part because heroism is stunted by outside circumstances. If identity is entirely a construct, if people are made up of selves they absorb from other people and their circumstances, the stamp of the heroic has little meaning; on the other hand, romance still requires adversity for the test. Pressure against one's character produces heroism, but it also has the potential to erase the meaningfulness of heroic action. The solution for James involves a reimagining of influence itself, by making the constructed identity one that depends on the assumption of responsibility and freedom in one's own construction. This bridges romance and realism, connects the heroic stamp of choice in the one with the rooted familiarity of the other.

The stakes of such choices turn out to be those "sharpest hazards" James likes in romance. Mrs. Touchett is right to worry about Isabel being "gifted." People in James's fiction don't merely receive character as a gift; they can also offer it— and the character in the novel with a "gift" to extend is Madame Merle, whose knowledge of "how to feel . . . was, indeed [her] great talent, her most perfect gift" (181). Isabel embraces transfer of personality: she moves quickly from admiring "the talents, the accomplishments, the aptitudes, of Madame Merle" to "desiring to emulate them, and in this and other ways Madame Merle presented herself as a model" (182). Isabel sees these qualities as something both inborn—talents, aptitudes—and transferable, an emulable gift. By deliberately placing herself "under an influence" (182), she begins to receive far more from Madame Merle than she intends. The specifically sinister attributes of such an influence come out when the same sentiment is expressed to Isabel by Pansy: "You will be my model; I shall try to imitate you—though I am afraid it will be very feeble" (343). Isabel is more confident than Pansy in the quality of her emulation, but the statement crystallizes all the sadness of Pansy's too-perfectly-influenced character and shows the dangers that lurk in the attempt at imitation. Pansy's "absence of initiative, of conversation, of personal claims, seemed to her, in a girl of twenty, unnatural and even sinister" (471–472). Pansy is someone, to use the language of James's description of mirroring narrators, who has no "other passions" to interfere with the constant influx of others' desires and outlooks: she makes no claims for herself and fails to have a character of her own.

If Ralph, Henrietta, and Mrs. Touchett all fundamentally agree that Isabel's uninfluenced identity is important, Madame Merle stands for the opposite perspective: that identity is inseparable from one's surroundings. She asks of the self, "Where does it begin? where does it end? It overflows into everything that belongs to us—and then it flows back again" (193). She views the self as composed all of things external to it—and fluid, at that; she is the threatening current that

Henrietta fears will take Isabel out to sea.[14] Along with Gilbert Osmond, she has come to the conclusion that transfer of personality expresses the self: she wishes to express herself in others—principally, Pansy and Isabel. The language she uses of overflowing and expression arises from a sense of limitation, of being influenced—of being subject to those "sordid and squalid" hazards associated with the real (appearances, movements, engagements, society) that James thought failed to give rise to the heroic. She has built herself through other selves—other people's things, and the access to society they provide—and desires in turn to reproduce that self in those around her:

> "I call your life—your ambitions," said Osmond.
> Madame Merle looked a moment at Pansy. (228)

Her outlook, personalities, and experience all flow together into one unified image of how people act; she fails to account for differences between characters. When she hears of Isabel's inheritance, she cries, "The clever creature!" (201). She is seeing Isabel as an exact mirror of herself, assuming a similarity of identity because she knows how she herself would have been calculating in similar circumstances—and to her, circumstances are everything. Unlike Strether or Maggie, both of whom ultimately come to rest in self-conscious knowledge of what they will take and reject from those around them, she foregrounds her own lack of freedom. Isabel thinks she knows what she is getting from Madame Merle, but doesn't.

Madame Merle's fluid self is set in the novel against Isabel's romantic ideal self, the "clever girl" her aunt sees. Mrs. Touchett reads character like Austen's narrator in *Emma*—seeing identity as defined only in terms of itself, not "hideously relative."[15] In James's fiction, none of the traditional strategies—an omniscient narrator pronouncing the nature of things and people; a romance convention by which identity is immutable within and intrinsic to an individual—offers a meaningful way of understanding who people are. But this does not mean that he views all conceptions of distinct identities and individual personalities as meaningless or illusory; instead, he seeks to find new ways of representing identity, precisely by challenging the old conventions that made it seem so suspect. Out of relativistic perspective meaning arises: destabilization of perception and confusion of reference become, for James, not ways of undermining fixed concepts—of character, of truth, of morality—but ways of defending fixed concepts using newly responsive and contingent vantage points. In his fiction, not saying something explicitly allows characters to pinpoint more precisely what it is, and changes in personality are the most meaningful building blocks for character.

When James describes the real as "*related*" and "measurable," he points to a key connection between these problems of genre, characterization, and literary form. "Related" deliberately hovers between the sense of being told or narrated and being connected (as to the "vulgar communities"); being connected to and impinged upon by other people also involves knowing a little too much about them. The romantic, as James imagines it, involves independence and freedom; it also is inherently, on some level, intangible: "The romantic stands, on the other hand, for the things that, with all the facilities in the world, all the wealth and all the courage and all the wit and all the adventure, we never *can* directly know" (II. xvi).[16] In these pages early in the *New York Edition*, James sets out to claim the obliquity of his style as a defense of romantic truth. It is not a mere acknowledgment of truth's slippery status, but a strategy for trying to hold on.

"Somebody Else": Perceptions and Personality in The Ambassadors

The most intangible romantic truth in James is the persistence of an individual's identity. When Strether first sees Chad Newsome, he thinks: "What could be more remarkable than this sharp rupture of an identity? You could deal with a man as himself—you couldn't deal with him as somebody else" (84). James's "somebody else" is an odder phrasing than the alternatives available: "someone different," "someone new." "Somebody else" carries a suggestion of an alternative, not just a transformation. Chad is not just different from before; he is a *specific* other person. Maria Gostrey, as we have seen, insists to Strether that the transformation is so specific that looking at Chad is a way of judging Madame de Vionnet. But despite the "sharp rupture of an identity," the young man from Woollett returns, by the end, to being "none the less only Chad" (369). There is a core of self that is much more difficult to alter. Isabel Archer has a similar realization about her marriage: "He had thought at first he could change her, and she had done her best to be what he would like. But she was, after all, herself" (411).

James's Americans in Europe constantly confront the specter of losing their individual identities in the vivid scene of European culture and personality; just as often, they discover that, despite their best efforts, not everything can be shaped into new experiences and roles. Chad's being "only Chad" and Isabel's being "after all, herself" are tautological formulations that render the quality under discussion intangible, but also unavoidable: we do not read those sentences as devoid of meaning, even though they do not point to a precise sense of what "Chad" and "herself" are. This suggests a particular habit of James's late style: by undermining denotation, James validates connotation. Chad's being "only Chad" makes the core of character into the material of romance: it is something we never can directly know, but it endures in the emptiness of the forms and phrases that replace it.[17]

Being foreign, especially being American in Europe, like Isabel or Strether, often acts as a ready-made exceptional status. The challenge for the characters is to use this status to become protagonists—not merely representative of a foreign type, but vividly distinctive as individuals. In *The Ambassadors*, individual identity—both shifting and fixed—is set against ideas of moral and national type. At the beginning of the novel, Strether is still a virtual record of Woollett's opinions; when Maria asks him about Chad, "Of what type and temper is he?" his replies are all in terms of moralized categories: "Well—the obstinate. . . . I'm thinking of his mother. . . . He has darkened her admirable life. . . . He has worried her half to death" (33). These are the tones of Woollett's gossiping unanimity, confidently identifying the intrinsic moral worth of an individual.

This analysis may seem to be tending toward an argument that, in *The Ambassadors*, there is no such thing as character, all morality is suspect, and that the key thing to do is to embrace precisely the things that the novel implies are European, rather than American, cultural features: James in *The American Scene* refers to feeling in America the absence of the "romance of costume, . . . of amusement, of social and sensual margin, overflow and by-play" (393). Many critics focus on this opposition. Unlike both *Wings of the Dove* and *The Golden Bowl*, *The Ambassadors* is not a novel that foregrounds a large moral category like "evil"; it therefore draws many interpreters eager to find an uncomplicatedly one-sided affirmation of complication and a wholesale rejection of all moral terminology.[18] It becomes an example of "Derrida's logic of supplementarity,"[19] or a gesture of aborted fin de siècle escape from Victorian didacticism,[20] or a lesson that enthrones openness to experience as the source of freedom.[21] *The Ambassadors* has long been celebrated as a novel that seems decisively to valorize the openness of identity and consciousness to others. But if consciousness and knowledge can be safely shared tacitly in James, identity is a much riskier, and cannot easily be assimilated to the "utopian image of communitarian possibility" that David Kurnick discerns in James's late style (152).

The novel's approach to its various central contrasts,—the schema it sets up opposing American and European attitudes—does not come to rest firmly on one side. The novel contains pointed critiques of both sides of Strether's inclinations—and offers one potential conclusive formation. I don't wish to minimize the famously open endings for which James is known, but to argue that the structure of openness he provides bears, itself, a particular meaning: James is denying the generic qualities of moral schemes while defending the idea of moral value it-self. Just as the conclusion of *The Beast in the Jungle* offers narrative satisfaction while denying Marcher the specific experience he expected, the endings of James's novels take the form of a mismatch between plot and apparent moral. Isabel's re-turn to Rome is not a suggestion of the virtues of Osmond, or of some likely future happiness in their marriage. In *What Maisie Knew*, Maisie's choice to stay with the moralizing Mrs. Wix is not a direct rejection of adultery but arises instead out of the sense that Mrs. Beale, as a specific character, cannot be fully devoted to caring for Maisie herself. In *The Bostonians*, Verena Tarrant goes with Basil Ransom—but again, not to a happy marriage, and not because Basil's view of fem-inism is validated. And despite the way the entire plot of *The Ambassadors*—from the unnerving arranged marriage of Madame de Vionnet's daughter Jeanne to the climactic discovery of Chad's relationship with Madame de Vionnet—seems to offer all the external ingredients of a moralistic condemnation of Europe (logically leading to Strether's return to Woollett), the novel deliberately presents that story as insufficient.

This mismatch of plot and significance, a sense that the action is, in T. S. Eliot's terms, the objective correlative to a story different from the one we're given, con-sistently denies James's readers a general moral. Instead, morals are tied up in far more specific and elusive ways with individual situations—perhaps with Olive Chancellor's violation of the Jamesian instinct to privacy, with Mrs. Beale as an individual being an unwise choice of mother, or Caspar Goodwood a poor fit as a partner to Isabel. The narratives disallow the obvious meanings—but the process of denial consistently relies on strong oppositional, if unplotted, meanings that push the reader to reject the standard conclusions we might draw from characters' choices (we don't see Strether's return to America as a complete rejection of Europe). James is shifting the final significance of the novel into the same oblique space as character, romance, and all those truths that can never be spoken aloud in his fiction: it must be apprehended instead through readerly reactions to plots.

Such strategies defend the validity of searching for things that can only be expressed obliquely. James is not reacting, in his fiction, only against Woollett's morally definitive types, but also against the limited form of realism exemplified in the perfect mirror. Early in the novel Strether thinks, after talking with Little Bilham and Miss Barrace, "He must approach Chad, must wait for him, deal with him, master him, but he must not dispossess himself of the faculty of seeing things as they were. . . . Bilham and Miss Barrace threw so little light. So there they were" (72). Strether contrasts the idea of imposing his own will upon the situation (mastering Chad—in this context, likely according to Woollett moral outlooks) with a more restrained approach ("seeing things as they were") that turns out to imply complacency. The underlying opposition between his capacity for action and his ability to perceive is registered by the slip from the idea of approaching Chad to the idea of waiting for him. This is a chapter ending and—with "So there they were"—a foreshadowing of the ending of the novel as a whole ("Then there we are!" [395]). By the end, both the mirror and moral mastery seem like bad alternatives, and the final line becomes another instance of undermined denotation—the ostensible referent of "There" in "Then there we are!" is Marie's comment about being unable to resist Strether, which, we know, means little, since he is about to depart: there they are, about to bid farewell.

Perceiving the World and Creating a Self

What Strether views early on as the romance of Paris turns out to be a refusal to pick among perceptions. All he wants, he thinks, is to achieve "the common, unattainable art of taking things as they came" (51). *Take* here is closer to the sense of *taking a blow* than *seizing*. In the passages that expand upon his early impressions of Paris, this "taking things as they come" manifests as a refusal to analyze or "select under some sense for something":

> Almost any acceptance of Paris might give one's authority away. It hung before him this morning, the vast bright Babylon, like some huge iridescent object, a jewel brilliant and hard, in which parts were not to be discriminated nor differences comfortably marked. It twinkled and trembled and melted together; and what seemed all surface one moment seemed all depth the next. (55)

This passage mingles elements of the Woollett judgment ("authority," "Babylon") that currently constitutes his personality with the growing ethic of nondiscrimination, of lack of manipulation of the things he perceives—he refuses, here, the "difficult, dire process of selection and comparison, of surrender and sacrifice," which James claims as essential on the part of an author (I.viii). Strether here manifests another instance of the American negative definition of self—self by exclusion of other things—combined with a passive embrace and refusal of analysis of Paris. He sees Paris as unitary but unfixed, rather like having a simplifying idea of a refusal to simplify. He does not see the depth via the surface, but refuses to sort out the surface and the depth from one another.

Once again, *The American Scene* offers a useful comparison, as James models his own thought processes in a situation analogous to Strether's. There are many moments of similarity; James at one point speaks of "a mild warm wave that broke over the succession of aspects and objects. . . . It floated me, my wave, all that day and the next" (358). Strether finds himself "remembering on what current of association he had been floated so far" (56). (Being "floated," of course, sounds suspiciously like Henrietta's "drifting.") Paris as a vast bright jewel is comparable to New York as a vast monster (418) knitting everything together. Yet after that description, James writes,

> Each of these huge constructed and compressed communities, throbbing, through its myriad arteries and pores, with a single passion, even as a complicated watch throbs with the one purpose of telling you the hour and the minute, testified overwhelmingly to the *character* of New York—and the passion of the restless analyst, on his side, is for the extraction of character. (424)

The "passion of the restless analyst"—this can hardly describe Strether. "Extraction" was also James's word for the way the "lucid reflector" would find the "finest importance" of his subject in "The Novel in *The Ring and the Book.*" It is James's rescue work: the removal of a lasting essence from the ephemeral, and akin to the "concentrated" character Strether sees in Notre Dame in Madame de Vionnet. Strether, in the "vast bright Babylon" passage, is an instance of what might happen were James to arrest himself in the warm wave and never try to "extract" from it anything specific. "I would take my stand on my gathered impressions," James says in the preface to *The American Scene* (353)—language diametrically opposed to how Strether speaks of his impressions, both in the activity of "gathering" rather than taking and, as we shall see later, in framing them when challenged by Sarah Pocock.[22] James's language associated with the "painter of life" is itself heroic—taking a stand, high honor. Over the course of the novel Strether represents first naive (and moralistic) insensitivity to subtle impressions of the exterior world, then a kind of obsessive reluctance to do any violence to those impressions, before finally developing a way of *making* a sense of the raw material of his experience.[23] At the climax he finds himself "supposing everything" (357)—recognizing that refusing to suppose is its own kind of limitation.

In the "vast bright Babylon" passage, James exposes a similarity between a moralizing view that has no desire to find out or see anything (because the outside is a moral threat) and a wide-open sensitivity to anything (which will not assume that there is any deeper meaning than the splendid play of surfaces). James is subtly undermining the latter: supposing nothing is no less a preconception than the American outlook so obviously satirized from the opening. The arc of the novel is a defense of the attempt to know, to take in both surface and depth and begin to understand the distinctions between them.

As we have seen, James calls Strether a "mirror of miraculous silver," and at one point in the book the character considers his own role. As Little Bilham expresses contentment with the idea of growing into someone like him, Strether is skeptical:

> Little Bilham continued to think; then at last he had a smile. "Well, you *are* amusing—to *me*."
>
> "*Impayable*, as you say, no doubt. But what am I to myself?" (136)

Mirrors, of course, are nothing to themselves; Little Bilham doesn't answer the question. This exchange contrasts a comic sense of type, being a broadly drawn "character" in someone else's field of vision with the familiar function of a center of consciousness as a perfect mirror of the complexities of others' various existences (nothing to oneself). The task of James's artistic project—and the task his characters face within it—is to make his fictional people both complicated and coherent. This is also the task of making oneself fit for being the perceiving center of consciousness in a novel while also fit to be the hero of a story. James's desire is to make the inequities of the character-system (to borrow Alex Woloch's terms) seem just, to portray the capacities characters have to assign themselves to the role of hero or of minor character. If the problem of Dickens's fiction, according to Woloch, is the tension between a "weak protagonist" and strong secondary characters—in other words, between characters who deserve to have all our attention and those who are capable of holding it—the problem of James's fiction is characters learning that they must be both capable of seeing and worthy of being seen.[24] There is a tension between being that charismatic protagonist who holds all our attention and the literary technology of the center of consciousness; a character's status as an interpreting observer both places him or her to the side of the action and, simultaneously, at the center of our attention. The story of *The Ambassadors* is Strether's learning to reconcile being a focalizing central consciousness with being the central character of a novel.

Not Being Worldly: Character and Moral Choice

The subsumption of his personality that impedes this process is a consequence of the ethic of taking things as they come. Faced with Sarah Pocock's accusations late in the novel, he says, "I don't think there's anything I've done in any such calculated way as you describe. Everything has come as a sort of indistinguishable part of everything else" (312). *Everything has come* to Strether, who wanted to *take things as they come*: his reaction is not just to her strident terms but to the emphasis on his having deliberately *done* something.

At the end of the novel, he changes his idea of taking once more, finally using the phrase to assert a separation between himself and the outside world. He talks to Maria: " 'I'm not,' he explained, leaning back in his chair, but with his eyes on a small ripe, round melon—'in real harmony with what surrounds me. You *are*. I take it too hard. You don't. It makes—that's what it comes to in the end—a fool of me' " (391). That lengthy speech tag separates him syntactically from what surrounds him—separates him, principally, from her, since his eyes are (oddly) on the melon instead. His mind is, at last, separate from that of others; his context is different from theirs. For most of the novel he is in harmony, taking in surroundings and people without taking them "hard": he is responsive and accepting. This insistence on matters being ultimately serious rather than light is a legacy of Woollett, not Paris.[25] Strether's realization that he is something to himself, not just a mirror of Parisian phantasmagoria, is also his discovery of some sense of moral judgment.

In *Portrait of a Lady* Isabel has a thought about Madame Merle that connects to Strether's concerns about being something to himself: "Isabel often wondered what her relations might be with her own soul" (185). The line anticipates Strether, wondering what he is to himself; but it adds an implication of moral doubt. This uneasy association between a self open to the world and a self morally at risk remains in *The Ambassadors*. Madame de Vionnet talks with Sarah Pocock about enjoying Paris:

> ". . . The great thing, Mr. Strether will show you," she smiled, "is just to let one's self go."
>
> "Oh, I've not let myself go very far," Strether answered, feeling quite as if he had been called upon to hint to Mrs. Pocock how Parisians could talk. "I'm only afraid of showing I haven't let myself go far enough." (243)

Sarah's moral perspective might be too extreme, but once again the language of the relative soul, the self absent or loosed, is nervously associated with moral laxity. Strether wants to ascribe it to "how Parisians could talk," as though there is no meaning behind it; but ultimately he too will feel that he has to recover a little bit of himself, has let himself go too far. He can't let the suffering and injustice pass—the marriage of Jeanne de Vionnet, the abandonment of her mother. He has realized that he can't merely take in things as they are, that he must, inevitably, both analyze and judge them.

The announcement of Jeanne's marriage—a marriage of convenience—is an especially telling moment, where Strether finds that his reluctance to see into and know things becomes problematic:

> Vaguely and confusedly he was troubled by it; feeling as if he had even himself been concerned in something deep and dim. He had allowed for depths, but these were greater; and it was as if, oppressively—indeed absurdly—he was responsible for what they had now thrown up to the surface. (265)

Suddenly, the actual content of the depths has become relevant—they cannot remain as oblique suggestions. This is the clearest moment where the ethic of passive nonanalysis fails: Strether has discovered that he can't just "take" things, that he has a substance of his own that must meet them. This is one of the most important points about James's mirror characters: with a few exceptions—like Pansy—they discover that the development of their own character is inevitable even when they do not desire it. Chad and Isabel are, after all, themselves; Strether can't forever put off reacting more to some aspects of life than others.[26] He has become "responsible for" Jeanne's marriage not in the sense that he has actually caused it, but in the sense that he has become an actor on behalf of Madame de Vionnet, has taken her perspective (which leads to the marriage) into his own without fully realizing it. Only when he sees the consequences outside himself does he realize how little he wants that to be his entire personality.

Thus, at the conclusion of the novel, Strether chooses neither Europe nor America, and the novel refuses to affirm an ethic associated with either place. Strether, too, is, after all, himself: out of harmony and out of context in every surrounding. When he leaves Madame de Vionnet for the last time, she tells him that she had wanted to have him as a friend. "'Ah, but you've *had* me!' he declared, at the door, with an emphasis that made an end" (371). His response has at least three dimensions: first, that he was her friend; second, that she has "had" him in the sense of playing a trick on him; and third, that she "had" him in the sense of her spirit possessing him, making himself into an extension of her will just as she had influenced Chad. Strether's simultaneous gesture of sympathy, reproach, and honest self-awareness—all adding up into the singular significance of an "end"—is what all James's characters seek to find. Strether rejects the romance of mirroring the glitter of the social scene—the social world that would also give up Jeanne de Vionnet, and whose expectation of careless ethics regarding women Chad Newsome absorbs so fully that he ultimately rejects the woman from whom he absorbs it. Instead, romance resides in characters who choose to make meaning—and the plots with their endings, and their own personalities—for themselves.

Practically Passionate: The Failure of Fatalism in The Golden Bowl

Strether tried to make passive appreciation of aesthetic experience into a high ethical value; similarly, in *The Golden Bowl*, characters try to make their own lack of freedom into luxurious aesthetic experience—to base romance on imprisonment. Whereas Isabel Archer overestimates the ease of her free state, in *The Golden Bowl* Charlotte, the Prince, and, even, for a time, Maggie are all eager to state their own imprisonment—even, in some moments, acting in order to forestall their own freedom. The novel is built around two marriages— Maggie's with the Prince, and Charlotte Stant's—Maggie's friend—with Maggie's father, Adam Verver. Neither Maggie nor her father knows that Charlotte and the Prince had been in love years before, unable to marry due to poverty. In this novel, where marriage and financial constraints have genuinely imprisoning effects, James lays out the disastrous consequences of failing to claim control of the materials of one's personality.

In the second paragraph of the novel, the Prince thinks, "Shortly before, at three o'clock, his fate had practically been sealed" (XXIII.4–5). The novel, it seems to him, is over before it has begun; and the terms in which he thinks mingle the very prosaically real ("at three o'clock"; "practically") with the melodramatically grandiose ("fate . . . sealed"). The realist touches indicate the Prince's sense of ironic detachment from the romantic notions that might very well be alive here, and signal a note of contradiction that haunts the whole of his affair with Charlotte: they are trying to turn their sense of their own imprisonment and choicelessness into the source of their significance, replacing *freedom* with *fate*. In showing the frustration of their relationship, James insists that romance plot lines depend on the choice and expression of character, not the spectacle of character straining against limiting circumstances.

The Golden Bowl takes sharp aim at a trope treated much more explicitly and sympathetically elsewhere in James's fiction—the theme of belatedness, epitomized in *The Beast in the Jungle* and threaded throughout *The Ambassadors*. By thinking of themselves as having had all the choices made for them, Charlotte and the Prince get the story wrong: just as the Prince assumes his fate is decided for him at the outset, much later in the novel Charlotte has the "wrong volume" of a novel in hand. Maggie corrects her in offering the right volume: "*This* is the beginning" (XXIV.311). Obsessively seeking endings—like Kate Croy and her "broken sentence"—they fail to recognize the potential of beginning, the possibilities of their own responsibility. It is by claiming the freedom to begin that characters in James become capable of making endings—by, finally, denying that endings have been made for them.

At the opening of the novel, the Prince is faced with two separate visions of romance, one associated with Maggie, the other associated with Charlotte. There is already an internal conflict regarding his marriage. On the one hand, his "fate" is "practically sealed"; on the other, he says to Fanny Assingham: "You talk about rest—it's too selfish!—when you're just launching me on adventures?" (XXIII.27).[27] The Prince's idea of his marriage depends on viewing it as a kind of adventure, and he is in general eager to see things as about to happen: when he detects that Fanny has news, he comments, "I somehow see volumes in it" (XXIII.37). On one level, this ends the incongruity that greeted the reader when he claimed that his fate had been "sealed" at the outset: now a new element will upset that sense of settledness. But the Prince's romantic "adventures" are passive; the volumes he sees now, it is implied, are not ones that he is writing but ones that are writing themselves in Fanny's mind.

The Prince, then, simultaneously sees his future life as having been predetermined and as a "new adventure." At one point he conceptualizes a life that "constituted our young man's 'romance'" (XXIII.16) with Maggie: "a familiarity with 'lines,' a command of 'own' cars, from an experience of continents and seas, that he was unable as yet to emulate; from vast modern machineries and facilities whose acquaintance he had still to make" (XXIII.15). The parallelism is deflating: each clause seems to move onward "from" the Ververs' experience—but is consistently brought short by his inexperience. This type of romance is all a movement outward, but it is also something foreign to his own mind. The "lines" and "'own' cars" have to appear with inverted commas because they are only hypothetical to him.

Charlotte, by contrast, embodies a similar type of romance—one based on travel—in which the familiar and the strange are inextricable. Charlotte has

> the air of her adventurous situation, a reference in all her person, in motion and gesture, in free vivid yet altogether happy indications of dress, from the becoming compactness of her hat to the shade of tan in her shoes, to winds and waves and custom-houses, to far countries and long journeys, the knowledge of how and where and the habit, founded on experience, of not being afraid. (XXIII.45)

This is a vision of the romance of travel that makes intuitive sense. It bridges the externals of countries and dress with the central personal characteristics of knowledge and fearlessness. Charlotte, like the actress Miriam Rooth, triumphantly makes the distant related to herself. If Maggie and her father have "familiarity" and "command" of the mechanisms of travel, Charlotte has "knowledge"—a more sympathetically resonant word—of not only travel's mechanisms but also its objects; moreover, they are in her person, not merely part of manipulable surroundings.

Charlotte appears to present a successful détente between realistic and romantic character, between the external and the internal—a figure compounded of experience, but experience taking the form of the power of knowledge and fearlessness rather than the limitations of helplessness. But as the novel continues, Charlotte becomes invested in viewing her fate as out of her hands; she evokes the distance of romance while refusing to make choices herself. When the moment of crisis regarding her potential marriage to Adam arrives, she offers the Prince's telegram to Adam, not only to avoid guilt for deceit but also to remove her own will from the action. " 'I'll give you,' she simply said, 'what you ask' " (XXIII.239): not *I will marry you*. She does not choose to marry him; she chooses to obey him. Like Strether's attempt to take things as they come, Charlotte's act raises her restrictions to an ethic of their own.

The action of the novel shows the gradual souring of Charlotte's romance as she rejects her own ability to choose it. Maggie, by contrast, builds her romance out of Charlotte's romantic personality fused with her own growing willingness to assume agency and control. Charlotte's lack of agency has, of course, an external source: the Ververs' material power and marital possession of her. But as Charlotte finds herself in this particular prison, she begins to weave together the romance of knowledge with a new romance of being unfree. Charlotte, granted money and a large social stage at last, feels that wealth perfectly suits her: she enjoys

> the other perfections of aspect and arrangement that made her personal scheme a success, the *proved* private theory that materials to work with had been all she required and that there were none too precious for her to understand and use—to which might be added lastly, as the strong-scented flower of the total sweetness, an easy command, a high enjoyment, of her crisis. (XXIII.246)

She seems to enjoy equally her sense of fulfilled personality and her sense of "crisis"; she takes "command" of her own imprisonment. Like Madame Merle and Kate Croy, she views the subject of her tragedy as her own powerlessness and her placement in social contexts.[28] All three of them are self-consciously romantic: they try to write grand stories for themselves; and all three of them view the grandeur of their stories as residing in the ways they lack freedom.

Forms Imposed: Imprisonment and Essential Character

Just as the Ververs have perfectly accommodated what they view as the fixed selves of their spouses, Charlotte and the Prince's affair begins when they decide to preserve what they view as the selves of the Ververs. Like Maggie and her curatorial father collecting Charlotte and the Prince, the Prince and Charlotte are interested in preserving and highlighting what they view as the Ververs' essential qualities. Everyone seems to agree on who everyone else is: Charlotte is the social genius; the Prince offers antique, historical richness; Maggie and her father are innocent and good. Though they all recognize personality as meaningful in the romantic sense, they see it as given rather than chosen. The novel resounds with every character pronouncing the identity of the others: if romance lies in "the things that . . . we never *can* directly know," it is by assuming that characters are knowable that they all fall into errors. Most clearly, of course, Fanny, Charlotte, and the Prince all underestimate Maggie. Fanny pronounces at the beginning: "She wasn't born to know evil. She must never know it" (XXIII.78). Charlotte, speaking with an irony she could not predict, claims just as the affair commences, "I can't put myself into Maggie's skin—I can't, as I say. It's not my fit—I shouldn't be able, as I see it, to breathe in it. But I can feel that I'd do anything to shield it from a bruise" (XXIII.311). By the end of the novel, Charlotte will be very much in Maggie's skin—through Maggie's doing, through Maggie's learning from Charlotte. Speaking to her husband, Fanny Assingham calls Charlotte and the Prince "victims of fate," encapsulating the errors all the characters share at the middle of the novel. Maggie and her father, she says, have "forms":

> ". . . those they *impose* on Charlotte and the Prince. Those," she developed, "that so perversely, as I say, have succeeded in setting themselves up as the right ones."
>
> He considered—but only now, at last, really to relapse into woe. ". . . Whatever they, all round, may be in for now is at least the consequence of what they've *done*. Are they mere helpless victims of fate?"
>
> Well, Fanny at last had the courage of it. "Yes—they are. To be so abjectly innocent—that *is* to be victims of fate." (XXIII.391–392)

The forms are both imposed and are "the right ones": the characters impose visions on each other that are actually in accordance with their characters. All the characters *did* know each other quite well; but it's not enough to know. "She ought to have *known* you," says the Prince to Maggie about Charlotte: "She doesn't know you now." But Maggie responds: "Ah, yes she does!" (XXIV.347). Maggie's idea of "knowing" is predicated on also not-knowing, on being able to guess without actually being certain or having confirmation. It is the elusiveness of partial knowledge that generates romance. Charlotte knows her better, Maggie implies, when Charlotte knows that there is something elusive and unknowable about her.

In a sense, *The Golden Bowl* is series of dazzling variations on George Eliot's famous declaration that character is destiny, but not the whole of our destiny (514); character in James is the ability to wrest some degree of freedom from destiny. If Eliot examines the interactions between character and exterior circumstances in producing events, James examines the interactions between oneself and one's circumstances in producing character. When the characters in *The Golden Bowl* place "fate"—or destiny—at the center of their self-conceptions and interpretations of events, they risk letting destiny become character.

The rote fatalism of the idea of "victims of fate" is the one that enables the affair—but dooms romance in the larger, generic sense: "What else, my dear, what in the world else can we do?" (XXIII.297), Charlotte repeats shortly before they "passionately sealed their pledge" with a kiss (XXIII.312). "Passionately sealed their pledge," though it might seem like a moment of decision, is haunted not only by "What else?" but also by the echo of the much earlier line about "fate . . . practically . . . sealed"; "practically" here shadows "passionately" with a much more prosaic valence than it would otherwise have. The tragedy of Charlotte and the Prince is that because they do not admit that they're stuck in realist situations—dictated by the brute forces of money and power—and instead claim that their restrictions are romance, they can never escape them. If *The Ambassadors* suggests that Strether begins "supposing everything" (357) actively, rather than taking things as they come, *The Golden Bowl* warns its protagonists of the danger of supposing they already know everything. In *The Golden Bowl*, the romantic aspects of character adhere when characters can start to suppose—but flexibly, always willing to modify their positions. James's famously elliptical style is here a way of pinning down the romantic around its edges, of mediating the necessarily unknowable by the knowable, just as character—individual and interior—is mediated by the elements of personality transferred between characters.

The Uses and Abuses of Romantic Obliquity

In *The Golden Bowl*, the unstable situations of the novel's characters are produced by their assumptions of stability. On a formal level, the same strange inversion applies: characters become insightful perceivers not by objectivity, but by becoming self-aware about their own passions and predilections. And the clearest visions of "character" occur not by explicit statement—Maggie is innocent, Milly is a dove—but by acknowledgment of the failure of such statements.

James's formulation that romance is what we never can directly know has a corollary in his fiction: when something potentially romantic becomes "known," is explicitly spoken out, it tends to degrade into the prosaically real. The romantic is not just defined by its unknowability, it depends on and is constituted by it.[29] When Maggie wants to give the Prince a moment to "arrange" his face after the bowl has smashed (XXIV.181), it represents a revolution in characters' relations to one another in this novel—Maggie is both closer to and more distant from the Prince in this moment than all the earlier instances of characters assuming what other people are or are not doing. She privileges a space for conscious, deliberate self-presentation and communication—and allows for both self and communication to select and to exclude.

When Maggie becomes aware of the existence of the things Jamesian obliquity is designed to protect—love, identity—she also becomes aware of her own consciousness as a malleable thing—and promptly tries to become someone like Charlotte. "She would go to balls again—that seemed, freely, even crudely, stated, the remedy" (XXIV.8). Despite the apparent triviality of the decision, it springs out of her sense of being excluded from a world Amerigo and Charlotte occupy; she is taking elements of Charlotte's personality. The word *again* implies that, although Charlotte is her model, dancing and social activity are not foreign to her nature; dancing is "a matter of remembered steps that had grown vague from her ceasing to go to balls" (XXIV.8). The state of affairs at this point is *not* a perfect expression of her identity; it is an artificially exaggerated and simplified version of her personality.[30]

When Maggie initially begins to strike out from her assigned role, the model she picks is Charlotte.[31] When she finds herself at a party, she suddenly begins to see people not as art objects to be appreciated passively, or arranged curatorially, but as active materials infused into herself—rendering them both more vulnerable and more potent:

> She could concern herself at present absolutely with no secret but her own. What occurred was simply that she became aware, at a stroke, of the quantity of further nourishment required by her own, and of the amount of it she might somehow extract from these people; whereby she rose of a sudden to the desire to possess and use them. (XXIV.49)

Personality, in this scene, is oblique in the sense that it is "secret," and because she must "extract" it from other people and through their perspectives. On one level, the "nourishment" required by her "secret" refers to the material for analysis required by her new interest in determining the nature of her life; on another, it refers to the social experiences required to become the sort of person who would go to balls again. Character construction and analysis of others overlap very closely, here, as everywhere in James's fiction.[32]

The mutual recognition of others' complexity does not dissolve character but constitutes it. And this recognition implies the existence of a choosing mind beyond the social roles and categories on the surface.[33] While Charlotte and the Prince—like Kate Croy or Madame Merle before them—rely on characters *not* seeing, Maggie's obliquity is designed to convey information, to make others look back and see her. She makes the gesture of "engaging them all, unconventionally, almost violently, to dine with her in Portland Place" (XXIV.51)—inserting herself into Charlotte's place as hostess ("the initiative obviously belonged to Mrs. Verver" [XXIV.49]). What would be a conventional action for Charlotte becomes startling for Maggie; in her, her stepmother's personality changes in significance.

When Maggie follows Charlotte out into the garden for their climactic confrontation, she seems to perceive all the thoughts of her adversary:

> She hadn't been pursued, it had quickly struck her, without some design on the part of her pursuer, and what mightn't she be thinking of in addition but the way she had, when herself the pursuer, made her stepdaughter take in her spirit and her purpose? (XXIV.310)

Charlotte and her wrong volume have gone out, "fantastically at such an hour to cultivate romance in an arbour" (XXIV.308). The cultivation of romance—here not just her reading, but her desire for self-renewal, not so distant from Madame de Vionnet in Notre Dame—is Charlotte's marker of helplessness, and Maggie relies on it throughout the conversation that follows. This passage contains a familiar pun on "take": here "take in" clearly means both the common idiom of "understand" and also the Jamesian idiom of "absorb as part of her personality"; like Strether, Maggie absorbs, but unlike him she also transforms to a new purpose. "Spirit," too, has a double meaning of "intent" and "self." Maggie understood Charlotte's intent; she has also made herself over to be like Charlotte, to become a Charlotte-like social creature willing to test the limits of others' views in veiled and pointed conversation.

Maggie and Charlotte, in this passage, have become almost the same person, locked in reduplications of forms of *pursue*, and in a loop of personality flowing back and forth. But in this contest—making other people understand you, and finding yourself in them—both characters have some degree of knowledge, confronting each other through the social veil they both wish to preserve. In the confrontation, Maggie perceives Charlotte composing herself on Maggie's arrival: "To be doomed was in her situation to have extravagantly incurred a doom" (XXIV.312). Yet this self-consciousness is not mere posturing; it is Charlotte's very instinct for the romance of her own suffering that leads to the successful outcome for Maggie: Charlotte is forced to produce Maggie's victory because she is committed to the image of fates being sealed by factors she can see clearly but are beyond her control (in this case, the relationship between Maggie and her father, which she presents as so fixed that she must depart with Adam for America immediately). Maggie, by contrast, is victorious because playing her classic role—being wretched and ignorant—brings about the outcome she desires without requiring her to justify it.

Charlotte, like Madame de Vionnet—and unlike her close cousin Madame Merle—is successful at presenting a strong identity of her own; and like Madame de Vionnet, her end is tragic. In both cases, a character with a surplus of social charisma and a deficit of power in society, capable of fascinating all around her but lacking resources beyond that ability, finds that her romance collapses into a reality of constrained options. (Christina Light, becoming the Princess Casamassima at the end of *Roderick Hudson*, shares many of the same outlines.) James has a tendency to extend sympathy to economically disempowered characters—particularly disempowered female characters—while offering them almost no acceptable options for establishment of the kind of free identity he grants to his protagonists, who usually either are men (Strether, Roderick Hudson) or have money (Isabel, Maggie, Milly Theale). It is notable that even in *The Ambassadors*, where there is no abuse of trust on Madame de Vionnet's part equivalent to those of Charlotte, Madame Merle, and Kate Croy, and where Madame de Vionnet's dependency on Chad echoes Strether's dependency on Mrs. Newsome, Madame de Vionnet's final abandonment is something done to her by others, while Strether chooses to separate himself. Such disparities reflect one of the limitations of James's vision of the interactions between class and gender: a habitual plot pattern in which the achievement of romantic identity, finally, is dependent on possessing some privilege relative to those around you.[34]

And yet while that might be what the stories James tells mean—especially fixed to the social context of James's novels—it's not what they do to their readers. The terms he sketches out for free establishment of identity are revivified decades later, in the debate among African American writers about whether characterization in fiction ought to evoke the restrictions of socially constructed identity, or the distant possibilities of freedom.

Mirrors Can Only Lie: Character
and Baldwin's Protest

Although Henry James is seldom the first author to come to mind when discussing the modernist influences on African American fiction, James Baldwin was not alone in acknowledging his usefulness.[35] But Baldwin's use of James is especially far-reaching. On Baldwin's list of "ten books that had helped him break out of the ghetto," James is the only author besides Dostoevsky to make more than one appearance; the novels are *Portrait of a Lady* and *The Princess Casamassima*.[36] Baldwin once produced an unpublished sketch of American types that took James's Daisy Miller and J. Ward Moorehouse (of Dos Passos's *U.S.A.* trilogy) as exemplars of "Le male et la femelle d'une espece"; both characters, in this argument, stand in for the failings of American society.[37] At one time Baldwin began to write an introduction to *The Ambassadors*: he never finished it, writing to his agent that it was difficult "because I owe him so much and am so afraid of him; and talking about the sexuality in James is a dangerous thing to do—though I think it should be done."[38] His leading biographer and a friend while he was alive, David Leeming, interviewed him in the pages of the *Henry James Review* in 1986, in which they collectively attempt to reconstruct the lost manuscript of the *Ambassadors* introduction.

Baldwin, then, was a close and emotionally invested reader of James, and his use of Jamesian motifs and forms can help to sketch out the kind of reading experience and uses James's fiction might provide in a startlingly different social and political context from their first appearance. The Jamesianess of Baldwin has itself become part of Baldwin's later-day reception: Colm Tóibín, another Jamesian novelist, wrote an article about Baldwin in the *Guardian* dramatically declaring that "Henry James had come to Harlem."

I have suggested that James's idea of novelistic character was a strategic attempt to balance an ideal of individual, vivid character and agency against a sharp awareness of the way personality is influenced, shaped, and limited by society through other characters' influence. It is easy to say that James's love of the vivid character is a legacy of the Victorian age and his awareness of character instability an anticipation of modernism, poststructuralism, and a host of other convenient later ideological formations. But Baldwin's use of James upsets these associations; outside influences, with their shaping effects on character, are a source of normative social assumptions at odds with the varieties of individual experience. This is Baldwin's version of W. E. B. Du Bois's famous evocation of "double consciousness." Where Du Bois translates the interior/exterior dichotomy into the overlapping categories of being black and being American, Baldwin holds the imagery closer to the question of the individual. Ken Warren points out a strange conjunction: Du Bois used the phrase in 1897 and more famously in 1903; in the same year, James features it in the second paragraph of *The Ambassadors* (Warren 12). There, James describes Strether as having a "double consciousness": "There was detachment in his zeal and curiosity in his indifference" (2). In James, the term refers to the relationship between a character and the world around him. Baldwin's double consciousness fuses the Jamesian preoccupation with interiority with the racial vision of Du Bois.[39]

In Baldwin's unpublished sketch of American types, the dichotomy between self and world is central: Dos Passos's characters have "no lives and no identities of their own," and Daisy is condemned because "the sum of her gestures makes no ensemble" (James Baldwin Papers, Folder 42.17, pp. 8, 2). Although his intensely negative judgment on Daisy is unusual among critics, Baldwin's critique of American character occurs in intensely Jamesian terms.[40] Daisy seems to embody, simultaneously, a failure to construct an identity of her own out of too-various materials and a refusal to let the world have enough of an impact on her identity. Her status, in the passage quoted earlier, as a "fly on an infinite sheet of glass" is precisely a failure to combine detached indifference with curiosity and zeal.

Characterization in James is always constituted by either a contest or a balance between a variety of external forces—social pressures; the influences and the visions of other characters—and a more elusive core of identity defined mainly through the power of choice over societal influences. As in James, Baldwin's characters find their sense of themselves challenged by potential new social worlds—and as in James, they must balance both openness to change and faith in some identity of their own.

In Baldwin's *Giovanni's Room* (1956), the protagonist, David, can be described in typically Jamesian terms. An American in Paris, he wants to maintain his sense of a strong national identity in the face of myriad temptations and potential influences offered by the city, primarily the possibility that acknowledging his own homosexual desires will fundamentally alter his relation to the American future he has long imagined for himself. He begins an affair with the charismatic but impoverished bartender Giovanni—an affair disrupted when his American fiancée Hella arrives. The novel is structured as a flashback; on the evening before Giovanni is to be executed for a murder he committed in desperation after David left him, David recalls, alone, the events of their time together.

Jamesian echoes abound in the novel. For instance, early in *Portrait of a Lady* James highlights the viewpoint of his heroine, Isabel Archer, in an exchange with her aunt:

> "I always want to know the things one shouldn't do."
> "So as to do them?" asked her aunt.
> "So as to choose," said Isabel. (63)

The chapter ends here, leaving the line ringing prominently—but also into a void.[41] Isabel does not yet have material to make her choices. But knowledge of the world constitutes pressure, one way or the other, on the choices themselves. It is in this charged interaction that characters form themselves in James's fiction.

Baldwin picks up the irony of Isabel's empty choice. In his first conversation with Giovanni, David and Giovanni collaborate to produce an echo of James's prominent chapter ending. Giovanni says,

> ". . . The big fish eat the little fish and the ocean doesn't care."
> "Oh, please," I said. "I don't believe *that*. Time's hot water and we're not fish and you can choose to be eaten and also not to eat—not to eat," I added quickly, turning a little red before his delighted and sardonic smile, "the little fish, of course."
> "To choose!" cried Giovanni, turning his face away from me and speaking, it appeared, to an invisible ally who had been eavesdropping on this conversation all along. "To *choose!*" He turned to me again. "Ah, you are really an American. *J'adore votre enthousiasme!*" (35)

David's belief that he can choose his place in the world (and his companions), like Isabel's desire to make an independent choice, turns disastrous for protagonists and supporting characters alike.

The "Le male et la femelle" sketch refers to Daisy's "absolute metaphysical freedom" (James Baldwin Papers, Folder 42.17, p. 5) as part of what precipitates the disaster. Baldwin's description of James's novella anticipates *Giovanni's Room* in many respects: he highlights Daisy's deathbed declaration that she was not engaged to the disreputable Giovanelli (whose very name begins to seem ancestral to Giovanni in this document) as signifying her refusal to surrender to the possibility of soul-altering love—precisely the gesture that David will make in the novel, refusing to admit that his relationship with Giovanni is anything more than a distraction while his fiancée is away.[42]

In some ways it might be easy to read *Giovanni's Room* as a sharp riposte to the dangerous delusion of individual identity: David believes his rejection of Giovanni is a product of his own choices; in fact, he's wrong. In the scene of their final breakup, Giovanni figures David's pathology as a delusion of individual (sexual) purity: "You will never give it to anybody, you will never let anybody *touch it*—man *or* woman. You want to be *clean*. You think you came here covered with soap and you think you will go out covered with soap—and you do not want to *stink*, not even for five minutes, in the meantime" (141). From this perspective, *Giovanni's Room* might seem to embrace precisely that sense of outside influence James recognizes and shows his individual characters learning to control. David tries to be merely an individual untainted by others' influences; instead, he irrevocably entangles with them and cannot remain "pure." As in Baldwin's reading of Daisy, the delusion that one can be "contaminated by nothing" is destructive. Ross Posnock, for instance, reads Baldwin as finding "a mode of being that encouraged choice and invention rather than fidelity and authenticity" (235). But what's most evident as the tensions of the novel play out is that the sides of the opposition meet: choosing and inventing a self requires also recognizing the existence of an authentic self. In other words, if Baldwin is undermining the use of "authenticity" to describe an individual's relationship to one's culture, he does so in order to replace *culture* with *self*.

James's characters often realize only belatedly how attenuated their selves have become; Baldwin's often actively insist their contexts are their selves. The point is not that David believes in his own individual self, but that he hasn't realized yet what his self really is. His belief is destructive not because he misses the way society can hem in one's decisions, but because his ideal of his own individual character is incorrect. Baldwin's equivalent of Jamesian tautology (e.g., "She was, after all, herself") is even more strained: "What Europe still gives an American—or gave us—is the sanction, if one can accept it, to become oneself" (*Collected Essays* 668).[43] The self is both harder to get to in Baldwin and a much more stable, powerful thing than in James. Where Maggie Verver discovers that to be herself she must adopt part of Charlotte's character, and where Strether discovers that in order to be himself he has to pick and choose the best of American and European people and ideas, David discovers that his self is quite other than what he thought it was. In other words, Daisy and David alike meet with disaster not only because they refuse to open themselves to love, but because they are all too open to other forms of influence and incapable of meeting social surfaces with selves of their own.

In some ways, *Giovanni's Room* is the story of a love affair between a realist character who is a construction of society and a romance hero whose identity is wholly his own. David's failure, in the end, is that he is all too merely a reflection of American values; Giovanni's attraction and the cause of his death is that he cannot be anything but his vividly distinct self. Giovanni's singular identity, his charisma as a character, is precisely the alignment of interior and exterior that David lacks. And just as, in *The Golden Bowl*, Charlotte Stant's charismatic romance of the social genius whose form is both her own and imposed upon her ultimately falters before Maggie's assumption of agency, Giovanni's fascinating self-possession, confronted with realism's economic and emotional limitations, devolves into the brutal ugliness of melodrama.

Identity, then, is actually somewhat more solid in Baldwin than in James, though it is also more concealed and often goes unrealized. Baldwin's characters do change—particularly when love is involved—but his way of mapping out their selves relies on postulating an individual self far fuller than the faculty of choice on which James focuses. David's buried homosexual desires are a part of him; he can't get rid of them at all—whereas, the novel suggests, his ideas about remaining pure reflected the false consciousness of a broader culture could have been jettisoned in order better to "become" himself. This transposition is clearest in Giovanni's shifting comments about what David feels. A few moments into their first conversation, the following exchange occurs:

> "People are always saying, we must wait, we must wait. What are they waiting for?"
>
> "Well," I said, feeling myself being led by Giovanni into deep and dangerous water, "I guess people wait in order to make sure of what they feel."
>
> "In order to make *sure!*" He turned again to that invisible ally and laughed again. (37–38)

Giovanni initially mocks David's paralysis in the face of his uncertain feelings. Yet much later, in their final conversation, David says,

> "What in the world do you want me to do? I can't *help* the way I feel."
> "Do you *know* how you feel? *Do* you feel? *What* do you feel?" (141)

Over the course of their relationship, Giovanni discovers the ways people can deceive themselves about what they feel: he has switched from finding it absurd that David would have trouble figuring out his own feelings to finding it absurd that David thinks he has figured them out. When David says, "I can't *help* the way I feel," he appeals to a rhetoric of individual identity while missing its content: he is, in fact, wrong about the way he feels, but he is right that he can't help it (as his fiancée Hella will shortly discover). In *Giovanni's Room*, one has to recognize the restrictions on one's freedom in order to recognize one's emotions and self. David is confronted by the fact that his obsession with his own purity is precisely the aspect of himself that is *not* himself.

If David resembles Strether, an American in Europe who discovers that the moral hazard of his situation is not where he thinks it is, Giovanni owes something to Isabel—he might ridicule the idea of choice where she embraces it, but like her he is an object of immediate attention, attraction, and fascination, and it is ultimately the fascination he exerts on others that destroys him. James's free indirect discourse and characterization strategies are designed to unite the passive eye with the vivid whole personality; Baldwin's first-person instead heightens the contrast between the narrating David, unable to become a character of his own and formed too much by social contexts, and the narrated Giovanni, whose perfection as a character in someone else's vision leads to his objectification by those around him.

In the two passages on what people feel, both David and Giovanni let the referents remain indistinct: "what they feel" and "the way I feel" are never stated directly. Baldwin, in general, is not only more sexually explicit but more direct than James was by the end of his life—characters make generalizations about love and sex; they offer lovely New Critical explications of their own imagery; only rarely does the Jamesian social surface assert itself. But the noun clauses in these crucial moments allow all the characters to leave indistinct what they're actually talking about: queer romantic love (explicitly: not just sex, but an ongoing commitment and love). As queer theorists have long pointed out, James's obliquity of style might itself constitute a queer habit—when no one says anything explicitly, the "love that dare not speak its name" can be implied.[44] Kevin Ohi, in *Henry James and the Queerness of Style*, offers a comprehensive account of the way the "queerness of Henry James's writing resides . . . in its systematic challenging of the presumption that desire can be, or ought to be, represented" (2–3). In this sense, queerness is inextricable from the genre of romance itself: the things that can't be said directly.[45]

In both passages above, Giovanni asks questions—leaving room for explicit answers or inexplicit flirtation—while David makes statements, fending off the possibility of love. Yet as the conversation winds to its tragic conclusion, Giovanni, too, resorts to the mannered circumlocutions of noun clauses:

> "But I'm a man," I cried, "a man! What do you think can *happen* between us?"
> "You know very well," said Giovanni slowly, "what can happen between us. It is for that reason you are leaving me." (142)

This is a classic demonstration of the use of romantic obliquity: it protects the seriousness of romance against the humiliation visited upon it by the world. If "talking about the sexuality in James is a dangerous thing to do," this is where that danger comes out: once you start talking, you risk making the ideal less significant than it might have been, risk becoming Flaubert (whose "charmlessness" produces an "eloquent plea for the ideal"). David and Giovanni get to hold onto the social surface of Jamesian fiction for their final conversation and all the dignity it offers. But only between themselves: David suggests that becoming *known* precipitates the loss of Giovanni's chance at employment and the murder that follows: "Giovanni . . . has lost his drawing power. Everything is known about him, his secrecy has been discovered" (156).

The legacy of Jamesian literary form is often thought of as a set of institutionalized rules: Mark McGurl, for instance, speaks of the "shackles of the Jamesian and New Critical model of narration" (*Program Era* 208); Jameson talks about James's "tyranny of 'point of view'" (*Antinomies* 82). But as Baldwin's example shows, what he's after is as much the *effect* of the forms as the forms themselves; in this novel—indisputably one of his most Jamesian—he is not even using James's classic focalized third person. But the structures of characterization, and the manipulation of the reader's response to characters, remain the same. Outside of the institution, in the realm of amoral authors taking what they need, James doesn't offer rules but resources.

If the problem in James is getting the right balance of social influences to construct one's identity, the problem in Baldwin is finding a social context in which one can express it—and the courage to do so. What Baldwin takes from James is not the doubts about the idea of people as having their own identities but the sense of the drama of a struggle against the outside pressures upon identity. Baldwin's unfinished piece on *The Ambassadors* was entitled "The Self as a Journey"; in the 1986 *HJR* interview he says that Strether "learns as the novel progresses that to live costs something" (50). Living costs, in Baldwin's terms, a loss of innocence, but the loss leads to a gain in knowledge. "Innocence," in the interview, is the great stigmatized term: "Freedom and innocence are antithetical"; innocence is "the 'general failure'—the failure to touch, to see" (54). More than that, it is the failure to see that one's connections to other people have costs and incur obligations.[46]

Strether in *The Ambassadors* undergoes two shifts—one from an American, closed-off attitude that rejects outside influence (but entirely internalizes American social attitudes), to a Parisian attitude of openness, flux, and refusal of judgment (Madame de Vionnet can welcome Sarah Pocock; Sarah cannot return the favor). His second change is to realize that along with openness must come the construction of a self, through a degree of judgment about which influences one wishes to adopt (Strether sympathizes with Madame de Vionnet, but is uncomfortable about the way she marries off her daughter). In Baldwin's view, these movements occur together, even when characters don't realize it: when you jettison received ideas and begin to connect your self to people around you, the previously caged self emerges.

Mirrors of Character and Art

Baldwin's image for the prison of societal norms is also James's: the mirror. Where James shows how the individual uses the building blocks of others' personalities to construct his or her own personality, Baldwin shows how the variegated connections and contexts of lives provide different circumstances for the emergence of an inner self, as affected as it may be by its environment. The Jamesian image of a mirror frames *Giovanni's Room*: as he remembers Giovanni and awaits the moment of his execution, David is staring into a mirror. "My reflection is tall, perhaps rather like an arrow, my blond hair gleams. My face is like a face you have seen many times," he says (3). Looking at his reflection makes him indistinguishable from a group, from an ideal of white American identity—"perhaps rather like an arrow" not quite going so far as to say "straight as an arrow," but wistfully implying it. Mirrors record society's trap. When David first encounters Giovanni, Giovanni gives him a look: "And this look made me feel that no one in my life had ever looked at me directly before" (36–37); the man who seems like every other face has at last been looked at.

David describes the "germ" of his flight from homosexual desire through his reflection in a window: "Of course, it is somewhere before me, locked in that reflection I am watching in the window as the night comes down outside. It is trapped in the room with me, always has been, and always will be, and it is yet more foreign to me than those foreign hills outside" (10). The paradoxes of this image—being trapped with him, yet foreign—express the way social constructions of identity invade their subjects. At the end of the novel the mirrors become more explicitly invidious: "I do not know what moves in this body, what this body is searching. It is trapped in my mirror as it is trapped in time . . . I long to crack that mirror and be free" (168). Mirrors have become not merely an alienating experience of effaced identity, but a "trap." Reflections are images of social expectations—they show an individual looking like his surroundings, blending in to what is thought by others. Like Strether, David discovers that mirrors are nothing to themselves, that he has an identity struggling against the trap.

Mirrors show up again and again in Baldwin's various efforts to adapt the novel. In one movie script a shot is described as from the perspective of a mirror (James Baldwin Papers, Folder 14.8, p. 156), and David's reflections in windows are used to fade from one scene to another (4). In one draft dated to 1982—very late in Baldwin's life—David's reflection in the window is used to cut to Giovanni looking through the bars of his (literal) prison (Folder 15.1, p. 169). David's inability to escape his own reflection fades into the far more brutal fate society has in store for Giovanni.

Mirrors are one of the recurring images throughout Baldwin's fiction and non-fiction. In the essays, they tend to stand for the force of societal categorization—particularly in its construction of the self-image of white Americans. For instance, in *The Fire Next Time*, he writes,

> A vast amount of the energy that goes into what we call the Negro problem is produced by the white man's profound desire not to be judged by those who are not white, not to be seen as he is, and at the same time a vast amount of the white anguish is rooted in the white man's equally profound need to be seen as he is, to be released from the tyranny of his mirror. All of us know, whether or not we are able to admit it, that mirrors can only lie, that death by drowning is all that awaits one there. (341)

White Americans are nothing to themselves, but can't admit it. The perspective of black Americans—and of black artists—is more accurate for being distinct from them; as with Ellison's jug, their exclusion enables them to see clearly. James wanted the artist to be an outsider, to have separation from his social context; Baldwin says that those who are outside have, as a result, particular resources they can bring to bear both on society and on art.

Baldwin's emphasis on individualism underwent a dramatic rhetorical shift after his Henry James enthusiasm began when he arrived in Paris. In 1946, an early version appears in a letter, and his theorization sounds very different, expressed in skepticism about the "glib theory . . . that people are environment and environmental changes, presto, change the people."[47] Other letters of the period also talk about the importance of respecting individual difference. David Leeming suggests that Stanley Geist, a literary historian Baldwin met in Paris in 1948, "introduced" him to the works of Henry James (*James Baldwin* 61).[48] Regardless, around this point, mirrors enter his symbolic language, and they never leave. James, it seems, offers a model to continue advocating for expressive individualism, while acknowledging the pressures and powers of social environment.

Generally, in Baldwin's work, mirrors and drowning are related, and they stand for confusion between the interior and exterior of one's character, for the ways a context can become the mold of a soul. If mirrors and "death by drowning" are only invidious in *The Fire Next Time*, they have a stranger resonance in his near-contemporaneous novel *Another Country*. There, two protagonists' single sexual encounter is described complexly: "It was strangely and insistently double-edged, it was like making love in the midst of mirrors, or it was like death by drowning.

But it was also like music, the highest, sweetest, loneliest reeds, and it was like the rain" (385).[49] Mirrors and drowning appear once again, but this time they suggest a salutary lowering of barriers, an absorption of context from another individual rather than from a generalized societal perspective. As in James, picking and choosing others' personalities as models is a force for developing one's own self. Mirrors and drowning, most consistently, represent a self that is open to change—and if in their negative version they represent the self being rewritten in the conventional image of society, they can also capture the way love opens individuals to experiment with becoming one another.

The passage above from *The Fire Next Time* continues,

> It is for this reason that love is so desperately sought and so cunningly avoided. Love takes off the masks that we fear we cannot live without and know we cannot live within. I use the word "love" here not merely in the personal sense but as a state of being, or a state of grace—not in the infantile American sense of being made happy but in the tough and universal sense of quest and daring and growth. (341)

The masks here owe something to the "cage of reality"; but the value placed on love—typical for Baldwin—also sheds light on the potential positive view of mirrors in the *Another Country* passage. If mirrors are usually one form of the mask of society, love stands for the possibility of bringing the interior self into communion with the world. The language of romance—quest, daring—emerges here in order to defend the idea of choosing to develop one's own self, and, as with James, images of discovering a preexisting self blend with images of new development: to remove a mask is to grow.

Characters' struggles to mirror and to do more than mirror society also reflect the complex tasks of the artist. What begins, in *The Fire Next Time*, as an apparently specific point about American racial dynamics shades into a broad claim about how the perspective of an outsider allows better understanding than the "tyranny of [the] mirror." Mirrors can only lie; transformative vision is only possible from a perspective that is outside the object of perception. In *The Fire Next Time*, Baldwin says, "To accept one's past—one's history—is not the same as drowning in it; it is learning how to use it" (333). Novels that, like the protest novel, offer a mirror of circumstances, merely drown in the past. The shift from drowning in the past to actively using it is parallel to the change from merely mirroring present-day social expectations to learning how to become oneself within a world defined by them. When Baldwin critiques Wright and the protest novel for a failure to be more than a mirror of "confusion," he aligns a Jamesian ethic of novelistic craft with a political point about the dangers of seeing people through categories rather than as individuals.

In the Howe-Ellison polemics, which were an early-1960s echo of Baldwin's polemics on protest novels, Ellison adapts Baldwin's critique of a viewpoint that does not allow for an individual's ability to elude social categories into a more explicit defense of the value of a particular kind of art. Ellison rests his argument for the aesthetic possibilities of African American literature on dual claims of representational faith and artistic transformation. On the one hand, he says, "The view from inside the skin is not so dark as it appears to be from Howe's remote position" (177). This is a reminder of the claim that the jug is transparent: the view is *from* the inside, not *of* the inside. On the other: "If *Invisible Man* is even 'apparently' free from 'the ideological and emotional penalties suffered by Negroes in this country,' it is because I tried to the best of my ability to transform these elements into art. My goal was not to escape or hold back, but to work through; to transcend" (183). These two claims, of representation and transformation, echo the contrast between Woolf's author faithfully tracing the atoms and James's agonizingly selective embroidery of the flower. Ellison's claim of transcendence, of art as effortful working-through, in contrast to a representational rigor by which reality doesn't need to be "worked through," is, like Baldwin's aesthetic theory, a repurposing of the project of recuperative modernism—of selection and distillation, rather than faithful representation.

Baldwin's Universalism

Like Ellison, it is a central tenet of Baldwin's work that the art, as well as the artist, is not entirely in sync with the details of social realities, and that abstractions and general truths undergird those details. Baldwin's and James's shared investment in the idea of the individual character and individual identity—as opposed to categories of race, nation, or gender—is ultimately an investment in a kind of universalism: an expression of the ability of the novelist to say, for instance, that people ought to give up innocence for freedom (Baldwin) or that they ought to learn to acknowledge the separate desires of other people (James)—even as, in both cases, they maintain sympathy with their characters (David, Madame Merle) who fail to do so. It is not that either will say that human nature is all one thing, but they think individuals' minds and experiences have a recurring structure, even if the materials making up the structure may be different.

Baldwin's attachment to universalizing generalization is paradoxically a way of defending his ideal of the strangeness and power of the individual, and multiple modernist styles overlap in the service of this goal. In *Giovanni's Room*, modernist echoes interlock with biblical tones; these high, generalizing registers are made personal by the first-person narrator. In the following passage, Baldwin isn't alluding with particular density to any one source, but a variety of voices weave together:

> And these nights were being acted out under a foreign sky, with no one to watch, no penalties attached—it was this last fact which was our undoing, for nothing is more unbearable, once one has it, than freedom. I suppose this was why I asked her to marry me: to give myself something to be moored to. Perhaps this was why, in Spain, she decided that she wanted to marry me. But people can't, unhappily, invent their mooring posts, their lovers and their friends, anymore than they can invent their parents. Life gives these and also takes them away and the great difficulty is to say Yes to life. (5)

Here Baldwin's use of James goes beyond the specific problem of character and identity to a broader sense of the value of recuperative literary experiences. This passage from the beginning of the novel sets up at the start an impression of revelation: *that* fact was our undoing, *this* was why something happened. It is a string of explanations prior to the representation of the problem. The generalizations above become the tools characters have to interpret events—in Jamesian terms, to "make a sense."

In this case, there are a few Jamesian moments in different senses. "Nothing is more unbearable, once one has it, than freedom," with its abstracting "one," and its interrupting comma clause, takes a great deal from James. There is Conrad, too—whose part in this story will be discussed in the next chapter—with his rhetorical expansiveness and carefully planted sentence endings: "people can't, unhappily, invent their mooring posts, their lovers and their friends, anymore than they can invent their parents." James and Conrad are the source here not of epistemological doubts but of styles for expressing rhetorical certainties. But where a Conrad novel begins with a puzzle—e.g., why does Jim the water-clerk, who seems devoted to his job, keep on quitting?—and slowly works through question after question to fragmentary universal phrases ("Nobody, nobody is good enough" [*Lord Jim* 240]), Baldwin starts with the universal phrases, setting up the novel as an explanation of how one could arrive at a coherent vision. This passage illustrates the central survival mode of modernism's recuperative tendencies: it lives on in its epigrams and its revelations, in its hard-fought moments of victory over skepticism, rather than in its critiques and insecurities.

There are thematic connections to modernism too—"the great difficulty is to say Yes to life" feels a little like Molly Bloom's triumphant *Yes* in *Ulysses* mixed with echoes of prayer ("Life gives these and also takes them away") and of Jamesian expressive agonies ("the great difficulty is . . ."). Baldwin's is a much more direct an expression of optimism than either James or Conrad would allow. Isabel Archer retreats from the "cup of experience," calling it a "poisoned drink" (143), and modulates the image into something vaguer ("I only want to see for myself"); Conrad's novels are full of climaxes that list multiple optimistic words before ending with something like "illusion" (see, e.g., the ending of *Youth*, or that of chapter 21 of *Lord Jim*).[50]

Yet for Baldwin it is a general image of mankind as a multitude of various individuals, all with much in common, that is alluring about his predecessors' art. Jamesian character is valuable to him because James values the idea of a distinct character or self, but represents just how tough it is to grapple with the irreducible strangeness of being an individual nonetheless. And this is absolutely necessary to the kind of political points Baldwin wants to make: to his claim that categorization is invidious, and even to his wish to allow for "the perpetual achievement of the impossible" (*Collected Essays* 346)—a phrase that, like so many of Conrad's, ends with a negative word, but in such a context that it seems like a thrilling challenge rather than a dark intimation of doubts.

Baldwin ultimately views the literary past in much the same way as he does the historical past: once accepted, it can be used; but it cannot simply be imported whole into the present. In passages like this one he weaves together the characteristic effects of multiple genres as well as multiple individuals—and rebalances the emphasis for his own moment and own uses. James's recuperation of romantic identity is useful to Baldwin precisely because the terminology and purposes James had are no longer present; the contrast between realism and romance echoes in, but is not exactly the same as, that between protest novel and the novel of "the human being" (in Baldwin's phrase). Neither *Giovanni's Room* nor the similar points made in *The Fire Next Time* are themselves of the genre of romance. But they do testify that James's recuperation of an older genre, his desire to see the outlooks and literary effects of the past as not merely to be dismissed for new times, could invigorate and be reinvigorated by readers not merely in his own time, but the future as well.

And that future is our own. The aspects of Baldwin I have highlighted—just like those of James that Baldwin himself finds useful—might seem like features most of his time. After all, perhaps it's no coincidence that, in the American context, the literary works that pick up most visibly on recuperative modernism are mid-century works: the individualism and freedom highlighted by Baldwin and, we'll see later, Kesey, might be yet another bit of Cold War ideology lurking in everything of its era. Yet, just as James's privileged romance shows surprising new uses, Baldwin's vision of the responsibilities of freedom shows up in unexpected places today.[51]

Baldwin is having a moment of widespread revival. Young African writers are finding excitement in his work, completing a connection that never took flight back in the days of the Conference of Negro-African Writers and Artists—a 1956 event where Senghor and Césaire, Wright and Baldwin, sought and for the most part failed to find common ground between the descendants of slaves and the rising anticolonial artists of Africa.[52] The offset of a few decades has created that missing connection. In part, today's new generation of African writers is enacting the Jamesian—and Baldwinian—journey in reverse. The Ethiopian-American Maaza Mengiste cites Baldwin as one of her key influences and as part of the "American literary traditions" standing behind her first novel, which is set entirely in Ethiopia. Chimamanda Ngozi Adichie, who now resides half the time in the United States, lists *Another Country* as one of her favorite novels (*Half of a Yellow Sun* postscript 7). One of the major themes of Adichie's *Americanah* is how awkwardly Ifemelu, its protagonist, gets along with most African American individuals; at the same time, she's finding inspiration in African American literary heritage, reading Baldwin's works from start to finish when first she arrives in America, beginning with *The Fire Next Time* (166). The old dream of diasporic connection, in other words, develops its resonance for her at a distance, tranhistorically. Alain Mabanckou, a French and Congolese writer now living in the United States, wrote a poetic biography of Baldwin in the second person in which he focuses on Baldwin's desire to produce lasting works of art, works that, implicitly, would find their way to him: "Until your last day, until your last breath, you hammer away at the keys of your typewriter, as if to engrave your final wishes, to write the sentence with which posterity would remember the name" (127). Mabanckou's book, *Letter to Jimmy*, is both a literal form of "writing back"—a letter to the dead past—and a revitalization of it, narrating the *you* (*tu*) in the present tense, forcing the reader to inhabit the ghostly shell of Baldwin's presence.

Adichie has never demonstrated any particular interest in Henry James, but her use of Baldwin is of the most Jamesian things in Baldwin: the feeling of being outside of everything and alien everywhere. In fact, she adapts Baldwin's "love" back in the direction of James. Ifemelu writes on her blog after she reads *The Fire Next Time*:

> The simplest solution to the problem of race in America? Romantic love. Not friendship. Not the safe, shallow love where the objective is that both people remain comfortable. But real deep romantic love, the kind that twists you and wrings you out and makes you breathe through the nostrils of your beloved. And because that real deep romantic love is so rare, and because American society is set up to make it even rarer between American Black and American White, the problem of race in America will never be solved. (366–367)

This is, of course, an echo of Baldwin's passage on love in *The Fire Next Time*: like him, she juxtaposes a negative, too-easy vision of love ("infantile American sense of being made happy"; "safe, shallow love") against a substantive, challenging form that demands ethical commitment and development of one's identity ("tough and universal sense of quest and daring and growth"; "twists you and wrings you out and makes you breathe through the nostrils of your beloved"). Ifemelu, like Giovanni, valorizes love that doesn't let you stay clean.

And if Baldwin is concerned to escape the categories imposed by American racial history, Adichie's protagonist feels even more acutely the strangeness of being assimilated to a racial category that isn't her own. She is black in America, but not a descendant of enslaved peoples. (At one point she titles her blog *Observations by a Non-American Black on the Subject of Blackness in America*.) The absurdity of racial categorization as an experience stands out all the more harshly when seen by a Nigerian outsider; as Ifemelu moves from one relationship or social scene to the next, she is continually cast in roles that don't quite fit her, from the obvious—the white woman who feels *so sorry* for anyone from Africa—to the subtle—the African American boyfriend whose confidence in every particularity of the ideologies of social justice seems to obscure the complexity of her experience. And the progress of the novel is her discovery what she must simply reject, and what she can make use of, in others' views of her identity. Some of those relationships are too safe and shallow; others, having the potential to change her, require her to pick and choose the changes she wants.

All Ifemelu's commentary about race in America leads in the end to her choice to return to Nigeria. She's an outsider there, too, now. Yet, in an old romance paradigm, she ends the novel by reconnecting with an old boyfriend—another Nigerian returned from ambiguous experiences abroad. They have exchanged, like Baldwin, like James, innocence for freedom, but, in the rekindling of their relationship, they are, after all, themselves. *Americanah* is an intensely Jamesian novel, a twenty-first-century *Portrait of a Lady*, the story of a woman finding her identity abroad through her romantic entanglements—though, unlike *Portrait*, Ifemelu seems to reach a traditionally happy conclusion. If a contemporary writer claiming to be influenced by James Baldwin ends up writing a novel that looks like a nineteenth-century marriage plot, the substrate of James might be part of the reason why.

Americanah carries few direct lessons for American politics today. But I'd like to suggest that Adichie's interest in Baldwin's views on love have more immediately forceful counterparts. Baldwin quotations circulate on social media as part of Black Lives Matter; Ta-Nehisi Coates, one of the most notable nonfiction writers in America today, is happy to acknowledge his profound debt to Baldwin—his book *Between the World and Me* is a structural and stylistic re-enactment of *The Fire Next Time*, from its title to its syntax. He's also written multiple blog posts with the title "Is James Baldwin America's Greatest Essayist?"; these coincided with a period spent living in Paris.

Coates credits Baldwin with helping him to synthesize a space between black nationalism and old-school nonviolence: Baldwin, he finds, offers "the black pride of nationalism fused to the undeniable morality of integration. . . . These are some of the coldest American sentences every written," he writes in the second blog post, quoting Baldwin's fiercer statements about why white people are so eager to see nonviolence as a virtue in black activists. Yet, he continues, "After all of this—after all his hard talk—Baldwin is still talking about love." The "coldness" of Baldwin's love, its demanding moral dimension, is, of course, exactly where its political efficacy lies.

It's also what some readers have long disliked about Henry James, saying that some of the relationships in his novels sacrifice passion on the altar of justice. For instance, Robert Pippin reads the conclusion to *The Golden Bowl*, where Maggie is victorious over Charlotte in her contest for the Prince: "What love? There is very little substance or passion in this love" (Pippin 78). But now look at the terms of his critique: Maggie, he says, doesn't want love; she "wants above all not 'to have been' a fool, to *assert herself as an equal*" (emphasis added). And if Maggie's assertion of equality might fit uneasily in a marriage to which she brings all the financial power, the language of Pippin's criticism suggests a more sympathetic side. Mabanckou, discussing the critical reception of Baldwin's *Another Country*, describes a critic "bewildered by the analytical approach of the characters and by the stark portrayal of racial prejudice" (80). For Mabanckou, the characters' analytical qualities are precisely what makes them more *real* rather than artificially distant from human beings.[53] The exacting love of James's privileged people, in other words, has different uses when the power relations run the other way. This may seem cold love; but it's the kind of love Baldwin needs.

Baldwin's use exposes the way James's novels seek to found passion on a difficult process of mutual moral recognition. This is where Baldwin's love is a little different from more familiar evocations of love in the context of nonviolence: this is precisely *not* King's love that "seeks nothing in return"—its redemptive power lies in how much it demands, of both lover and beloved. It is love as call to action and awareness and responsibility; individualism as a call to recognize how implicated in society any one person is.[54] And when, in *Between the World and Me*, Coates talks about his intellectual development and his realization that he needs to cast a critical eye on the conception of black culture he had already formed, he writes: "I had thought that I must mirror the outside world, create a carbon copy of white claims to civilization. It was beginning to occur to me to question the logic of the claim itself" (50). The Baldwinian mirror returns. Coates, like Adichie, never expresses an interest in James, but, through the mediation of Baldwin, his diagnosis of the cultural effects of white supremacy appears here in the same language James used to diagnose the limits of Trollope's and Flaubert's realist aesthetics.

Baldwin needs an ideal of the individual on behalf of whom he can call for political change, and a model of love that is exacting rather than accepting, and finds it in James; Coates needs a model of moral commitment that demands accepting the past without drowning in it, and finds it in Baldwin. Reparations, he says, "would represent America's maturation out of the childhood myth of its innocence into a wisdom worthy of its founders" (71). As Baldwin said of James: Americans must learn that their lives cost something. James's old hint that America's innocence was its limitation and the source of its corruption helps Baldwin to develop the terminology with which he can call for growth and political awareness; and in turn, Baldwin's terminology is Coates's language for grappling with history. "The Case for Reparations" is an indictment of those who would forget the evils of American history; it is also a call for an action that requires cool distance on that history. One of the final images of the article is of the debate in Israel about postwar reparations from Germany: "Survivors of the Holocaust feared laundering the reputation of Germany with money, and mortgaging the memory of their dead" (70). Dealing with the great genocides of history today requires leaving behind some of the incommensurability of their losses. Action today can never fully reckon for the still-gaping injuries of the past; we have to choose what from it can spur just action to repair the wound as much as possible in the present.

The history of the readers of these texts shows, in part, that the large historical social structures onto which some of James's novels provide a glancing window sometimes have little effect on the shape of the novels' impact and use. When readers respond to these novels, they pick and choose history to suit the political needs of their own purposes and periods—and structures of literary experience are often the most adaptable tools. James's attempt to write away from his own moment—to make the novel into art by limiting the degree of social detail he allows into his fiction, to suggest that individuals are after all themselves rather than expressions of their time—helped make him useful, in a way he could not possibly have predicted, to new political debates and other political moments. And Baldwin's own commitment to abstract terms—love, innocence—has helped make him generative to Adichie and Coates.

One of the reasons we tend to make allies of past literary works by discerning in them forms of critique and ambivalence is that commitment seems more time-bound, more likely to go out of date. Ambiguity is eternally beguiling; anything you commit to will inevitably disappoint you. But here, the object of commitment is less important than the process of committing and the role that object fills. The exact content of Isabel Archer's identity, or Lambert Strether's, isn't very useful to Baldwin; the process by which James *constructs* the identity, however, is. Baldwin's use of *innocence* is often about individual knowledge, Coates's about society-wide awareness and action—but the rhetorical move is the same, as is the call to commitment.

This is the history to which this book seeks to make our criticism more responsible—the history of texts' persistence and their malleability, the ways new writers remake the past to reach their own present and the unknowable future. In between the universal implied reader and the local study of particular reading communities lies the history of literary works. This is also the world of today's writers: responding to the past, creating instruments to move the present and the future. We need not drown in the contexts of the novels of the past if we turn instead to who has used them, and how.

3. What Chronology Demands of Us

The Kenyan writer, critic, and activist Ngũgĩ wa Thiong'o, contemplating the rise of African fiction, comments, "Perhaps the crucial question is not that of the racial, national, and class origins of the novel, but that of its development and the uses to which it is continually being put" (*Decolonising* 69). Like Baldwin, Ngũgĩ focuses on present-day use; if Baldwin sought to negotiate between drowning in and accepting the past, Ngũgĩ comes close to suggesting that the past can, in a literary context, be swept aside. This idea runs counter to many of literary criticism's reflexive habits of thought. We have learned always to historicize; we examine the ways literary forms and works are shaped by the racial, national, and class contexts he suggests are irrelevant. To do otherwise, we worry, would suggest a vision of art as disengaged from history, would see literature through the prism of a white, privileged Anglo-American aesthetic experience.

But Ngũgĩ approaches the novel's relationship to history from the other end—from the perspective not of production, but of future use. He decenters Eurocentric literature not on behalf of the erased past of colonized peoples, but on behalf of their present and future. Literary studies often ricochets between two persistently appealing, yet persistently opposed, premises. On the one hand, literature is political and historical, a product of and comment upon complex social forces in its own times. On the other, novels cross historical boundaries and are read in distant times and places.

This book contests both the yoking of political relevance to the context of production and the presumption that such relevance is incompatible with transhistorical significance. Ngũgĩ's reading and appropriation of Conrad—my example here—both dehistoricizes the older author and deploys him for a later-day political effect. For Ngũgĩ, Conrad's appeal is not historically specific—it lies in content that is transposable across different times and places (like themes of guilt and betrayal) and in the effects of literary form on its readers. This is not a move against the value of history—it is a denial that English history is what matters.

Conrad's use of nonchronological narration tends to demand particular kinds of mental work from his readers. Conrad's novels are often analyzed in terms of what their structures represent or mean, but seldom as sequential reading experiences, and it is as experiences that Ngũgĩ finds them politically useful. The novels ask their readers to seek knowledge, however contingent it may be. Conrad's most famous statement on writing is that the task of art is to "make you *see*"; great attention has been paid to its seeing, but relatively little to the fraught dynamic implied by the idea of "making" the reader do something in the first place.[1] Modernist novels, with their difficulty and their fragmentation, may seem on one level to have scorned the idea of reader manipulation we associate, say, with a serial installment's cliffhanger ending, but their literary innovations—in the cases I will discuss in this chapter and the next—are as invested in controlling the attention, curiosity, and sense-making capacities of their readers as any mystery novel. A broken chronology, after all, is also a demand that the reader attempt to piece it back together—as narratologists who examine detective fiction have pointed out for a long time.[2] And this process, which is galvanized by confusion and uncertainty, does not come to rest in the metaphysics of irresolvable contradiction, or in the deconstructive acknowledgment that nothing can be known for certain, but instead shows the inevitability and the value of committing to one idea rather than another, or seeking knowledge even if it will always be partial.

Barring a few postmodern experiments, we read from start to finish,[3] and the linearity of the novel as an art form is at odds with the time schemes Conrad furnishes for his novels, which tend to show time in recursive loops, or reshuffleable like a deck of cards. The interaction between these aspects of Conrad's art—the sequential experience of reading, and the disruption of our ordinary view of sequential time—forms the reader's experience. In these works, we seek not the future tense but the past: the urge to see what happens next is replaced by the urge to see what *happened* before, to put together the materials of a past already hinted at by the things that followed it. These novels don't just involve retrospection and memory for the characters; as in James's work, they also unite the reader's inquiry with the characters' own, emphasizing the process of looking back, of distancing one-self from what has happened through repeating it as an effort of understanding. In James, characters had to be dislocated psychologically and socially from their surroundings in order to gain understanding of them; in Conrad, the saving sep-aration is chronological.

Yet this distancing move is a statement of the importance of the events being described, of the stakes of coming to a conclusion about them. As we'll see, one of the lessons of *Nostromo*, for instance, is that an ironically uninvolved perspec-tive on the history in which the novel takes place is unsustainable. It is in this respect that Conrad's techniques are useful to Ngũgĩ, whose work addresses the moral stakes of involving oneself in political events, and particularly reproaches those who think they can stand aside as history happens. Narrative puzzles and bewilderment, in both authors, are modes of generating readers' investment in events—even if their ultimate political purposes are very different. Conrad's achronology is at times a rearguard action: it demands that its readers engage with concepts of value that seem to have become obsolete or untenable in shifting social conditions. Ngũgĩ's achronology is advocacy of political revolution: it forces its readers to take a stand rather than standing by from historical events. Both authors, in the end, carve the possibility of knowledge and commitment out of the risky ambiguities of multiple perspectives. These novels make claims for one perspective rather than another, for interpretation of events rather than passive experience of them.

Postcolonial literature has long been alert to the ways literature can compel political commitment rather than instilling forms of doubt and critique. Neil Lazarus, for instance, notes that "the vast majority of 'postcolonial' literary writings point us . . . towards the idea not of 'fundamental alienness' but of deep-seated affinity and community" (19). Indeed, Edward Said, in critiquing *Heart of Darkness*, does so precisely on the grounds of its apparent representation of irresolvable subjectivity: "If we cannot truly understand someone else's experi-ence . . . there is no use looking for other, non-imperialist alternatives" (*Culture and Imperialism* 24). Said is hardly alone among critics in attributing to Conrad a skeptical affect, but he flips the political significance he attributes to it: here, undermining the possibility of knowledge is quietism in the face of oppression, rather than a disruption of received norms. For Ngũgĩ as well, Conrad's political limitations arise from his skepticism and his too-easy assertion of the impos-sibility of knowing or achieving anything. For Conrad's political uses we must look elsewhere, must look beyond the quotable declarations that the world is incomprehensible.

This is an older tradition in Marxist criticism—going back to Lukács, where modernism, because it offers only the "surface of life," lets reality remain "opaque, fragmentary, chaotic and uncomprehended" ("Realism" 39). Jameson declares, by contrast, that "realism requires a conviction as to the massive weight and persistence of the present as such, and an aesthetic need to avoid recognition of deep structural social change" (*Antinomies* 145). The debate over whether modernism or realism is intrinsically conservative is unlikely to be settled anytime soon. But it's worth noting that Jameson and Lukács tend to share presumptions about the epistemological habits produced by realism and modernism: realist form produces certainty, whereas modernism and the forms that follow progressively offer greater gestures toward the unknowable and incomprehensible. The only real question is which variety of literary experience is more useful; one generation detects political critique in the demonstration of what can't be understood; another finds political commitment in knowledge. This book has suggested not only that different effects are useful in different historical moments, but that the formal features that produce them are more various and unpredictable than is usually acknowledged.

Despite the formal distinctions, in other words, the effects of the narrative strategies of Conrad and Ngũgĩ resemble the towering omniscient narrators of the nineteenth century. They refuse some of the liberties of speech traditionally granted to the narrators of fiction in the tradition of Henry Fielding, the right to pronounce authoritatively from a stance that presumptively acknowledges the author as the creator of the universe. Yet Ngũgĩ and Conrad both reinforce in their novels the authority of quasi-authorial voices, holding out the possibility of moral certainty as a hope or a political necessity. These complex chronologies elude realist explanation—they often can't be reduced to the arrangements of embedded narrators. Yet the novels maneuver their readers into recognizing some of these voices without origin as speaking with interpretive authority by their conclusions.

The various narrative devices that foreground the constructedness of Conrad's fiction—achronology, rhetorical ostentatiousness—are all ways of demonstrating such a selectiveness of vision, of defending the role of the artist as far from faithful reporter. All the way back in 1966, Ngũgĩ declared, "In Africa today, no matter who you are, you cannot be content with simply reflecting the conflict—you must be prepared to suggest" (*Ngũgĩ wa Thiong'o Speaks* 23). Art as mirror, for Ngũgĩ, may not be a lie, but it is an abdication of responsibility—a waste of the power of the artist to write history by attending to the future as well as the present.

Refusing to Represent: Conrad's Challenge to Readers

Ford Madox Ford claimed that both he and Conrad wished novels to mimic the "general effect" life makes on the reader (*Joseph Conrad* 180). This is a vision of modernism's formal experimentation as a form of realism, whereby the task of the artist is strictly circumscribed by the experience of life, by the partial views of men and the impossibility of omniscience. The opening pages of *Nostromo* seem to bear this out. Conrad sets up a deliberate clash between the author and God: speaking of locals' comments about the darkness of the Placid Gulf, the narrator comments, "The eye of God Himself—they add with grim profanity—could not find out what work a man's hand is doing in there; and you would be free to call the devil to your aid with impunity if even his malice were not defeated by such a blind darkness" (7). On the one hand, this passage displays a world haunted by its own emptiness, by the dominion of blind nature over the most powerful of human and super-human visions.

On the other hand, the rest of the novel implies that the artist is a perfectly adequate replacement for the eye of God: this darkness will become the scene of the central sequence of the novel, the night voyage of Nostromo and Decoud out into the gulf to take a treasure of silver away from the armies converging on Sulaco, during which the absolute blackness leads to a slow-motion crash. This moment stands as a sly assertion of the tremendous power the artist has: even the devout may think God nods, from time to time; the artist's vision never fails. The task of the artist is not to convey the effect life makes, but to convey exactly the effects life does not make, to convey the scenes hidden to any ordinary (or extraordinary) view. Even as Conrad denies the possibility of a divine outlook, he develops a conception of the artist's power that flaunts its authority, its distance from ordinary experience.

It is commonplace to see Conrad as somehow dismantling the view of the author as a reflection of God, as though only belief in a divinity-suffused world could justify an author's claim to make authoritative statements about people and life in general. The artist, in this case, starts to look like another faithful imitator of life—like Woolf, avoiding the introduction of the "alien and external," and, like Ford, limited to the perceptual capabilities of people. Mark Wollaeger, for instance, views Conrad's work as a dialogue between a prior tradition of empiricism in fiction and a newly ascendant tradition of philosophical skepticism—a dialogue in which skepticism usually wins. But Conrad takes the dialogue further than Wollaeger allows: the latter's chapter on the role of art in *Lord Jim* concludes,

"Conrad ultimately sacrifices the emerging artist-god on the altar of his skepticism" (*Joseph Conrad* 119). But this isn't the point at which Conrad's conception of art *ends*; this sacrifice is the principle with which he starts, and it is characteristically the openings of his novels that present the most skeptical stances about the possibility of knowledge, as in the chronological convolutions of *Lord Jim* and *Nostromo*. The task of Conrad's fiction is revivifying the speaking voice of the author, even if it is no longer quasi-divine. Conrad views the artist not as a fallen God but instead as the supreme example of what man can do instead.

What, then, *does* it feel like to read *Nostromo*? And the same might be asked of *Lord Jim*, which includes a realist and objective explanation for the disorder of time (embedded narrators engaging in out-loud retrospection), but famously proved so confusing to one early reviewer that he mistakenly asserted that the *Patna*, the ship at the center of the novel, had sunk.[4] (The *Patna* at one point seems likely to sink, causing the young Jim to join his fellow officers in abandoning ship; in fact, the ship stays afloat, and its survival reveals the cowardice of its officers.) These are, in other words, confusing novels. But they bewilder in order to demand of their readers an ability to survey life that approaches that of the lost omniscient narrator. To feel confusion, in Conrad, is to learn how to know. One answer to the question of what it is like to read a Conrad novel is that it is constantly to feel the presence of a forceful shaping mind at work. The chronological manipulation is a way of foregrounding the work of organization and synthesis the artist does—and consequently of laying bare what exactly art can do to its readers.

Ford famously gave a brief example of the technique he claimed was practiced by both himself and Conrad in *Joseph Conrad: A Personal Remembrance*, describing the theoretical case of a neighbor's actions:

> Life does not say to you: In 1914 my next-door neighbour, Mr. Slack, erected a greenhouse and painted it with Cox's green aluminum paint. . . . If you think about the matter you will remember, in various unordered pictures, how one day Mr. Slack appeared in his garden and contemplated the wall of his house. You will then try to remember the year of that occurrence and you will fix it as August 1914 because having had the foresight to bear the municipal stock of the city of Liège you were able to afford a first-class season ticket for the first time in your life. You will remember Mr. Slack—then much thinner because it was before he found out where to buy that cheap Burgundy of which he has since drunk an inordinate quantity though whiskey you think would be much better for him! (180–181)

The situation Ford imagines involves the deliberate suppression of two figures usually crucial to models of literary experience: the artist and the reader. The speaker
for Ford is a "neighbour," someone involved in events, who is thinking to himself
rather than trying to present a story to someone else. The difference between the
way Ford builds Mr. Slack's greenhouse and the way Conrad does, say, the failed
bomb plot against the Greenwich observatory in *The Secret Agent* is that for Ford
the sequence of associations has a *realist* source—Ford explicitly tells us that his
method arises out of a desire faithfully to reproduce the movements of a mind, of
an observer telling his story to no one in particular. The fact that the story is a work
of art has to be concealed: the mind must not be seen as deliberately presenting its
movements to an outside audience. But for Conrad, the deliberation of art is crucial, and rather than Ford's concealment of the author's movement and statements,
Conrad foregrounds the presence of authorial action and choices while making it
extremely difficult to pin down the motive and meanings behind the choices. For
Ford, the mind is at the mercy of its random processes of association and chron-
ologically disordered because of them; for Conrad, I will argue, achronology is
a tool for sorting out the random associations. Conrad's art does not reproduce
what life says to a character, or to a reader; instead, he manipulates chronology and
rhetorical structures in order to have characters and readers arrive at particular
interpretations of life.

The narrative momentum of Conrad's novels is the process of the reader's
attempts to put the material of the novel together, to make sense out of the strange
experience of the story as presented, much as in a James novel it is the characters'
growing understanding of the forces that have gone into their own existences and
selves. "Spatial form," Joseph Frank's conception of the difficulties of modernism,
suggests that in modernist fiction the novel is a work of art designed to be viewed
from above as a complete whole: "A knowledge of the whole is essential to an
understanding of any part" (*The Idea* 21). The idea has obvious relevance to the
endless rereadings for sly and subtle detailing demanded by *Ulysses*; but Conrad's
works reward the tactics and phenomenology of reading for the plot, of retrospection going on *within* and throughout the novel rather than in conclusion.[5] The
characters, not just the external reader, strain toward a broader understanding,
and the unfolding of the novel over the distance from start to finish is as meaningful as the apparent view of the whole reached at the end: we search for "that
which makes us . . . want and need plotting, seeking through the narrative text as
it unfurls before us a precipitation of shape and meaning" (Brooks, *Reading for
the Plot* 35). Conrad the novelist goes out of his way to imply that the whole you
see at the end may not mean anything at all. The novels turn out to be about the

experience of moving away from the immediate moment of impression toward a distanced view possessing greater understanding of it—though never any final, total revelation. As in James, the novels are acts of selection, "selected under some sense for something"—and as in James, the act of selection is more important than the "something" they are selected for.

Neither an exalted perception of spatial form by which all the pieces of plot lie next to one another to be pieced together by a reader marveling at the concealed wisdom of the author, nor the simple evocation of a phenomenonology of confusion, does justice to the experience we have reading these novels. In reading Conrad, aesthetic experience has propositional force, force often at odds with the apparent implications of the story and the statements of narrator and characters alike. Where James usually aligns the rhetorical experience of his sentences and images with the meanings they convey, Conrad often sets these on a collision course. By playing sequential aesthetic form against nonlinear content—stories out of order, statements that contradict rather than build upon one another—Conrad tests the idea of a fragmentary, senseless reality—and finds it wanting.

Conrad's presentation of time is hardly understudied; the "most discussed aspect of Conrad's narrative technique is achronology" (Peters 108). Yet the discussion habitually leans toward the teleologies of fragmentation and skepticism, as well as toward explanations that focus on "subjectivity" in some form. Ian Watt's important study *Conrad in the Nineteenth Century*, for instance, focuses on the way the "break with linear temporal progression in the order of the narrative ultimately reflects Conrad's sense of the fragmentary and elusive quality of individual experience" (357). This is a salient feature of Conrad's early work, but starting with *Lord Jim* and moving into the twentieth century, Conrad's methods would shift decisively *away* from a focus on representation of experience. For instance, the "delayed decoding" Watt illuminates in *Heart of Darkness* does represent the mind-in-process—or, more precisely, the retrospecting narrator seeking to represent the atoms of his own mind in process.[6] The classic example of Marlow describing himself being pelted with "sticks" and only afterward realizing that they are arrows is not at all far from the momentary impressions that flicker across the minds of Woolf's and Joyce's characters in their most characteristic stream-of-consciousness moments; but it is a mistake to treat this feature—which becomes much less prevalent in *Lord Jim* and virtually disappears in the later novels—as a microcosm of Conrad's use of retrospection in general, which more and more often refuses to give past moments the stylistic impact visible in the "sticks" in *Heart of Darkness*.

The focus on the representation of subjectivity as the source of achronology in Conrad's work leads to misreadings of these later works, where it is no longer true that "achronological narration locates the narrative at a single point of view and represents the way an individual encounters phenomena" (Peters 109). Such readings take Ford Madox Ford too much at his word and miss what is going on in Conrad—and they also take Marlow as the defining device of Conrad's fictive practice. The restructurings of time in *Nostromo* and *Secret Agent*, far from being evocative of the experience of an observer, seem to frustrate the possibility of any observer's sharing the perspective of the reader; they deliberately move us away from what it is like to live through an event. The tremendous pressure Conrad puts on the reader's faculties of understanding has an estranging effect: when the novel presents time as full of holes, we become aware that we are not experiencing time as we usually do. We do not, in reading Conrad, recognize the confusing state of mankind's limited existence in personal time as opposed to clock time; instead, he makes confusion strange to us, forces us to react against it. The time kept at the Greenwich observatory within *The Secret Agent* looks very much like our ordinary experience, compared with the temporal structures the novel follows.

Conrad in some respects might seem to be much less amenable to my argument than James or Faulkner: my claim of artists hewing to a more conservative optimism about character and epistemology seems ill at ease with his reputation as among the most skeptical and pessimistic of the modernists, remorselessly annihilating old sources of consolation without offering the alternatives that later authors like Joyce and Woolf do. We like to see Conrad, in his late-Victorian pessimism and his vivid consciousness of a mechanistic universe in which people are helpless pawns of society and nature alike, as contemporary with all our anxieties, as seeing exactly with us: perhaps he seems even more pessimistic. For instance, Wollaeger writes:

> In its hesitancies, ellipses, and repetitions, the style of Marlow's narration marks a fall away from the impossible omniscience of a sovereign power—impossible because to Conrad too (not just from our historical retrospect) the idea of a reliably omniscient narrator must have seemed a doomed effort to banish a multitude of unreliable ones. (*Joseph Conrad* 20–21)

That parenthesis gives the subtext: *our* historical retrospect. When we turn to Ngũgĩ's writing later in this chapter, it becomes evident that a different vantage point shows different uses in Conrad. The "impossible omniscience of a sovereign power" neatly blurs the boundaries between the author and God, as though the only two alternatives were either a confident assertion of omniscience that relies on a theistic universe or the constant undermining of such a view, a third-person omniscient narrator ("reliably omniscient") or a chaotic clash of many voices notable only for their limitations.

Conrad's forms produce a different set of effects. The inhuman omniscience of the narrator of *Nostromo*, for instance, is not consistently authoritative; his voice slowly converges with the events of the novel, shifting from ironic distance to sympathetic affiliation. The hesitancies, ellipses, and repetitions—and the assertions, expansions, and parallelisms—of Marlow's style in *Lord Jim* are not irresolvable ambiguities but training in their resolution. In other words, Conrad may know that all narrators are unreliable, but the point of the style and narrative form he develops—in both embedded narrators like Marlow and the faux-omniscient figures who speak in *Nostromo* and *The Secret Agent*—is to develop a way of approaching as close as possible to something like a comprehensive vision. As in my treatment of James, one line of argument throughout this chapter will be the way techniques that seem to invite the possibility of insoluble ambiguity become modes of defending choices and discriminations among alternatives. Conrad's, and Marlow's, statements of the unknowable, like the juxtaposition of events from different parts of time, are ways of defending the attempts of readers and characters to reach an understanding—an understanding not, perhaps, fully reliable, but maintaining reliability as a goal. The possibility of communication is a valuable, even inevitable investment—but can only be made responsibly if it is always shadowed by acknowledgment of its difficulties. John Guillory makes a similar point about mediated communication in general: "The assertion of the possible rejects its alternative, the actual, in recognition of the inherent difficulty of communication" (357). Conrad may never represent a "true" understanding effectively communicated, but he insists on the importance of continually seeking its possibility.

When his literary forms are always read with an eye toward the representation of a rupture from the past, any moment of clarity or generality becomes either a readerly delusion (Conrad doesn't really mean a single thing Marlow says)[7] or an unfortunate and uninteresting side note (Conrad had certain romantic sentimental predilections that sometimes interfered with his skepticism).[8] But he demands a more subtle attention to the multiple possible significances of the connection between literary form and historical change.

High modernist readers of Conrad in some respects echo the major binary in Conrad's thought. On the one hand, Conrad stands for proto-existentialist refusal of illusions; on the other, he stands for the simple worldview of adventure literature.

These views part ways in the famous contrast between Eliot and Pound: Eliot sees a Conrad worthy of excerpting in epigraphs for bleak evocations of mortality and horror; Pound doubted that Conrad was "weighty enough" for Eliot's citation (Eliot, *Waste Land* 125). The latter view is, in a more sophisticated form, also that of Virginia Woolf, who loves Conrad precisely for his old-fashioned certainties: "He must be lost indeed to the meaning of words who does not hear in that rather stiff and somber music . . . how it is better to be good than bad, how loyalty is good and honesty and courage" (*Essays* IV.228). On the one side Conrad is a partisan of the romance of men bound together against the sea, distrustful of the powers of a skeptical intellect and tempted by the idea that great things may be accomplished by heroic action; on the other he is a revolutionary skeptic, dissolving conventions of morality, idealism, communication—and narrative.[9]

In showing art as a way of getting beyond a tyrannically chaotic reality without succumbing to misty complacency, he defends the refusal to submit to skepticism, and the responsible effort at imposing order—and keeping on with the imposition, after every attempt (inevitably) fails. I've referred to the fragmentation of time in Conrad's novels, in part because confusion is a genuine part of the reader's experience of the fiction: but it is more accurate to say that Conrad *orders* reality by rejecting the disorder created by temporal sequence. He is not breaking apart a life artificially ordered, but fitting together the pieces of an experience that—by the happenstance of chronology—appears absurd, nonsensical, chaotic.[10] Achronology and the complicated narratorial constructs that generate it are ways of forestalling too-obvious and disillusioning readings of events.

Politically inflected readings of Conrad tend either to critique his moral longing or to see him as questioning moral ideals and undermining the too-confident assumptions of a knowable world associated with realist fiction.[11] Jed Esty has recently modulated this formulation, suggesting that modernist experimental novels "break up and reorganize—without seeking fully to banish or destroy—linear, historicist time as the organizing principle of form, biography, and history itself" (*Unseasonable* 213). But what happens if we reverse the emphasis? Conrad, we might see, begins with chronology and knowledge already broken and uncertain, and his novels use alternative chronologies to lead to new forms of knowing. Recent criticism tends reflexively to privilege disruption and critique; we find that the most interesting thing for Conrad to be doing is to upset worldviews, or to show them as irreconcilably opposed and subjective. If Conrad were to be asserting a general way of viewing the world, so the thinking goes, then he would be doing violence to the complexities of reality, particularly the experiences of colonized peoples. Edward Said has said, "Any comprehensive vision is fundamentally conservative"

(*Orientalism* 239). If "comprehensive vision" means something like complacently settling on a worldview and refusing to change it, this is probably true; but seeking out a vision that you then leave open to revision and change is perhaps a preliminary necessity for most forms of political commitment and activism.

"Undiminished Light": Conrad's Temporal Structures

The meanings I attribute to our experience of Conrad's temporal restructurings are clearer in contrast to other experiments of modernist fiction. Ford, for instance, uses structures that have real similarities to Conrad's; but John Dowell's role as narrator in *The Good Soldier* is very far from Marlow's or that of the English teacher in *Under Western Eyes*. By showing Marlow's impression of Jim's appeal slowly and painfully meet with facts that seem alternately to undermine and to validate it, even as he constantly acknowledges the inexplicable nature of his interest in Jim and its attendant convictions, Conrad defends the process and effort of making sense both of events and of intangible impressions. By showing Dowell's impressions utterly collapse in the face of the facts, Ford remorselessly undercuts the human mind trying to understand events.

"It suddenly occurs to me that I have forgotten to say how Edward met his death": Dowell begins the final scene of the novel with this shocking offhand announcement of the death of the title character (276). There are many similar flourishes throughout, indicating Dowell's inability to put together the events of the novel. Ford associates Dowell's dislocation in time with claims of mimesis and fidelity to the way the mind remembers things. But Conrad's ideas about the mind's use of memory are much more optimistic than Ford's. Dowell's disorderly associations, ostentatiously at odds with what the reader thinks would be important or memorable, stand in sharp contrast with Marlow's self-conscious argument for the importance of what he chooses to privilege.[12]

Even Conrad's omniscient narrators partake of this ordering sensibility: the narrator of *The Secret Agent* does not seem to evoke the patterns of any characters' minds. The stranger the narrative choices seem to be, the less realist and the more artificial they become. Their very alien quality foregrounds the work done by the artist. Conrad's narrator estranges the artist from readers and characters alike: by contrast, Ford's mimesis of a mind searching for answers, either in the miniature version of the greenhouse or in the elaborate convolutions of *The Good Soldier*, creates the appearance of alignment between the artist's arranging work and that of the characters' minds. Whereas the defining opposition in Ford is between the truth of experience, what it feels like to be an individual human being, and a stigmatized "objective" truth that is not faithful to how the mind works, Conrad refuses to adjudicate whether subjectivity or objectivity constitutes a better realism. For him, a strict report of reality, experiential or external, is not faithful to the truth.

The inexplicability of the narrators here is not a way of evoking confusion and disorder but of manipulating the reader into generating order and convincing him or her of the presence of an order soon to be disclosed; as in the analysis of Faulkner's syntax in chapter 1, a comprehensive vision comes not as a received whole from the past but lurks around the corner in the future. The most distinct jump in time and space in *The Secret Agent*, for instance, occurs between the third and fourth chapters, when the scene shifts from a despairing Verloc going to bed with his wife Winnie to a faux-medieval gathering, to the side of which sit Comrade Ossipon and the Professor. This is also a jump in time—the bomb has exploded, and Ossipon is trying to figure out who planned the attack. Over the course of the following scene, they come to the conclusion that the dead man in the park must have been Verloc; only slowly does the reader deduce otherwise. Conrad does not signal the leap in time in opening the fourth chapter: "Most of the thirty or so little tables covered by red clothes with a white design stood ranged at right angles to the deep brown wainscoting of the underground hall. . . . Varlets in green jerkins brandished hunting knives and raised on high tankards of foaming beer" (52). The passage introduces a completely unknown scene; the only familiar element is the knives, which echo Winnie Verloc's comment in the preceding scene, "I had to take the carving knife from the boy" (50).

The reader (anecdotally: most readers to whom I have taught this novel and questioned about their experience) encountering this transition will grasp, soon enough, that the bomb to which the preceding events seemed to tend has gone off, and is probably the "news" (53) Ossipon has heard; once we have the sense of a mystery to solve, our minds know what to do with the material as we encounter it. But this opening paragraph, purely descriptive of a scene that seems to have no relation to our story, is disorienting because we have nothing to grab onto—the narrator is both insistently explanatory (all the characters are tagged with multiple epithets; here, for instance, we have "the robust Ossipon" [52]) and silent about matters that it would seem natural for any storyteller to clarify. Ford seemed to elide the situation of artistic organization in having Dowell speak without the capacity to reorganize his retrospections; Conrad's narrator occupies a position of assumed knowledge, as though we've heard far more of the story than we actually have. Rather than the difficulties and confusions of Ford's narration, full of material Dowell hasn't fully acknowledged, the narration of *The Secret Agent* drops us into a universe where, it seems, parts of the story have already been told but not to us, a universe so carefully ordered that the organization becomes confusion.

Instead we grasp the small cues we can find: for instance, the knives reduplicate Stevie's implement in multiple. And this connection, we feel, must be absurd: there is no meaning in the juxtaposition between the knife at home and the knives here. The effect is to extend the life of that first reference to the knife: the failed connection draws attention to the implement. Thus, when it returns many pages later in the climax as a murder weapon, we can see Winnie's action as part of a universe with knives in every shadow, ready at hand. The varlets in green jerkins brandish to no purpose and no threat; but their parodic recreation of a violent feudal universe is actually a parody of modern reality. The grandiosity of their scene and action is fake, but what they point to is real. Marlow's "And this also . . . has been one of the dark places of the earth" from *Heart of Darkness* (45) is transfigured into an even more cutting claim: this London, *still*, is one of the dark places of the earth.

Something of Ford's idea of impressionist fiction lurks here: a random association, a coincidence like the "cheap Burgundy" that helps signify the passage of time in Mr. Slack's greenhouse. But there is no mind that could be the source of the random association, no characters present at both scenes, and not even a narratorial gesture—for example, *Knives were raised, too, above thirty small tables*—of the sort we might see in the narration of *Nostromo*. The sheerly inexplicable quality of this transition points to the fact that this is a *novel*, highlights its status as a constructed object. It makes a claim that narrative means more than the random associations of Mr. Slack's mind. And the temporary incomprehensibility of the nature of the construction does not, ultimately, make the reader suspect that all logical order is breaking down, but instead points toward perpetually hidden orders that we might slowly uncover.

Reading Conrad's achronology as rhetorical rather than representational is another way of shifting our understanding of literary forms from questions of production to questions of future use. Rather than asking us to contextualize textual production within the world of the novel—say, answering the question of whose perspective or what psychological state of mind produces a shift in time—*The Secret Agent*, like *Nostromo* before it, uses its chronological contortions to force readers to think in particular ways. *The Secret Agent*'s temporal dislocations are not a representation of the buffetings to which consciousness is subjected in modern experience, nor evocations of the chaotic subjectivity of the individual mind. They are an alternate means of postulating omniscience—of implying the artist's ordering hand without having to say anything that explicitly claims it. As in Flaubert's famous dictum, one feels the author everywhere, but never sees him.[13]

The novel bears the marks of obscure artistic choice in every sentence, from the epithets remorselessly dogging characters to rhetorical flourishes such as the cab-horse that becomes a "steed of apocalyptic misery" (128). And this sense of an obscure—possibly malicious and knife-ridden—ordering force behind everything drives the experience of the novel. The author stands aside, able both to mock the grandiosity of phrases like "apocalyptic misery" and to subtly assert it.[14] Conrad's letter on life as a meaningless knitting machine ends, "I'll admit however that to look at the remorseless process is sometimes amusing" (*Letters* I.425). This sounds a little like merely an ironic sting: all we can do is watch. But it does offer a signif-icant change to the image—it sets Conrad aside, someone able to look on, not in the process of being knitted in or out. This is the characteristic role of the artist in Conrad—free to observe only by his disillusionment about the efficacy of acting.

Yet the act of observation has power. In the final paragraph of the novel, the Professor—a bomb-making nihilist who walks about with his hand on a detonator he plans to set off should any policeman come to arrest him—suddenly ceases to be the apparently ridiculous figure he had been throughout the novel:

> And the incorruptible Professor walked too, averting his eyes from the odious multitude of mankind. He had no future. He disdained it. He was a force. His thoughts caressed the images of ruin and destruction. He walked frail, insignificant, shabby, miserable—and terrible in the simplicity of his idea calling madness and despair to the regeneration of the world. Nobody looked at him. He passed on unsuspected and deadly, like a pest in the street full of men. (231)

"Madness and despair" are a repurposing of a newspaper article's phrase about Winnie Verloc's suicide; here they become like a classical deity's attendant helpmeets.[15] They also seem to connect the anarchist Professor with Mr. Vladimir, who wishes to use public despair for his own political ends. The phrase "calling madness and despair to the regeneration of the world" also describes Conrad's art, which, perpet-ually evoking both madness and despair, nevertheless claims to be "rescue work." The inexplicability and confusion Conrad creates in the process of reading are never ultimately ratified, but are occasions for his readers to become aware of their own impulses to understand and order. And at this last moment of a novel so dense with ugliness, the terror Conrad evokes has a consoling function. In disdaining his own personal future, the Professor becomes terrifyingly indelible as a character.

Conrad's nonrealist narrator works toward such moments: Ford's valorization of the "general effect" life makes on the reader does not allow space for a Professor whose "idea" can appeal to the imagination while his self remains trivial inside and out. Throughout the novel, Conrad's rhetoric—the epithets, the grandiosity of the "steed of apocalyptic misery"—has worked to signal the artistic mind as a being outside of the world of the characters; in this last moment it has another quality central, ultimately, to the conclusions one takes from the work. It is beautiful—beautifully ordered, that is. Drawing together phrases repeated in prominent places all over the novel—*force*, *miserable*, and *madness and despair*—the passage substantiates the author's capacity to discern connections between disparate parts of his material, making parallels between the interests of newspaper copy and of the Professor, much the way the narrative as a whole juxtaposes the anarchists and the police.[16] That juxtaposition locks all parties into a pointless, absurd struggle, signaled by the Professor's grandiose gesture of carrying dynamite with him always to prevent arrest; at the same time, if the individual parties seemed absurd, the fact of their sameness remains unnerving.

Conrad's tendency to evoke grandiose darkness in order to deny the triviality of human action often takes this form: stylistic splendor in service of a pessimistic statement. I will return to it in more detail in analyzing *Nostromo*, but the important aspect here is the sense of a sudden breakthrough of real significance upon a landscape of suffering that up until this moment had seemed ruthlessly trivialized and absurd. The Professor ought to be absurd but isn't; and it is by purely aesthetic means—stylistic splendor, gestural connection to epic—that Conrad accomplishes this. Once more, artistic organization tells against a reality that seems empty of meaning.

In drawing attention to his work's status as ordered art, Conrad is not making a claim for aestheticism—rather, he is deploying the specifically aesthetic effects of literature to speak to thematic questions within the works, including political ones. *The Secret Agent*, when viewed not as an experience of subjective fragmentation but grimly rigorous order, becomes ever more merciless in its implications that police, spies, and terrorists are all playing the same game.[17] We'll see later in this chapter how the specific structures of rhetoric underpinning Conrad's syntax have similar effects.

Conrad's insistence on an aesthetic ordering principle anticipates the kinds of proto-New Critical aesthetics visible in something like Eliot's essay "*Ulysses*, Order and Myth," where he describes Joyce's myth-based structure as "simply a way of controlling, of ordering, of giving a shape and a significance to the immense panorama of futility and anarchy which is contemporary history" (*Selected Prose* 177). Notably, Eliot's own sentence throws far more emphasis on the "immense panorama of futility" than on "shape and significance." Conrad, I'm arguing, is up to something a little different: not merely finding an aesthetic form that can contain anarchy but using aesthetic form to question and undermine futility and anarchy as a paradigm.

Woolf's writing might be described using similar terms. But even she refuses Conrad's centering of the ordering hand of the artist. Woolf's rejection of the "alien and external" (*Essays* IV.160–161) is a "philosophy of anonymity" by which "the creative mind consciously absents itself from the work" (DiBattista 63). Conrad's artist, in the essay "Henry James: An Appreciation," is supposed to "interpret the ultimate experience of mankind in terms of his temperament, in terms of art" (*Notes on Life and Letters* 17), but interpretation is exactly the power that Woolf suggests individuals—and even, to some extent, the artist—should give up in order to do justice to the fluidity of the people and things around them. "She would not say of Peter, she would not say of herself, I am this, I am that," thinks Clarissa Dalloway. In *The Waves*, Woolf's style permits all the minds it occupies to interpret themselves, rather than putting any pressure of interpretation upon them. "This is poetry if we do not write it," says Neville (168), and though Woolf goes ahead and writes it, his sense of the potential violence writing could do to the world is her own. By contrast, for Conrad the poetry is *only* in the writing, never the world.

When Conrad died, Woolf wrote, "One opens his pages and feels as Helen must have felt when she looked in her glass and realized that, do what she would, she could never in any circumstances pass for a plain woman" (IV.227). Woolf has no desire to have her own style pass for plain. But for her, style is a joint construct between character and author: in *The Waves*, all the characters tend to have similar syntax but are marked by different imagery. For Woolf, this shared effort is an attempt to cut down the potential irresponsibility of artistic decisiveness: the author's power to pronounce authoritatively on events, like the arrangement of incidents in a creative time structure, is a potentially suspect external imposition upon reality. Woolf's discomfort with Conrad's style springs from her sense of its cold inhumanity; in her sense of its frozen stillness is a sense of its being alien to the quick of human experience. She criticized *Nostromo*, detecting "something inanimate and stationary in the human figures which chills our warmer sympathies" (II.228). For Woolf, like Conrad, style is the site of the author's appearance, the means of establishing a skillful creator. But she also has aspects of Ford's desire to limit the novel to characters' experiences. By contrast, Conrad uses style to force his readers—if not always the characters themselves—to confront the possibility of a comprehensive vision next to which individual perspective shrinks in scale.

Lord Jim: *Inevitable Divisions*

In *Lord Jim*, these questions of about whether a comprehensive vision is possible are central to the generic instability of the novel; as in James, romance clashes against realism. This novel has always seemed a divided work. Jameson, in *Political Unconscious*, introduces the novel by describing Conrad as "floating uncertainly somewhere in between Proust and Robert Louis Stevenson" (206). Critics have generally been more skeptical of the second half, the "romantic" Patusan section, while lauding the more polyphonic first half. The favored Conrad is the one who affirms nothing, whose sense of the heroic is only ironic. The various critical approaches to the divide see it as either a literary flaw or a temperamental one. The idea of a problematic division goes back to contemporary reviewers, but one of the early critical statements on the subject was by F. R. Leavis: "The romance that follows, though plausibly offered as a continued exhibition of Jim's case, has no inevitability as that" (190).[18]

Yet inevitability is exactly what the novel offers as justification for the romance. The novel presents its division as a motivation for the existence of the story. Marlow tells the story precisely because Jim's nadir and zenith are both known to him already; it is the improbable combination of the two that makes the story notable. The novel is best viewed not just as divided, but as a puzzle and provocation that takes the shape of division: a puzzle to Marlow that he passes on to his oral audience at first, and to which he adds additional pieces later. The real question of the novel is not whether it is realist or romantic, Proust or Stevenson, but just why exactly the oscillation between these two viewpoints should be so irresolvable—and therefore so aesthetically productive. Jim's story has, Marlow says, an "uncanny vitality": "an extraordinary power of defying the shortness of memories" (107). That is, it has that to which all art aspires: "the permanence of memory" (*Notes on Life and Letters* 16). The consolation of art is itself a kind of achronology—the ability of the material of life to span time beyond the shortness of human experience.

Marlow's narration occurs in approximately three large parts: his reconstruction of the *Patna* incident, which also incorporates into itself Jim's successive peripatetic employment troubles (chapters 5 through 18); his retelling of Stein's and Jim's early history in Patusan (19 through 35), which includes Jim's most triumphant successes; and the subsequent history conveyed to the "privileged man" who receives a written communication from Marlow (36 through 45), which describes Jim's downfall through the machinations of Gentleman Brown. The division between the first two parts is entirely content-based; the most romantic and most experimental parts of the story are formally continuous with one another, both part of Marlow's speech. Yet it is this division that has occupied critics for decades. Certainly with the arrival of Patusan there appears a new tone in the narrative ("Remember this is a love-story I am telling you now," says Marlow [224]). But the tripartite structure suggests something more complicated than a head-on collision between realist *Patna* and romantic Patusan. The extreme high point at which Marlow's oral narrative ends—Jim fantastically, unbelievably successful—is meant as a challenge, an unfinished story. The last section is the means of getting out from between the insoluble oppositions to something more complicated. The tension between the two ways of dividing the narrative—by content, between *Patna* and Patusan, or by form, between oral and written narration—complicates Conrad's general outlook on the issues raised by both forms of division. The division between Patna and Patusan is real; the Jim who gives a "Homeric peal of laughter" (201) seems genuinely at odds with the Jim of the first part.

Yet at the same time the pause at Jim's zenith is equally substantial; formally, it is much more clearly marked. The audience breaks up "as if the last image of that incomplete story, its incompleteness itself, and the very tone of the speaker, had made discussion vain and comment impossible" (254). Each man leaves with "his own impression," carried "like a secret" (254)—understanding is individual, incommunicable. That last image they receive, of Jim "at the heart of a vast enigma" (253)—Jim seeming heroic and triumphant, despite his failings—has given them all some final and individual summation. Inconclusiveness and ambiguity here *foreclose* conversation, rather than generating it.

The last section is ultimately a refusal of precisely this incommunicable, unspeakable solution. For all Marlow's rhetoric about Jim's being "under a cloud," for all his claims that telling will never do justice to an event, his final narrative writes over the blank space of mystery; he refuses to leave events unspeakable, refuses to let the enigma rest. "There is never time to say our last word—the last word of our love, of our desire, faith, remorse, submission, revolt" (171). He seems to deny the possibility of speech—and then goes on, a haphazard Samuel Beckett. The existence of the mind faced with an insoluble problem to which no last word will be fit inevitably generates endless attempts at the last word.

Lord Jim begins by demonstrating the limitations of a third-person omniscient narrator: early in the novel, before Marlow appears, the narrator tells of Jim's tendency to quit dockside jobs: "To his employers the reasons he gave were obviously inadequate. They said 'Confounded fool!' as soon as his back was turned. This was their criticism on his exquisite sensibility" (10). The narrator seems to be mustering ironies against the employers—*to them* this was obvious; perhaps an explanation of Jim's reasons will follow. Instead the irony cuts against Jim, with that mocking phrase "exquisite sensibility"—unlikely to be the thoughts of the employers, with their colloquial register. This third-person omniscient narrator, Conrad is showing, *can't* speak with sincerity. Corrosive irony creeps in.

In fact, the figure who possesses "earnestness" in *Lord Jim* is neither human nor textual: specifically, the alternative to human authorship of events is that *nature* is responsible for them. Nature is a kind of wicked author whose influence the human author must contest:

> Only once in all that time he had again the glimpse of the earnestness in the anger of the sea. That truth is not so often made apparent as people might think. There are many shades in the danger of adventures and gales, and it is only now and then that there appears on the face of facts a sinister violence of intention—that indefinable something which forces it upon the mind and the heart of a man, that this complication of accidents or these elemental furies are coming at him with a purpose of malice, with a strength beyond control, with an unbridled cruelty that means to tear out of him his hope and his fear, the pain of his fatigue and his longing for rest: which means to smash, to destroy, to annihilate all he had seen, known, loved, enjoyed or hated; all that is priceless and necessary—the sunshine, the memories, the future—which means to sweep the whole precious world utterly away from his sight by the simple and appalling act of taking his life. (14)

This is one of the passages that Jameson reads as an example of a "containment" strategy whereby a surface theme hides the workings of history: the passage is "coded for us in existential terms, the sea, the source of this mindless violence, becoming the great adversary of Man" (*Political Unconscious* 216). There is something rote about this straw man opponent: after all, the whole point of Conrad's passage is precisely to convey the way in which nature does *not* seem mindless: rather than seeming like existential absurdity, this presentation is of "intention" and "purpose"—of a terrifying coherence and logic in nature's violence. And this is precisely what the narration will go on to show happening to Jim—as with the famously unlucky protagonists of Hardy's fiction, his most disastrous choice comes about when a sequence of improbable events seem to conspire against him.

The long sentence offers a miniature story, an abstraction of all the elements of novels' plots: hope, fear, loss, memory. Throughout the lengthy clauses, Conrad carefully refrains from making the human figure the target of violence. The sea can "tear out of him" emotions; it can smash the things in the world he has experienced—but only in the final word is it clear that the means of destroying the world is destroying the self. The consequence is that death looks even more unbearable than we expect it to: rather than the grandiose image of a Job-like figure whose life has been ruined by "elemental furies," we realize instead that nothing so individual and narratively complicated is available: "simple and appalling" death is the only option. This isn't a story of existential suffering; this is actually a story of near-instantaneous death.[19]

Jameson says of the "existential" reading that "this ostensible . . . 'theme' of the novel is no more to be taken at face value than is the dreamer's immediate waking sense of what the dream was about . . . such a theme must mean *something else*" (217); this is one of his explicit calls for symptomatic reading. But in all its miniature dramas of reversed expectations, we might look at this sentence less for what the themes *mean* and more for what their slow unveiling *does*. Jameson tells us to look for what isn't in the text. But there are also things the text *asks* its readers to think against its own apparent meaning, as well as things it is hiding from readers.

For instance, the reversal, nasty though it is, also contests nature's authorship of events. Without our quite being aware of it, Conrad has temporarily rewritten what nature does, made an act of senseless obliteration into a complex story of suffering and loss. The reversal at the end undermines this, but it also foregrounds what the author of the *sentence* has done, makes the complexity of his manipulation clear. It has seduced us with the story we think we're getting: the protagonist first loses hope, then suffers suicidal despair, then begins losing the external elements of life, and so on. This paragraph sets up the reader to look for a story that doesn't fit the facts, that provides some meaning beyond the obliteration with which it ends. It makes the "simple and appalling act" a disappointment, an insufficient story.

This is, of course, precisely what Marlow, and the novel as a whole, will do with Jim, insisting that there is more than the "facts" that are "visible" to the men of the inquiry (29). Indeed, the narrator says, those facts suggest a "whole" that has "a directing spirit of perdition that dwelt within, like a malevolent soul in a detestable body" (30). This "directing spirit" and "malevolent soul" has a lot in common with the "violence of intention" and "purpose of malice"—something intangible, something in contrast to immediate and precise realities. *Lord Jim* is a novel that again and again trains us to look away from what is solid, to seek out what is difficult to grasp.

This kind of turn is not merely a repeated gesture in *Lord Jim*. In the opening of *Heart of Darkness* Marlow is described as seeking meaning "not inside like a kernel, but outside, enveloping the tale which brought it out only as a glow brings out a haze" (45). This looks like one more way in which Conrad undermines the idea of easily conveyable morals. But it also represents his reaction in the direction of romance and toward ideals about belief that could transcend a harshly skeptical view of reality. In *Victory*, the narrator comments about Axel Heyst, "It is not the clear-sighted who lead the world. Great achievements are accomplished in a blessed, warm, mental fog, which the pitiless cold blasts of the father's analysis had blown away from the son" (87). Like the kernel, clear, solid vision is contrasted with something more hazy—and rejecting the solidity and precision of facts allows not only meaning but decisive action. Conrad's contestation of nature's authorship, in other words, is also a way of training the reader to perceive beyond what seems immediate and inescapable, to see local facts as significant for a hazy envelope that surrounds them. And as a literary experience, this is often not an erasure of local politics, but a gesture toward a larger political reality.

That, for instance, is how Ngũgĩ uses a similar gesture. In his *Petals of Blood*, one protagonist, Wanja, is visited by two old friends after a long absence; she has opened a brothel in order to keep her land in their rapidly industrializing town. As they depart, she stays still:

> She remained sitting in one place, truly queen of them all under the electric light; her head was bowed slightly and it was as if, under the bluish light of her creation, the wealth she had so accumulated weighed on her heavily, as if the jewelled, rubied cord around her neck was now pulling her and her very shadow to the ground, so that she would not rise to say goodbye, or to shut the door. (349)

This is a thrilling sentence: Wanja is utterly lost to the other characters and at the same time, in the scale of her fall, is more impressive than either of them. Viewed spatially, the image in this sentence might look redundant: "remained," "sitting," and "in one place" are overlapping phrases; the wealth weighs on her, and also her necklace seems to pull her to the ground; she is in light both electric and bluish; the cord is both jeweled and rubied.

Yet there is no experience of redundancy. The repetitions follow a pattern: they move from a relatively simple, literal phrase to a more figurative and suggestive one: "electric light" becomes "bluish light of her creation"; "her head was bowed" first becomes the simple simile of "wealth . . . weighed" before the more specific image "the . . . cord . . . was now pulling"; generic "jewelled" becomes "rubied," suggestive of the blood in the title of the novel. The repetitions reveal what is hinted at by the repeated *as ifs*: that the scene, which is simple (Wanja sits with her head bowed while they leave), contains layers, suggestions, and symbols requiring elaboration, that literal physical description is again and again insufficient. The unexpected temporal extension of clauses forces the reader to confront a large-scale way of viewing the world.

This swerve away from the literal toward the general, the weightily symbolic—the sudden opening up of new significances within apparently familiar figures—is similar to Conrad's refusal to let facts seem to speak for themselves; the "directing spirit" behind them needs to be discerned. Like the unnamed figure whose suffering is created by Conrad's syntax where the events itself don't quite testify to it, Wanja's impressiveness is not just in the grandeur of her individual fall but also the way her very posture suggests the warping of her life by market forces. And a reader's experience of that moment is not just of what the words and objects represent, but also the feel of the connection snapping into place. This is not a direct allusion, unlike the examples in Ngũgĩ's work I'll discuss later, but Conrad's shift toward the abstract tones of human mortality resonates in Ngũgĩ's pointed reminders of the workings of global capitalism. The mental moves these novels ask of their readers can point to a Marxist vision as easily as to a liberal individualist one. The similarity is not in the content, nor in what the style represents, but in the experiences the sentences create for their readers. The struggle to see a clarifying vision beyond immediate facts is, structurally, not that distant from the totalities of Marxism.

In this sense, *Lord Jim's* mysterious figures of ordering intentionality—from sinister nature to Marlow to the narrator's contestation of nature's authorship—are not desperate evasions of political truths; they are models of precisely the kind of thinking that enables people to access larger, sometimes conceptually challenging frameworks for understanding. This is not something Conrad's form hides; it is something Conrad's form helps make possible. And throughout Conrad's work, these same gestures—turns away from the semantic, valorizations of the intangible—become the fragile sources of understanding and commitment.

Nostromo: *"An Obscure Instinct of Consolation"*

Nostromo is dominated by various forms of search for understanding: the reader's desire to figure out the plot; some characters' attempts to figure out the power structures dominating their lives; and other characters' desire for moral ideals that might actually change society. The novel begins, like *Lord Jim*, in confusion and uncertainty: Conrad foregrounds the omniscient narrator whose inescapable ironizing had been so problematic in *Lord Jim*. Each of the novel's three sections mixes wildly contorted chronology with periods of sequential plot development. The first section is by far the most convoluted, presenting the reader with the history of a fictional country (Costaguana) through multiple revolutions and regimes, told as though the reader is already familiar with the broad outline of events. The second part gradually begins to coalesce around the central few days of the novel, ending with the night voyage into that dark Placid Gulf, as a political revolution occurs on land. The final section continues the events of those days before jumping ahead in time with the action not yet resolved, and slowly fills in the intervening days while a final romance plot takes shape. As in *Lord Jim*, the manipulation of chronology in *Nostromo* foregrounds the shaping hand of an artist who stands outside the subject of the work—the artist qua artist, who has the capacity to see things that the characters cannot. In *Nostromo*, at the beginning, characters have knowledge the reader lacks and desires; and the reverse is true as well: characters and readers alike are struggling to discern events as they unfold—just not asking the same questions.

The primary stylistic difference between the narrative technique of *Nostromo* and *The Secret Agent*—aside from the greatly expanded scale of the former—is that *Nostromo* adds apparently irrelevant explanations for its temporal transitions. Unlike the absence of comment that foregrounds the gaps in time in *The Secret Agent*, here there is always some gesture of connection. The transitional commentary tends to be more diffidently phrased than many of the narrator's comments, as though less significant, less certain. The first drastic contextual shift occurs between chapters 2 and 3, where we shift from a complex overview of the flight of the President-Dictator Ribiera through Sulaco (the town where most of the action takes place), to a specific scene elsewhere at the time. The transition involves two distinct varieties of narrative juxtaposition: between events at different moments in time and between events that occur at the same time in different places. The last paragraph of chapter 2 reads,

> Such leadership was inspiriting, and in truth all the harm the mob managed to achieve was to set fire to one—only one—stack of railway-sleepers, which, being creosoted, burned well. The main attack on the railway yards, on the O.S.N. offices, and especially on the Custom House, whose strong-room, it was well known, contained a large treasure in silver ingots, failed completely. Even the little hotel kept by old Giorgio, standing alone half-way between the harbour and the town, escaped looting and destruction, not by a miracle, but because with the safes in view they had neglected it at first, and afterwards found no leisure to stop. Nostromo, with his cargadores, was pressing them too hard then. (15)

This passage is characteristic of the confusions the reader faces when reading the opening sections of this novel. We get details—just one stack of railway-sleepers set on fire, and why it burned well. But there is no context for the details we have;

no sense of why, for instance, we might be interested in whether or not the desultory attack included one instance of success (the fire). The intricacies of the attack and its chronology are assumed—we casually move from Ribiera, to the Custom House, to the mob going first one way past Giorgio's hotel and then back the other, as though we ought to be familiar with the local geography. This is our first reference to silver in the novel, though the title of the opening volume, "The Silver of the Mine," prepares us for its importance. In this context, however, it's jarring: a page earlier, the attack on the Custom House was described as haphazard: "The repulsed mob devoted its energies to an attack on the Custom House, a dreary, unfinished-looking structure with many windows two hundred yards away from the O.S.N. offices, and the only other building near the harbour" (14). This is a page before the end of the chapter, and the clear implication is that the mob attacks the Custom House because it is deprived of its main object (the President-Dictator) and, as mobs do, goes after the nearest structure: Cinna the Poet to Ribiera as Cinna the Conspirator. Instead, we discover offhandedly a page later, the attack has a motivation: the "well-known" treasure. Meanwhile the overview of consequences also compresses into itself a recapitulation of the whole attack, in relating the fate of the hotel: we have not heard of it before, either, though typically in this novel it is introduced as though we ought to be familiar with: "*the* little hotel," is kept by a character familiarly called "old Giorgio," as though we might know him.

This passage sets up many characteristics of the opening pages: misled expectations; important details mentioned for the first time without comment; and casual refusal to be linear in narration. There is also a constant air of explanation ("In truth") that is belied by the failure to explain any of the things that are actually confusing: the character of the mob, the political background and stakes of the conflict. These are all the materials that are most difficult and fraught to pronounce on decisively, that would require the narrator to take a political stand and make a perhaps irresponsible generalization.[20] All the context we slowly discover—that Ribiera is a philosophical ruler aspiring to justice, but supported primarily by the wealthy—would potentially do violence to the complexity of any situation being described, so the narrator forces the reader to see how such working generalizations are necessary parts of comprehending life and history. In leaving out such information, instead of foregrounding the difficulty the omission causes, the narrator proceeds as though we already know this, already have the general context of the history of Costaguana, if not, perhaps, Sulaco in particular. Over the course of the rest of the introductory time changes, Conrad keeps introducing new details of the history of the country (e.g., in chapter 6, "the time of Guzman Bento" appears, and is explained a few pages later [45]), and explaining them only when more confusions have arisen that will need further explanation. Brian Richardson writes about Conrad that critics should not "presuppose an exclusively mimetic conception of the narrator. . . . To get at the root of Conrad's achievement in narrative technique, we must ask, 'What is the narration doing now?' rather than 'Who is speaking here?'" (216). And the narration of *Nostromo* confronts its readers with broad political implications for which we have not only no evidence, but also no explicit statement.

Chapter 3 opens, "It might have been said that there he was only protecting his own" (16), referring to the hotel that Nostromo's efforts protected on the preceding page. At this point, the narrative at last drops into a specific scene, rather than a broad overview of events. We also get the first glimpse of a narrative hint of significance, in that "there," setting up a contrast between "his own" at the hotel and the fight over the Customs House. This distinction, between acting for others who are not "your own" and acting on behalf of people with whom you have a personal connection, will become crucial to the action and themes of the novel. In context, it also echoes Captain Mitchell's comment describing Giorgio's family as "his own countrymen" (13) to Nostromo; and the distinction between obligation to country and obligation to personal representatives of it becomes crucial with regard to Decoud, who enters ridiculing "his own country" (152), but before long is risking his life over his love for one particular resident of Sulaco. Like those apparently insignificant knives early in *The Secret Agent*, we are being given a glimpse, though we don't know it, of something soon to be crucial in the novel, and the ambiguities attendant upon it. The juxtapositions of chronology, the text signals ("*there* he was only protecting his own"), are meaningful—but we have no way, as yet, of seeing how. The overall impression is of an order inaccessible to the reader—a history the characters know but do not realize they need to disclose, a conversation you are assumed to be part of but do not understand. The sense of order giving rise to confusion, of background knowledge assumed but unspoken, sets up the reader's relation to knowledge as one of denied access: we know there's something that will make sense of this; but we can't see it—yet.

The Eye of God: Nostromo's *Narrator*

The omniscient narrator is one of the more maligned characters in fiction. Identified with a monologic author-god and swept aside with contempt by the modernist revolution, an unidentifiable speaker pronouncing judgments and producing *sententiae* can seem inseparable from the mistakes of an imperialist, complacent Victorian age.[21] In *Lord Jim* Marlow develops ways of making sincere statements unavailable to the narrator; in the more rhetorically visible narrator of *Nostromo*, Conrad works out a way of making the omniscient narrator sincere. The narrator of *Nostromo* is very much not Flaubert's author—everywhere felt and seen, he is no less mysterious for his presence.

Conrad's narrator in *Nostromo* evolves from an ironic voice to a dramatic pronouncer of precisely the sincerities he mocks in the opening. Specifically, his character changes with the death of the skeptical and ironic Decoud shortly before the conclusion of the novel. Immediately after the narration of Decoud's suicide, the narrator announces a self-conscious second beginning in the middle of the final section of the novel:

> Sulaco outstripped Nostromo's prudence, growing rich swiftly on the hidden treasures of the earth, hovered over by the anxious spirits of good and evil, torn out by the labouring hands of the people. It was like a second youth, like a new life, full of promise, of unrest, of toil, scattering lavishly its wealth to the four corners of an excited world. (504)

This is a deliberate echo of the opening of the novel as a whole, which in similarly authoritative tones took a different outlook:

> In the time of Spanish rule, and for many years afterwards, the town of Sulaco—the luxuriant beauty of the orange gardens bears witness to its antiquity—had never been commercially anything more important than a coasting port with a fairly large local trade in ox-hides and indigo. (3)

The later version frames the novel as the story of how the town went from an old, sleepy era to a new and commercially lively one. The period of this narrative also entails a change in the way time works in the town: from "many years" of unchanging stasis to "swiftly" growing wealth and worldwide fame. Yet the apparently natural progression—it's not surprising that commercial growth is exponential—is rendered unnatural by the metaphor. Sulaco's period of speed is a temporal inversion, a "second youth"—and not, notably, a "second youth" in the sense of senility. The second youth is a *narrative* youth: the skeptical narrator, carefully hedging his bets ("it was well known," "it might have been said") has now taken on an old storyteller's cadence, in part through the buildup of phrases over the course of the novel that now have a ritual familiarity: "the hidden treasures of the earth," "the labouring hands of the people." We have met these words before; they usually had skepticism attached to them, and now they are free. That is, the words no longer sound like an ironic evocation of a voice that would use "labouring hands of the people" with no consciousness of the suffering and deaths of the owners of those hands. The narration now sounds like a voice unironically incorporating that awareness as a given part of the phrase. Narrating the story of the novel and its tragedies has earned the narrator the right to sincere knowledge and generalization.

The clearest and most telling contrast comes in regard to those "spirits" haunting the treasure. There were spirits in the narrator's opening too, in his relating the lore of remote and rocky Azuera:

> The poor, associating by an obscure instinct of consolation the ideas of evil and wealth, will tell you it is deadly because of its forbidden treasures. . . . the two gringos, spectral and alive, are believed to be dwelling to this day amongst the rocks, under the fatal spell of their success. . . . They are now rich and hungry and thirsty—a strange theory of tenacious gringo ghosts suffering in their starved and parched flesh of defiant heretics, where a Christian would have renounced and been released. (4–5)

The narrator distances himself from the legend. It is a product of superstition—and a particularly historically situated superstition, at the crossroads of poverty and piety. He condescends to it and to those who believe in it: it is merely consolatory illusion, a pathological "obscure instinct" rather than anything more resonantly telling. The spirits hovering around treasure are individuals: folklore and local myth. By the time of the later reference, they have become generalized: "the anxious spirits of good and evil" of Sulaco's "second youth" echoes, a few pages earlier, the way "the spirits of good and evil that hover about a forbidden treasure understood well that the silver of San Tomé was provided now with a faithful and lifelong slave" (501). This—a pronouncement of Nostromo's fate, in thrall to the treasure he has hidden—has none of the skeptical irony attached to the legend of the gringos. By being general and even metaphorical the spirits become *serious*—and the narrator, whose voice seemed to generate without will a skeptical negation, ratifies rather than undermines the idea.

The skeptical narrator, always haunted by irony, dies, in other words, with Decoud. Decoud's suicide, the death of the ironist left alone with his own thoughts, plays out to its furthest limits the refusal to take abstract ideals seriously—and provides a warning that permits the narrator to start doing so. Decoud had originated the plan of separation (by which Sulaco would secede from Costaguana) out of self-interested love for Sulacan Antonia, but presented it as an idea dictated by geography and culture; after his death independence has taken hold on the terms in which he did not even believe. As with the spirits of good and evil, by moving away from a specific past myth the narrator finds a present haunted by a fictively generalized version of the past—the real effects of which, through the telling of the story, have become clear.

This does not imply that all ideals are particularly desirable. The great idealist in the novel is Charles Gould, whose faith in his silver mine and in "material interests" (e.g., 84 *et passim*) as a civilizing force drives the plot of the novel. But the problem is not, in the end, ideals. *Nostromo*, as dramatically as any of Conrad's novels, comes to a singular and decisive moral conclusion in the voice of Dr. Monygham:

> There is no peace and no rest in the development of material interests. They have their law, and their justice. But it is founded on expediency, and is inhuman; it is without rectitude, without the continuity and the force that can be found only in a moral principle. Mrs. Gould, the time approaches when all that the Gould Concession stands for shall weigh as heavily upon the people as the barbarism, cruelty, and misrule of a few years back. (511)

It's possible to describe Conrad's novels as contests of different types and forms of ideals. In this passage, the "material interests" stand both for the ideology of global capitalism as a civilizing force and for imperial missionary zeal in the form of the Protestant investor Holroyd. Passages like these point to why *Nostromo* has become so influential and lasting a critique of neocolonial economic power structures. But it's worth pausing over the alternatives listed here: "rectitude," a "moral principle." These are the terms that in *Lord Jim* and throughout Conrad seem to be under assault. They don't stand here for precisely the same thing— the "moral principle" here certainly isn't the code of seamanship next to which Jim fails; the phrases sound conservative, but in fact they're virtually empty of meaning—not because they have *lost* meaning but because they have yet to gain it. Neither Monygham nor his listener, Emily Gould, knows how to solve the tangle of complicity, history, and power that define neocolonial economies. (Nor, for that matter, does Conrad.) But those vague phrases are a call for precisely that. They are a demand of the future—of the reader, declaring the necessity of a moral principle that can found a new form of action.

Eloquence against Itself

Most of Conrad's generalizations, on their surface, seem primarily negative and skeptical; moments like the one above that explicitly call for a new commitment with no detectable irony are rare. But the alluring decisiveness of his phrases—"the immense indifference of things," "we live, as we dream, alone"—can obscure the way his style throws these into question. Conrad's sentences are elegantly balanced, rippling with luxuriant polysyllables, and there is often a disjunction between the ostentatious gorgeousness of a sentence and its ugly, implacable semantic content:

> A victim of the disillusioned weariness which is the retribution meted out to intellectual audacity, the brilliant Don Martin Decoud, weighted by the bars of San Tomé silver, disappeared without a trace, swallowed up in the immense indifference of things. (*Nostromo* 501)

The sentence makes several claims, apparently on behalf of the narrator and not just within Decoud's mind: intellectual audacity leads to disillusioned weariness; things are immense and immensely indifferent. But this is an entirely unindifferent sentence: energetic, without a trace of weariness. In itself, it is carefully balanced— long modifier clauses at the beginning, middle, and end, alternating neatly with subject ("the brilliant Don Martin Decoud") and verb ("disappeared without a trace"). Beyond its syntax, it functions to highlight the large-scale organization of the plot—the silver that "weighted" Decoud down is also a weight on Nostromo and eventually will weigh upon Sulaco as a whole. Such intricate devices generate a propositional force that contradicts the claims the sentence seems to make. By foregrounding the care of the construction of a sentence—and of a novel as a whole—Conrad uses the self-consciousness of his own artistry to present the opposite of an indifferent world.

Critics often present rhetoric as stigmatized in Conrad's work, precisely because it has a startlingly visceral effect on readers' thinking. At its most extreme form, the suspicion of rhetoric in Conrad views Conrad himself as culpable (rather than as an ally in unmasking the evils of rhetoric); this was a key part of Chinua Achebe's famous critique of racism in *Heart of Darkness*, which accuses Conrad of "inducing hypnotic stupor in his readers through a bombardment of emotive words and other forms of trickery" (3). This Platonist critique of rhetoric is easy to critique—Achebe's charged essay itself might be said to indulge in the "trickery" of "emotive words"—but nonetheless does capture just how intense the sensation of encountering Conrad's rhetoric can be, precisely because it is inextricable from what appear to be his important abstract statements.[22] But rather than induce stupor, the rhetorical splendor is unsettling: it flaunts the gap between its meaning and its rhetorical tone. The work of the artist, I said, provides some form of consolation. Conrad himself says it: "I am inclined to think that the last utterance will formulate (strange as it may appear) some to us and now utterly inconceivable hope" (*Notes on Life and Letters* 17). In historical context, this phenomenon sometimes has the effect Achebe identifies as problematic: Conrad is a "purveyor of comforting myths" (3). But, more often, the tension between meaning and rhetoric—the implication of significance the words deny—has *no* particular hope attached to it. The sentences valorize the idea of myth—and it's up to the reader to decide which myth might be useful. Once they are out of context, the tools Conrad fashions are, as I will show with Ngũgĩ, useful precisely in their capacity to compel assent to political commitments.

A longer version of this passage shows the same tensions on a larger narrative level:

> A victim of the disillusioned weariness which is the retribution meted out to intellectual audacity, the brilliant Don Martin Decoud, weighted by the bars of San Tomé silver, disappeared without a trace, swallowed up in the immense indifference of things. His sleepless, crouching figure was gone from the side of the San Tomé silver; and for a time the spirits of good and evil that hover near every concealed treasure of the earth might have thought that this one had been forgotten by all mankind. Then, after a few days, another form appeared striding away from the setting sun to sit motionless and awake in the narrow black gully all through the night, in nearly the same pose, in the same place in which had sat that other sleepless man who had gone away for ever so quietly in a small boat, about the time of sunset. And the spirits of good and evil that hover about a forbidden treasure understood well that the silver of San Tomé was provided now with a faithful and lifelong slave.
>
> The magnificent Capataz de Cargadores, victim of the disenchanted vanity which is the reward of audacious action, sat in the weary pose of a hunted outcast through a night of sleeplessness as tormenting as any known to Decoud, his companion in the most desperate affair of his life. (501–502)

I have quoted at length because the mode of narrative transition here specifically contrasts linear chronology with other forms of narrative organization, particularly one based on rhetoric. This is ostensibly a linear sequence—atypically linear. Decoud leaves; and "then, after a few days," Nostromo arrives. The linear narrative, however, seems oddly insufficient—the pause of a few days shows how little the time actually matters to the point of this particular contrast. Instead we are overwhelmed with the parallels between the men, made here partially by explicit statement—"nearly the same pose, in the same place." Yet this decisive statement about them is also not quite right—the physical comparison is the least important part of the parallel.

Instead, the most prominent points of the passage—and the most important parallels structuring the temporal transition—are rhetorical and literary in nature. The parallel sentences that ostentatiously head the opposing paragraphs, the phrases like "spirits of good and evil" that are woven throughout the novel from start to finish—these devices do point to the meanings hidden by chronology—to, for instance, an evocation of a broad idea of human greed and rapacity in those generalized spirits.

Even given all these connections, the semantics matter less than the rhetorical impression created by the parallels: I have mentioned the disjunction between the "immense indifference of things" as an idea and the very unindifferent construction of the sentence in which it appears. Stanley Fish, in *Self-Consuming Artifacts*, contrasts two sentences by Walter Pater and A. N. Whitehead, both on the obscuring power of language, which ostensibly mean the same thing. Then he goes on to say,

> But as individual experiences through which a reader lives, they are not alike at all, and neither, therefore, are their meanings.
>
> To take the Whitehead sentence first, it simply doesn't mean what it says; for as the reader moves through it, he experiences the stability of the world whose existence it supposedly denies. (394)

Rhetoric in Conrad also does not mean what it says, or at least does not do what it says. This is not a cause for bemoaning its slipperiness; rather, it is a cause for celebrating rhetoric's power. Robert Browning once offered a succinct statement of the method of dramatic monologue: "Art may tell a truth / Obliquely, do the thing shall breed the thought, / Nor wrong the thought, missing the mediate word," he wrote in his own voice near the climax of *The Ring and the Book* (XII.855–857). Conrad's sentences—and, as we've seen, Faulkner's—*do* things in order to breed thoughts—and, often, part of the point is to contrast what they do with the erroneous "mediate word" they appear to convey.

The "immense indifference of things" presents a worldview that is *Nostromo's* version of nature as a bad author in *Lord Jim*. Here, rather than being malevolent, nature is simply indifferent. Nature effectively makes people indifferent to each other, too: it is in darkness that the ships crash, with no evil human or meteorological interference. This kind of author is encapsulated in the narrator's early, skeptically ironizing stance. But Conrad does not rest on this particular vision of late-Victorian pessimism, and instead allows the accumulation of the events of the novel slowly to permit sincerity. The accumulation of clauses and rhetorical effects has a similar effect in altering the way the statements are read.

To take another example, the slightly earlier chronological shift that introduces the sequence leading to Decoud's death exhibits the same distinction between rhetorical force and semantic content. This shift occurs following Nostromo's bewilderment after inspecting the island where he had left Decoud and finding it empty.

> "But, then, I cannot know," he pronounced, distinctly, and remained silent and staring for hours.
>
> He could not know. Nobody was to know. As might have been supposed, the end of Don Martin Decoud never became a subject of speculation for any one except Nostromo. Had the truth of the facts been known, there would always have remained the question, Why? Whereas the version of his death at the sinking of the lighter had no uncertainty of motive. The young apostle of Separation had died striving for his idea by an ever-lamented accident. But the truth was that he died from solitude, the enemy known but to few on this earth, and whom only the simplest of us are fit to withstand. (496)

This lengthy, subtle transition from free indirect discourse to direct authorial narration involves a slow escalation in style, so carefully handled that it is not entirely clear when Nostromo's thoughts cease to encompass the matter of the text. The first two short sentences seem like his thought patterns, staccato and composed of easy, sharp logic.[23] "As might have been supposed," however, seems like the historicizing persona, the one who derives his information from the *Fifty Years of Misrule* manuscript. Here that persona seems to be pulling back for a historical view, but the initial thoughts are all ones that could have occurred to Nostromo— the line about "no uncertainty of motive" has the sound of someone's picking a convenient story, in keeping with the dilemma facing Nostromo at the moment; "Nobody was to know" similarly echoes the problem of the secret silver, and has the short ring of Nostromo's usual thought patterns. "The truth of the facts" is ambiguous; it might refer to the fragmentary evidence Nostromo finds, or to the whole story of what happened to Decoud (since that story, arguably, still leaves a suspended "Why"). In the next sentence the view seems to solidify into a mock-epic style, ironic and grandiose, with the epithet "young apostle of Separation" and the funereal formulaic phrase "ever-lamented": this seems the historical record, assuming the "accident" of the boat crash to be the end of the story.

In the last quoted sentence, however, the irony falls away completely, and the voice can no longer be the simple historian persona, because indeed, "Nobody was to know." No character within the novel will ever know Decoud's fate; only the narrator (and his readers) can. That last sentence generalizes so universally and so quickly that it has the quality of veils of fiction falling away: Conrad has managed to create an effect whereby he suddenly seems to speak in his own voice, just in time to make a sharp accusation about the nature of a universal human vulnerability. The force of the sentence lies in its remorselessness: it demands acceptance as a statement that has no source other than complete understanding. There is no nonauthorial vantage point to which to assign it, and Conrad deliberately leaves it hanging as an absolute psychological law that dares challenge.[24]

This transition—this historically and psychologically impossible transition—is entirely an act of authorial will. Its effect is a reassertion of an authorial persona's complete knowledge and control, *as author* rather than as narrator with access to history books. But that meandering, exacting sentence does invite challenge, through the strange and characteristically Conradian syntax: "But the truth was that he died from solitude, the enemy known but to few on this earth, and whom only the simplest of us are fit to withstand." The sentence, grammatically, could easily end at either comma—though neither would have provided so satisfactory a conclusion as the period at which it finally arrives. This is additive syntax: Conrad adds clauses to answer questions raised by the preceding clauses, but none of the questions sustaining the momentum of reading ever actually are answered. Just like the novel's plot, raising new questions just when a parenthesis has seemed to answer the old ones, the rhetoric puts confusion where you expect an answer and an answer where you expect nothing of importance. In the sentence here, the question invited by the first clause—"the truth was that he died from solitude"—is how one could die of solitude, not how one can withstand it. The end of the next phrase—"the enemy known but to few on this earth"—offers no answer, and raises new ones, such as what particularly rare and lethal variety of solitude is under discussion. Yet the final clause answers nothing.

Despite, then, its gesture of broad revelation, "the truth was" offers no single and specific "truth" as an answer. The gesture of revelation, with the absence of final truth, is another way of provoking readerly questions. Because pessimism is always, in Conrad's work, the generalization, eloquence stands in for consolation. It represents the process of organization freed from any particular organizational content. Thus, while acknowledging in rational terms that illusions—of communication, of heroic action, of orderable generalities about the world—will always fail, Conrad validates and even valorizes continuous straining toward generalization and meaning. In the example from *Nostromo*, the illusion being undermined is itself the failure of illusion—Decoud is lost in the "great unbroken solitude of waiting without faith" (498). Skepticism becomes subject to a skeptical analysis of its claim to absolute authority. The sentence in *Nostromo* deliberately frees itself from any source of truth and significance in its context; the only remaining source of meaning is in its impression of *sounding* significant, in its implication of the organizing force of the author. Conrad's fiction may tell us, again and again, that "every discovery of a center or an origin is subject to a decentering, or, to put it another way, every disclosure of a ground is subject to the recession of that ground" (Meisel 239). But that doesn't mean, for Conrad, that it's possible to stop seeking grounds. His world is unstable; it has no center. But seeking (provisional) centers is not a valueless act for him.

The additive syntax, with its continual shifts of ground, and its always provisional final formulations, models the role—for Conrad—of eloquence, of the work of the artist in general, faced with such a universe. Readings that emphasize the lack of centers make Conrad into a static portrayal of the state of the world, focus on the world as something that *happens to* people: Conrad, rather, shows how the artist can respond to the world.[25] That's the force of rhetoric—to exhort, to inspire, and to provoke.

"There is never time to say our last word," says Marlow in *Lord Jim*, before offering love, desire, submission, revolt, and others as possible last words. Never time to say it—but there is always time to offer a surplus of candidates in advance; never time to say it—because speaking a sequence of potential last words without ever having to end is the best hope possible. The consolations may be purely rhetorical, but they are not *merely* rhetorical: two sentences after the stilled workshop of the earth occurs the evocation of the "utterly unconceivable hope" that the artist will offer.

Conrad discloses no rescued meanings that are not themselves subject to incipient loss, but the process of searching for them, the "rescue work" he speaks of so eloquently, always drives his fiction, and his readers, forward: to another clause, another sentence, a new scene, the next novel—and to new eras. The lasting power of Conrad's work is not in offering specific commentary about the philosophical or social issues at stake in his work; it is in his relentless isolation of the interest of the literary, of rhetoric as pure syntax rather than bearing content. For Conrad, the artist is obliged not to represent reality or even phenomenal experience, but instead to rescue it, by demanding interpretation from anyone reading a sentence of his from start to finish.

Ngũgĩ's Use of Conradian Time

T. S. Eliot famously declared that an artist's "significance, his appreciation is the appreciation of his relation to the dead poets and artists" (*Selected* 38). The reverse is more accurate: Ngũgĩ's significance does not lie in his relationship to Conrad, but Conrad's significance lies in his relationship to Ngũgĩ, and to all who read and react to his work decades and continents away from its moment of production. Influence study has fallen out of fashion, because, after Eliot, it has tended to see earlier authors as defining their successors, and controlling critical readings of them. Nicholas Brown, for instance, has suggested that the study of "influence," especially with regard to postcolonial fiction's use of European fiction, can lead to privileging European influencers over later postcolonial authors.[26] Yet for Ngũgĩ, influence can as easily allow the present to dominate the past as the reverse; in the context of the debate about the language of African fiction, he suggests that African writers "'prey' on the rich humanist and democratic heritage in the struggles of other peoples and other times" (*Decolonising* 8).

To be later, in other words, is an advantage. Many critics are suspicious of seeming to see postcolonial authors as "belated" responses to a European tradition. "Europeans were acted upon, not always acting subjects" (6), Wendy Belcher reminds us.[27] Although these critics valuably broaden the range of aesthetic connections under discussion, actual instances of African use of European fiction often differ substantially from the quasi-Bloomian anxieties that such critical models impute to them. Ngũgĩ in particular seems to have no sense of belatedness.[28] Influence study should not be discarded as a topic, but it must reflect this reversed power dynamic: rather than suggesting a revised view of Ngũgĩ in light of his Conradian interests, influence study can ask criticism of Conrad to take into account Ngũgĩ's critical and aesthetic use of him.

As the predatorial imagery suggests, rendering European and African literatures as separate species, Ngũgĩ's attitude toward European literature does not fit into most of the classic theories of influence, which, ranging from Harold Bloom's vision of contest to Christopher Ricks's gestures of gracious homage, presume a shared tradition between past and present—an assumption inapplicable to postcolonial fiction. These theories tend to take tradition and originality as their key opposing terms, neither of which looms large in Ngũgĩ's thinking on the subject. He neither fears that his works will be derivative in some invidious way, nor expects that their value will rise in proportion to their newness.[29] He also tends to view literature in Kenya as free to draw from both European and African traditions—or to reject them. Ngũgĩ conceives of his use of European literature not as an African novelist trailing behind a European vanguard, but instead as an African novelist turning the tables on colonialism and repurposing the resources of the center for the benefit of the periphery.

Ngũgĩ clearly had a very powerful experience reading Conrad, an experience that had relatively little to do with the African content of Conrad's novels; for him, *Heart of Darkness* is a relatively minor Conrad text.[30] This experience helped shape his conception of what the novel as a form could do for (and to) its readers. The Conradian period of his career was relatively brief: *A Grain of Wheat* (1967) and *Petals of Blood* (1977) are the only two novels of his with a recognizably Conradian time structure, and the connections with *Petals* are less specific. But even as his fiction became more politically decisive, the narrative effects he attributes to Conrad reappear in new shapes.

In *Decolonising the Mind*, Ngũgĩ conceives of the history of the novel primarily in formal terms:

> The first question has to do with how the novel as a form has developed. Defoe is different from George Eliot, certainly from Balzac, Zola, Tolstoy and Dostoevsky. What about Joseph Conrad, James Joyce, and Faulkner with their handling of points of view, time, character and plot? The Afro-European novel itself had produced a whole range of approaches: from the linear plot development in Chinua Achebe's *Things Fall Apart* to Wole Soyinka's *The Interpreters* which almost dispenses with plot. (75)

He seems to picture himself surveying the works of the past and present from on high, picking and choosing. Literary forms, and the interplay between them, are instrumental rather than symbolic of their historical origins. They can be picked up and employed for one's own purpose. Modernism, including Conrad, is merely one more element on a colonial school curriculum that could be made useful. Rather than displaying what the discourse of a European novel does to colonized and oppressed peoples, Ngũgĩ illustrates how those peoples have repurposed, and thus changed, the European novel.

When we separate postcolonial appropriations of Conradian content (representations of colonized people, the theme of the "heart of darkness") from postcolonial uses of Conradian style and form, the reactionary tendencies of the Conradian yearning toward generalizable pronouncement become far from inevitable. Even as he delved deeply into Conradian form, Ngũgĩ consistently critiqued Conrad's depiction of the thematics of empire: "Conrad," he says, "always made me uneasy with his inability to see any possibility of redemption arising from the energy of the oppressed" (*Moving the Centre* 6).[31] His emphasis on optimism and redemption as the missing ingredients in Conrad's politics show the inadequacies of readings that locate the political force of Conrad's literary techniques in disruption and uncertainty; rather, the apparently backward and nostalgic qualities of Conrad's style, the longing for knowledge and for meaningful action, can be repurposed for a new, anticolonial politics. The problem is not that at the end of *Nostromo* Conrad calls for a "moral principle"—it's that he can't offer one or believe in the possibility of people putting into action.

A Grain of Wheat and *Petals of Blood* do not write back to Conrad or respond to him as in a dialogue, in the manner of Achebe or Naipaul; the meanings of his texts do not depend in any way on recognizing allusions. Yet the connections are deep. It has long been noted that *A Grain of Wheat* bears marked plot similarities to Conrad's *Under Western Eyes*, a novel about Russian revolutionaries.[32] In *Under Western Eyes*, a student named Razumov betrays a fellow student, Haldin, to the authorities following Haldin's assassination of a repressive official. Razumov is welcomed as an ally by the revolutionaries, but eventually confesses the truth to them. *A Grain of Wheat* is set during the Mau Mau Uprising and in the days immediately surrounding independence. All of the characters remember a Mau Mau leader named Kihika, who, after assassinating a British officer, had been betrayed by the acquaintance in whom he put his trust—the protagonist, named Mugo. Mugo, esteemed as a hero by his village, publicly confesses the truth at the Uhuru (independence) celebrations at the climax of the novel.

Though Ngũgĩ took his plot from *Under Western Eyes*, he rewrote it to make the novel resemble *Nostromo* in form, adding a broader historical perspective and removing the frame of a single narrating character.[33] These adaptations turn literary form into a means of provoking and channeling readers' judgment of events. In 1971, he described *A Grain of Wheat* as resulting from "my preoccupation with the time structure and the problem of judgment. . . . in the problem of judging an action, you have to take into account the spatial and also the historical dimensions" (Sander and Lindfors 51). In another interview, he says: "At the beginning of the novel, there are so many things we do not know about my characters. But as we go on in the novel, you go on discovering certain aspects of their past history which make you change your judgment, or revise your judgment" (Blishen). This reader-centric analysis of the form suggests that his evocations of the novel's "uses" rather than its "origins" applies as much to his own writing as to past works: how novels represent the past matters not for its own sake but because those representations have consequences.

Judgment reappears often when Ngũgĩ's discusses fiction. In one of his most detailed comments about Conrad's influence on him, he confirms that his interest in Conrad is primarily formal and deeply related to the problem of judgment:

> *Nostromo* was my favourite. I still think it is a great novel, but on the whole I found Conrad's vision limited. His ambivalence towards imperialism—and

it was imperialism that supplied him with the setting and subject matter of his novels—could never let him go beyond the balancing acts of liberal humanism. But the shifting points of view in time and space; the multiplicity of narrative voices; the narrative-within-a-narration; the delayed information that helps the revision of a previous judgement so that only at the end with the full assemblage of evidence, information and points of view, can the reader make full judgement—these techniques had impressed me. (*Decolonising* 76)

Ngũgĩ's tendency to see the literary past as a tool for present use, rather than as a microcosm of its own social world, is visible in the split between the "great novel" and the "limited vision": he likes the fact that Conrad's novels create readerly judgments, without necessarily liking the particular judgments to which Conrad points his readers. The vessel is useful, in other words, so long as it can be emptied out. In addition, when he discusses the form, judgment is not only deferred, but more decisive for the deferral. As in Conrad's novels, the place of greatest authority is at the end: multiple versions do not throw the whole into doubt, but provide as much information as possible en route to a final call for judgment.

Discussions of Ngũgĩ and Conrad often focus on a particular moment in one of Ngũgĩ's earliest interviews, in 1964, where he is usually quoted as declaring himself interested in "the way he [Conrad] questions things, requestions things like action, the morality of action, for instance" (Sander and Lindfors 4).[34] The quotation is often used to point to "the skeptical or ironic strain in Conrad that manifestly informs *A Grain of Wheat*" (West-Pavlov 165). This quotation is, however, a mistranscription. Ngũgĩ actually said, "he questions things—he questions things like action" (Duerden).[35] Rather than intensifying, the repetition is a slight hesitation: he is trying to isolate what exactly Conrad questions, and the rest of the response regarding Conrad is a careful tacking back and forth between Conrad as skeptical and affirming. Asked by the interviewer, "Doesn't he question man's ability to have any control over his own destiny?" Ngũgĩ responds,

No; yes and no, because while he questions man's ideas and ability to control his destiny, at the heart of Conrad is a feeling that man is great, and reading Conrad one feels struck by man's capacity for bearing suffering, but much more than this, he questions what appears on the surface. . . . you find that some characters in Conrad fail to do something, but their failure to do something is a moral decision with Conrad. (Sander and Lindfors 4)

This has a distant kinship to Woolf's evocation of Conradian cliché-ideals—"Man is great" (a statement he emphasizes heavily in the audio) might stand next to "Loyalty is good and honesty and courage." Ngũgĩ values a certain type of questioning here, carefully delimited, and avoids presenting the questions as mere negations that would undermine the possibility of taking action.

The language about judgment grew stronger as he came to have a more politicized notion of the role of art; if the earliest interviews are concerned with the problem of forestalling erroneous judgments based on limited information, the later ones focus more on the idea that after all perspectives are visible, "full judgement" is possible. *A Grain of Wheat* appeared at a transitional moment in his career; at Leeds University, where he wrote the novel, he was discovering Fanonist Marxism and more politicized literary theory at odds with the traditional, more aesthetic and abstract criticism he had been taught at Makerere University.[36] The shift toward stronger notions of readerly judgment is also a move toward conceiving literature less as a passive object of analysis and more as a political tool. *A Grain of Wheat*, I will argue, reflects a commitment to the uses of Conradian form as political, but does not yet fully imagine the broad audience, including those not literate in English, that became so crucial to his later, more specific, political and cultural purposes.

In grappling with Kenyan history in *A Grain of Wheat*, Ngũgĩ conceives of the juxtaposition of multiple perspectives and worldviews as a way of enabling judgment on the past. Addressing an African and global audience of English-language readers, he wants them to struggle with and cast judgment on the ethical dilemmas and historical events of decolonization, rather than to see them as a tragic farce from afar. To the extent that the novel got immediate European attention, it worked: early English reviews praised the way its elaborate form could draw out the "sympathies" of Western readers.[37] They also do not question its portrayal of the controversial historical events of the state of emergency, and seem on some level to value its perspective on them.[38] After *A Grain of Wheat*, Ngũgĩ's subject matter and his intended audience shifted decisively; his later works treat not the conflicts between European and Kenyan characters but the rise of a neocolonial African elite, and he became ever more focused on the power of literature to rouse its audience to direct political action in a local Kenyan context. As a consequence, Conradian techniques aimed at an elite audience steeped in European traditions became less useful. However, as I will discuss shortly, the later works continue to place readerly judgment at the center of their aesthetics.

Paradoxically, Ngũgĩ's strategy in *A Grain of Wheat* is to out-Conrad Conrad by increasing the formal disruption. The time scheme, for instance, is even more complicated than Conrad's. Unusual among Conrad's novels, *Under Western Eyes* is mostly linear: its first section tells the story of Razumov's betrayal of Haldin; its later sections play out the aftermath, with a few belated detours covering the time in between. Ngũgĩ's novel is far less linear and moves through a greater variety of perspectives: over the course of a few days surrounding Uhuru, many of the protagonists recall earlier events in their lives, usually out of order. Mugo's betrayal occurs in the earliest days of the uprising but is revealed only late in the novel, whereas Razumov's is the first major action in *Under Western Eyes*.

This reversal crucially changes the relation of narration and plot. Razumov's betrayal of Haldin is a psychological puzzle and an insoluble ethical dilemma; the rest of the novel searches for ways to understand and terms on which to judge his actions. By contrast, Mugo's betrayal appears as the solution to the novel's mysteries, and Ngũgĩ, while ensuring sympathy for Mugo, avoids any suggestion that the betrayal might have been "right." Ngũgĩ's more achronological structure, in other words, allows the confession to feel meaningful in a way that Conrad's structure does not. Peter Nazareth points out that Mugo's confession has both a broader audience and greater consequences in the plot than Razumov's ("Teaching" 169); these elements align the readerly process of solving the mystery with the historical crisis of an entire community. All his characters, on the eve of independence, have found that their history has not led where they thought it would. At the end Mugo disappears into darkness (and, it is implied, execution), and it is precisely because the past has become comprehensively knowable that the ambiguities of Kenya's future can now be faced.

Many of the events and characters entice the reader into making judgments using the specific techniques Ngũgĩ attributes to Conrad: "the multiplicity of narrative voices . . . the delayed information." Here, for instance, is a sequence of references, which give progressively greater information about a crucial event in the novel. First comes a passing thought in the mind of Margery, wife of the British officer Thompson:

This was soon after the Rira disaster. (37)

This first reference is dramatic enough to ensure notice. Another brief, still-enigmatic reference follows shortly, this time with Thompson comparing a present-day interaction to the past:

He remembered the detainees at Rira the day they went on strike. (42)

Next, an outline emerges, still from Thompson's perspective:

> Like Rira. There the detainees had refused to speak. They sat down and
> refused to eat or drink. The obduracy was like iron. Their eyes followed
> him everywhere. The agony, lack of sleep, thinking of how to break the si-
> lence. . . . At Rira, the tragedy of his life occurred. A hunger strike, a little
> beating and eleven detainees died. The fact leaked out. Because he was the
> officer in charge, Thompson's name was bandied about in the House of
> Commons and in the world press. (46)

"A hunger strike, a little beating and eleven detainees died": the missing verbs
suppress both agency and causality, and are clear pointers to Thompson's
incapacities. Soon comes a broader, non-British perspective, where it becomes
clear that the events at Rira involve other familiar characters:

> Two days later, people were to talk about Mugo in the eight ridges around
> Thabai: they told with varying degrees of exaggeration how he organized
> the hunger-strike in Rira, an action which made Fenna Brokowi raise
> questions in the British House of Commons. (63)

For the first time, the incident appears for its own sake—rather than being
introduced as an explanation or context for a character's state of mind. Finally,
much later, the whole story is retold from multiple perspectives.

> Learned men will, no doubt, dig into the troubled times which we in Kenya
> underwent, and maybe sum up the lesson of history in a phrase. Why, let
> us ask them, did the incident in Rira Camp capture the imagination of the
> world? (131)

The following pages give a full description of the events at Rira, including
Thompson's mental state and an analysis of the way Mugo, suffering beatings in
silence because "numbed" by guilt, "gave . . . courage" (134) to the other inmates.
This sequence of references is Ngũgĩ's version of a classic Conradian device—
compare, for instance, the revelation of Father Beron's torture of Dr. Monygham in
Nostromo, where references similarly grow in detail.

The narrative thus moves toward improved perception. The final section
juxtaposes the individual with the global, the intimate with the historic—and it
gives the sense that this is, at last, the truth. This account ends by reiterating an
outside perspective: "What occurred next is known to the world. The men were

rounded up and locked in their cells. The now famous beating went on day and night. Eleven men died" (134). No causal conjunctions have intervened, but the greater detail makes them unnecessary. Ngũgĩ has ensured that the beating is "now famous" to us as well as the world, because we've been within the characters' minds. Just as the reader's understanding of Nostromo's theft of the silver gives meaning to the image of spirits hovering over treasure, the slow buildup of multiple perspectives fills with sympathy and significance phrasing that had before seemed grotesquely empty.

The framing of these passages suggests the pan-African and global audience of literary-minded people Ngũgĩ is interested in at this point in his career. "The world" recurs again and again in the final treatment of Rira: "capture the imagination of the world," "is known to the world," and so forth. Along with recalling the way the Rira hunger strike has become known to the novel's readers, these phrases also allude to a historical context that was then widely known: Fenner Brockway, a Labour MP, really did speak out (among others) about the Hola Massacre, a beating at one of the camps during which eleven men died. The allusion to a larger, global perspective has behind it both the force of reading experience, recalling the knowledge gained through reading the story, and the force of real-life recognition. Whether we assume a readership aware of Hola or not, the slow accretion of knowledge demands recognition, by the end, of the "knownness" of the event, rather than its unknowability or illegibility.[39]

Ngũgĩ, we might say, employs Conradian techniques as political tools rather than political symbols. Evan Mwangi has criticized "a persistent tendency to see African art to be nothing but a rant against colonialism and a counterpoint to Western aesthetics" (256). The readings to which he refers tend to see African novelists' uses of modernist literary form as allusions to Western viewpoints, which writers call upon primarily in order to refute. For instance, Byron Caminero-Santangelo argues that the first-person plural narrator's prominent use in the climactic Uhuru celebrations in the novel is a gesture of postcolonial rewriting—a collectivist rebellion against the regime of Western individualism and its literary hegemony (65). Yet this narrator disappears in the final four chapters; the novel does not mark an unambiguous move toward collective speech; it uses collective speech for a collective event, and other forms of speech for other events.

Although Ngũgĩ is not trying to reject a symbolic form of Western narration, the emphasis on group action does get at the point where Ngũgĩ thought Conrad's vision "limited." Ngũgĩ's emphasis on collective activity as a response to social evils differs sharply from Conrad's image of self-interested individual revolutionaries; Mugo confesses to his entire community rather than a caricatured cabal. The novel does not particularly privilege collective narration, but it does use Conrad's tools to create a collective reader response. Indeed, collectivity is far more notice-able in Ngũgĩ's fiction, not in the person of the narrator, but in the situation of narration: one individual might be talking, but invariably *to* a specific group of people: the members of a village, or sometimes even a smaller group.

Take a passage in *Petals of Blood*, Ngũgĩ's last English-language novel. Like *Grain of Wheat*, it is densely Conradian in form, although it does not directly adapt the plot of any particular novel. Echoes resound throughout the novel.[40] The opening of *Nostromo* provides material for the second part of the novel, which begins with a history of Ilmorog:

> Ilmorog, the scene of the unfolding of this drama, had not always been a small cluster of mud huts lived in only by old men and women and chil-dren with occasional visits from wandering herdsmen. It had had its days of glory. (145)

This appears to be another omniscient narrator, who has come in after the first section of the novel to provide the fuller history that the opening did not provide. This narrator, like the opening of *Nostromo*, sounds distant: the present measures up badly against a heroic past. But a few pages later, we read: "Thus Nyakinyua talked to them" (149). The whole passage is belatedly revealed to be narrated by a specific character in one of the main timelines of the novel. This kind of gesture—a frame narrative that is only revealed as frame at the end—is often destabilizing (e.g., "It was all a dream"). In this case, however, the effect is opposite: Nyakinyua's history has more significance because it is being told to a specific audience in dire straits as an explanation of how their town has ended up in its current situation. What seems like distant omniscience becomes intimately connected to individuals we know—both the speaker and the audience. And yet the effect is not to under-mine the perspective because it is not the narrator's; the effect, rather, is to raise individuals' efforts of interpretation to the status of an intervention in history.

Ngũgĩ's Authority

One of the most important formal differences between *Under Western Eyes* and *A Grain of Wheat* is a matter of tone that complicates the arc of Ngũgĩ's career. Conrad's novel has a prominent satirical element; Ngũgĩ's does not. In *A Grain of Wheat*, even potentially farcical moments remain intensely serious. Thus, at the climactic Uhuru celebrations, two characters, Gikonyo and Karanja, who are rivals for the love of Mumbi, the female protagonist, end up in the lead of a village-wide footrace. Then, one of them trips, and they both fall down. It is a ridiculous ending—and yet, in the moment, there's nothing even darkly funny about it. Gikonyo has broken his arm; Karanja is wrongly suspected of Mugo's crime and may shortly be executed. At the same time, Mugo's sense of guilt is coming to a climax. Everything seems so fraught and fateful that, in this novel, tripping over a rock can't break the tension. Yet from *Petals of Blood* forward, Ngũgĩ, like Conrad, inclined increasingly to satire, culminating in the pointed political satire of *Wizard of the Crow* (2006): why, then, did he deliberately avoid satirical touches in his most Conradian work?

Conradian satire is at odds with the purposes to which Ngũgĩ eventually turned the form. Conrad's revolutionaries are caricatured, and Razumov's dilemma has the appearance of a dark farce, complete with an inconveniently drunken peasant who was supposed to help with Haldin's escape. Both *Under Western Eyes* and *The Secret Agent*, Conrad's other novel about revolutionaries, create the impression of a purposeless struggle between legal forces and revolutionary ones that seems only intermittently to touch the society in which they exist; part of the humor arises from the contrast between the ideology of revolutionaries and the lives of the people on whose behalf they speak (Haldin exclaims of the peasant, "A bright spirit! A hardy soul!" [21]). In both novels satirical distance eventually gives way to real terror, just as skepticism gives way to authoritative statement in *Nostromo*.

In *A Grain of Wheat*, by contrast, the satire was never there to begin with. Kenya's state of emergency does not permit anyone to remain on the sidelines of struggle. In a talk given at the time (1966), Ngũgĩ suggests that the writer of satire "gets away unscathed" (*Homecoming* 65): it permits critique without commitment. The excision of satire thus underscores one of the political themes of the novel: Mugo betrays Kihika because he fails to see that everyone would inevitably soon be involved in the conflict, whether in detention or imprisoned in their own village. To join in activism or to stand by (until events come to you) is a crucial question throughout Ngũgĩ's work, while in Conrad's revolutionary novels most people stand by, and the plot lines happen on the margins of society. In *A Grain of Wheat*, there is no position outside of the plot line of the novel from which to mock the characters. In Ngũgĩ's eyes the radical potential of the novel form—even difficult modernist form—lies precisely in its sincerity: not in the way it questions the possibilities of knowledge, but the way it forces the reader to assume knowledge and take sides. Ngũgĩ started writing satirically when he came to see how satire can compel commitment rather than ridicule it.

Ngũgĩ eventually abandoned most of his Conradian forms; after his 1977–1978 imprisonment, he focused on advocating the literary use of African languages and structured his novels with more clearly Kikuyu narrative techniques to address a Kikuyu population who could not necessarily read English: political efficacy required speaking to the people from whom he hoped change could arise. Yet though the different audience required different tools, the purpose remained the same, and the language of gaining knowledge in order to make a judgment that Ngũgĩ uses to describe Conrad in *Decolonising the Mind* (1986) actually echoes phrases within his first Kikuyu (and highly satirical) novel, *Devil on the Cross* (1980). The opening of the novel—in his own translation—frames the work as a written example of *gĩcaandĩ*, a form of poetic oral performance:

> And then Warĩĩnga's mother came to me when dawn was breaking, and in tears she beseeched me: Gĩcaandĩ Player, tell the story of the child I loved so dearly. Cast light upon all that happened, so that each may pass judgment only when he knows the whole truth. Gĩcaandĩ Player, reveal all that is hidden. (7)

As in *Nostromo*, the artist sees within the darkness, presents a vision that can form the foundation for renewed authoritative understanding. At the end of the novel, this image reappears when its protagonist finally obtains both personal and political revenge against an upper-class man who has wronged her: "She began to speak like a people's judge about to deliver his judgment" (253). This is a much more explicitly activist novel than *A Grain of Wheat*: it not only portrays the process of coming to judgment in its characters but also demands judgment from its readers, and that judgment is meant to compel political action. Ngũgĩ has switched from trying to affect one type of audience to trying to affect another, but the same arc toward judgment that he attributes to Conrad and puzzled over in the form of *A Grain of Wheat* remains.

Notably, Ngũgĩ's argument about the language of fiction is as much about efficacy and audience as it is about history and cultural capital. He advocates African languages because they will better reach an oppressed proletariat audience. In other words, it's less about where language comes from than who speaks it today. Back in *A Grain of Wheat* he had claimed that everyone—even the isolated villager Mugo—will need to take a stand. Conrad's narrative experimentation makes tenuous ideals and hopes—for the possibility of change, for the existence of moral ideals—appear in the interstices between juxtaposed scenes or in, as Woolf says, the music of the prose. These tenuous and abstract ideals, once scenes and narrators have been sliced up and remixed even more dramatically, become Ngũgĩ's political and moral imperatives.

Modernist Reconstructions

Historicist and theoretical scholars widely share the persuasion that modernist disruption of formal norms and resistance to conventional plot structures is politically subversive. Jessica Berman, for instance, describes the Indian modernist Mulk Raj Anand's *Untouchable* in these terms: "The experimentalism of *Untouchable* and the other narratives I will take up in this book is crucial to their ethicopolitical power, exhibiting the incommensurate experiences, uneven relationships, disrupted perspectives, and political uncertainties that characterize Bakha's modernity" (23). Incommensurability, disruption, uncertainty: these are all words critics commonly use to link modernist form with political radicalism. They are valid words for this purpose, of course, but their opposites—recognition, construction, knowledge—are what Ngũgĩ sees as politically useful in Conrad.

Most recent criticism that questions the marriage of disruptive form to radical ideology does so by calling for a de-emphasis on modernist innovation, either defending the political efficacy of realism or critiquing the inaccessibility of experimentation. Simon Gikandi, for instance, points out that "when modernism was taken to the margins of the modern world-system, its mandate—its concern with the spasmodic and subjective—was often at odds with the colonial writers' desire for a reality effect in which the colonized could be rehabilitated as sovereign subjects" ("Realism, Romance" 316). The formal effects considered most revolutionary in modernism, in other words, had more limited potential for subversion outside the metropole; the particular views they were good at undermining were not the ones that haunted colonial subjects.[41]

Yet the political impact of modernist literature never did reside solely in critique, and the "spasmodic and subjective" is far from the primary effect of modernist experimentation. Conrad's literary forms, as we've seen, are less about subjectivity than they've long been thought to be. Conrad, in all his strange and startling innovation, has political use to Ngũgĩ precisely through his techniques for seeking knowledge rather than deconstructing it. And Ngũgĩ's use of Conrad shows that these functions are not merely vestiges of Victorian outlooks that more radical authors would shed, but essential to Conrad's formal innovation, political use, and continuing literary appeal.

Emphasizing abstract ideals is dangerous when criticism treats abstraction as the endpoint, when the drawing of universal lessons never proceeds to see how the universals act in particular situations. But Ngũgĩ tends to see the antidote not in unmitigated suspicion of any kind of general statement, but in generality as bridge between particulars; and even as he inveighs against the failure to particularize, he delights in the rhetoric of boundary-crossing relevance. "Works of imagination refuse to be bound within national geographies; they leap out of nationalist prisons and find welcoming fans outside the geographic walls" (*Globalectics* 58). This is not a recent development: in 1981's *Writers in Politics*, he declares, "The African writer and Joseph Conrad share the same world and that is why Conrad's world is so familiar. . . . They have known Hola camps, My Lai, Algiers, Sharpeville, the Arab mother and child driven from Palestine" (77). If the colonial school system built only half-bridges, the answer, for Ngũgĩ, is to finish the bridge: not to read books primarily in their own contexts, but to be attentive to the context in which they can be read later, to make the abstraction a path toward the particular.[42]

The abstractions that Ngũgĩ found most useful in Conrad were not a particular statement or worldview, but a structure of readerly experience that could be aimed at producing a political response. By increasing the formal disruption of realist norms beyond where Conrad went, Ngũgĩ found a new way to turn some of the most familiar effects of realism to his own political purposes—the reader's sense of a strong narratorial moral compass and judgment, the deep sympathy with characters' struggles that Conrad seems to render as a perhaps-impossible dream.[43] In treating authors' formal disruptions only as politically progressive repudiations of the epistemological outlooks of the nineteenth century, modernist studies does not fully capture their manifold effects and uses. Ngũgĩ's use of Conrad implies that sometimes the most exciting and appealing thing about modernism's ever-more-elaborate narrative structures is their ability to find a stronger foundation for old ways of viewing the world—and that this defense of one social order can furnish the tools for revolution against another.

Yet this potential use for Conradian form is only visible if we temporarily hold attention to its early twentieth-century political context in abeyance. Form doesn't have political meaning; it has political use, and its uses are many. The abstractions in which Conrad's novels culminate are designed to be applicable beyond Conrad's historical context. When Conrad discusses his readers, he consistently renders them as indistinct; art, for instance, is "the appeal of one temperament to all the other innumerable temperaments" (*"Narcissus"* ix). These readers in their "innumerable temperaments" are as vague as the moral impressions Woolf and Ngũgĩ receive from his novels: that loyalty is good and man is great. Conrad was probably incapable of imagining the wide African audience that would read his work; but he did understand that he could not predict who his audience would be. His readership is another empty vessel, an invitation to be filled out by the unknown future.

Pausing over the stage of analysis in which literary forms have effects on their readers that might seem abstract helps to explain some of the vagaries of reception history. Achebe and Ngũgĩ, for instance, clearly evaluate Conrad differently, but neither of them sees him as a source of epistemological instability. Achebe's discussion of him as a "purveyor of comforting myths" in this respect isn't that distant from Ngũgĩ's discussion of how "the reader makes full judgment"—both focus on the way the novels produce certainty rather than doubt. They disagree radically about the political implications of this literary effect—Ngũgĩ clearly finds it useful, Achebe sees it as invidious—but the contours of their literary experiences are shared.

Although critics are rightly skeptical of erasing the particularities of different readerships, the aspiration to write for the future implicitly relies on some sense of continuity between present and future reading communities. A full understanding of literary history requires doing justice to works' attempts to speak to an unknowable future without falling into New Critical visions of autonomous art objects unmoored from the messiness of history. Studying transhistorical readership requires attending to what is portable in a work, to what is particular about the uses to which it has been put rather than the historical context from which it springs. Hans Robert Jauss, arguing for attention to the long history of reception, envisions "a chain of receptions from generation to generation" (20). The completist vision he imagines—surveying the whole history of a work's reception from its appearance to the present moment (see, e.g., his sample reading of Baudelaire [171–185]) seems now impossible; the splintered reactions to Conrad even within Africa, let alone the rest of the world, suggest Conrad's reception will never form a coherent whole or a single chain.[44] Yet still Ngũgĩ, describing Conrad, recalls the phrases and impressions of Woolf; and, in turn, the Ugandan critic and writer Peter Nazareth attributes to Ngũgĩ his own discovery of the uses Conrad could have for him.[45] It remains both possible and important to discern the patterns that unite at least a few diverse moments of reception. Only then can we understand not only what a work means, but what it has already done—and what it still might do.

4. Needing to Narrate

"It is my ambition," declared Faulkner, "to be, as a private individual, abolished and voided from history, leaving it markless, no refuse save the printed books" (Blotner, *Selected* 285). Faulkner's imagination of futurity expresses the same concern as James did about Flaubert's letters, that the private details of a life matter infinitely less than the public achievement of the work, and we might pay for the knowledge of the former by obscuring our sight of the latter. But Faulkner's statement doesn't merely demand biographical obscurity. It also, strangely, conjures an image of history itself being blank: "leaving it markless" rather than "leaving no mark." For a moment in that sentence, Faulkner's desire for his art to eclipse his life means that history itself must go dark.

The letter is from 1949, after Malcolm Cowley had already edited *The Portable Faulkner*, which made Faulkner's American reputation. *The Portable Faulkner* constructs Faulkner exactly opposite to his inclination here: it revels in Faulkner's novels as themselves a form of history, arranging them according to thematic headings: "The End of an Order," "Modern Times," "The Undying Past," among others. If Faulkner liked the idea that books could blank out history, Cowley implied that they did so by offering a suitable replacement.

The subtle difference between these two ideas haunts Faulkner's reception since, where his capacity to appear to elude historical limitations and his sustained engagement with a particular local history compete to center our analysis of him. Faulkner stands in our eyes always half-embedded in his historical context, a frieze mixing high- and bas-relief. His relationship with Jim Crow is not unlike Conrad's with British imperialism; like Conrad, he is ambiguously turned partially away from a massive oppressive system, critiquing its monstrosities while partaking of its fallacies, only possessing a limited ability to see beyond it. And like Conrad, his work constantly turns from the local to the universal, from the immediate to the distant. If in Conrad, universal phrases are fragile, tentative, and paradoxical things, shadowed by darkness and undone by the very rhetoric that conveys them, in Faulkner—and in Kesey after him—multiple forms of universal principle compete. The difficulty is sorting them out.

Faulkner, more persistently and explicitly than James or Conrad, is an anatomist of the past's power over the present, the author of perhaps the most famous American aphorism on the subject—"The past is never dead. It's not even past" (*Novels 1942–1954* 535). James's America is almost unnervingly pastless (to its detriment); his characters are free to pick and choose the bits of European history they want because they lack American options. Conrad's heroes often find themselves unexpectedly free of the past anywhere but their own mind—Jim, Razumov, and Nostromo all manage fresh starts where their previous transgressions might be erased, only to discover that the crimes live on within them. But Faulkner's characters carry the past inside and out. They're haunted in their own mind like Conrad's, but also in the eyes of others and in the scars the past leaves upon the landscape, like the hulking antebellum mansion decaying in the backdrop of *The Hamlet*, whose conjectured backstory drives the final twists of the plot. The idea of a markless history is attractive to Faulkner precisely because it seems so impossible. In Faulkner's novels the past's influence on the present is consistently invidious: Quentin Compson's brain taken over by his own delusions of sexual purity and his father's invidious skepticism; Gail Hightower in *Light in August*, his life and sanity forfeit to Civil War stories. "An echo," says Ken Kesey in the spirit of Faulkner in *Sometimes a Great Notion*, "is an inflexible and pitiless taskmaster" (325).

Conversely, Faulkner's sense of a present held in the grip of the past is reflected in his much greater confidence about the possibility of the novel to last into the future. Faulkner's easy talk of "the old verities" as the source of the novelist's power is the optimistic side of the hauntings his characters suffer: the persistence of the past suggests the possibility of the literary persistence of the present. Faulkner's strong sense of both the evils and the inevitability of the past's haunting drives his analysis of the stakes of striving for literary futurity. Faulkner's novels on both a literary and a historical level think through what can be taken from the past and what can be left behind; what can be offered to the future from the present and what must be erased from present-day context.

It's a tired truism to point out that a recurring vice of American political thought is a refusal to acknowledge the continuing impact of the violence of the historical past—alongside a desire to claim its glories. The history of Faulkner's reception is an oscillation between seeing his literary achievement as one of those glories and seeing his novels as useful warnings of its shames. This oscillation suggests something counterintuitive: that Faulkner's real continuing use is in the ways he strains against the influence of the past. If he provides terrifyingly precise sketches of the undead hand of history strangling the present, he does so in order to place at the center of our attention what it means to make a usable past rather than suffocating one.[1] He's a model of the necessity of fighting this influence—however doomed the task might be. Faulkner's "lost cause," in other words, is not nostalgic longing for a monstrous antebellum world, but instead a longing that it might be possible truly to leave behind the worst parts of that world—that the marks of history might someday be blanked out. Faulkner—and, I will show, Ken Kesey after him—asks not that we believe the past is dead, but that we be willing to struggle against it when necessary. The struggle to decontextualize is not a complacent erasure of the evils done before, but an attempt to recognize and repair them. As David Minter writes, "His fiction not only assimilates, preserves, and transmits the past; it also openly and even aggressively transforms the past, in part by showing it to have been multiple" (101). If James's characters struggle to pick and choose social influences to construct their identities, Faulkner's characters struggle to select what aspects of the past they must commit to and what they must reject.

This sense of connection and of distance between present and past unites him with Kesey. "I *still* don't understand what happened," says an outsider to the town, near the end of *Sometimes a Great Notion*. "Maybe that's because it's still happening," replies a former outsider who's lived there long enough (714). Kesey takes for granted that the past is both dead, incomprehensibly different, and always still present. This is a world not timeless, but enmeshed in startlingly powerful connections across time. As James's novels are about his characters coming to understand and control the connections between their minds and others', Faulkner's and Kesey's are about his characters understanding and controlling their own relation between the past and the present.

One way of describing this is that his novels explore characters' different strategies for placing themselves in time as well as in their social worlds. Some orient themselves at a distance from the past but connected to it; others reduplicate it as though it were still present; still others seek entirely to escape, erase, or reject the past. Faulkner's novels turn toward the universal, in other words, not in order to get to a space without or outside of time, but to see multiple times in relation to one another, to face both the differences and the inevitable connections between eras.

Faulkner, literary inheritor, in one sense, of Joycean stream of consciousness, is often thought of as another artist of the present in all its chaos and confusion, of the mind riven by insoluble complexities and contradictions, unable to make sense of itself. But the movement of his novels is usually toward ever-increasing understanding (for his characters as well as the reader) about the large systems structuring the world of Yoknapatawpha County. Rather than highlight as inevitable the failures of his characters to make sense of their lives and history, his novels mercilessly raise the stakes of that failure.

The temporal and perspectival experiments of Faulkner's novels are designed to get their readers to a place where they can have some distance on events without dismissing them: where we can recognize the past as dead, but still acknowledge its continuing effects. Faulkner, like James, is invested in stories of charisma—narratives where one character occupies an outsize place in the minds of others. The whole of *Absalom, Absalom!*, in which Thomas Sutpen's story is repeated and reimagined by others who never knew him decades after his death, is the most notable example. And like Conrad, his novels are shot through with abstract invocations of mortality and fate, coming from characters who double as narrators and slice up the story to tell it out of order. As we saw in chapter 1, sometimes those abstract pronouncements use the same syntax and language as Conrad.

These novels, in other words, are dramatizations of what it means to try to see one's life in novelistic terms—to become a narrator for another's story, to try to be a protagonist, to try to see one's life as having a larger meaning. In Faulkner, it is when power is unknowable that it *has* power; to know and understand, to impose narrative order on the world, is a countervailing subversive activity. Will Varner, owner of that decaying big house in *The Hamlet*, will ultimately lose to the subtle plottings of the incomprehensible Flem Snopes. To survive is to seek to understand and to recognize the larger design of the story you're in.

By striving to impose meaning on the past and present, Faulkner's characters see the way the past is sedimented into the present, but they also see it as no longer identifiable with themselves. In Kesey, this connected yet separate past is represented by various aspects of the natural world: "A shiny new ax, taking a swing at somebody's next year's split-level pinewood pad, bites all the way to the Civil War" (227). For Kesey, the past is imminently present precisely because it is dead—and therefore transfigurable. Making the future—a different future—exposes the hidden past.

And the literary history in question raises the problem of the boundary between past and present as well. *Sometimes a Great Notion* fits firmly into the category of the "neglected masterpiece." It's a novel that a generation remembers reading when it came out (and generally remembers fondly); that those growing up in the Pacific Northwest (I am one) are still informed is the Great Regional Novel. But it is very seldom read today: lengthy and formally complex, alone in its region, alone in its period as neither realist nor postmodernist; stuck as the second novel to *One Flew Over the Cuckoo's Nest*—overshadowed by its cultural resonance, and shadowed by its misogyny. *Sometimes a Great Notion*, then, is perhaps more stuck in its context than Baldwin or Ngũgĩ, who are now enshrined firmly in canon. Yet with its 1960s tensions between expressive individualism and collective politics, it also has obvious relevance to similar debates today. Faulkner's novels required a few years to achieve their fame, but have rested firmly in their status since; *Sometimes a Great Notion* found only temporary status despite the ready-made celebrity of its author.[2]

In the great coniferous forests where *Sometimes a Great Notion* is set, occasionally you will see several massive, century-old trees arrayed in what seems to be an unnaturally straight row. Or perhaps a tree's roots will have grown into an arch, leaving space underneath the trunk so that it appears perched on a giant's tripod. Invisible in the fog of the past is a tree from centuries before that, which died, decayed in place, and eventually crashed to the ground through branches and bushes and moss. This tree, called a nurse log, provided nourishment for the saplings that eventually grew into that straight row; its continued decay left empty the arch beneath their roots.

If Baldwin sees the literary past as tools—with all the love and workmanship that implies—and Ngũgĩ sees it as prey to be converted to a new purpose, Kesey's use of Faulkner suggests a middle way: this is the literary past as nurse log, as source of nourishment. The violence with which that trunk fell is no longer part of its life and its use; it is merely now a piece of landscape and regenerative sustenance for a seed that happened to fall upon its bulk.

The literary past is the ground and the decaying substance from which the literary present grows.

"Things That Just Have to Be": Faulkner's Designing Characters

In *Light in August*, the character Gail Hightower is famously stuck in time: "born about thirty years after the only day he seemed to have ever lived in—that day when his grandfather was shot from the galloping horse" (443). Hightower, obsessed with one day, offers one model of the transhistorical: the past is always present; in fact, the present is merely the past in another guise. In this light, the transhistorical looks sinister: the dead haunting the living, the myths of the past warping the present.

Hightower's ruined life is a devastating critique of one form of thinking beyond a single moment. In seeing the past in the present, he erases the present—he's a bad minister, whose congregation is continuously mystified by the presence of that dying grandfather in their sermons; he's virtually unable to see his wife, who eventually kills herself. We might see Hightower as a parody of one form of the transhistorical, where time is stopped; in the name of a mythic eternal moment, the past dominates the present. This is, in one sense, the classic mode of spatial form, whereby repeated structures become eternal and allow access to a world outside of time.[3] *Light in August*, in general, is obsessed with characters whose lives seem attenuated into a sequence of repeating gestures: Lena Grove, finding herself in a new town in search of her feckless lover; Joe Christmas, forever fleeing and, like Hightower, in thrall to a pernicious origin story. This is the danger of a mythic world: that it erases any temporal difference, makes the present only another image of the past, often supported by a kind of nostalgia for that past.

Hightower's life is also a commentary on a classic kind of modernist novel. After all, Faulkner never did write a novel that takes place over a single day, but we might consider Hightower's life a kind of parodic inversion of the form. If Woolf and Joyce select a day and then represent it as shot through with moments from the whole life leading up to it, Hightower's whole life has been shot through by a single day—a single lethal moment from a past that predates his entire life.

Hightower is a jaundiced vision of what it really looks like to define a life by a single day—not the intense presence and attention to the contingent and ordinary highlighted by Woolf, but the ossification of detail into fixed myth. Hightower is life reduced to spatial form or symbolist image. Jameson distinguishes in *Antinomies of Realism* between the temporality of "everything having happened already"—the temporality of destiny and of linear time—and the temporality the "perpetual present," between the "tale" and "daily life" (*Antinomies* 27–28). The literary history he tells tends to be the supersession of the former by the latter. The lineaments, for instance, of a transition from romance to realism's everyday, from realist plot to modernist antiplot, are clear. But Hightower's temporality unites these two: it is both eternal present and always already happened.

Mrs. Dalloway and *Ulysses* have always simultaneously occupied two contrasting stances toward the historical and transhistorical: deeply rooted in particular times and places, refusing to exclude any extraneous atoms of detail; and yet turning constantly toward visionary moments that expand beyond. Jameson describes *Ulysses* as "a stubborn and hard fought attempt to hold onto the absolute being of the place and day, the untranscendable reality of a specifically limited secular experience" (*Antinomies* 216). The "absolute being of the place and day" of Hightower's grandfather's death is indeed stubbornly "untranscendable"—but at the cost of sacrificing the open, contingent present to what has already happened.

If Conrad's work draws attention to the impossible artifice of authorship, to the perspective and ordering work that no individual can reach, Faulkner goes a step further and examines what it means to replace untranscendable reality by a transcendent truth that in fact has little relation to reality. Indeed, the very reality of Hightower's grandfather seems to be part of what makes it pernicious—far less damaging, for instance, is the hold the dead Thomas Sutpen has on Quentin and Shreve in *Absalom, Absalom!*, in part because they are far less bound to anything real. Recall Shreve on "things that just have to be whether they are or not" (266); and Kesey, making it even more explicit in *Cuckoo's Nest*: "It's the truth even if it didn't happen" (8).

Perhaps the most successful instance of self-narration in Faulkner is Lena Grove of *Light in August*, whose narrative is peculiarly powerful because it never has to become true; it determines only her own actions. First pregnant, then a single mother, she wanders into new worlds after the father of her child. Constantly saying things we know aren't true—that Lucas Burch intends to return to her—she finds herself in a narrative as cyclically repetitive as Hightower's, yet the outcome is constant movement and the perpetual discovery of generosity in those around her. Lena Grove's wrong narrative distorts the present and the past, but—like fiction itself—it is unfalsifiable. Precisely because she is perceived to believe sincerely her own false story, those who encounter her help her on her way.

The vast majority of Faulkner's characters' narratives are tested by a different standard: whether they adequately take the perspectives of others into account. Hightower erases everyone in his life; Sutpen discounts anyone beyond his or her fitness or lack thereof for his design. Faulkner's novels are recurrently about the ways characters try (and often fail) to find large-scale frameworks for understanding the world, about the ways they think they've escaped history only to fall into it, about the ways the realist precision of the present gives way to generalities that can be either invidious delusions or moments of clarity. In other words, these are characters who fail or succeed on the adroitness with which they impose ways of seeing on reality—not by making their visions come true, but by developing narratives that do not require them to reflect the world for good outcomes to occur.

Joseph Urgo has proposed that in Faulkner there's an intimate link between narrative and capitalism: "Land becomes valuable only once it is invested with narrative significance, and someone who buys land buys a story as well—the story of the land's value, the promise it holds for habitation, cultivation, or re-sale. Narrative alone transforms land into property" ("Faulkner's Real Estate" 445). Faulkner's novels are contests of narrative—from Caddy's brothers' attempts to define her life in *The Sound and the Fury* to the intricate games of salesmanship and scamming that lead inexorably to Flem Snopes's rise in *The Hamlet*. If James's characters must figure out *what character are you?*, Faulkner's must confront *what story are you in?*

Urgo's argument dovetails neatly with Lauren Berlant's account of "cruel optimism" under contemporary capitalism, whereby "something you desire is actually an obstacle to your flourishing" (1). One of the most common types of narrative in Faulkner is precisely Berlant's cruel optimism—characters tell themselves a story about their own future success in which the means of success is the very thing that will destroy them. These are precisely the terms Faulkner uses in his interviews: *Absalom, Absalom!* is a "story of a man who wanted a son and got . . . so many that they destroyed him" (Gwynn and Blotner 71). The men of Frenchman's Bend in *The Hamlet* want the dream of heroic freedom represented by the wild "spotted horses" up for auction, but the horses will only destroy what they care about—and, in the end, are yet another means by which Flem Snopes will enrich himself. Stuck in an unjust social world, these characters lack the ability to change its terms (*The Hamlet*) or the capacity to see beyond them (*Absalom, Absalom!*).

Berlant ends by turning toward a more powerful, productive form of optimism, looking for ways that it might "be possible to imagine a potentialized present that does not reproduce all of the conventional collateral damage" (263). And the solution in Faulkner is not to refuse narrative. That's the way of Gail Hightower, of the world as one mythic day in which everything can only happen for and within an instant. Faulkner's unusual literary forms are often ways of dramatizing what happens when characters try to refuse narrative. Quentin Compson, for instance, finds that syntax itself breaks down when he seeks the "cool eternal dark" instead of the linear time represented by tolling bells:

> The first note sounded, measured and tranquil, serenely peremptory, emptying the unhurried silence for the next one and that's it if people could only change one another forever that way merge like a flame swirling up for an instant then blown cleanly out along the cool eternal dark instead

of lying there trying not to think of the swing until all the cedars came to have that vivid dead smell of perfume that Benjy hated so. (*Novels 1926–1929* 1012)

When a sentence in a Faulkner novel like this one ends halfway through, or when halves of two separate sentences run into one another, what happens? This sentence has a joint near the beginning: somewhere in the run of words "and that's it" one sentence becomes a different sentence. The piece before and the piece after the "that's it" each are coherent as possible parts of sentences (despite the missing punctuation in the second part), but they each seem incomplete when placed next to each other. When the reader of *The Sound and the Fury* encounters this sentence, near the climax of Quentin's section, he or she is already well used to grammatical oddities; in fact, the wholeness and punctuation of the first part of the sentence come as something of a surprise in context. This sentence is a good example of a typical Faulkner structure of break and juxtaposition—a calmly narrated present (in past tense) is interrupted by a confused rush of memory (in present tense). The intrusion of the past shows a lucidly clear present to hide a multitude of ambiguities, confusions, and traumas. Yet if Quentin seeks "eternal dark," the timeless is immediately replaced by a sequence of disparate moments in time and place, "lying there trying not to think . . ."

This interruption is also a continuation—a continuation of the thoughts of the previous paragraph, where, also without commas, Quentin imagines his grandfather conversing with death in the afterlife. "That's it," as we read it, isn't only an interruption of comfortable clarity; it is a revelation to Quentin— his image of his grandfather suddenly made more resonant by the way he connects it to his generalized longing for the "cool eternal dark." I argued in the last chapter that Conrad refused linear time in order to show the orders that could be made to appear when linear time is upset; here, Faulkner sets the grammatical, chronological notes marching, without urgency, in order, against the rushing process of thoughts that places many time periods next to one another in order to generate a moment of understanding: *that's it.* We read this chapter of *The Sound and the Fury* for growing understanding, in order to grasp Quentin's mind and life; at the same time, Quentin's own grasp seems to be slipping away, his moment of revelatory "that's it" a contingent wish, immediately changed to the "if only . . ." of his fantasized incest. The rushing movements of fragmentary thoughts in Faulkner are where the plot happens—where the explanations and ordering structures that readers seek appear. As with James, where the search for understanding is the major heroic undertaking of both the characters and the reader struggling through syntax, Quentin's search for some kind of stable formulation of his own desires and life is the reader's search as well.

I asked *what happens* in such a sentence, rather than *what does it mean*, because, just like Conrad's nonchronological narration, Faulkner's strange fragmentary structures mean things primarily through what they do—through the mental patterns they encourage in their readers—rather than what they are. A fragmentary sentence is not a representative example of the fragmentation of experience; it is an invitation to fill in the gaps, to see what isn't being said. It generates readerly desires, disappointments, and triumphs as much as it reflects those of Faulkner's characters. Yet these sentences have durational existence not only in the experience of one reader but also in the sequence of generations of readers who interact with them in turn. Faulkner, theorist of the future for his "printed books," represents the interlocking of these durations, the way authors' uses of the sequential form of the novel to create an individual reader's experience are also the means of ensuring the novel's own lasting presence. The techniques by which novelists generate readers' thought patterns in time are also the novelists' strategies for making their works relevant across time.

The Faulkner passage above is, among other things, about trying to reconcile the past and the present—about not just the way in which memories roil up and intrude, but also the way in which the complex variations and changes of life make impossible any form of eternal ideal. The "cool eternal dark"—a static eternity, associated with the lost delusions and horrors of antebellum southern society—and the "measured and tranquil" notes of the bell—impersonal, linear time—are equally insufficient ways of figuring experience, equally insufficient modes of imagining the passage of time, and each alike leaves Quentin unable to imagine a future.

The juncture between sentence halves, then, sets out a clash between two equally untenable alternatives. Yet the experience of the juncture for the reader is neither of these alternatives: for the reader, the process by which Quentin's mind interrupts itself creates not chaos but an order by which we come to understand, for instance, the way in which Quentin connects incest to the prospect of an ideal apotheosis. The fault lines of Quentin's uneasy mental movements reveal the tectonic shapes underlying them, and the movement of the novel is the slow outlining of these plates, of the network of associations and abstractions that connect the various themes of Compson experience. Time for the reader moves forward without being linear, and it aims toward future insight without positing eternity. In other words, the novel's response to the challenge of modernity—in this case, to Quentin's sense of an irreconcilable difference between past and present—is to restore continuity to time through retrospective analysis. The novel makes the present past (not just embraces the past as present), makes it distant enough to be clearly seen and analyzed. Sartre thought that Faulkner's temporal manipulations showed man as having no future: "Nothing happens, everything has happened" (227). In his view, Faulkner is too pessimistic, but his formula is an inversion of Faulkner's: for Faulkner, everything is still—and always—*happening*.[4] This can have elements of the fatalistic pessimism Sartre discerns, but it also provides a model for existence beyond immediate bodily life—for remaining present while absent, as Caddy Compson is to her brothers, and for remaining alive while dead, as Thomas Sutpen and his connections are to Quentin Compson. It's true that such presences can impede life in the moment—Quentin Compson is perhaps the clearest example—but they also provide troves of material for mental activity and organization of the kind that establishes one's own consciousness and life for Faulkner, in the same way others' personalities do in James. Peter Brooks says of *Absalom* that the narrative is "an enterprise apparently nostalgic, oriented towards the recovery of the past, yet really phatic in its vector, asking for hearing" (*Reading for the Plot* 312). The past is still happening—and narrating it is always part of negotiating relationships in the present. It is still happening *because* it is being narrated.

In what follows, I return to the two major themes of my previous chapters on James and Conrad—characterization and temporal dislocation—in order to argue that Faulkner's techniques, from local syntactical features to the broad patterns of narration, work to generate readers' desires for understanding and order; they seek to demonstrate not only the inevitable limitation of any particular order but the necessity for continuing to search for one. Faulkner, like Conrad and James, seeks to find his way back to modes of understanding that are under attack: the image of a coherent, vivid character; the possibility of the interpretation of underlying causes and the grander meanings of an event.[5] He breaks more sharply than either Conrad or James with traditional modes of representation; at the same time, he does so in order to represent personality as less fluid than James does and to use narration as a greater tool for authoritative communication than Conrad allows it to be. Faulkner's radicalization of literary forms is a way of demonstrating the force and use of our habit of interpreting other people as vivid whole personalities, and of enticing his readers to enter into the kind of analysis and interpretations his characters are constantly making—and to learn from their mistakes.

"The Homemade, the Experimental": Designing Narrative

This depiction of life—activity generated and defined by the story-forming capacities of oneself and others—is not, in Faulkner's work, a way of setting up an opposition between the unnarrated raw material of life and the layers of anticipation and interpretation formed on top of it, but a way of contrasting different types of narrative activity. Story-seeking and story-forming are inevitable; the question is how one goes about forming a story; and ultimately this is the type of question that sets Faulkner very much in line with the acts of selection and interpretation in James and Conrad. As in their work, the problem becomes how to select and order the most important of the materials in one's experience and consciousness, and like James and Conrad, Faulkner presents this activity as inevitable but risky: it is possible to choose the wrong materials to exclude, and be haunted later.

The acts of selection and exclusion these authors perform seem so potentially problematic for precisely the reasons Faulkner's novels foreground: characters persistently fail to fit members of marginalized groups into their narration. Sutpen's design makes no provision for a mixed-race wife; Quentin Compson cannot cope with the reality of his sister's life and sexuality because it upends his mental narrative of family honor and the existential significance he had founded on that narrative. But the point is not that all acts of exclusion are suspect, but that the only way to survive in Faulkner's world is to develop skill at sorting out the types of exclusion that will be useful—like Lena Grove's narrative—from those that are damaging and unstable.

Faulkner's revisions of the narrative of his own writing and career help bring into focus the revisions characters perform within the novels. His creative practice is full of interpretive anticipation and rewriting, of designs and their revision, that echo the concerns of his characters. Short stories become novels; novels gain new parts; novels' events are revisited in sequels years later. This circling, revising process is a habit not just in content and in publication history but on a syntactical level: Faulkner's hypotactic style is the means by which he conveys his commitment to interpretation.

In 1945, sixteen years after the publication of *The Sound and the Fury*, Faulkner added an appendix, "Compson: 1699–1945." Here he sets forth one more version of the Compson family story he had told so many times before. When he was asked to write a preface to the appendix, he constructed, in the third person, a theory of art:

> He still didn't know enough about people to finish out his own, and so the
> book was actually not unconsciously willful tour de force in obfuscation

but rather the homemade, the experimental, the first moving picture projector—warped lens, poor light, undependable mechanism and even a bad screen—which had to wait until 1946 for the lens to clear, the light to steady, the gears to run smooth. (Meriwether 183–184).

Trying to make light "steady" points to a key feature of both the appendix and the novel as a whole: the novel traces a movement from Benjy's extreme confusion to realist lucidity in the third-person section assigned to Dilsey. The appendix itself is stylistically obsessed with the shift from multiple alternate interpretations to a single, most likely interpretations. These patterns suggest that the *reduction* of confusion and the slow attempt to clear the lens of fiction is a central topic of Faulkner's fiction: never willing to present a perfect lens, he uses fictional representation to map out the modes by which people can cope with the warped and undependable mechanisms of perception and understanding—and to improve our use of them as much as possible.

Faulkner's appendix, for all its pragmatic origins, has an urgent energy about it. Modernism is full of paratextual provisions offered by authors to supplement reading practices—Eliot's *Waste Land* annotations, Joyce's schema of *Ulysses*. But where Eliot's response to a request for more material to fill up a book was essentially to mock the idea of annotating his poem, Faulkner's response to a request for a summary is to give himself another try at communicating his story. Eliot parodies annotations by glossing some allusions, often not the ones of greatest importance or difficulty. Faulkner's appendix has the form of a parody—of the idea of a character-list appendix—but it works by generating a sequence of stories that seem to overwhelm the form that contains them, that make the form more meaningful rather than undermining it.

This kind of sincere effort of comprehension struggling through complication is most clearly seen in the syntax of the appendix, which encapsulates the always-provisional mode of clarification endemic in Faulkner's work. Throughout the appendix, Faulkner uses correlative conjunctions to make his points: Quentin Compson's entry begins by saying that he "loved not his sister's body but some concept of Compson honor" (1131); his entry ends by informing us that he completes his year at Harvard before committing suicide "not because he had his old . . . grandfathers in him but because the remaining piece of the old Compson mile which had been sold to pay for his sister's wedding and his year at Harvard had been the one thing, excepting that same sister and the sight of an open fire, which his youngest brother, born an idiot, had loved" (1132). Faulkner's correlative conjunctions are acts of exclusion, picking one interpretation over another. They raise alternatives but always indicate an imminent rejection. The rejected alternatives here are more standard narratives: Quentin in love, Quentin faithful to familial sense of duty. The clauses that follow "but" tend to emphasize what is more specific and unusual: Quentin has a peculiar and obsessive conception of family honor; his loyalties are to his siblings rather than his ancestors.

Yet it is also clear that the two statements here, which begin and end Quentin's entry in the appendix, though not exactly contradictory, pull against one another. Quentin may not love his sister's body, but a form of individual sibling loyalty appears in the second of the two contrasts. He may love a concept of Compson honor, but not because he has much of the Compson family mindset that gives rise to the honor. The two "not . . . but . . ." statements interlock with one another, each hinting at the value of precisely what the other excludes. The statements do not actually contradict but rather refine and explicate one another: they are a model of how, when repeated, the act of exclusion can head off the problem of the return of the repressed that so consistently destroys his characters. While giving the syntactical sense of constantly getting closer to some form of truth, Faulkner shows that getting at a synthesized truth requires incorporation of the memory of the excluded factors.

A parallel process in the appendix is a similar yet opposite syntactical construction: "not only . . . but also . . ." If "not . . . but . . ." zooms in closer to the truth, "not only . . . but also . . ." is the equivalent of pulling back and revealing a wider set of alternatives. At the same time, the shared periodicity of the structure—in both cases, the initial conjunction lets us know what the second half of the sentence will do—makes both constructions ways of substantiating authority, of demonstrating speakerly knowledge. Caddy loved "her brother despite him, loved not only him but loved in him that bitter prophet and inflexible corruptless judge" (1132). Although the semantics of this are opposite to the "not . . . but . . ." examples, they ultimately give a very similar impression: the "but also" clause comes to seem like the most important aspect of the phrase, reproducing the impression of focusing in on a particular point. It may have an element of zooming out, but it is the kind of broader view that reveals a menacing shadow in the corner of the frame. What these phrases do is reshape *emphasis*: they are ultimately less about what is in and out of the frame than what is in focus within it. Christopher Ricks says of a line of Tennyson's poetry, "You cannot employ the English language to say 'Nor winks the gold fin in the porphyry font' without our glimpsing—through the interstices of the negative—the winking fin" (*Tennyson* 192). Similarly, you cannot write that Quentin "loved not his sister's body" without raising the possibility of the breaking of the incest taboo: what the appendix claims, ultimately, is not that seeing some form of incestuous connection in Quentin's psyche is false, but that within the complex network of Quentin's feelings about Caddy's sexuality direct incestuous desire is not the most important one—not the key explanatory factor with which to conclude his brief entry in an appendix, though important enough to lead it off. These syntactical constructions create a process by which all the alternatives are made present and put into orders of greater or lesser importance.

This is the internal logic by which interpretations appear in the appendix itself, and not exactly the same as the relation between the interpretations of the appendix and those of the novel on its own. The appendix has an ambiguous scholarly status, missing from many current editions of the novel, and often derided as a kind of reader's aid written for commercial purposes on Faulkner's part.[6] Philip Cohen, for instance, even while arguing for its importance, describes it as having "simplified and sanitized" both Benjy's character and the "complex and innovative" version of Quentin in the original novel, about whom the appendix "does not do justice to the richness of his earlier characterization" (246, 247). The successively clearer parts of the novel itself must be charged with a similar simplifying power. I have no wish to argue that the appendix presents a *more* complex version of Quentin than the novel, but I wish to make two claims in defense of its literary consonance with the original: first, that its explanatory qualities merely continue the trend traced from Benjy to the third-person narrator of the final section of the novel; and second, that the means by which it portrays characters as less complex than they are in the novel (probably inevitable, due to its brevity) is itself a complex process, one that foregrounds, acknowledges, and defends its own acts of exclusion.[7] On the issue of Quentin, Cohen discusses the "not his sister's body" line I have analyzed already in order to argue that the appendix suppresses the incestuous undertones of Quentin's psychology (246–247). It is not that the appendix eradicates the incestuousness but that it represents a different balancing of the elements of the novel. The novel of 1929 and the appendix do not, for the most part, present fundamentally incompatible stories; the appendix, however, does continue the trend—evident in the movement from Benjy, to Quentin, to Jason, to third person—toward an ever more stable equilibrium between alternative interpretations.

In the first chapter, I suggested that the second part of *The Sound and the Fury* represents the failure of Quentin Compson to respond to the voices invading his mind: Caddy's, his father's. The problem goes beyond the particular voice of pessimistic abstraction associated with Conrad—it is that Quentin's mind, in this novel, does not have the capacity to make narrative out of his life. "It's nature is hurting you not Caddy and I said That's just words and he said So is virginity and I said you dont know. You cant know and he said Yes" (965–966). When the elder Compson says that virginity is "just words," Quentin's fallback response is a relativistic distinction between his perspective and his father's—essentially, saying that his father doesn't understand him. When his father responds "Yes," what he means is that the state of not-knowing, of unknowability, is the whole point. Quentin's father converts pessimistic skepticism into a philosophy, into an ordering principle that he can use to understand almost any statement: it is similar to the later moment in *Absalom, Absalom!* where his response to Quentin's statement that he could make out an old letter without moving inside was to say, "Perhaps you are right . . . Maybe even the light of day . . . would be too much for . . . them" (73–74). His assertions of gulfs blocking communication can answer almost anything Quentin says, whereas for Quentin uncertainty does not rise to the level of abstract ordering principle. Quentin dies before his father, is unable to find a comparatively stable mental state, precisely because he views his father's philosophy as destructive, as disabling of response rather than enabling of it.

The trend toward explanation, the slow development from the world of Benjy, with almost no analytical capacity and very little sense of narrative, through Quentin's failed attempt to synthesize his life into a narrative, all the way to the appendix with its presentation of a historical story of southern decline, shows the way in which the novel plays with the possibilities of narrativization: the novel is not only concerned to represent complex people but also to explore what can be achieved by simplifying and trying to explain. Faulkner's explanation of the change in tone—his claim that the original was "not unconsciously willful tour de force in obfuscation but rather the homemade, the experimental"—chimes with a recurrent theme of his descriptions of his work. The differing interpretations offered by the different stages of the text are mapped onto a process of apprenticeship, of gaining writerly skill and human wisdom.

Faulkner liked to talk about his own ineptitude as an author, using lack of skill as a metric not just for his own career but for that of the writers he most admired. In 1957, asked about similarities between his works and Conrad's, and "Conrad's effort to surround an event by throwing light on it from past and future as well as present," he offered the answer:

> I'm inclined to think that all writers do that, only most of them, except Conrad and me, may be a little more clever about it. Probably Conrad was because he deliberately taught himself a foreign language to write in. And

mine may be because I never went to school enough to save myself the shortcuts of learning English. That we both are a little more obvious than the others for that reason. (*Faulkner in the University* 142)

Such responses, in Faulkner's interviews, have many sources: in part he may have been trying to avoid answering a question about which nothing immediately occurred to him to say; in part he enjoyed presenting himself as the folksy backwoods storyteller. In this particular case, the answer has the strong tone of a dodge—in the recording, he pauses for an unnerving period over the word *never*, which he actually repeats ("English Department Faculty and Wives"). Faulkner was invested in the myth of his own virtuosity, but also his haphazardness; he may have been fond of describing *As I Lay Dying* as a tour de force, but he also claimed that the four parts of *The Sound and the Fury* were necessary because the first three couldn't get the story, or the character of Caddy, right.[8] His idea that Benjy's section might be printed in multiple colors, along with his fatalistic sense that publishing couldn't fulfill his dream, is a good example: he was merely picking among possible shortcuts to indicate time. Faulkner presents writing as an act intrinsically full of complexities that good writing makes appear simple; at the same time, he never makes it appear simple himself.

He also often criticizes other writers who *lack* the features of apparent ineptitude. Joyce was a case of "a genius who was electrocuted by the divine fire" (*Faulkner in the University* 53): raw talent—"more talent than he could control" (280)—has its own disadvantages. Meanwhile, Hemingway "has no courage, has never climbed out on a limb."[9] He does not, in other words, seek out writerly tasks of great peril and difficulty. For Faulkner, writing good novels was an act of risk and of potential failure. Whereas James traces in his career a trajectory in which certain themes and techniques become ever more fully developed and expertly deployed, and Conrad shuffles a repertory of devices in different combinations (embedded narrators, omniscient narrators, heavily ironic narrators, achronology), Faulkner's great works seem to start afresh each time: *Absalom, Absalom!*'s lack of differentiation between the styles of different speakers and the narrator is utterly unlike *As I Lay Dying* and *The Sound and the Fury*; *As I Lay Dying* is an oasis of relatively linear chronology amid novels constituted by disordered drifts of time. James and Conrad take the techniques they already have and try to do more with them; Faulkner puts his down and tries new ones.

From the perspective of readers of Faulkner's fiction, it is hard to imagine that making his temporal strangeness less "obvious" was ever a guiding principle of his work. Faulkner's works seem to flaunt the strangeness and obscurity of their construction. Many old and new treatments of Faulkner's form agree that the primary function of the style is as an impediment to communication, a way of foregrounding its impossibility: Faulkner makes communication difficult because crossing the boundaries between minds is essentially impossible; his style, in this reading, is a constant warning about the limitations and partiality of our knowledge of others.[10] I want to introduce the paradigm of ineptitude and skill to this discussion: rather than viewing communication as a strictly epistemological issue—what people can make others know—it is a question of trying, and failing, and trying again, to communicate. In other words, Faulkner is neither failing to communicate nor presenting failure as the most important aspect of communicative attempts: he is enquiring into the skills it takes to communicate as much as possible—and to receive communication.

Shreve's comment about what "has to be" is as bracketed as Sutpen's story, and bracketed by acts of communication: on the one hand, it comes from someone else—"Because listen. What was it the old dame, the Aunt Rosa, told you . . ." (266)—and on the other, it is being told back as a tool for persuasion. Rosa told this to Quentin, who told it to Shreve, who is telling it back to Quentin. Interpretation happens in transfers—transfers from past to present, from one person to another. Interpretation is what Faulkner's characters communicate.

The laboratory of his fiction produces not just a set of experiments proving the hypothesis that fully expressing a coherent thought to another is impossible; it examines the ways in which vivid images can suddenly communicate themselves, the way coherence itself is a cause for shock. A good example is the way single phrases impress themselves upon Quentin's mind in *The Sound and the Fury*: his father's "*Harvard my boy*"; Caddy's "*poor Quentin.*" The world is full of communication; the problem is not to be drowned by it. Like Henry James's characters at sea amid the influences of strong personalities, Faulkner's characters face a world where uncertainty, ambiguity, and discontinuity arise out of the strong connections between people, rather than, as in Conrad's works, their isolation.

Faulkner's interest in striving for clarity and explanation is the other side of ineptitude. The world seems full of strange elements that demand the novelist develop new and different ways of making the reader see the story; Faulkner's discussion of ineptitude is a way of acknowledging the challenges presented by modernity to the artist. Forging communicative connections between characters is not difficult—what is difficult is making that communication bear the weight of the "old verities" Faulkner sought to represent in fiction. Faulkner, even more than the authors I have already discussed, has been read for his representational skills—and by this I refer not only to his realist presentation of action and character, but also to his structures of symbolism and metaphor, the ways one thing in his novels can represent another.[11] Close readings of Faulkner tend to focus on what imagery and symbolic figures *mean*, whether in theoretical or historical terms, rather than how they create experiences for the reader. Readings of Faulkner's syntax and narrative structures similarly see the discontinuities and fragments as representing, standing in for, or reflecting various sorts of breakdown—of Enlightenment forms of knowledge, of the possibility of communication, or of southern racist culture. However, if we read these not for their static form but for the sequential experience they generate, a different picture emerges: rather than a broken sentence representing a break, a broken sentence incites an attempt to connect. The ellipses and confusions of communicative processes open up the space for the next narrator, or for the reader, to come in and bridge the gap. The experience of reading Faulkner is of constant revisions, both to what we know and to what we want to find out: the characters whose narratives can succeed are those who, unlike Hightower, develop narratives flexible enough to encompass the sudden eruption of new characters and new events.

How Not to Be a Hero: Absalom, Absalom!

Absalom, Absalom! (1936) is full of distance and sudden closeness. Characters find themselves unstably ricocheting between past and present, between the specific and the abstract, between immediate impressions and irremediable absences; abstractions appear from nowhere and narratives are upended in instants. Yet it is also a novel obsessed with apparently inevitable stories, with the foreordained reversals of fortune in classical genres like tragedy. As in James, Faulkner's novels associate the heroic dimensions of older genres with characters' abilities to make sense of their lives.

Thomas Sutpen's attempt to narrativize his life—to found his own wealthy plantation dynasty—fails catastrophically, damaging him, his family, and anyone else who happens to interact with them. In this sense, it might seem that Sutpen is an object lesson in the dangers of attempting to impose a pattern on the recalcitrantly various material of one's life. But Sutpen is not the only one attempting to impose a pattern on his life: Quentin Compson, like all the other narrators, is engaged in understanding the puzzle of his actions. And the reader is offered Faulkner's juxtaposition of all those narrators attempting to understand.

The novel, then, offers a profusion of different kinds of design for the reader to evaluate. At the same time, it never allows its readers a conclusive final pattern that satisfies everything, foregrounding instead the pattern-making impulse itself.

Yet in all cases, this impulse relies on a particular premise: that Thomas Sutpen is an interesting character, or at least that his story is in some way significant. Otherwise, why would all these attempts to understand his life story be worth the effort?

On a syntactical level, Faulkner allies the reader with his characters' search for understanding. Early in *Absalom, Absalom!*, Quentin Compson listens to Rosa Coldfield, who has summoned him to hear the history of long-dead Thomas Sutpen. This paragraph follows a lengthy parenthesis containing a speech from Quentin's father setting out a convoluted family history that might explain Rosa's desire to speak to him:

> Whatever her reason for choosing him, whether it was that or not, the getting to it, Quentin thought, was taking a long time. Meanwhile, as though in inverse ratio to the vanishing voice, the invoked ghost of the man whom she could neither forgive nor revenge herself upon began to assume a quality almost of solidity, permanence. (10)

The style of this passage teaches us what kind of explanations for the mysteries of this novel we should seek. By the end of the preceding parenthesis, so many baroque details had been mentioned that the opening drop into colloquial language, "Whatever her reason," is a welcome reminder of what the occasion for the parenthesis actually was. It signals that there is a through-thread to this story: a reason for its digressions and a continuous motion forward. More distantly, the reference to the "vanishing voice" calls back the first description of Rosa—"Her voice would not cease, it would just vanish" (5)—an image that, at the time, seemed to imply Quentin's loss of concentration on the story. Now it becomes clear that while the voice may vanish, the material it conveys—Thomas Sutpen—is becoming even more vivid. These sentences are signals of increasing clarity and continuity: we may not know everything, but patterns are forming.[12]

The reading experience consists of not only the order in which we encounter content but also the syntax's effect upon our ability to understand it. Faulkner's style is difficult precisely because it constantly pulls its reader forward. These sentences may contain phrases connecting back to earlier moments, but they also distribute their meaning asymmetrically: more information is available in the second half of each sentence than the first. Subordinate clauses appear before subjects and main verbs. This asymmetry—the periodic syntax—presses the reader again and again through a process of confusion transformed into order, of miscellaneous clauses set into their right places by a verb. *Meanwhile* something is happening, something *as though* connected to the vanishing voice—but what? Reading along the length of a Faulkner sentence like this one involves the reader in a continuous attempt at sense-making—we read in search of an explanation that always seems just about to arrive. When, at the end of the sentence, the figure of Thomas Sutpen begins to appear to Quentin, it is not just fascinating to him; it is also the solution to the reader's syntactical woes. Sutpen becomes a source of explanation and meaning—both in the syntax and in the plot.

Faulkner's sentences are not a rebuke to our desire for plot and character, but a means of heightening our investment in the story and training us to figure out whatever we can—however contingent and partial our knowledge must be. As much as we might critique the grandiosity of its characters, the novel forces us to partake of the fascination they exert in order to understand it on a line-by-line level. Viewing the sentences spatially, as static forms, we discern involute impediments to knowledge. If we view them instead as scripts for specific readerly mental activity in time, they become a way of training the reader into desire for and expectation of a particular kind of understanding.

Critical readings of the structure of this novel have tended to argue that the embedded narrators represent the impossibility of truly knowing Sutpen's story, associating this novelistic structure with doubt and skepticism.[13] Yet the credulous excitement with which the first-time reader can puzzle out the lineaments of Sutpen's character and story is not an error to be dispelled with rereading; it reasserts itself when the text is examined more closely. Rather than undermining the reader's desire to make sense of events, Faulkner uses that desire to instill in his readers a particular attitude toward his characters and their narratives.

This kind of reading—reading to recapture the effect of a first-time reader's helplessness before the sentence and plot—changes how we understand the novel. It is not just that knowing how the story ends makes us feel more distant and less invested in the story and the character; it is that knowing the answers to all these questions makes it more difficult to see the methods by which Faulkner ensures that the first-time reader will be interested. Under such circumstances, it becomes easy to see Sutpen's story, and Quentin's, as *only* critiques—of idealizing narratives of heroic tragedy, of the possibility of full knowledge. On rereading, rather than experience the process of investment in and alteration of our understanding of the plot, we risk focusing more on the gap between Quentin's or Rosa's early views and the later knowledge that we have. Attending to the stylistic features of first reading, we can see that this modernist innovation, far from rejecting or undermining the pleasures of plot or narratives of heroism, is designed to preserve it.[14]

In cases like this one, modernist fiction's simultaneous allusion to and critique of potentially overidealizing genres—dynastic revenge tragedy in *Absalom,*

Absalom! or, for instance, adventure literature in *Lord Jim*—becomes especially slippery.[15] A first reader of each of these novels partakes of the thrills and investments of these genres; on a second reading, often only the critique of genre convention is visible.[16] Even as reader-centric a critic as Wolfgang Iser tends to see the critique first. He sees modernist technique primarily as reproaching its readers' presuppositions, describing Faulkner's form in *The Sound and the Fury* as forcing the reader constantly to form and then abandon expectations of where understanding will be found, ultimately bringing home to the reader "the senselessness of life" (219–221). But a certain degree of contemplative distance is necessary to form the kinds of expectations Iser discusses (for instance, that the missing element in Quentin's chapter is "action"). The syntactical difficulty together with the complex time schemes often works precisely to prevent such distanced perception.

One later reader who felt that intense involvement was Toni Morrison, whose take on Quentin is that, paradoxically, he never let the Sutpens become more than relics of the past, never let them be quite magnetic *enough* to him: "They are ghosts and he has no feeling of affinity for them." Quentin, she says, "lacks human sympathy" (Wofford 28, 29), and this absence dooms him, leaves him bereft of anything but abstract ideals. The theme of the too-cold, uninvolved narrator shows up in Morrison's own work: the narrator of the last section of her novel *Jazz* says of the story that has just passed, "I missed the people altogether" (220). Morrison's reading of *Absalom, Absalom!* centers on reader involvement and expectations: she describes, for instance, how "as a reader you have been forced to hunt for a drop of black blood that means everything and nothing" (*Conversations* 74). The formal achievement of the book, in her reading, is in the ways it directs your attention and curiosity over time.

The novel deploys all this magnetism in order to cast a peculiar form of irony against Sutpen's design. Sutpen's horrific amorality arises from the limitation of his aspirations, from his inability to see a dream beyond that of his social worlds. He apparently patterns his entire life's hope on one rich man who insulted him as a child—deciding not to overturn the society that exploits him but to join it. Tragedy takes the form of the self-limitation of characters' aspirations; the tragedy of Sutpen is not just that he did terrible things, but that all that demonic energy was *wasted*. The best dream he and his world can imagine is too small—like Quentin's inability to find meaning in life in any other form besides that of the family honor resting on his sister's virginity.

This type of plot is even clearer in *The Known World*, by Edward P. Jones, one of Faulkner's many literary descendants, where the son of a freed slave seeks to rise by becoming, himself, a slave-owner. This plot line is not a strictly modern invention, but it is distinct from classic nineteenth-century patterns of social aspiration, such as *Vanity Fair*, where irony against Becky is not intrinsic to the position to which she aspires but associated with the means she employs to get there, or *Great Expectations*, where aspiration itself seems morally suspect. In Jones and in Faulkner, the irony against the aspiring figure is that by subscribing to the oppressive structures of his society, he not only will fail but turns out not to have aspired *enough*, to imagine another way of being. As Ramón Saldívar points out, Faulkner's work goes out of its way to suggest paradigms from other countries that offer alternatives to southern racial codes (8–9).

The lesson here is not that Sutpen is wrong to try to aspire, to make meaning from his life; it is that he is absurd to import his narrative design wholesale from specific and local social standards by which the presence of racial difference in his wife—even if known only to him—would destroy his design. He fears that such an act would be a "mockery and a betrayal of that little boy who approached that door fifty years ago" (226). There is no intrinsic reason that this should be so—that the little boy fifty years before should need a success exactly in the reverse image of his original trauma. Faulkner presents Sutpen's desire on this point as a crucial flaw in his character, as a disappointment.[17] As in James, it is dangerous—and deflating of heroic scale—to reflect society in one's own identity.[18] Lena's narrative in *Light in August* seems to generate a better outcome for her life, where Sutpen's seems only to damage his, precisely because hers does not need to come true: she only needs to use it as a mode of self-presentation that will gain sympathy from the people she encounters. Sutpen finds the "lie" of whiteness too intolerable; Lena believes in what is obviously untrue but is in fact a better, less venial world—and this belief helps bring into being better actions on the part of those around her, even if it will never change Lucas Burch. The most important aspect of the narrative is perfectly within her control: she is sincerely searching for the father of her child. Sutpen, on the other hand, needs factors beyond his control—other people and the happenstances of biological sex and imaginary race—to align.

Faulkner wants the novel to have its heroism and to criticize it too, to explore the glitter and grandeur of a superhuman character while showing its danger. The question raised by this structure is whether any better ends are imaginable in Faulkner's world. The end that most often seems to succeed is narration—characters either gaining knowledge and the ability to grasp those around them, or becoming parts of others' narration. The end of Lena Grove's story is narrated by someone she met only for a few days who doesn't even know her name. Quentin in *Absalom, Absalom!* is both audience and confident recreator of Sutpen's life. What characters *can* safely aspire to, in Faulkner's world, is knowledge, the ability to narrate a story—and, perhaps, to learn by doing so what story they are themselves in. This never leads to a final understanding, but Faulkner's desire to represent the possibility of truth leads to his endless deferral down the chain of storytelling: truth, like a narratively perfect life, can exist only as an absent object, but the contagious effects of the search for it testify to its possibility. The distance crucial to Faulkner's method is not an instance of deliberately holding subjects at arm's length. It arises because, despite the most heroic of efforts, those subjects never can be reached. Quentin and Shreve have no qualms about narrativizing Sutpen's life, and they need none because no matter how bold their explanation, it will always be partial.

How Not to Be a Minor Character: The Hamlet

In 1958, Faulkner's *The Hamlet* (1940) became a movie—in a manner of speaking. The title is *The Long, Hot Summer*, which is the title of one section of the novel. Familiar names from the novel appear—Varner, Quick, Littlejohn, Eula, Jody. So do familiar plot points: buried treasure that turns out to be planted, a wild horse auction, an interloper taking over a family business, a familial history of barn burning. The plot points, however, are all displaced onto characters who are themselves amalgams of figures in the original: the victim of the buried treasure plot is Jody, not Ratliff, Armstid, and Bookwright; the interloper is named Quick rather than Snopes. Perhaps the most crucial difference is that there is not a Snopes in sight. *The Hamlet* is today thought of as the first work in the "Snopes Trilogy" (followed by *The Town* and *The Mansion*), which narrate the rise of the ruthless Snopes family—led by Flem Snopes, a boy at the start of *The Hamlet*—from tenant farmers to positions of power and prominence all over Jefferson. Yet the movie cuts the Snopeses out entirely. Rather than the structure of the novel—where entirely separate plot lines are strung together on Flem Snopes's story like gaudy beads on a thread scarcely visible between them—the movie mixes the stories together into one narrative of a summer of desire and greed in a small town.

The movie, I'd argue, *has* to eliminate the main story of the novel (the arrival and rise of the Snopeses) in order to make a coherent narrative of *The Hamlet*. Many film adaptations combine or eliminate a novel's profusion of minor characters to suit a film's length; here, the minor characters survive and the protagonist disappears into them. In the novel, the Snopeses make up the only constant element in a wildly disparate array of short stories, many of which focus on different groups of characters that do not reappear in other parts of the novel. For instance, in book 2 of the novel, the first chapter is concerned primarily with the schoolteacher Labove and his education. When he returns to town to become the local teacher, he becomes infatuated with Eula Varner. Her sexual development becomes the plot line picked up in the next section, describing her many suitors, and ultimately winding its way back to Snopes when she becomes pregnant by another man and Flem's willingness to marry her further enriches him. The movie's drastic alterations indicate the fragility of the coherence of this novel—the sense that it scarcely takes shape as a single narrative, and that Flem is a peculiarly thin thread of a protagonist. Though nearly every critical treatment of *The Hamlet*—including my own—focuses on Flem Snopes or the Snopes family, Flem's absence from *The Hamlet* is very different, and in some ways much more total, than those of Faulkner's other absent centers. It is almost impossible to construct a coherent narrative focusing on Flem's predatory rise because the rise itself is predicated on the way the society of the novel fails to see and understand it as a coherent narrative.[19]

Caddy's physical absence is a defining feature of her role in *The Sound and the Fury* and of her relationship to other characters. By contrast, Flem Snopes's physical presence in *The Hamlet* is continually mentioned—he is always behind the counter at Will Varner's store, described primarily in terms of his physical features and accessories: "the straw bag, the minute tie, the constant jaw" (870). Unlike Sutpen, he steps into the present-tense scene of the novel, his actions narrated by a third-person narrator rather than through the remove of multiple embedded narrators. Yet Flem *is* an absence—a mysterious being whose interiority is never suggested and scarcely speculated about. If *Absalom, Absalom!* dramatizes the compulsion to explain lives, to see Thomas Sutpen at a distance in order both to acknowledge his particularized inscrutability and to apply a universal narrative to him, *The Hamlet* demonstrates how the short-circuiting of that compulsion can allow Flem to exploit the people around him. Absence, obscurity, and ambiguity are not an authorial mode of representing the uncertainty of life; in this novel, they are Flem Snopes's strategy for gaining control of those around him.

The Hamlet, in other words, adopts a narrative strategy opposite to that of *Absalom, Absalom!* Here, characters do not seek out narratives bridging local life with grandiose themes; instead; they ostentatiously fail to do so, fail to see the larger patterns of their lives, and their mistake is disastrous for themselves and for their community. Particularly, they fail to construct narratives around Flem Snopes: they miss the scale of his ambition and insist instead on seeing him in localized terms, in relation to themselves and their interests. Rather than *Absalom*'s strategy of enlisting the reader's excitement in characters' attempts to develop narrative patterns, *The Hamlet* works by generating ever-increasing unease over the limitations of the characters' narratives.

The last section of *The Hamlet* is titled "The Peasants" and opens with the story of the auction of the "spotted horses" arriving in Frenchman's Bend from Texas at the same time as Flem Snopes's return. The men watch the wild and untamable horses the evening before the auction:

> "He aint said they was his yet," Quick said.
> "He aint said they aint neither," Freeman said.

The men see the horses at first in terms of whether or not they belong to Flem; not knowing for certain allows room to change the narrative. Even Ratliff, usually quick to blame Flem, acquiesces, responding:

> "I see," Ratliff said. "That's what you are holding back on. Until he tells you whether they are his or not." (988)

Ratliff implies that whether or not the others buy the horses should not have anything to do with whether or not the horses belong to Flem, an unusual indifference, since throughout the novel he is usually careful to detect any connection to Snopes in the dealings of the community. The departure from his usual habit turns out to be a mistake: it lets in a discussion of how Anse McCallum brought a similar team of horses back from Texas and they were useful. Ratliff's commonsensical approach—consider that those horses, which, at this moment in the plot, are running around so wildly that they crash into the sides of their pen, are clearly useless to you; therefore it makes no sense to purchase them—puts the problem in personal, immediate terms that, paradoxically, allow Flem to benefit.

In fact, after they buy the horses, which, inevitably, escape and cause widespread damage, the members of the community are prevented from getting satisfaction precisely because they failed to see that these horses aren't just any wild horses, but Flem's. It is ambiguity about the ownership that allows the Texan auctioneer, who is ostensibly in charge of them, to feel guiltless about some of his sales techniques, thinking that the buyers will be able to get justice from Flem later. It is because the men try to see the narrative with reference to themselves— whether or not the horses will be useful to them—that they are swindled and injured. Henry Armstid's horse is the prime example: he attempts to bid, and his wife chides the Texan for taking the money she has earned. Not wanting to make a scene—Armstid is fiercely insistent that no one can stop him from buying the horse—the Texan tells Armstid's wife to retrieve her money from Flem later. It is precisely because people suspect but don't know Flem's involvement that Flem is insulated from the consequences of his actions: Armstid's wife is unable to sue him for the money the Texan promised.

Ambiguity, in other words, becomes the weapon of Flem's predations and exacerbates the vulnerability of his victims. Because they let the ambiguity lie without trying to resolve it, they are left with no recourse after the disastrous attempt to catch the horses. Flem's inscrutability—he is depicted through a flat affect and a collection of tics—and his resistance to being the kind of object of analysis that Sutpen is, becomes the source of his power and a demonstration of the limitations of a particularist view of events. The other characters participate in large narratives they do not understand—and they get wrong the local narratives they think they're in. The transactions that are the recurring features of *The Hamlet* are contests of narrative—about what benefit will come from a horse, or what history a house might have that makes it valuable.[20] The final contest of the novel— where Ratliff is fooled by Flem—involves the intersection of Ratliff's assumptions about Flem's narrative, local lore, and Flem's active creation of a narrative to manipulate others.

The men who lose narrative contests to Flem are rounder characters than he is—we see them more fully; their passions and their feelings are both clearer and more complex. Like the Victorian works Alex Woloch examines, *The Hamlet* uses the distinctions between major and minor characters to negotiate problems of economic and social power. But rather than the Dickensian problem of a protagonist losing vividness because of his complexity, surrounded by supporting characters who lack complex interior life, we are given here the form of a supporting character as our protagonist and the form of a protagonist in all the supporting characters. Flem *must* be complex; he cannot be nothing but the clean shirts and chewing jaw that characterize him. But they are all we have, and, just as a Dickensian minor character would, Flem stays in the background of the novel.

Where James attempts to balance the disparities between major and minor characters through the narrative work performed by his focalizing consciousnesses, Faulkner highlights the disparities and the confusions of narrative. Faulkner's reversal of the paradigm Woloch illuminates reflects a typically modernist variation on these dynamics: Faulkner uses the interaction between character and narrative form to generate the reader's concern with Flem's rise—to make the reader construct the narrative the characters are missing. Woloch's "narrative asymmetry" is defined as "narrative subordination of potentially full human beings" (44): here, it is the minor characters who *are* full human beings, who are granted a sympathetic and complex interiority. The fact that the novel is structured as a sequence of short stories works to make a relatively generous argument for the minor characters, whose interiority is more sympathetically visible to us as "potentially full" than is Flem's; we can see, from their perspective, how they are not merely minor characters in a novel but protagonists of short stories. Houston, for instance, a relatively wealthy farmer, has a complex backstory of romantic tragedy, and the story of his past is narrated just in time to tell the moment of his murder (922–933). All these characters are the heroes of their own lives, for a time; major characters for the length of a short story, if not of a novel.

What this novel then demonstrates is the limitation of a particular kind of interiority and roundness as a model for being a protagonist and center of attention in a novel; if James ingeniously reconciled the two, Faulkner pushes the paradox to its limits. Where Woloch's work assumes that all characters implicitly aspire to be round and to be protagonists, that to be otherwise is a loss, Flem's power is in this respect similar to the fascination the Sutpens exert over the Compson family: "simpler and therefore . . . more heroic" (74). Flem refuses existence beyond the collection of familiar and consistent features, like the constantly chewing jaw. He also, however, fills no standard model for the simple and consistent protagonist: he is neither a romantic idealist (like Ike Snopes) nor a cynically insightful storyteller (like Ratliff). The template he adopts so perfectly in his public interactions—the stickler-for-rules store clerk—doesn't seem to be likely to produce the narrative of his rise.

Flem's absent, incomprehensible interiority is the organizing principle holding the novel's many vignettes together. And it is because the other characters give up on or are bad readers of his interiority that he is able to beat them. But it is also important that Flem's rise is dependent less on any particular skill as a manipulator or reader of others than on his perfect ability to embody his own character. His victory is as much a product of his absolute consistency in his own character as anything else—in the incident of the spotted horses, he merely stands by silently during the auction and afterward refuses to admit that he had any part in the whole affair. The other characters, in other words, lose because they believe that Flem is more complicated or less consistent than he is. Ratliff has it right when he generalizes to a single law of interaction: "I'd just as soon buy a tiger or a rattlesnake [as one of the horses]. And if Flem Snopes offered me either one of them, I would be afraid to touch it for fear it would turn out to be a painted dog or a piece of garden hose" (990–991). The rule, quite simply, is never to trust Flem (or any Snopes), because he will come out ahead in any bargain. And, as Ratliff will discover by the end of the novel, this simplified view of their world would be much more helpful to the residents of Frenchman's Bend than the localized complexities they tend to look for. The other characters don't need to discover complexity in Flem's character to win; they merely need to understand his absolutely consistent role in the narrative.

The novel is a demonstration of the importance of skilled reading of the world as on some level ordered. Flem's rise is a kind of constant law of the universe of the novel. The other characters think they are subject to the same narrative laws as Flem; in fact they are as condemned to minor status as any Dickens character. The spotted horses spur the characters' attempts at miniature narratives, not just about the horses' potential use as work animals, but as a kind of larger dream of expansive freedom. One of the horses "seemed not to gallop but to flow, bodiless, without dimension. Yet there was the rapid light beat of hard hooves on the packed earth" (988). The horses represent to the men the dream of a connection between earth and the unearthly, the alluring hope of intangible grandeur on one's own soil—a classic object of cruelly optimistic desire, destined for "collateral damage." This passage—one of many similar passages describing the horses—represents a note only sounded in the novel version of the story; the original short story, narrated by Ratliff, makes the focus on Flem much clearer. "Yes, sir. Flem Snopes has filled that whole country full of spotted horses," the story begins; the next paragraph opens with a sentence fragment: "That Flem Snopes" (*Uncollected Stories* 165). The introduction of the omniscient narrator in the novel version engages the narrative in Flem's tactics, causes the novel, on some level, to contribute to his schemes. For instance, after the exchange where Ratliff ridicules the men's obsession with who owns the horses ("That's what you are holding back on"), the men agree on the unreliability of Snopeses.

> "That's a fact," Ratliff said. "A fellow can dodge a Snopes if he just starts lively enough. In fact, I dont believe he would have to pass more than two folks before he would have another victim intervened betwixt them. You folks aint going to buy them things sho enough, are you?" Nobody answered. They sat on the steps, their backs against the veranda posts, or on the railing itself. Only Ratliff and Quick sat in chairs, so that to them the others were black silhouettes against the dreaming lambence of the moonlight beyond the veranda. The pear tree across the road opposite was now in full and frosty bloom, the twigs and branches springing not outward from the limbs but standing motionless and perpendicular above the horizontal boughs like the separate and upstreaming hair of a drowned woman sleeping upon the uttermost floor of the windless and tideless sea.
>
> "Anse McCallum brought two of them horses back from Texas once," one of the men on the steps said. He did not move to speak. He was not speaking to anyone. "It was a good team. A little light. He worked it for ten years. Light work, it was." (988–989)

The reiteration of the simplifying rule about Snopeses introduces a pause. The passage that follows feels out of place—and its strangeness is part of the point. A classic epic simile takes a moment in the plot—legions of devils lying on the burning lake in *Paradise Lost*, for instance—and compares it to something apparently quite distant, before expanding the context of the comparison in ways that far exceed the original: autumn leaves, seaweed, armies drowned by the ocean (I.301–313). Faulkner's simile is strange not just because of the expansiveness of its simile, but because it has such an absurdly small excuse in the outer plot—that pear tree has never been mentioned before; none of the men actually seems to be looking at it. It is a simile made almost as a purely rhythmical gesture from the narrator, inserting a break in the narrative all the more forceful for the great distance it takes us from landlocked Frenchman's Bend.[21]

Yet in that pause, something important and entirely unstated happens: the men shift the conversation from Flem Snopes and dealing with Snopeses to the possible merits of the horses (Anse McCallum's team); the local narrative takes over. Like the unearthly horses, the narrator's lyrical interludes provide occasion for the interpolation of narratives in which they are the immediate heroes. Ratliff's form of the Snopes rule, always a last word, creates pauses that men fill with other narratives; they cannot answer him directly. The digression on the pear tree makes no sense if we think of it as representing anything in particular—it is probably not in the thoughts of the characters—but it succeeds in setting the reader's mind to the same epic expansiveness that lurks beneath the men's talk. The narrator's intrusions from a higher register set up, in other words, the dream for these men of a connection between their lives and life on an epic scale. Yet the problem is not that they dream of epic grandeur, but that they reduce the grandeur to a local, halfhearted form—the "light work" of Anse McCallum's team.

This dream directly contributes to their own downfall. They buy the horses; later, Ratliff, Armstid, and Bookwright buy the house from Flem. The characters' bad readings of their lives work the way Sutpen's design does in *Absalom*: even while the novels demonstrate the problems involved in specific narrativizations of life, pattern always lurks somewhere and can't be avoided entirely. Flem is always on the edges of the story; there is perpetually a more immediate narrative in the foreground. The stories generally don't involve Flem from their beginnings: he tends to prove more crucial at the end of each section than at any other part. After the narration of Eula's adolescence, Labove's infatuation, and the host of other suitors she attracts, the entire plot line of book 2 is resolved by her marriage to Flem. Flem's rise, in other words, happens not only because the other characters fail to see his overarching narrative, but because they consistently find themselves in abortive or unstable narrative positions that leave him openings. They are, in other words, poor plotters.

Modernism has often had a somewhat tenuous relationship to plot as a topic; in the same article where she introduces the term "stream of consciousness," May Sinclair lays down a series of principles by which she claimed Dorothy Richardson was operating: "She must not tell a story or handle a situation or set a scene" (443). The apparent structure of *The Hamlet*, the set of interlinked short stories that so many of the characters seem to think define their lives, can superficially seem akin to this modernist preoccupation: full of people telling stories, the novel shows how all the actual outcomes of their lives seem to follow none of the plots they see. The novel seems to meander, to be a mere portrait of life in the titular hamlet. All of the miniature narratives are frustrated plots. The mock-romance register of Ike Snopes and his cow, for instance, can be seen as pastiche in a Joycean tradition, drawing on a chivalric style in order to mock its conventional arcs. Ike has his moment of heroism—rescuing his beloved cow from the fire—but ultimately the real denouement of the story is in neither the consummation nor the tragic denial of his passion. It is instead in the social world constructed around him: the peep show and the way Ratliff turns to the rest of the Snopes family—ultimately, of course, to Flem—to get the show stopped. On a local level, Flem Snopes acts to frustrate plot—to show that attempts to build narratives out of one's life will be resolved by forces outside one's control. Thanks to him, plots never seem to go anywhere. But on the level of the novel as a whole, he *is* the plot.

This is, of course, an ugly, pitiless view of events—in which the desires of women and actions of poorer characters who are not Snopeses ultimately are revealed to be meaningless. Recognizing narrative, in this sense, looks like learning to know one's place—to know that those horses *don't* offer the dream of freedom they seem to represent so perfectly, to know that Eula striking out for sexual liberation will only enclose her in a loveless marriage. The tragedy of *The Hamlet*, then, is somewhat different from that of *Absalom, Absalom!* If the workings of *Absalom, Absalom!*'s syntax ensure that its ironies produce reader investment in better, broader ambitions, the structure of *The Hamlet* seems to train the reader in the hopelessness of seeking to write your own story. These characters have never seemed to find a clear way to aspire; the unfocused nature of their aspirations—those intangibly desirable horses, for instance—makes them particularly susceptible to Flem. If Ngũgĩ thought Conrad didn't have enough confidence in the ability of the oppressed to liberate themselves, *The Hamlet* seems like an even worse case: even to think of an alternative life is potentially destructive.

In the final episode of the novel, even the most knowing of characters falls prey to these ugly laws: Armstid and Ratliff think they have a way to beat Flem Snopes and become wealthy. Throughout the novel, Ratliff has been offering Snopes-centered narratives that attempt to counter Flem's pervasive influence. Yet he has only a limited success at gaining from the narratives he constructs—his negotiation with Flem over goats is only a small victory, rather than the decisive one he had hoped for. At the end, he finally thinks he sees a way to win that is consistent with the narrative he has told about Flem from the start. His feeling that there must be treasure at the Old Frenchman house arises precisely out of his conviction that Flem wouldn't make a bad business deal—"I knowed it for sho when Flem Snopes took it" (1045)—that Flem wouldn't have accepted the house if he hadn't thought it profitable. Flem manipulates both the old myth about treasure and the idea Ratliff has constructed of him in order to make it appear that he had believed there was money but has just recently given up. Ratliff, Armstid, and Bookwright buy the house when Flem seems on the verge of selling it to an outsider.

In all the entangled narratives, the fact Ratliff misses is one more bit of order in the cosmos: the "new face" at Varner's store, Eustace Grimm, "a young tenant-farmer living ten or twelve miles away in the next county" (1058), who seems to be Flem's other prospective buyer for the house, turns out to be another Snopes: Grimm is part of Flem's scheme to get Ratliff to buy the house quickly. Ratliff ignores a "click" in his mind about Grimm "because now he believed he did know, that he saw the pattern complete" (1060). He is so enamored of one pattern that he is willing to admit the random element of a suddenly appearing stranger without trying to fit it in.[22]

Ratliff, in other words, loses to Flem because he settles for a narrative that doesn't explain; he lets one ordering of the world stand without trying to revise it. When he figures out the truth, the valuelessness of the house, the importance of the contingency of narrative becomes clearer: the spectacle of Armstid's ceaseless digging, with which the book ends, suggests that unwillingness to revise narrative ends in madness. Ratliff, realizing that the original coins they found had been planted recently by Flem, walks over to Armstid to inform him, only to be threatened with the edge of shovel (1070). This is Ratliff's last appearance in the novel; the final few pages contrast Flem's departure for town with the crowds that watch Armstid dig. The narrator describes his "gaunt unshaven face which was now completely that of a madman" (1075). Armstid has gone from a complex character with a family and a life to having as little complexity and detail as Flem's collection of tics. He has made himself flat, and it happens because every attempt he has made to write his own narrative has instead made him a tool of Flem's.

Ratliff's role at the end, however, seems to hint at another way narrative can become something more than a negative though inevitable force. His ability to see the patterns of Frenchman's Bend, and later of Snopes (and Snopeses) in Jefferson, leads to his futile attempts to prevent others from becoming Flem's victims. Like Lena, he is capable of constructing narratives that cast people as better than they might otherwise be—kind and hospitable in Lena's case, canny and perceptive in his. Faulkner's world is full of pernicious narratives; but it is impossible to try to live without them, and disastrous not to learn to recognize them. The slim hope the novel holds out in such characters is that narrating inevitably involves characters in the lives of their auditors; Ratliff can deliver his warnings, can do his best to keep people out of the way of the predatory protagonist of the novel he's stuck in. Recognizing narrative laws becomes a form of collectivity: it connects people to their world and, rather than estranging them from others as in Conrad, it allows them to make human connections that aim toward the future instead of the past.

Faulkner's Voices Multiplied by Kesey

Ken Kesey's *Sometimes a Great Notion* forms a useful comparison with *Giovanni's Room*. Baldwin's novel appeared in 1956 to an uneasy but generally appreciative reception. *Sometimes a Great Notion* appeared in 1964, to mixed reviews that consistently compared his work to Faulkner's. Each novel is its author's second, and both authors are now better known for their nonnovelistic pursuits—Baldwin for his essays and his role in the major debates of the civil rights struggle; Kesey for his place in the transition from 1950s beatnik to 1960s hippie counterculture. And while each author's first novel had been more clearly connected to its author's broader cultural place—Baldwin's *Go Tell It on the Mountain* as an examination of African American experience; Kesey's *One Flew Over the Cuckoo's Nest* as an outraged cry of youthful rebellion against social conformity and repression—these second novels turn to subjects that are less obviously continuous with the broad cultural movements that popular perception associated with these authors in their own time.

At the same time, these novels turn to personal subjects—Baldwin's homosexuality; the Pacific Northwest childhood that Kesey did not share with his Stanford associates.[23] They are ambitious, self-consciously literary novels—and they address themselves to precisely the concerns of their authors that were least in step with the broad social movements of their eras. Kesey, I will argue, uses the unexpectedness of his subject matter—the way in which it will frustrate readers' and reviewers' preconceptions about his work and cultural context—in order to help generate his claim for universal significance. The novel's untimeliness, its orthogonal relationship to its own historical context, is part of its literary strategy. Kesey wrenches Faulkner out of context in order to get some distance on his own.

When *Sometimes a Great Notion* was scheduled for publication, its appearance occasioned a cultural event that has, in some senses, eclipsed the novel that occasioned it. The Merry Pranksters undertook the cross-country trip aboard a psychedelic school bus (its destination "Furthur"), at first in order to attend the publication party in New York. This conjunction encapsulates the weird dichotomies of Kesey's first two novels. Kesey was writing experimental modernist fiction and was welcomed as a writer by many leading critics and authors of an older generation, including Faulkner's editor and friend Malcolm Cowley. Cowley had helped bring to the public both Kerouac's *On the Road* and the *Portable Faulkner*—and he had taught Kesey.[24] But the Furthur trip was a very different kind of event, arising out of Kesey's extracurricular cultural production while at Stanford, and part of Kesey's shift away from fiction writing. The destination of the bus gestures expansively toward an opening vista of a future; at the same time, it was a presentist project—like many forms of performance art, it incarnated its utopian thinking in the present rather than seeking to create objects of use to the future. It raises an obvious question about Kesey's novel: why, when setting out to follow the phenomenal success of *One Flew Over the Cuckoo's Nest*, did Kesey turn away from the cultural milieu that had defined him and that he would help to define?[25] Hippies, Beats, buses, and acid tests: none of these make an appearance in *Sometimes a Great Notion*; Kesey left them to Tom Wolfe. Instead, he turned to a personal version of Faulkner's Yoknapatawpha: the fictional town of Wakonda, Oregon. *Sometimes a Great Notion*, unlike *Cuckoo's Nest*, is a work not quite at home in its historical moment: it takes up the tools of the literary past and aims to last into the future.

Kesey, I am suggesting, is another figure incongruously outside of everything and alien everywhere. On the one hand, he seemed to be the next Great American Novelist, as Robert Stone, his classmate at Stanford, wrote in 2004. Cowley's

> endorsement . . . seemed to connect him to a line of "heavyweight" novelists, the hitters, as Norman Mailer put it, of long balls, the wearers of mantles that by then seemed ready to be passed along to the next heroic generation. . . . [A]n Olympic-calibre athlete with an advanced academic degree, he had inherited the progressive empowerment of centuries. (72)

In this sense, Kesey seems to fit in poorly with Baldwin—let alone with Ngũgĩ. But this vision of ready-made inheritance obscures how incongruous his melding of the disparate parts of his life was. Being an "Olympic-calibre athlete with an advanced academic degree" was, in Kesey's vision, a tension producing exclusion: he liked to describe his college life as shuttling between the two opposing camps of the wrestling team and the drama or writing departments, each of which could not understand how he would associate with the other (Perry 39). Kesey certainly benefited from all the privileged attributes Stone describes; but the way he benefited from them is a little different than Stone implies. Kesey's power as a character—as a character in *The Electric Kool-Aid Acid Test*, as a dominant personality in his social group—was precisely in the way he couldn't fit in with any group, the way he stood out as bizarre and alien, even *within* a group defined by its freewheeling countercultural resistance to conformity.[26] Wolfe describes Oregonian Kesey as delightfully exotic next to his Perry Lane compatriots: he has a "strange up-country charisma" (8). *Sometimes a Great Notion*, in a sense, is an exploration of the strange charisma of an isolated rural world. Its strategy for aspiring to a broader aesthetic reception is the deliberate dislocation of any local cultural identity its readers might wish to attach to the author.

Like Conrad, Faulkner criticism already has a rich tradition of attention to later authors' politicized responses to him.[27] African American writers from Ellison and Baldwin to Morrison and beyond acknowledge that Faulkner's novels remain powerful in spite of their persistent racism. This stance echoes Ngũgĩ's relationship with Conrad, in which delight coexists with critique.[28] That said, these writers engage much more directly with Faulkner on the grounds of race as a shared context than Ngũgĩ does with Conrad's portrayal of Africa. Faulkner's abstractions are not what makes him alluring to them; they instead attend to the deep enmeshment between form and context. They are an example of the ways contextual reading continues to have its appeal: precisely by attending to the contexts of Faulkner's society do they continue to see his relevance. "As for Faulkner," says Morrison, "I read him with enormous pleasure. He seemed to me the only writer who took black people seriously. Which is not to say he was, or was not, a bigot."[29] Unlike Baldwin's use of James, the titans of African American literature engage with Faulkner on the ground of shared history and context.

Yet they do read him recuperatively, reparatively. Morrison's MA thesis, for instance, contrasts Woolf with Faulkner: Woolf "suggests that by isolating oneself into the fragmentary experiences and sensations as they come . . . [o]ne can live outside time, as it were" (Wofford 23). This is Woolf's faithful record of the atoms as an emblem of ahistorical spatial form. By contrast, she reads Quentin's suicide against the Nobel oration to argue that despite his failings, Faulkner distances himself from such pessimism: "Neither order nor hope is denied" (35). The possibility of finding a pattern is, for Morrison, an optimistic one—and the source of Faulkner's interest for her.

The attempt to discern a pattern and order in the apparently chaotic is also the structuring principle of Kesey's form. His fiction trades on the way new and unfamiliar voices intrude upon literary forms, on the contrast between a grandiosely heroic mode of storytelling and characters who seem as if they don't qualify as heroes. In this contrast, of course, Kesey is drawing on Faulkner—on the epic scale of the Bundren family journey, on the sense of outraged inexplicability with which the town of Jefferson views Sutpen. *Sometimes a Great Notion*, which stages a conflict between eastern urban intellectual skeptical hipness and western rural physicality and faith, makes use of this complex positioning in order to write a novel both new—infamously fired by hallucinogenic drugs, using the modern Pacific Northwest in a new way—and old, drawing on the canonized techniques of the previous generation to tell a multigenerational family tragedy with story elements as old as Homer. It is the novel experimental in very familiar ways.

Yet the several decades between Faulkner and Kesey made for a crucial change in the path to the universal in fiction. Where Faulkner's work could be defiantly apolitical—even at times antipolitical—Kesey's fiction does not perform the same move of turning constantly from the immediate to the abstract. Instead, local politics becomes the basis for generating readerly reactions. *Sometimes a Great Notion* presents a case for the uses of universalism in fiction made under the strong awareness of the powerful countervailing claims of the individual setting and social context. For Kesey, like Baldwin, universalism is a bid for respect for characters; in making that bid, it simultaneously trades on the sense of people as being familiar and as being unimaginably foreign.

Kesey traces his crucial moment of literary development to a formal revelation. In an oft-told story, he says that *One Flew Over the Cuckoo's Nest* fell into place as a novel when he realized that his narrator would be Chief Bromden, rather than a third-person narrator.[30] It's very easy to trace such an inspiration to Faulkner, whose *The Sound and the Fury* and *As I Lay Dying* both feature first-person narrators of questionable sanity. But *Sometimes a Great Notion* is far more densely Faulknerian, both in style and in subject matter. Where *Cuckoo's Nest* focuses on a particular time— its psychiatric ward tensions encapsulate a 1960s confrontation between order and chaos, between society's rules and the forces of life they repress—*Sometimes a Great Notion* focuses instead on a particular place, a small Oregon logging town, itself fictional but surrounded by nonfictional place names. Much as *Absalom, Absalom!*

seems to owe its form and plot to *Lord Jim, Sometimes a Great Notion* owes its form and plot to *Absalom, Absalom!* Kesey, unlike Baldwin and Ngũgĩ, has not left a full record of interviews and essays testifying to his literary affiliations, but in his *Paris Review* interview Faulkner looms large among the authors he mentions (*Beat Writers* 221–222). The parallels, in form and content alike, are dense enough (like those of *A Grain of Wheat* and *Under Western Eyes*) to be sure that they are not coincidence. Lee Stamper, the younger Stamper son, stands in for Quentin, off at an Ivy League institution for college and haunted by his small-town childhood. But where Quentin's suicide attempt will eventually be successful, Lee's fails, and he ends up back at home, trying to understand his own family with much the same fascination and bewilderment that Quentin would apply to the Sutpens. Like Quentin, endlessly discussing the Sutpens with his Harvard roommate Shreve, Lee writes a lengthy framing letter to a college friend depicting his family. And like Quentin, Lee is obsessed with the sexual activity of a female relative (Lee's mother, standing in for Quentin's sister). As with Quentin, declaring at the end that he doesn't hate the South, the plot of the novel revolves around Lee's attempt to figure out what his relation to his own family and West Coast life actually is.

Where in *Absalom, Absalom!* any drama in the present day is confined to the playing out of revelations from the past, in *Sometimes a Great Notion*, the conflict between Lee and his brother Hank, heavily freighted with childhood resentments, occurs simultaneously with the primary plot of the novel: a present-day conflict with the local logging union. Lee is called home for a family crisis—the union is on strike, and Hank Stamper, Lee's older brother, has contracted the family logging outfit to supply timber to the logging company in defiance of the strike, to the outrage of the town.

The form of the book is as experimental as anything Faulkner tried. The novel regularly shifts perspectives, switching from third to first person, from one perspective to another, from one time to another. The novel traverses half a century of convoluted familial history, compacting decades into parentheses, and its various perspectival shifts often happen in the middle of a paragraph or even a sentence. Usually the reader has to keep track of multiple perspectives, locations, and timescales at once as the novel alternates between them, like an epic musical composition in which multiple themes harmonize. The largest flashback bounds almost the entire novel—taking off as Viv, Hank's wife, tries to explain Hank's reasoning to Draeger, the union representative from Portland. Like Faulkner's successively clearer lenses, the structure is all about coming to understand: the great narrative circle is welded at the joint by the phrase, "You must go through one of these winters to have some notion" (15, cf. 713).

Kesey's narrative explores not the changing vagaries of retelling, but the surreal possibility of total knowledge. Information and narrative proliferate far in excess of what Viv would offer Draeger and even what she could know. *"Reality is greater than the sum of its parts"* (16), the narrator says at the end of the first section of the novel, which is this novel's version of "It's the truth even if it didn't happen" from *Cuckoo's Nest* (8). These phrases are formally and thematically parallel: they register an instinct, like James's "Facts themselves are often falsifying," to move beyond what happened.

In this novel, the twistier and more multiplicitous the perspectives and time periods get, the more authority accrues to the statements the characters make. Here's a typical example:

> *You can make a mark across the night with the tip of an embered stick, and you can actually see it fixed in its finity. You can be absolutely certain of its treacherous impermanence. And that is all. Hank knew . . .*
>
> As well as he knew that the Wakona has not always run this course. (Yeah . . . you want to know something about rivers, friends and neighbors?)
>
> Along its twenty miles numerous switchbacks and oxbows, sloughs and backwaters mark its old channel. (You want me to tell you a thing or two about rivers?) Some of these sloughs are kept clean by small currents from nearby streams. . . . (Funny thing is, I didn't learn this thing about rivers from the old man or any of the uncles, or even Boney Stokes, but from old Floyd Evenwrite, a couple years ago, that first time Floyd and us locked horns about the union.) (113)

This is the introductory passage to a lengthy sequence juxtaposing two lines of narrative. In parentheses is a first-person account of Hank's meeting with Floyd Evenwrite, the local union representative, "years ago," which remains fragmentary and difficult to follow; we don't quite figure out what they are arguing about, and not until many pages later do we discover that the meeting with Floyd is "years ago" from the specific moment Lee Stamper arrives home and Hank meets him in the middle of the river; the whole passage is retroactively framed as Hank meeting Lee thinking back to the conversation with Evenwrite. The other main narrative is the third-person account—beginning with this narratorial image of the ember and the description of the river—of the story that is occupying Hank's mind during the union meeting (an anecdote from his childhood about bobcat kittens). But we don't realize that connection immediately: he eventually tells us in the parentheses that during the meeting he "got to thinking about the bobcats I found in the berry vines" (115). Outside the parentheses and in third person, we follow the childhood story without a clear understanding why or for what. At the climax of *that* story the third person becomes italicized and then switches to first person. At this point the parentheses disappear, leaving only first-person Hank in the river with Lee recalling a moment of realization (the meeting with Floyd) from several years before, which took the form of a memory from childhood (the bobcats), the meaning of which he has suddenly determined. We discover that the reason for the narration—which, in the italics above, began as an apparent narrator's description—is to explain Hank's suspicion about the river. "So as close as I can come to explaining it, friends and neighbors, that is why that river is no buddy of mine" (124). The voice within the parentheses is now outside them.

I analyzed a passage from *Absalom, Absalom!* where Faulkner has a similar movement into and out of parentheses, and in that case as well the voices seem to merge and come to an agreement, but Kesey's version introduces the appearance of narrative objectivity to the mix. All Faulkner's voices seem to be those of characters; by contrast, the third-person voice here seems to be something like a traditional external narrator, who speaks in noncolloquial sentences with lyrical language. The omniscient narrator steps in to provide a surplus of material that is still within the possible confines of the characters' thoughts. The structure of memory and recollection, rather than reflecting the mind's revisions and confusions, as Faulkner does, is smoothed into objectivity—we're given something we can assume strongly resembles what actually happened with the bobcats, ratified by the narrator's precise and leisurely descriptive habits, such as those above of the river and its channels. The narrator steps in to provide what Hank's own process of recollection does not, but it sticks with the material he was describing himself as recollecting. This is not Faulkner's dialogue and oscillation, but a much steadier movement: the voices run straight until they intersect, and Hank suddenly speaks with particular authority. After summing up his feelings about the river, he gets to the moment with Lee, but is already once again anticipating the future: foreshadowing how Lee's arrival will "show me there are *other* ways of winning" (125). The third-person narrator sets up authority for Hank's voice to generalize about what the meaning of the events in the novel will be.

After the narrative is finished, we get Hank's voice commenting on it, as though he had been responsible for the narration all along: "So as close as I can come to explaining it . . ." The narrative structure, in other words, persuades us that Hank's self-understanding is accurate, even as we also get the benefit of seeing him from the outside. And we only discover the motivation for recollection and retelling— the local context of the memory's narration—after the fact, so that the memory is allowed to stand independent and valid, not predetermined by its narrative purpose.

The form of *Sometimes a Great Notion*, in other words, looks impossibly complicated at first; it often requires the reader to hold a great deal in mind while waiting for a long-delayed clarifying convergence between narrative strands.[31] But the convergence always arrives; more than that, the effect of the juxtaposition is usually, as in the example above, to offer readers greater security in their knowledge of what the events in question actually are. At times they also work to validate characters' gestures at larger narrativizing statements—Hank's "That is why that river is no buddy of mine" implicitly casts himself as a self-conscious hero of his own story.

Yet it's not entirely obvious why any of the characters should be so confident in their status as protagonists of their stories. As in *The Hamlet*, the novel is in part about characters who mistake what story they are in: Lee, in particular, thinks he's involved in an elaborate unspoken contest with and vengeance against Hank, while the remorseless juxtaposition of perspectives reveals not only that Hank is entirely unaware of Lee's sexual psychodrama, but that Hank's story is the one Lee is stuck in. In a scene at the town bar, Lee is convinced that the hostility he senses is part of a setup Hank has arranged to humiliate him; he misses that in fact the hostility is directed at Hank about the union business (379–388). The multiple perspectives work as correctives to each other, not as ambiguous alternatives.

In this novel, these problems about what kind of story the characters are in take the form of a contest between different forms of universal statement. On the surface, the novel seems to be a contest of the abstract and the concrete. The Stamper family values of autonomy and stubbornness—expressed through their credo, NEVER GIVE A INCH (*sic*)—face off against the local claims of friends and fellow loggers. On the face of it, the other loggers and the family members who do not wish to break the strike are sympathetic. As the novel proceeds, Hank's defiance becomes more and more absurd and impractical; being a scab in this case does not even produce profit.

The choice of scabs as heroes puzzled the novel's first reviewers; *Time* commented parenthetically, "This may be the only novel about workingmen in which the strikers are villains" ("The Strength of One"). But by activating the sympathies of local associations, Kesey also defuses them: we as readers can tell that in every practical and immediate respect, Hank and the Stampers are on the wrong side. Unlike in *Cuckoo's Nest*, where the fellow patients seem to be helpless and benefit from McMurphy's tactics, Hank's stubbornness is catastrophic for family, friend, and foe alike, climaxing in a logging accident that results in a death and a maiming. As the familial strife and natural disasters become more daunting, the novel becomes an inquiry into what the value of such a principle as Stamper autonomy can be when the human connections that ought to sustain it fall away. Like Sutpen's design, the abstract commitment to NEVER GIVE A INCH becomes interesting precisely because of its apparent lack of merit: it challenges the reader to examine why, exactly, this story might be worthy of our fascination. In this novel, the very clarity with which the local, collective claim can be made sets up an inquiry into the nature of the appeal of the universal and individual.

An explicit appeal to the universal appears in the early pages of the novel, which at first seems to stage a conflict between stubbornly chaotic individualism and universalist ideals. The novel begins with Draeger the union outsider, called up to the Stamper house by Floyd Evenwrite with the news that the Stampers are apparently reneging on their agreement not to supply logs to the Wakonda Pacific Logging Company while the other loggers are on strike. Draeger is furious and puzzled, and his question of how Hank could make the decision he does sets in motion the sequence of flashbacks that constitute most of the novel. Draeger habitually in sleeping "slips off to dream of a labeled world" (65): to him, Hank's final resistance is

> a deliberate refutation of all he believed to be true, *knew* to be true about Man . . . that the fool Man will oppose everything except a Hand Extended; that he will stand up in the face of every hazard except Lonely Time . . . will relinquish his *firmest stand* for Love. (10–11)

The capital letters are a way of separating the principles from the situation, separating a Hand Extended from both the person doing the extending and the person to whom the hand is reaching—not to mention the context: say, that the extender may have knocked the extendee down five seconds before. Draeger is an outsider who has come to Wakonda thinking he has a principle that will hold in and against all circumstances. There is, then, a possible surface reading of the novel in which the local prevails—in which characters like Draeger who wish to assimilate people at the peripheries of society into happy similitude with civilization are frustrated. By this reading, the whole point of the Stampers' credo is the refusal of general principles—they will follow nothing but their own desires.

Yet the very object that has provoked Floyd's call to Draeger is, in the words of the narrator, a "rigid and universal sentiment" (10), and a shocking one: a raised middle finger, attached to a severed arm on which all the other fingers have been tied down. This is the image that begins the novel: grotesque and comic, and above all puzzling. It is also an image for the connection between the abstract and the particular that the novel demands the reader forge: a universal sentiment, it is also clearly the result of some highly specific sequence of events leading to the moment (the logging accident that severs the arm will not occur until page 571). Wondering how a severed arm comes to be displayed over a strange house across a river is the major motivating factor that propels the reader into the book. Reading the novel is a process of developing an answer to the question not just how the arm got severed, but how the same history that leads to the severing of an arm leads to unbudging adherence to a particular set of principles. The opening sequence aims all the reader's curiosity and interest at understanding the Stampers' act of defiance as the culmination of local plot and history. Kesey is not presenting the Stamper's universal credo as a self-evident fact; he is presenting it as an incomprehensible one, a phenomenon in need of an explanation, similar to the way Conrad has Marlow present Jim's fascination for him.

The Stampers' "universal sentiment" is an affront to Draeger's "truths about men, and Man" (11). The novel turns out to be less about the conflict between local connection and abstract principle than about the conflict between multiple kinds of appeals to the universal. Draeger's telling slide from "men" to "Man" reveals his principles to be at odds with actual individuals; his capitalizations are labels, boxing plural people ("men") into singular identities ("Man") from his perspective. The Stamper motto, perpetually represented in all capitals, stands against a horde of Draeger-like phrases distinguished only by their initial capitals.

"Never give a[n] inch" is a universal principle: but although it is phrased as an absolute, it assumes an origin point particular to an individual; you can only refuse to give an inch from wherever you happen to start. Draeger, in a central confrontation with Hank, phrases his universalism as descriptive, a matter of inevitable human nature: "I'm speaking of the *basic* loyalty, the *true* patriotism, the selfless, open-hearted, humane *concern* that you always find welling up from someplace within you—a concern you might almost have forgotten—when you see a fellow human being in need of your help" (412–413). Those italic modifiers are an out-loud equivalent of the capitals earlier. Even so bland a noun as "concern" becomes mystified when Draeger talks about it.

By contrast, the Stamper credo assumes nothing. By being prescriptive rather than descriptive, it acknowledges the possibility of different reactions and different starting points, even as it counsels a singular tactic. It has this in common with the other all-caps refrain of the novel, Lee's interior voice of warning, which constantly tells him to "WATCH OUT." The Stamper imperatives are goads to the self; they can be morally suspect (as both Hank's actions and Lee's watchful vengeance are), and they can be disobeyed, but they can't be falsified. Like Lena Grove's narrative, the Stamper credo does not require anyone else to make it true.

The source of the Stamper credo is a rewriting of a descriptive universal into a prescriptive one. After Jonas Stamper (grandfather of Hank and Lee) flees back to Kansas, leaving his wife and sons alone, he eventually sends a wall plaque bearing the biblical inscription "Blessed Are the Meek, for They Shall Inherit the Earth" (34). Like Draeger's principles, initial caps proliferate. His son Henry (father of Hank and Lee, former owner of the severed arm), in response, "laboriously lettered his own personal gospel over the raised copper words of Jesus":

> He stood up, right pleased with his work, and walked across the room and nailed the plaque into the wall over the enormous crib he and the boys at the mill built for Henry Junior. (Where the goddamned ugly outfit hangs, all the time I'm growing up. NEVER GIVE A INCH! In Pa's broad, awkward hand. . . .) (35)

"Right pleased with his work" is poised between sounding archaic and sounding backwoodsy, between the immediate setting and an implication that this really is an alternative to the gospels. The all-caps "personal gospel" is also intertwined with the emphatic subjectivity of the first person—the phrase appears in the parenthetical interjection from Hank's perspective. The phrase knits together multiple perspectives while only appearing in the one.

The idea of never giving an inch repeats itself throughout the novel. The Stamper house itself is an emblem of that tactic: the family has refused to move the house from where it perches, precariously, at the end of a ramshackle peninsula of their own construction as the river has swallowed up the bank, leaving the house alone and isolated midstream. The first foreshadowing of the phrase in the novel occurs in the narrator's voice: "this single house that acknowledged no zone of respect for *nobody* and surrendered seldom a scant inch, let alone a hundred or so yards" (5). Jonas had fled to Kansas because there was "*no* permanence" (24) in Oregon, and his descendants have set out ostentatiously to prove him wrong: to make themselves permanent, even as the land shifts around them, monumental in a landscape whose only constancy is its contingency.

The universals in this novel, then, are essential to its regional and particularist claims: in the context of making a logging life in the Pacific Northwest, the "universalist" theme of an individual human confrontation with nature is simply much more immediate and local than the kind of historical contexts that are easy to assume belong to this novel. In this novel, the union and nature come to seem the same: "In my novels and stories," Kesey said, "evil is always the thing that seems to control. . . . In *Sometimes a Great Notion*, it's the symbol of the river, eating away, leveling, trying to make that town the same" (*Beat Writers* 222) The river an eternal leveler, but more as a force than a feature of the landscape: "The river roams the fields like a glistening bird of prey" (166). We might want to say that in this novel the Stampers oppose the river because the river, connected to the union, reflects a broader national Cold War anti-communist rhetoric about American individualism. But we might just as easily say that the reason in the novel Hank stands for individualism and against the union is that the union has too much in common with the river, which he's been fighting all his life. And, importantly, this is a fight that he is absolutely doomed to lose. The only thing timeless in this novel is change: rot and regeneration, erosion and rust. Nature is neither benevolent nor tameable: it is merely there. The passage in which Hank recalls his childhood lesson about why the river is "no friend of mind" while arguing with the union is an emblem of this parallel.

Kesey is a strange amalgamation of individualism and investment in groups and communities. After all, as many critics have noted, Kesey may make the institutions the villain and iconoclastic individuals his heroes, but Kesey himself was a group-builder, a theorist of the terms on which small groups of people commit to each other.[32] And even McMurphy of *Cuckoo's Nest* is heroic precisely because of the way in which he forges a community within the asylum: not because he individually defies Big Nurse, but because his defiance creates a social world in which the other inmates flourish. *Sometimes a Great Notion* may make the union a villain, but its form and plot aim toward unity: toward the possibility of consciousnesses merging and coinciding with one another. Even Hank and Lee, whose comic contrasts of perspective drive much of the humor of the novel, find themselves coinciding in someone else's vision at the end: they are indistinguishable, just "two tiny figures leaping foolishly from log to log" (714).

Sometimes a Great Notion revels in the alienness of its characters. But it also makes a point of forcing us to perceive that those characters are not defined by their local context. The novel entices the reader to recognize the diversity of types within this society by confronting us constantly with Lee Stamper's failure to see it. When he returns, he thinks of Hank merely as a characteristic product of his world, and misses both Hank's genuine overtures of friendship and his qualitative differences from those around him. The novel foregrounds the differences *between* characters in order that the qualities that differentiate them become intrinsic and valuable as traits associated with human existence more broadly. Universalism here, as with Baldwin, is also individualism, because believing that some things are not culturally determined—that there exist "universal sentiments"—also tends to foreground the differing ways and degrees individual people possess those sentiments. Thus, the emphasis on universals in human nature leads to the novel's tendency to undermine certain types of universalism—particularly universalisms that assume individuals are uniform products of their society.

The use of disparate local contexts to foreground "universal sentiment" and ideals about human nature is a peculiarly novelistic way of getting us to respect Appiah's "encumbered self . . . laden with all the specificity of its manifold allegiances" (xv). Novels often rely on the tension between our desire that a character do the right thing—morally right, or else just sane and reasonable given our understanding of circumstances—and our desire that a character play out his or her self-definition most perfectly. Hank Stamper will never give an inch, ghoulishly flipping off the union using his own father's severed arm, and completing his contract with the logging company, despite the death and dismemberment that have just occurred, despite the flood that makes it possible that taking the logs down the river could be a lethal task. Conrad's Jim, similarly, walks to his death in order to keep a faith, as he had always desired and never succeeded before in doing. Faulkner's Sutpen destroys his design out of his obsessive desire to preserve it.

The outsize heroic side of Hank is real: the way in which he seems like Paul Bunyan (able, in the novel, to hold a double-bitted axe straight out at arm's length more than twice as long as anyone else [372]), though a Paul Bunyan incongruously forced to deal with the vicissitudes of small-town politics. There are, within the novel, several explicit evocations of myth, usually as a meditation on repetition and the similitude of vastly different worlds. At times the whole story seems to be almost about overcoming differences: Lee slowly figures out how to help with logging; he also explains the myth of the Procrustean bed to his family, who know nothing of Greek mythology, and finds that with their interest, "The old myth feels fresh in his mouth, pure" (190). By this point the novel has already given us a live-action version of myth Lee didn't even notice, in his apparent recognition by an old dog of the family (135)—material straight from the *Odyssey*. It's given a comic valence by Hank's thought that "old Plover" died years ago and a college graduate should be able to do the math and figure that out, but as a character moment it remains—both for Lee's genuine sense of sudden and surprised familiarity and Hank's charitable failure to disillusion him.

Kesey's commitment to universals is also a commitment to artistic authority and to the manipulation of readerly experience. In a *Paris Review* interview, he sounds a note not too distant from Ngũgĩ's comment on how the author must not merely "reflect" but "must be prepared to suggest." Kesey was asked whether he believed "that an author imposes his own cultural vision on his readers." His response was, "I think that the artist should feel obligated to force whatever he can upon his audience and be the authority because if he doesn't, some advertising man will. . . . the older you get, the more you see people in the past who have thoughts that last. . . . As Faulkner says, there are the old verities. Revenge is about the same as it always was" (*Beat Writers at Work* 236).

5. Modernism Today, or The Author Becomes a Character

In the 2005 novel *The Typewriter's Tale* by the South African writer Michiel Heyns, Henry James tells his typist—here a fictional figure named Frieda Wroth—of a recent trip to Paris. She responds, "to see Paris I would give almost anything."

> He looked at her reflectively, as if it were occurring to him for the first time that she might have such aspirations. "Oh yes, my dear, you must see Paris. . . . you must go to Paris and you must live all you can."
>
> This was a stirring injunction, deficient only in not suggesting how it was to be executed by a single woman of limited means. It was a beautiful sentiment, but it was beautifully general. (87)

When, a few pages later, he dictates the famous passage from the preface to *The Ambassadors*, where the phrase "live all you can" appears, he breaks his usual habits, stops pacing, and "dictate[s] as if he were addressing her" (103).

This novel is in one sense an intent restoration of context to the general: it rebukes abstract statements with worldly particulars; it re-embeds James's famous statements back in a plot and world from which they might spring. It points out precisely how inflected by class James's ideal of romantic freedom is in its historical context.

But at the same time, Heyns's novel is an act of radical decontextualization, seizing James's entire world and serving it up for a modern audience. James's context, in other words, is out of context. Heyns's novel is one of many recent works taking this approach. Rather than resetting older themes, techniques, and plots in new times and places, authors have begun to write novels both set in their predecessors' times and featuring real authors as characters. Heyns isn't even the only novelist to write about James's typist: Cynthia Ozick's 2008 novella *Dictation* imagines a meeting between the typists of James and Conrad. Other works that have taken such an approach to the recuperative modernists include Colm Tóibín's *The Master* and David Lodge's *Author, Author*—two novels about James published in the same year—and Juan Gabriel Vásquez's *The Secret History of Costaguana*, a novel imagining the life of a Colombian exile who tells his story to Conrad, who then adapts it for the plot of *Nostromo*. Wai Chee Dimock describes *The Master* as a "host environment for Henry James" ("Weak Theory" 738)—an image that use-fully conveys that what these novels are up to is a switching of surround, a change in context; and in making James a "guest" (738), she foregrounds the way the au-thor travels rather than remains fixed in his time.

These novels are in dialogue most powerfully with the long tradition of post-colonial and feminist rewritings of classics, which often take as their target spe-cific *works*, and depend on a historicized oppositional relationship: Jean Rhys's *The Wide Sargasso Sea*, a prequel to *Jane Eyre*; Chinua Achebe's *Things Fall Apart* and its intimate relationship with Conrad's *Heart of Darkness*; J. M. Coetzee's *Foe* with its excavation of the silenced voices of *Robinson Crusoe*.[1] In this vein, Heyns and Ozick have both also written updates of James's *The Ambassadors*: Ozick's *Foreign Bodies* (2011) brings 1950s Americans to a fraying Paris full of pan-European war refugees; Heyns's *Invisible Furies* (2012) brings present-day South Africans to the glittery world of Parisian fashion. And Heyns and Ozick are, on some level, writing back: Ozick brings the James story into a merciless confrontation with World War II and its threadbare victims; Heyns directly exposes the subtle subtexts of James's treatment of sex and money.[2] Ozick's "An (Unfortunate) Interview with Henry James," discussed in the introduction, is an explicitly antagonistic text.

But this tradition is not the only one. Jeremy Rosen calls out critics for their "near-exclusive attention to intertextual works that endeavor to subvert their predecessors" (4). In their extended revisions of *The Ambassadors*, Ozick's and Heyns's opposition is less salient than their insistence on the continuing relevance of the past. Ozick's protagonist Bea (her version of Strether) has a composer ex-husband who stands in for both the selfishness and the improbably continuing appeal of trying to make great art. And Heyns's choice of the fashion/modeling world is a canny modern-day version of James's just-a-little-scandalous Madame de Vionnet. Madame de Vionnet's still-living husband causes Strether low-level uncertainty and anxiety that might not attach to the same circumstances today; but hearing that a favored son is involved with a supermodel might. These novels might look like writing back, but they also revivify the reading experience of James's novels.

They are also demonstrations of the push-and-pull negotiation of power relations between the past and the present. The dead hand of literary canon reaches out to drain the vitality of the present—or perhaps the hand really is dead, and no match for the living. "The appropriation of the living by the dead was an old enough tale," thinks Frieda in her novel (133)—but by the end being a medium for the dead becomes a strange source of power for her. Baldwin's use of James as tool, Ngũgĩ's view of cultural heritage as his prey, and Kesey's use of it as raw material are all examples of the power relationship reversed. Writing a novel about the literature of the past is an act of homage; it is also a revision and repurposing. To make a man into a character both animates and entombs him. The past is prey—and chasing it can define the life of the present.

The novels set in an author's time using the author as protagonist are even more powerfully committed to thinking through the continuing uses and appeal of the literary past. They explicitly bring authors back to fictional life for a new generation of readers, and in doing so they tend to place the authors into conflict with their own future and our present. They are, at the same time, meditations on the fact of literary influence and the history of their authors as readers; they bridge the gap between what an author finds in the literary past and what the reading public might see. Such novels of authorship, in addition to opening up the gap between fiction and life, tend to foreground the transhistorical side of writing fiction, by explicitly tackling the question of why an old novelist might be interesting to readers today. Not only do these works provide a way of analyzing later periods' encounters with modernist fiction; they also show the way later authors create new readers for older authors, and rely on the existence of a continuing readership for old novels. *The Master*, for instance, is among other things an eloquent argument for the continuing interest of Henry James the author as well as the character. Many of today's readers of James will have first been readers of Tóibín (or of David Lodge), and those readers will have a different experience of the older texts.

Tóibín's *The Master* is probably the most well known of the novels to feature a modernist novelist as a protagonist, and it provides a good case study in how these novels tend to imply or adjust readings of the original works. For instance, after James's beloved cousin Minny Temple dies in Tóibín's novel, Oliver Wendell Holmes tells James that he might have been able to save her by inviting her to Rome. " 'When she did not hear from you, she turned her face to the wall.' Holmes spoke as though it were a line he had been planning to say for some time" (112). The phrase "turned her face to the wall" is, of course, taken from the description of Milly Theale's decline in *The Wings of the Dove*, but when Susie Stringham says it in that novel, there is no explanation for its elliptical quality. On one level, this means that readers of *The Master* who later come to *Wings of the Dove* might be likely, in a vague way, to explain the oblique, artificial quality of the line by thinking that Susie too has been "planning" it, as opposed to other, equally valid explanations (that she likes melodramatic romance, or that she simply can't bear to say that Milly is dying). Or perhaps readers of *Wings of the Dove* will hear a stronger accusation than Susie is actually making in context, because Tóibín explicitly suggests that Holmes is accusing James. On another, simpler level, this means that such readers will see such Jamesian lines of dialogue and images as far more natural and realistic than they otherwise tend to seem to us today. Much of the pleasure of late James lies in that alien quality, in the sense of inhabiting a world where people do not speak as anyone ever has. Tóibín's novel cannot make the language less bizarre, but it strives to present Jamesian language as having very familiar emotional connections. *The Master* is full of allusions to Jamesian moments and themes, from Madame Merle's image of people needing the shells of their possessions (123) to the germ of the idea of *The Golden Bowl* (222). On one level these are allusions for the pleasure of Jamesians; on another, they potentially create new readers—and new modes of reading—for James, for expressing and substantiating the continuing use of his novels.

Allusions, like the one above, form one relation between today's texts and their progenitors. But when modernist authors become characters, their styles become personas—whole identities that their successors try out and experiment with. Not just riffing on James's famous lines, Tóibín fashions an entire style halfway between James and the present. This form of soft pastiche—neither parody nor faithful homage, but adaptation—is usually part of the game when authors write about other authors: beyond Tóibín, Joyce Carol Oates's *Wild Nights!* is a collection of stories that pastiche the styles of the authors who serve as their protagonists.

This becomes even more complex when Ozick takes on two authors as once, each with his own distinct style. Even the plot of her novella *Dictation* depends on the question of whether style is distinct and individual. In the novella, two women who work as amanuenses for James and Conrad—Theodora Bosanquet and Lilian Hallowes—meet and collude to transpose sentences from each writer's current project: a little patch of James's "The Jolly Corner" will end up in Conrad's "The Secret Sharer," and vice versa. Theodora is said to have "resplendently envisioned" a plan by which "two negligible footnotes" (the secretaries) end up "leaving behind an immutable mark" (49). The transportability of these authors' styles—into each other's works; into the authorial hands of the secretaries; and, ultimately, into Ozick's own work—is the premise of the novella. What happens, the novella asks, when we stretch the thread of connection between the moment of a sentence's invention and the moment it finds a reader to such attenuation that the act of authorship becomes obscure? The "immutable mark"—the transposition of sentences—is, after all, made only of the materials of the employers; it is a rearrangement of previously existing marks. The plot points to two opposing strands of thinking about literary authorship and literary endurance. Is authority in the unspooling of sentences before they are even transcribed—or transposed— by typewriter keys? Or is it in the editing, in the arrangement of material, from whatever source they might arise?

Meanwhile, in the novella, the authors themselves debate whether style confesses the soul or conceals it: "This observation led naturally to a discussion of style, and whether it remains distinct from the writer's intrinsic personality. Conrad thought not. The novelist, he argued . . . stands confessed in his works? On the other hand, James countered . . . , the artist *multiplies* his confessions, thereby concealing his inmost self" (11–12). The differing conceptions of style here are another version of the differing notions of what it means to make a "an immutable mark" reflected in the story—is style a patchwork, not tied to any particular identity or source? Or is it a matter of creation from nothing, hence reliant upon and tied to a creator?

The novella itself is on one level a patchwork, written in a mixture of Jamesian and Conradian styles, representing both the authors and the secretaries. Lilian's thoughts would never appear to her to be "resplendent" visions the way Jamesian Theodora's do. Theodora seems almost a perfect register of James's mentality—a demonstration of Jamesian transfer of personality. Lillian, meanwhile, sees herself as Conrad's "secret sharer," his words "in her ears, in her throat, in the whorls of her fingers" (28). She vacillates between the Conradian sense of the impossible gulf between souls and the attempt to bridge it: she insists again and again on the distance between herself and Conrad, even as she (in love with him) feels herself much closer to him than his own wife.

At the same time, Ozick's novella anticipates a world that had not yet come into being at the time of its setting. Free-thinking Theodora has a flirtation with young "Miss Stephen" (40; the future Virginia Woolf); the novella holds the works of James and Conrad in tension with the new generation that will succeed them. The works and worlds of James and Conrad, vanishing even as they penned their latest stories, were finding and shaping new readers whose ideas and interests were already very different; and it is this tradition that Ozick continues. She, and the audience for her novella, are new readers for Jamesian and Conradian style and form.

The novella itself, then, operates according to both models of authorship. On the one hand, it is new writing, deliberately opening a different perspective on the lives of these authors, that of female characters brought in to comment upon and alter a masculine world. On the other, it is also an editing job, with characters appearing to live in a Jamesian world spliced together with others in a Conradian one. Ozick takes style and content from both James and Conrad and uses them as she sees fit to accomplish Ozickian purposes. Her novella suggests that literary production is both ex nihilo creation—first there was nothing, and then there came stylish sentences—and skill in working with the material given, in the way one author's style of sentences can be turned to more contemporary purposes. Literary immortality, in this vision, is in part literary reproduction, the reappearance of authors' visions and styles in their readers—some of whom will be other authors. But only in part.

This distinction between editing and creation is not merely a matter of Eliotic tradition against Romantic individual talent; it more directly addresses the problem of literary works' place amid the changes of history. Part of the late-Victorian and modernist anxiety about literary production is the worry that the visions of authors will pass out of date with the times. The novels that turn authors into characters are demonstrations of persistence amid changes: the works and worlds of James and Conrad, vanishing even as they penned their latest stories, were finding new readers in a younger generation (Theodora Bosanquet / Frieda Wroth, Lillian Hallowes, Virginia Woolf) whose ideas and interests were already very different; and they still find readers convinced of their relevance decades later, in Ozick and the audience she creates.

It would be easy to describe Ozick's fusion of Conradian and Jamesian style as a postmodern aesthetic of bricolage; but something more subtle is going on here.[3] Ozick is, to speak broadly, more in keeping with neorealist authors like Franzen than pyrotechnic collage artists like Pynchon. But her collage in *Dictation* seamlessly produces character-driven storytelling. The delight of this novella, and the triumph of its style, is that it argues that the aesthetics of editing and of ex nihilo creation might be, in the end, the same thing. There is no thrill of contrast here, and no repudiation of or ironic distance on James's and Conrad's voices. Part of the pleasure of the novella, in other words, is that its relation to the authors it pastiches is obscured.

The actual style of its pastiche is deliberately a little out of focus, blurring boundaries between "Conradian" and "Jamesian" tones and generally using more hospitable sentence structures than either of them. Take for instance, this passage, in which Conrad contemplates with fear the prospect of Lilian and Theodora meeting:

> She was privy to his hesitations, his doubts, his reversals, and certainly his excitements; she was in the most crucial sense his double, since everything that came out of him she instantly duplicated on the Machine. His thoughts ran straight through her, unchanged, unmitigated, unloosed. Without doubt the same was true with respect to James and the spirited Miss Bosanquet: every vibration of James's sensibility ran through the woman who served and observed—how could it be otherwise? (15)

This passage is primarily free indirect discourse from Conrad's perspective. It begins in an entirely Conradian mode. The reference to the double and the evocation of an unthinking machine are familiar Conradian motifs. The lists, too, are Conradian in style and syntax. Compare, for instance, this from *Victory*: "For the use of reason is to justify the obscure desires that move our conduct, impulses, passions, prejudices and follies, and also our fears" (80). The "also" has the same rhythmic function as "certainly."

Yet the last sentence of the passage, in turning the subject to James, turns the style as well. The vibrating "sensibility," the formally phrased aporia to tag the end of a sentence—these sound far more like the author of the *New York Edition* prefaces. In other words, this is not just a matter of Conrad thinking in Conradian style; it suggests that style goes beyond the mentalities of the characters associated with it. Something about Henry James demands to be portrayed in Jamesian style, even when it is the mind of Conrad that is doing the portraying. (Elsewhere in the story, Conradian lists infect James's perspective when he is thinking about Conrad.)

Yet the feel of this passage, especially if you do not happen to be a literary critic deeply steeped in James and Conrad, is not one of shock or sharp contrast. That "served and observed" rhyme is neither especially Jamesian nor Conradian, but it does tie together the two sentences, echoing the Conradian anaphoric list. And this tends to be true throughout the story: the stronger stylistic contrasts are between narration and dialogue than between the Conradian and Jamesian forms of narration. By the end of this paragraph, the styles and perspectives are entirely muddled: two sentences, of parallel structure, using motifs from both authors, explain that each author fears his own reservations about the other's writing will become plain if the secretaries should be seen together:

> In Miss Hallowes's face, in her posture, in the very shape and condition of her shoes, James would detect, with the divining rod that was his powerful

instinct, the secret thing Conrad harbored against him: that the Master's cosmopolitanism, his civilized restraint, his perfection of method, his figures so
finished, chiseled, and carved, were, when you came down to it, stone. Under
the glow lay heartlessness and cold. And in Miss Bosanquet's face and posture
and perhaps even in the shape and condition of her shoes, Conrad himself
might recognize, frighteningly, the arrow of James's hidden dislike. (15)

This passage blends the authors' styles, picks out their most similar aspects in
order to frame the parallels. But it's much harder to pick out exactly what belongs
to whom. The "arrow" may be Conrad's (*Arrow of Gold*; Marlow's famously mistaken arrows); "were, when you came down to it" sounds more like James's combination of colloquialism and involution. But beyond that, here even the literary
critic's habits and experience fail me: take the central parallelism of the passage,
which draws attention to its distinctions:

> In Miss Hallowes's face, in her posture, in the very shape and condition of
> her shoes . . .
>
>   in Miss Bosanquet's face and posture and perhaps even in the shape and
> condition of her shoes . . .

Is one of these Conrad's syntax, and the other James's? I'm tempted to associate both
that emphatic "very" and the delicate "perhaps even" with James, while the habit
of list-making in general and the choice to modify the last element feel slightly
more Conradian. Then why are the passages even distinguished from another;
why is one excessive with *ands* and the other missing conjunctions? (Conrad's
lists tend equally toward polysyndeton and asyndeton.) Here Ozick is creating
the appearance of significant stylistic difference while denying specific referents;
it looks like bricolage but is in fact all Ozick's own. All those earlier passages held
clues for the partisans of her predecessor authors while blurring the line for a more
casual reader. Here the style draws attention to a subtle syntactic difference—but
it *doesn't* significantly map on to the different authors.

James and Conrad are identical at this moment, in their fear of the meeting of
the secretaries, in part because they see the secretaries as perfect registers of their
own thoughts. And as their styles merge in this passage, the novella reaches its
turning point: after the fateful meeting, we transition to the perspectives of the
secretaries themselves. It is because Conradian and Jamesian style have become,
in this work, softened and naturalized, blended and less distinctly their own, that
there is space for a later generation to speak for itself. The image of James's figures
being stone may actually owe something to the next generation: it's the real-life
Virginia Woolf who would write, as we saw earlier, that "the phrases lavished upon

them are beautiful enough to be carved for ever upon the pedestals of statues. But," she says, there is "something inanimate and stationary in the human figures which chills our warmer sympathies" (*Essays* II.228). Woolf's words, however, as we've seen, were about Conrad's characters, rather than James's. Ozick's passage, combining styles smoothly while pretending to contrast them, is a changeling stylistic gesture, like the scheme at the heart of the story. The very premise of Theodora's plot is that a sentence of James and a sentence of Conrad's can be switched without distinction. Here their styles have been made into one.

Style, on the surface, seems to be one of the least historically transportable of authorial features. If it is commonplace to talk about how a set of themes get repurposed from one period to another, and easy to discuss how narrative techniques find new uses in new generations, style in the more restricted, local sense is usually considered as an individual matter. One author's style appears in another as a form of disguise—as in parody, a thing held at a distance from one's own writing. Yet Ozick neither holds the styles of James and Conrad at a distance nor treats them as a neutral tool along the lines with which I've discussed larger narrative techniques. *Foreign Bodies* avoids the Jamesian syntax in *Dictation*, despite its Jamesian plot. Ozick takes James's and Conrad's styles and makes them her own; but only for a specific purpose associated with her need to represent and rethink their world.

Tellingly, the local style of these works is often treated uneasily by critics. Jesse Matz, discussing *The Master*, tends to find the moments of more Jamesian syntax a mere "pseudo-impressionism," less authentic than those moments where Tóibín writes in a more condensed, direct fashion. For instance, he approves as a "keen impression" the following: "He touched the muscles on his neck which had become stiff; to his fingers they seemed unyielding and solid but not painful. As he moved his head, he could hear his muscles creaking" (*Legacies* 247).[4] Though he is not explicitly talking about syntax, his examples seem to indicate that in his view syntax and sentence-by-sentence style is the thing that does not adapt across eras; it is somehow a betrayal of the *spirit* of the style. In order to "apply" modernist impressionism "to the new demands of postmodernity" (251–252), its actual textual incarnation must become radically different.

There is something lost if we consign authors' style in the local sense to the past. Given that, for both James and Conrad, syntax is one of the strongest impressions their works make, it seems odd that it should have no legitimate afterlife beyond the individual connections visible in, say, Faulkner's incorporation and revision of Conradian style within his own equally distinctive syntax, or Ellison's similar adoption of Faulkner. Style is, of course, always relative to its historical context: the singularity of the Jamesian sentence is important precisely so far as it departs from the sentences of James's predecessors and contemporaries. But style is also trans-historical; it does not merely mark the work as of the past; it marks it as struggling to be different from and untethered to its own time. Style is for the future.[5]

Ozick shows James and Conrad merging into one voice in order to make room for later generations; but those generations take their terms and their tools from the past. As the plot takes shape, Ozick writes:

> What Theodora was after was distinctly radical: she wished to send into the future a nameless immutability, visible though invisible, smooth while bent, unchangeable yet altered, integrated even as it sought to be wholly alien. And it was to be a secret. Nor could she accomplish it alone. It demanded a sharer, a double, a partner. (38)

The "secret" "sharer" (a Conrad title), scattered through this passage, shares space with paradoxical pairings that could be Jamesian.[6] But the title is split apart, and the Jamesian stylistic tic does not really sound like most instances of the same thing in James (the parallels are too clean and unadorned). The story has given birth to a new style—not modern, not identical to Ozick's syntax in other works; but not recognizably the same evocations of distinctly different authors that it was at the beginning. Ozick is not trying to write a Jamesian or Conradian no-vella; she sees the voices of James and Conrad as useful for something completely different.

Her novella uses literary style as always dislocated, as in part standing in for the dislocation of literary art itself.[7] Its historical context is always its material, but it is style because it cannot be identified with its context. At the same time, the style is not meant to free itself from history; instead, it is meant to open to history, to become something new in new historical contexts. Ozick, like the modernists she works with, is fascinated by the prospect of leaving something that will sur-vive into the future, whether or not it will ever be recognized. Rather than leaving monuments to an authorial name, her secretaries (and the style she develops for them) imagine literary sentences as marks without a single origin, which will con-tinue to shape the experiences of future readers—whoever, and however unknow-able, they may be.

Literary futurity is often thought of as fundamentally selfish. Lillian writes to Theodora of "the ambitiousness mortality confers" (39). But, consistently in the novella, this ambition has nothing to do with names or credit: Theodora wants her intervention to be secret; at the end, Ozick describes "her fingerprint, all unac-knowledged, to be eternally engraven, as material and manifest as peak and crater" (50). The dizzying shift in scale between a fingerprint and a mountaintop makes Theodora into a god, sculpting the world like clay. On a geological scale, the secre-taries have changed the landscape of literature. The idea of "making a mark" turns out not to be a signature, an enduring name, but simply the fact of having an im-pact, of having made a difference.

Ozick and Heyns, in using the figures of the secretaries, explicitly thematize the ways novels can invade the minds of their readers—and they each equally ex-periment with the shifting power relations between the past and the present. On the one hand, the minds of Lillian Hallowes, Theodora Bosanquet, and Frieda Wroth are superb records of others' souls, and it's easy to see this as a flattening of their own individuality, forced as they are by economic exigencies to become the conduits for others' thoughts.[8] Frieda's attempts at writing novels of her own are at first sad pastiches of James (84–86). The plots of Ozick and Heyns turn on strikes for independence: Theodora and Lillian have their swapping of sentences; Frieda has an affair with Edith Wharton's lover Morton Fullerton and steals letters on his behalf from James.

Yet passivity and receptivity are also, for Frieda especially, an act of choice and part of her attempts to regain power. Throughout the novel, she experiments with spiritualism: using her typewriter to act as a "receiver" for other minds living and dead. The conclusion suggests that this passivity is a deliberate choice. At the climax of her novel, Frieda thinks, "She knew how to become purely passive and expectant, a medium to another mind than hers, welcoming the invasion of an alien power" (233). Passivity is a form of knowledge, a skill. At the end of her novel, she feels that alien invader:

> There was, after all, something, a presence taking possession of her thoughts, moving her fingers on the keys, forming words, sentences:
>
> ```
> The worst part of taking dictation was the waiting.
> ```
>
> And Frieda, following the promptings of her fingers, began typing—for life, as it were. (233)

That's the first line of the novel we have just finished reading, suddenly made alien by its repetition in a typescript font. Frieda's failed attempts to write, this ending suggests, were merely "imitative"; now, she "would start anew, write her own tale, not his" (232). Yet writing "her own tale" involves learning a degree of openness to a mysterious other. After all, the last words multiply their literary connections: not only do they connect to Jamesian language about living all you can; they also echo more distantly David Copperfield's childhood, spent "reading as if for life." But now the literary past is not mere model; it is a tool to tell her own story, often snapping back at and critiquing senior literary figures. She may be taken over by an alien presence; but the presence becomes servant to her needs.

Baldwin's contrast between drowning in the past and learning how to use it resonates in the transition Frieda makes here and in Ozick's careful stylistic manipulations: in confronting the limitations of the literary past in its own world and context, these contemporary authors and their youthful protagonists take the past's continuing power as a source of renewed vitality for their own work and lives. Ozick and Heyns, with their careful attention to the limitations placed on their protagonists by gender and economic status, rebuke James's classism even as they appropriate the literary tools he created to expand the possibilities of drama and freedom beyond the wealthy characters he so often features. Frieda and Theodora are subject to far less irony than the protagonist of *In the Cage*.[9]

These novels too, then, are forms of writing back. But they also use the presence of fiction writing to complicate political stances; these novels put the ethical claims and risks of writing front and center. Again and again they set up situations where the claims of living individuals are at odds with those of the inanimate words: Tóibín's James benefits not from the open interchange of social knowledge in New York and London but from the "culture of easy duplicity" he finds in Paris: "He had never loved the intrigue. . . . He had learned everything from them" (5). He learns to be a novelist from precisely the social world he doesn't want to live in.

The political possibilities of this problem are thrown into high relief in Juan Gabriel Vásquez's *The Secret History of Costaguana*. On one level this a classic postcolonial writing-back story: the narrator, José Altamirano, expresses again and again his outrage that Conrad has taken the story of his life and his country (the separation of Panama from Colombia) for use as raw materials in *Nostromo* with no thought of any responsibility to the nonfictional originals. Facts, in this case, are silver taken from the mines in the colonies to enrich the colonial state—and an author of that state. In the first pages of the novel, Altamirano says that "here [in London] history had ceased some time ago" (6): English authors must prey on countries where history still happens.

Yet, on the other hand, Altamirano is presented as not entirely sane in his literal readings of the novel and in his obsession with distant intersections between his own life and Conrad's: he calls their meeting the "encounter for which my life was destined" (5). In other words, his political critique is valid only so long as we

are willing to read with credulous acceptance of the transparency and representational qualities of fiction—and the novel subtly encourages us not to be credulous.
The more skeptical the novel is, in other words, the less serious it is as a postcolonial critique. *The Secret History of Costaguana* is a fine-tuned machine for balancing between these two poles, for pushing us first one way and then the other. It
commits us to both the narrator's outrage and to his mistakenness, and the two are
constantly in tension. The final confrontation seems to make the tension between
art and life insurmountable:

> "You," I said, "owe me an explanation."
>
> "I owe you nothing," said Conrad. "Leave immediately. I'll call someone,
> I'm warning you."
>
> I took the copy of the *Weekly* out of my pocket. "This is false. This is not
> what I told you."
>
> "This, my dear sir, is a novel."
>
> "It's not my story. It's not the story of my country."
>
> "Of course not," said Conrad. "It's the story of my country. It's the story
> of Costaguana." (297–298)

The deeply personal outrage has nothing to do with any feeling that Conrad
has made any misrepresentations—that he's gotten wrong the fundamental relationship between expatriates and locals, or the role of financial investors in the
country. It's all about the specifics: that the Panama Canal became a silver mine,
and that, he, José Altamirano, has been erased from the story. He's outraged not
because Conrad gets the politics of his country wrong, but because it's not *his* story
and country. Yet, at the same time, Conrad's claiming of "my country" is an exact
description of the workings of colonialism and the postcolonial state, where fictional borders of convenience replace precolonial boundaries, and the institutions
and narratives of the colonizers replace those of the colonized. Fiction is fiction;
but historical fictions have always had a pernicious power.

Yet in *Secret History*, *Nostromo* the novel exerts little force: it has brought
Conrad fame, but it has made the fate of Panama no worse and popular perception of Western industrial investment no better. "I would go on remembering that
afternoon when I disappeared from history by magic" (301), Altamirano says,
at the end of a book where he has repeatedly alluded to an "Angel of History"
guiding his path of intersections and near-intersections with Conrad. He is himself a Benjaminian angel, carried backward into the future. If throughout the novel
history seems confused with authorship—with the kind of God-author who plots
destinies for characters—the ending is a revelation of the gulf between them.

Altamirano's outrage is replaced by a profound sadness—not over the literary re-incarnation of Panama and Colombia as the Sulaco and Costaguana, but over the tragic events themselves, and his culpable role in them. Altamirano realizes that he has not been erased from history—if only he could be!—but only from a novel. In his wry author's note to *Nostromo*, Conrad references his own fictional histo-rian: "my venerated friend, the late Don José Avellanos, Minister to the Courts of England and Spain, etc., etc., in his impartial and eloquent 'History of Fifty Years of Misrule'" (x). José Altamirano, like José Avellanos, is a fictional creation who represents an appeal to the reality of historical events—and in both cases their works are lost, supplanted by fiction. The nonexistent *Fifty Years of Misrule* shows up in Vásquez's own author's note too, right after Ian Watt's much more widely available *Conrad in the Nineteenth Century* (304). Altamirano's grounds of critique disappear out from under him; what remains is not a claim that facts can be stolen, but that fiction is responsible not to the facts but to the consequences of its fictions.

The consequences of the novels about modernist authorship are many, but one of the simplest is that they set contexts clashing against each other: Henry James in his time; his novels in ours. Joseph Conrad in his time; Conrad for readers today. In doing so, they revise and repurpose the older works. This same logic applies to the earlier novelists as well. Readers of Kesey will find Faulkner less alien; readers of Baldwin will see Jamesian character in a different light. Of course, the works of the past—whether they are difficult as late James or not—are always slightly alien. But the appeal of their work—the reason they are still read, the reason they have found such wide readerships—is in their ability to create vivid experiences for readers of those other times.

Studying influence, in this sense, is not a way of measuring later authors against the towering achievements of their predecessors, but a way of making visible what the literary past has already become in the present. Like James's characters, embracing the influx of others' personalities in order to adapt them for their own purposes, these later authors revise the techniques of the past to accomplish par-ticular purposes in the present. Recuperative modernists evoke connections with the past because believing in historical continuity allows them to aim their work at the future. Their successors demonstrate that they found their marks.

Zadie Smith has not yet written a novel about a modernist writer, but she has written several that are deep dives into modernist forms and plots. The most di-rect is *On Beauty*: a novel that resets the story of E. M. Forster's *Howards End* in contemporary Boston. In an essay, she comments, "Forster was never free from the anxiety of audience. . . . Joyce's ideal reader was himself—that was his purity.

Forster's ideal reader was a kind of projection, and not one entirely sympathetic to him" (17). What makes Forster interesting to her, in other words, is his theorization of an audience. In particular, he resisted the great divide between popular and elite literary forms: he wants to believe, in her reading, in an audience who might be surprised by how much they enjoy Valéry or D. H. Lawrence.

Modernism is often thought of as another turn of the screw on fin de siècle aestheticism. What else is aesthetic autonomy, after all, but another version of art for its own sake?[10] Modernism, it sometimes seems, is the period that to forgot to ask what art was for. As this book has demonstrated, modernism might just as easily be theorized as a moment when novelists in particular generated startling diverse theories about what—and who—art was for. Joyce offers professors; Forster an imagined mass-reading public. Conrad mows down every alternative form of the transhistorical (ideas, facts, theories) and stares into the abyss of the future of all those unknowable "innumerable temperaments."

This book has highlighted the ways literature can point away from context, content, and history. This is not to say that none of these features are part of the reading experience—but that experience does include more than representation. These novels demand of us particular kinds of thinking. Although they contain and strain after always-revised universalisms, they do not come to satisfyingly excerptable conclusions. James's extraction of identity, Conrad's search for meaning, and Faulkner's structuring narratives: these are all processes rather than endpoints, affirming the idea of a commitment rather than commitments to any final objects. The readerly reactions they create, therefore, are open-ended; and their successor novelists find that they can fill in the ends with a variety of political and philosophical commitments. But for them it's commitment that matters rather than negation and questioning. The recuperative modernists left open the possibility of new connections between transhistorical art and societal change. Literature is history; but it is not history alone. The living may turn and chase the dead. But the dead are undying. The novels remain, monumental skeletons of vanished fauna, source of tools for a new era.

Perhaps the past has two forms, and we choose between drowning in it or making something solid and useful out of it.

Or perhaps it is prey, and we grapple with it until it sustains us.

Or perhaps it is merely the landscape out of which we grow; we have no choice but to use it because it is all there is.

These novels, seeking to take from the past only what the future needs, suggest that if we want to understand what has happened in literary history, we must look for the moments where it is still happening.

Notes

Introduction

1. Rita Felski writes, "Our conventional models of context take these multidirectional linkages and cast them into coffinlike containers called periods" ("Context Stinks!" 590). A vampire canon, perhaps?

2. See, e.g., *Harry Potter* or David Mitchell's *The Bone Clocks*.

3. In both novels, a wealthy American (Mrs. Newsome in James; Marvin in Ozick) sends a poorer connection dissatisfied with his or her American life (the fiancé Strether; the sister Bea) to Paris to retrieve a son (Chad; Julian) who has become involved with a vaguely disreputable woman (Madame de Vionnet, separated from her husband; Lili, a Romanian refugee from the war). The ambassador in each case eventually becomes an ally of the wayward couple.

4. See, e.g., Joyce, *Ulysses* (28), and Eliot, *The Waste Land* (l. 430).

5. Susan Stanford Friedman provides one of the more consistent arguments for modernism as the "expressive domain of modernity" (476), where *modernity* stands for any form of sharp break from the past. Note the four headings she uses to organize her matrix of polyvalent modernities: "Vortex of Change," "Radical Ruptures," "Hybridity Heightened," "Phenomenology of the New and the Now" (479); all highlight the feel of an oncoming, rapidly changing present.

6. Other critics have shown just how historically inflected and politically engaged the ideal of autonomous art actually was. See Goldstone, Siraganian. Both, however, work primarily by rehistoricizing the idea of the autonomous art object itself: they show its political meaning as residing in a particular modernist moment from the past.

7. Although this position has few partisans in literary fields, strong contemporary advocates of it in philosophy include Martha Nussbaum and Kwame Anthony Appiah.

8. See, particularly, Walkowitz 2–3, critiquing prior versions of cosmopolitanism to clear space for her own. Other notable critical works that similarly examine the transnational in this register include Esty, *Unseasonable*; Berman, *Modernist Commitments*; and Kalliney.

9. Work on Morrison's use of Faulkner is legion. See, e.g., Weinstein, *What Else*, and Kolmerton and Ross. For further discussion of Morrison, Faulkner, and the literary past, see chapter 4.

10. Performance studies in some ways anticipates this attitude towards the transhistorical. Morrison's discussion of Faulkner might find a parallel in Joseph Roach's declaration about performance traditions: "Memory is a process that depends crucially on forgetting" (2).

11. In analyzing the "family resemblance" (*Through Other Continents* 73) between literary works, Dimock for the most part avoids founding her argument on reception or influence rather than resonances discerned in the act of criticism; in this book, I will be focusing exclusively on cases where the authors themselves are the readers who have already made the connections. Dimock also uses "form" and "genre" interchangeably (80), while I will usually mean something a little more local than that: the form of a romance character, for instance, who might nevertheless be stuck in a realist novel.

12. Modernism's fascination with rupture is only an exceptionally extreme form of a broader historicist tendency; Caroline Levine, for instance, describes encountering again and again the idea "that a historical perspective yields irreducible particularity, sheer *difference*" (xii).

13. As Lisi Schoenbach points out, our criticism remains dependent on "the ideology of rupture and opposition that defined the work of the modernist avant-garde" (3). Other recent critics who engage with ideas of the ordinary or the everyday include Phillips, Freed-Thall, and Olson. The everyday isn't the main subject of my analysis, for reasons I'll discuss in chapter 1, but the strength of this particular current within modernist studies suggests the variety of reasons to displace rupture from the center of modernist studies.

14. Faulkner's relation to "modernism," of various breeds, has been analyzed by many critics. See, for instance, Richard C. Moreland, *Faulkner and Modernism: Rereading and Rewriting*. In *Unknowing*, Philip Weinstein places Faulkner alongside Kafka and Proust, and privileges the undermining of old ways of knowing rather than the development of new ones.

15. The fullest work on the period is Christopher Butler, *Early Modernism: Literature, Music, and Painting in Europe, 1900–1916*. Peter Nicholls, in *Modernisms: A Literary Guide*, also extensively treats modernism's early years.

16. For more on Baldwin, James, and both the "individual" and "freedom," see chapter 2.

17. Susan Sontag's "Against Interpretation" is an influential earlier example of this dichotomy. Recently, Deidre Lynch takes the "long view" (*Loving* 2) on the whole problem, showing how the coolness of expertise and the warmth of amateurism alternate as normative affects of literary criticism.

18. See, for instance, the symptomatic reader par excellence Jameson recently discussing George Eliot's use of a "narrative formation . . . in order to undermine the ethical binary and to discredit the metaphysical and moral ideologies of evil" (*Antinomies* 137).

19. Terry Eagleton expands on her brief gesture in his review of *The Limits of Critique*: "In its disdain for the common life—for what is familiar, natural and habitual—critique is the true inheritor of high modernism. For both currents, everyday existence can be valid only if it is estranged, disrupted, dismantled, fragmented or penetrated to some deeper, more elusive level of being." Both the positive energies of critique and their failings, it seems, can be traced back to modernism.

20. See, e.g., Levine 18–19. For a specifically modernist example of this argument, see Jessica Berman, *Modernist Commitments* 15–16. I will discuss Berman's argument further in chapter 3. The most complex version of this debate has taken place in postcolonial studies, examined in the same chapter.

21. Best and Marcus use the word "modest" only once. Its popularity as an umbrella term stems from a review-essay in the *Chronicle of Higher Education* by Jeffrey J. Williams. Its accuracy as a descriptor of the various critical strands of this discussion is debatable.

22. In 1984, Spivak was particularly critical of those who "are busy protecting their theoretical purity by repudiating essentialism" (*Post-colonial Critic* 12). In 2008, Spivak declares herself to have "thoroughly repudiate[d] the idea of 'strategic essentialism'" (*Other Asias* 260).

23. Anthony Reed, in *Freedom Time*, offers one recent critique of what he calls "racialized reading": reading that prioritizes black literature as offering "testimony" about racial experience (7). He also highlights, as do I, the potential of later voices to redefine their predecessors: "How does our understanding of literary possibility change . . . when we consider dissident practices of citation of texts and forms as transformative of those forms rather than as rejecting or mocking them?" (5).

24. Nick Dormer, in *The Tragic Muse*, speaks of his painting: "The truth is that taking people's likenesses is a very absorbing inhuman occupation. You can't do much to them besides" (VIII.392).

25. In some ways this phenomenon is an inheritance from the Victorian aspiration toward "cultivated detachment" that Amanda Anderson has analyzed as an alternative to the valorization of the locally embedded (33). Certainly the contrast between Woolf's denigration of the "alien and external" and James's "alien everywhere" aesthetics echoes in today's critical debates about the legacy of the Enlightenment. But difference and alienation require a slightly different model: James (and Ellison) take distance as the starting point of their art; they do not *cultivate* detachment as an aspiration.

26. See, e.g., the edited collection *The Legacies of Modernism* (ed. David James); Jesse Matz, *Lasting Impressions: The Legacies of Impressionism in Contemporary Culture*.

27. Christopher Ricks declares his focus to be "the poet as heir" (*Allusion* 1). For Ngũgĩ, the development of African fiction requires no longer thinking of European fiction as a natural inheritance. As the Nigerian Niyi Osundare puts it in his poem "Ambiguous Legacy," "Oh the agony it does sometimes take / To borrow the tongue that Shakespeare spake." African authors borrow, appropriate, repurpose, or have thrust upon them European literature.

28. *Modernist Futures* 8. See also Martin Puchner's analysis of the "reactive avant-garde" (45)

29. This critique has special prominence with regard to postcolonial studies; I will discuss it at greater length in chapter 3 in treating the relationship between Conrad and Ngũgĩ. For critics who make this argument in decrying influence as a paradigm to analyze postcolonial literature, see Wendy Belcher, Nicholas Brown.

30. Sarvan 156. It should be noted that Sarvan argues precisely that Ngũgĩ's work *is* worthy, and goes on to compare his relationship with Conrad to that between Anouilh and Sophocles. Still, the rhetorical gambit indicates the underlying strength of the discourse valuing originality.

31. The most well-discussed locus of this shift is, of course, Romanticism, whose investment in ideas of originality animates critical debates from classics by M. H. Abrams and Jerome McGann to more recent work by Robert McFarlane on the Victorian responses to Romantic ideology.

32. The difficulty of describing modernist literary innovation is one demonstration of the problems of focusing on originality. It's easy to describe stream-of-consciousness narrative structures as innovative; it's in many cases impossible to demonstrate that no one had done them before. What we're really talking about when we highlight the innovation of modernism is a sequence of repeated departures from a continuing realist norm. It's not that any individual work was first; it's that each work continued to seem startling.

33. This book limits its analysis to the argument that literary influence can be used to give later authors power in determining the meaning of the past; it is a book far more about the earlier modernist authors than their successors. My next project lets the alternative claim back in: I argue that the direction of analysis can move in both directions without reducing later authors to afterthoughts; for an example from that analysis, see "*The Princess among the Polemicists.*"

34. See, e.g., Peter Mallios, Dale Peterson.

35. For an example of the uses and limitations of reception study with regard to these authors, see Lawrence Schwartz in *Creating Faulkner's Reputation*, which establishes quite convincingly that Faulkner's reputation in the United States rose because "he produced a commodity of enormous value as a cultural weapon in the early years of the Cold War" (210). But despite the unmasking tone of this argument, weaponry does not exhaust the uses and values of Faulkner—at mid-century or since, and I'll argue in chapter 4 via a reading of Ken Kesey that even Faulkner's individualism needs a broader context than the Cold War to understand its uses and effect on readers.

36. See, e.g., Neil Lazarus on the possibility of "*modernist writing after the canonization of modernism* . . . that resists the accommodationism of what has been canonized as modernism" (31)

37. Kalliney 4. On the Americanist side, critics tend to show the ways institutions seem more determinative of their participants' reading. See, for instance, just on the subject of Henry James: Amy Blair, and Merve Emre.

38. Sebastian Lecourt makes a distinction between literary forms and media to describe the dichotomy between institutional reading and the text's more startling consequences: "Where forms establish abstract shaping patterns that can be creatively reinterpreted, a text's medium carries particular kinds of prestige that subtly underwrite that interpretive activity" (670).

39. Mike Goode calls for a form of reception history bridging the gap between reader-response theory's "ahistorical implied reader" and reception history's focus "on particular identifiable individuals, groups, or traditions" (32 n. 20).

40. As observed above, the critique of critique has been notably less successful at coalescing around an alternative than it has in mounting a coherent argument for the need for *some* alternative. Most of the influential works on the subject are abstract polemics, focusing more on the underlying stakes of criticism than in giving substance to other methodologies. Felski's *Limits of Critique* is one example; the well-cited "Surface Reading"

introduction is another. Joseph North's *Literary Criticism*, which was published too late for me to deal with at length, follows the same pattern.

41. Friedman's argument depends on a strong form of historicist reading: if modernism cannot be defined alongside a definition of "modernity," then to limit "modernism" to a narrow period and geographic area is also to refuse to grant the status of modernity to other diverse cultural formations: "To resist the definitional expansions in modernist studies is to fight modernism's constitutive link with modernity" (474).

42. This is not to argue that, say, the Modernist Studies Association shouldn't welcome in scholars focusing on literary works from all areas of the middle of the nineteenth century to the present; just that declaring those works to *be* "modernist" should not be a price of admission.

43. For instance, see Esty, *Shrinking Island*; Genter; Tyrus Miller.

44. I borrow the phrase *singular modernity* from Jameson, of course, whose implication that the term "modern" appears in political contexts to naturalize and imply the inevitability of capitalist global modernity seems inarguable. But literary history runs on a shorter time frame, making distinctions that are only visible if we don't tie "modernism" quite so tightly to "modernity."

45. A nonexhaustive list of novels in this category might include many of Achebe's works; Abdulrazak Gurnah, *Paradise*; Zakes Mda, *Heart of Redness*; V. S. Naipaul, *Bend in the River*; Tayeb Salih, *A Season of Migration to the North*.

46. Perhaps the finest collection of metaphors for the literary text's relation to its readers comes from reader-response criticism: Iser's text as stars out of which the reader makes constellations (*Implied* 282); Jauss's reader "who performs the 'score' of the text" (145). If these critics highlighted more than we usually do today the power of narrative to script readers' responses, they also show how necessary some theory of texts' powers remains—even if it is no longer the endpoint of our analysis.

Chapter 1

1. See McGurl, *Novel Art*; the association of modernism with the rise of a "great divide" between popular and elite cultures is most influentially articulated by Huyssen.

2. Lee Edelman's critique of what he describes as "reproductive futurism" partakes of this logic. Edelman doesn't examine the particularities of literary futurity, but his critique of forms of the future that imply static reproduction of the present is applicable to notions of literary endurance that are about preserving the author rather than providing for an unknowably different future. These, however, are not the forms this book examines—nor should they be taken to typify the project of writing for the future more generally.

3. Cynthia Ozick's *Dictation*, discussed in my final chapter, is a novella that reimagines their friendship.

4. A few dual-author studies exist: see Nettels, *James and Conrad*; Branny, *A Conflict of Values* (on Conrad and Faulkner); and Reesman, *American Designs* (on James and Faulkner). Branny's study is strictly a philosophical rather than formal comparison, and while both Nettels and Reesman contain comparative readings of the novelists, neither attempts to place their work in the context of modernism more broadly, let alone its transhistorical reception.

5. See, e.g., Levenson's *Modernism and the Fate of Individuality*, or Matz's *Literary Impressionism in the Modernist Novel*; Walkowitz, *Cosmopolitan Style*, and Esty, *Unseasonable Youth*, make similar gestures.

6. *The Genealogy of Modernism* 10. Levenson then argues for a similar reading of James (20–22). More recently, Jesse Matz, in *Literary Impressionism and Modernist Aesthetics*, describes an impressionism in Conrad and James that is "an early, salvific, empathic Modernism; and it is the failure of it . . . that leads in Conrad and in Modernism more generally to the isolation, suspicion, and dread for which both are better known" (141). The rescuing impulse in these authors is always, in these critical narratives, doomed to give way to skepticism.

7. See Christopher Herbert, *Victorian Relativity*, for a history of nineteenth-century relativistic literature and its opponents: "The endeavor to suppress relativism in the name of 'absolute' values and of 'truth' constitutes in fact one of the abiding projects of the European intellectual tradition" (13). The authors I study are later than most of the history he traces; they accept relativism and then seek to found upon it a defense of human endeavors. Rather than using relativism to devise mental structures "radically emancipated" from sinister political influences (10), these authors use relativism to try to build back to more familiar forms of literary authority.

8. He had Marlow do exactly the same thing in *Lord Jim*: "Frankly, it is not my words that I mistrust but your minds" (171).

9. For the history of the tendency of formalist analysis in general to "give the impression of overcoming time," see Gallagher, "Formalism and Time" 231. The most notable exception is Peter Brooks, *Reading for the Plot*.

10. For a fuller analysis of this distinction, and the modernist period's theorization of different forms of readerly mental activity, see Bronstein, "On Not Re-reading Novels."

11. Conrad's letter was published in G. Jean-Aubry, *Joseph Conrad: Collected Letters* (1927), I.216, so it is possible Faulkner had seen it.

12. See Liesl Olson, *Modernism and the Ordinary*, for an examination of the importance of everyday life to the high modernists.

13. James was not the only author to turn to embroidery as an image of the transfiguration of the world. In Conrad's knitting machine letter of 1897, mentioned above, the image of a desirable alternative to knitting is of embroidery: "I am horrified at the horrible work and stand appalled. I feel it ought to embroider—but it goes on knitting" (I.425). Conrad is not describing art, but life—specifically, rebuking his friend R. B. Cunninghame Graham's statement of the value of trying to improve the world through political action.

14. This is an endpoint, but also a locus classicus: in the fourth century CE, Sallustius wrote of myths, "Now these things never happened, but always are" (*On the Gods and the World*, IV, qtd. in Murray 246).

15. I borrow this conceit from Michael Levenson, who makes a similar demonstration regarding the plots of *The Ambassadors* and *Heart of Darkness* (*Modernism and the Fate* 2).

16. See note 6.

17. Leon Edel is among those who suggest the influence ran from James to Conrad (5.54).

18. See Gordon 286, 324–325, for discussion of these parallels.

19. Peter Brooks has suggested a more conceptual Flaubertian model for *Beast in the Jungle*, in regard to both authors' investment in perspectival representation of a character's mental state of partial knowledge (*Henry James* 152–153). The parallel to *L'Éducation*

sentimentale, however, is more specific than that. Philip Horne has written a comprehensive account of James's engagement with that particular Flaubert novel over the years, which does not, however, discuss *The Beast in the Jungle*.

20. James's letter, alas, is lost, but the memory of it clearly stuck with Conrad: in 1904 when he sat down to write his tribute to James he elaborated his own metaphor on the subject: "I do not know into what brand of ink Mr Henry James dips his pen; . . . but I know that his mind is steeped in the waters flowing from the fountain of intellectual youth" (*Notes on Life and Letters* 15).

21. In some respects, Conrad, just like James, may be responding antagonistically to the example of Flaubert: Jameson compares the "light literature" passage in *Lord Jim* with Flaubert (*Political Unconscious* 211–213).

22. For another instance of the connection between *Lord Jim* and *The Beast in the Jungle*, see chapter 3, note 19.

23. Kevin Ohi, "The Beast's Storied End," points out that both Leo Bersani and Eve Kosofsky Sedgwick are troubled by the conclusion of the novella as a "sudden convergence of author and character" (1): that is, these critics see the rhetorical ending as reflecting James's endorsement of Marcher's dream. Ohi argues that the rhetorical extravagance of the conclusion should be seen with ironic distance, is in fact merely Marcher's attempt to salvage hope. I share his sense that the lofty style of the conclusion is not necessarily a convergence between author and character; however, for me the loftiness lands on the side of the author: the author provides the reader narrative satisfaction, while the character gets none.

24. The novella's mode of substituting literary form for the usual business of plot and content is suggested by Ruth Yeazell's formulation: Marcher is "a man obsessed with a metaphor" (37).

25. *Faulkner in the University* 50, 150. See also Faulkner, *Lion in the Garden* 21, 49, 110–111, 251. The only other writers in English to find regular places on any of these lists are Shakespeare, Dickens, and Melville.

26. *Notes on Life and Letters* 13. Citations to "Henry James: An Appreciation" in this section of the chapter follow the Dent collected edition rather than the recent Cambridge text, as the Cambridge text of the essay follows a manuscript that differs substantially from all versions published previously. Faulkner owned editions of Conrad that ultimately traced their texts back to the initial collected works published by Dent and Doubleday: see Joseph Blotner, *William Faulkner's Library: A Catalogue* 63–64.

27. Mallios argues that Conrad's passage was particularly relevant not just to Faulkner, but to a broader generation of southern writers (265–267, 325).

28. For gratitude, see Ricks; for rebellion, Bloom. Readings that foreground political differences are widespread, especially regarding Conrad and postcolonial authors; see chapter 3.

29. Stephen M. Ross, for instance, analyzes *Absalom, Absalom!* to show how Faulkner "improved upon" Conrad's "rhetorical procedures" in "push[ing] Conrad's use of conjecture to further levels of complexity"; the difference is "a matter of degree not kind" (Ross, "Conrad's Influence," 202, 204). Many critics acknowledge formal similarities between Faulkner and Conrad. In addition to those cited elsewhere, Albert Guerard, who peppers his work on each author with casual references to the other, describes Faulkner's techniques as "the next and natural" steps of novelistic development (*Conrad the Novelist* 269).

30. Philip Weinstein, *Unknowing* 192. For a classic reading of Faulkner's structures in this vein, see Kartiganer, *The Fragile Thread*: a Faulkner novel "can only be the precarious form that discloses the fact of its impending dissolution" (xv). He even makes *Absalom, Absalom!* sound like a Conrad novel: "At the bottom of this modern tragedy is the inability of one man to speak to another, some inviolable privacy at the center" (106).

31. For a comprehensive history of the composition of the Nobel oration and a response to critical dismissal of it, see Carothers.

32. See, e.g., Schwartz 33, Barnhisel 106.

33. A few other Conrad analogues have been proposed. Koc suggests *Almayer's Folly*; Glassman suggests *Chance*.

34. See Ross on the way Faulkner chooses to "enlarge the role" of the audience's impressions in constructing the story (204).

35. For the idea of literary experience as a strategy to "train" the reader, see Landy (10).

36. I borrow these terms from Felski's *The Uses of Literature*, where, along with "enchantment" and "shock," they form the matrix of categories of readerly experience she wants to recuperate.

37. See Said, *Culture*; Sorensen; Lazarus; and Cleary, introducing the issue of *Modern Language Quarterly* on "Peripheral Realisms."

38. Levine, in *Forms*, tends to treat aesthetic and cultural forms as essentially the same sort of thing, and therefore suggests they can be read similarly; at the conclusion of her book, characters in *The Wire* are said to "perform a reading of the social that is nothing other than a canny formalism" (150). Some distance, however, between cultural and literary forms is necessary to see the varieties of uses literary forms can have.

Chapter 2

1. This is an 1874 essay, published only a year before James's *Roderick Hudson* carefully presented a contrast between the sculptor of the ideal (Roderick) and of the real (Gloriani). Over the years the balance of James's attitude toward Flaubert evolved—in particular, he came to value Flaubert's stylistic merits more than he rejected Flaubert's outlook on life—but he remained hesitant to the last about the Flaubertian view of what life is. For more detail on James's attitude to Flaubert, see Peter Brooks, *Henry James Goes to Paris*, esp. 59–69.

2. Murphet's reading is based primarily on Woolf, though he does also suggest that "Henry James had . . . steered his form" in a similar direction (266).

3. Baldwin's interest in *The Princess* has far more to do with the twin contexts of 1950s and 1960s concern with the limitations of revolutionary utopianism and the general dilemma of the dispossessed turning to violence than it does to any racial elements in the text itself. See Sara Blair for a historicist account of such elements (90–93). See Bronstein, "*The Princess* among the Polemicists," for a full account of James's novel at mid-century.

4. Austen 7; James 16; Woolf 8–9.

5. We might see James's approach as closer to *The Waves* than *Mrs. Dalloway*, in which each character has his or her crucial phrase and gesture, seeking to sum up themselves and their impressions, which are almost exclusively conveyed through elaborately developed and repeated metaphors.

6. Felski, "Introduction" v. Felski is introducing a special issue devoted to themes of character; in addition, a few of the many major book-length studies on character include

Deidre Lynch, *The Economy of Character: Novels, Market Culture, and the Business of Inner Meaning*; Alex Woloch, *The One vs. the Many: Minor Characters and the Space of the Protagonist in the Novel*, and Blakey Vermeule, *Why Do We Care about Literary Characters?* I will discuss Woloch more fully later in this chapter and in chapter 4. See also David Kurnick's notion of "performative universalism" in James as balancing the structure of individual characters with their place in larger systems (144).

7. Butler has continued to evolve; work like *Giving an Account of Oneself* suggests greater potential individual agency in the performance of the self. Her career is evidence of how different moments demand different theories—and one of the many reasons that, when we look for the theoretical implications of literary texts, we do well to look for evidence of impact they actually had.

8. See, e.g., Blair, quoted above. John Carlos Rowe's *The Other Henry James* also focuses on multiplicity, describing "Jameses" that "are anxious, conflicted, marginal, sometimes ashamed of themselves": James "challenged ideas of literary authority" (xiii, x). I argue that James takes the challenge to authority as a given—he will not begin a novel, for instance "Isabel Archer, handsome, clever, and without a fortune . . ." The aim of his fictive project is to relocate authority, to defend a new form of it on new terms.

9. *New York Edition* III.287–288. This passage is garbled in the copy text used in the Cambridge edition; the editors emend it in a way that preserves less of the list (193; the original, on 763, includes the full list of elements James would later keep in the *New York Edition*).

10. As Richard Salmon says, "Strether experiences the sign of his name on the cover of the Review as an attenuation of identity" (154). This attenuation, crucially, is particularly associated with the structure of his personality at the beginning of the novel.

11. Other examples too numerous for treatment here appear in many novels: Nick Dormer of *The Tragic Muse* vacillates between art and politics under the influence of Gabriel Nash and Julia Dallow; Hyacinth Robinson and Verena Tarrant, of *The Princess Casamassima* and *The Bostonians*, find political ideology a kind of infection caught from more forceful personalities and ultimately foreign to their own characters. In *Wings of the Dove*, Merton Densher similarly oscillates between others' personalities—those of Kate Croy and Milly Theale—and is forced to a point of choice by the end of his novel.

12. Philip M. Weinstein in *Henry James and the Requirements of the Imagination* argues that "the exercise of the imagination on the part of James's characters plays an extraordinary role in molding the kinds of experience they undergo" (3). The importance of characters' imaginative attitude toward others goes beyond its effect on the imaginer and his experience; what occurs in James is a genuine warping of characters based on others' imagination of them, as well as their own of others, and the adversarial force of imagination against reality is not quite so unified in its import as Weinstein tends to see.

13. The nexus between the verbs *control* and *save* here suggests the complexity of James's view of the actions of consciousness. Sharon Cameron declares, "For James a phenomenology of consciousness is a phenomenology of its domination" (11), but highlighting consciousness as an exercise of power undervalues the degree to which the control is a rescue operation, saving and embracing rather than subjugating and enclosing.

14. Liquid tends to represent the threat of the self's dissolution—we'll see more examples of this in *The American Scene*—while air tends to be associated with romantic freedom (the

balloon, Ralph's "wind in her sails"). Baldwin, relatedly, persistently figures threats to identity as drowning.

15. Somewhat confusingly, James associates exaggerated, extreme characters with romance ("Who could pretend that Dickens was anything but romantic?" [*Literary Criticism* I.130]). By contrast, a long critical history associates nineteenth-century caricatures with realism: for instance, Lukács's discussion in *Writer and Critic* of the "extreme cases" of Balzac's characters (50), or Woloch's examination of Dickens's characters as forced into caricature by social forces (156).

16. James has this in common with Conrad. See, e.g., Marlow on Jim: "I affirm he had achieved greatness; but the thing would be dwarfed in the telling, or rather in the hearing . . . I could be eloquent were I not afraid you fellows had starved your imaginations to feed your bodies. I do not mean to be offensive; it is respectable to have no illusions—and safe—and profitable—and dull" (171).

17. Chad, unlike Isabel, seems a disappointment when he is only himself, and this is because his second change in identity—the reversion to Woollett—is not, it seems, consciously chosen. "He protests too much," says Strether late in the novel (393–394). Strether, on the other hand, will choose his final self consciously.

18. It is much more difficult to claim, for instance, that however sympathetic and complex Kate Croy is, moral transgression is not a key theme in *The Wings of the Dove*.

19. Rivkin 58. Rivkin reads the novel as a dogmatic rejection of American dogmatism: "Mme de Vionnet turns out to represent life as something far more problematic and plural than Strether's New England categories anticipated. . . . what Mme de Vionnet comes to reveal is that behind representation there is no firm ground, no singular, easily communicable and knowable presence of truth" (80). While I have no desire to claim James is defending singular, easily communicable truth, the destabilization Madame de Vionnet represents is itself subject to skepticism within the novel.

20. Jil Larson compares the novel to *Dorian Gray*: "Just as their characters find aesthetic means of evading responsibility, Wilde and James themselves sidestep didacticism—or even a more subtly identifiable ethics—through their evasive narrators, through the filters of their protagonists' minds, and through the aesthetic detachment afforded by a pastiche of generic conventions" (111).

21. Collin Meissner avoids absolutist claims, but still places all the evil on the side of American prejudice and suspicion: "*The Ambassadors* makes it particularly clear that the corrupting force resides in the New World's suspicion of experience as a way to understanding. . . . One can overcome, or at least have the illusion of overcoming, determinism, the 'illusion of freedom,' James seems to be suggesting, by cultivating an openness to experience" (*Henry James and the Language of Experience* 138, 155).

22. Sharon Cameron offers a forceful contrasting reading of the "I would take my stand" passage, in which rather than a sign of the mind's analytical capacity—extracting character from the impressions, resolutely valuing some over others (his sense "would react promptly in some presences only to remain imperturbably inert in others" [353])—this is a sign of James embracing randomness: the travelogue genre, she says, is a way of "*licensing* this randomness, providing James the opportunity to disengage his considerations of consciousness from anything but the most immediate context" (3). I see the determination as having more deliberation and less randomness than she does—hence the willingness to go to the stake for it.

23. Jesse Matz argues, "To Pater, James, Woolf, and the rest, impressions play a crucial *mediatory* role, standing somewhere between sensations and ideas, and likewise undoing other basic oppositions" (*Literary Impressionism* 17). In other words, the idea of the impression hovers between passive experience and active analysis. It is the proper balance between imposition of ideas and unfiltered sensations that his characters must strive to reach—much as they must balance their capacity of choice with the personalities of others in self-construction.

24. Woloch focuses on a sense of disparity between a character's role in the novel and the character's perceived possible potential. His phrase is "narrative asymmetry . . . the dynamic narrative subordination of potentially full human beings." Dickens's "weak protagonist" results from the way "minor characters persistently wrest attention away from any privileged, central figure" (44, 143). In James's work, being a minor character is not to be unjustly neglected; and, conversely, the hero must justify his or her status.

25. One critic who offers a warning against overly idealizing readings of the Parisian milieu of the novel is Tessa Hadley, who writes, "Into a world charged with a very masculine sexual energy and élan he intrudes qualities of gentleness and conscientiousness (Strether's 'enormous sense of responsibility about personal relationships') which read as coming rather from the Anglo-Saxon novel tradition" (107). Her distinction between the jaded, cynical storyline of adultery by which Madame de Vionnet's suffering is to be expected and the "responsibility" Strether feels upsets any easy alliance of Paris with romance and Woollett with the harshness of the real.

26. See Yeazell for an analysis of the way James's style suggests that characters' conscious knowledge arises out of subconscious awareness even when they struggle desperately against it (21–28).

27. Strether speaks of Chad and Madame de Vionnet in terms of a sense of his being doomed to uneventful life: "I mean they're living. They're rushing about. I've already had my rushing. I'm waiting" (270).

28. See Brannon W. Costello for an analysis of agency and determinism in *The Wings of the Dove* that points out the risks of this approach: "Although individuals are inevitably determined . . . they must behave as though they were free, for to do otherwise is to refuse the potential for meaningful engagement with the world and with others and to doom oneself to isolation and alienation" (174).

29. Salmon has suggested, about late-Victorian biography: "Regardless of whether the intention was to reveal or to conceal the privacy of the subject, privacy itself was invariably construed as the site in which truth was necessarily contained" (88–89). For James, truth of character is not just contained by a shell of privacy, but in fact generated and sustained by it. See also Brooks, *The Melodramatic Imagination*, on the ways Maggie avoids the temptations of melodrama (194–197).

30. Pippin misses this transformation in Maggie: "There is very little evidence that Maggie, however hard and willful she has become, will ever be able to fill that role, being the prim 'little nun,' 'Roman matron,' 'Madonna,' and 'doll' she has always been" (78). In claiming to resist moral conclusiveness in the overall structure of the novel, he is ascribing an unjust moral simplicity to the characters.

31. Kventsel puts the relation in psychoanalytic terms, describing "the reflexive element in Maggie's relationship to Charlotte, as if, like a virginal daughter, she were seeking a maternal pattern for her emergent sexuality" (185).

32. The importance of recognition of a fundamental estrangement between the self and others in James's fiction has long been a topic of criticism. Pippin places it in an ethical cast in discussing "the claims of others to be and to be treated as free, equally independent end-setting, end-seeking subjects" (29). Martha Nussbaum offered an earlier philosophical take on this approach in *Love's Knowledge*. On the literary side, David McWhirter in *Desire and Love in Henry James* uses it to argue for a Jamesian conception of love: "Instead of projecting onto the other the infinite variety of what *might* be, love embraces the other's limited and imperfect reality, and invites and accepts the binding and defining embrace offered by the other" (6). And John Bayley's *Characters of Love* (1960) argues for "the intense and curious apprehension of a separate being" as essential both to the representation of love and the creation of individuated characters (38).

33. Another general ethical account of this phenomenon is Butler's, which extends what Pippin (29) identifies in James beyond action to epistemology: "If letting the other live is part of any ethical definition of recognition, then this version of recognition is based less on knowledge than on an apprehension of epistemic limits" (*Giving an Account of Oneself* 43).

34. See Freedman 236–245, for a discussion of the political limitations of Jamesian aestheticism in *The Golden Bowl*. Seltzer's earlier suggestion that "in James's late fiction, love and power are two ways of saying the same thing" (94) is a forerunner of this line of argument.

35. For a fuller history of Jamesian aesthetics and mid-century African American writers, see Bronstein, "*The Princess* among the Polemicists."

36. See Eckman 168–169. The presence of *The Princess*, with its attention to the class politics of the dispossessed, suggests that Baldwin sought out not racialized discourse in James, but discourse that provided useful *analogies* to race.

37. This brief document is speculatively dated to 1949–1950 by the Schomburg Center (James Baldwin Papers, Folder 42.17).

38. Letter from Baldwin to Robert Mills from Istanbul; received March 28, 1963. Archived in the Robert Park Mills Papers, Folder 2.2.

39. For further analysis of Baldwin's conception of American identity as a mingled inheritance from Du Bois and (Henry) James, see Posnock 230.

40. Baldwin softened his negative view of Daisy at some point, referring to her as "poor Daisy Miller" in the interview with Leeming (52).

41. Millicent Bell describes Isabel: "It is the theoretical right of choice that she cherishes— to the point, indeed, of making no choice, and so preserving choice still longer" (111).

42. For years, Baldwin attempted to adapt *Giovanni's Room* for stage or screen, and in the process introduced more Jamesian echoes. See, for instance, one draft movie script of the novel (James Baldwin Papers, Folder 14.8). A few examples: after he is fired, Giovanni expresses his desire to decorate the room he and David share; David says, "*Vengo, vengo*" (100)—an echo of Charlotte's call to Amerigo in *The Golden Bowl*; like Charlotte and Amerigo, this is also the beginning of an attempt to found a romance on constrained circumstances. The movie script also uses numerous dashes to signal conversation trailing off, in circling dialogues that sound like many of those in late James: "HELLA: Oh. I've come to Paris to find out—! why have you come? / DAVID: Oh—to find out—!" (4)

43. Baldwin liked this type of formulation; compare, for instance, the climax of *The Fire Next Time*, when he evokes the possibility that Americans might "achieve our country, and

change the history of the world" (347). America is both already existing and in need of achievement.

44. See Sedgwick, *Tendencies* 75 for the locus classicus of this line of argument.

45. The Prince in *The Golden Bowl* observes that for Americans "duplicity, like 'love,' had to be joked about. It couldn't be 'gone into'" (XXIII.15).

46. Baldwin's stigmatization of innocence is similar to what Lauren Berlant describes as his critique of an aesthetics of passivity: "associating the human with the suffering actually limits the human to a mode of absolute passivity that, ethically, cannot embody the human in its fullness" (*Female Complaint* 57).

47. Letter of December 28, 1946 (James Baldwin Collection). This language sounds more like the other author with multiple books on Baldwin's list of ten novels that helped him escape the ghetto: Dostoevsky.

48. Whether or not Baldwin actually read James for the first time so late, Baldwin's sense of an individual identity starts taking on the language of mirrors, traps, and cages for the first time—suggesting a sudden shift in his understanding of the problem, a shift for which James likely provided some of the language.

49. Drowning hovers over this novel ominously: its opening section describes the descent into depression of Rufus, a black man in a relationship with a white woman and struggling with the shadow of stereotyped social roles cast upon the relationship. He kills himself by jumping off a bridge into water.

50. There are more specific *Heart of Darkness* allusions in the opening of the novel, and more in its drafts, that give greater support to the idea that he had Conrad in his ear while writing: the opening paragraph talks about "an ocean which faced away from Europe into a darker past" (3); in one draft, he writes, "The countryside will be still, there will be hanging over it darkness and intolerable mystery, terror, death"; in another passage two characters sit "at the black heart of the mystery" (James Baldwin Papers, Folder 14.3, pp. 2, 74). This particular passage sounds like Marlow: e.g., "We live, as we dream—alone" (70).

51. Baldwin's universalism was one of the most transmissible parts of his writing in odd ways even in his own time; Ross Posnock points out how Amiri Baraka, in describing Baldwin, finds himself "using a universalist rhetoric ordinarily inimical to his nationalism" (223).

52. For Baldwin's account of the Congress, see his essay "Princes and Powers." Perhaps symptomatically, Achebe's account of his meeting with Baldwin is also one of missed connections: Achebe was a longtime fan, but they didn't quite manage to meet until 1980 (172–173).

53. The French phrase is "le traitement sans fard" (87). The critic he's discussing is Paul Goodman, the *New York Times* reviewer, whose language does seem to echo old critiques of James: the characters of the novel "exist in a kind of vacuum," he complains (5).

54. The political scientist Jack Turner has recently argued that Baldwin is part of an undervalued tradition of American individualism focusing on "a commitment to examine oneself for complicity" (2).

Chapter 3

1. Conrad, *Nigger of the "Narcissus"* x. For an interpretation of the idea of "seeing" in this passage, see Jesse Matz, *Literary Impressionism and Modernist Aesthetics* 32. Ian Watt's

famous interpretation of this preface does say, in passing, "The force of the word 'make' is worth noting" ("Conrad's Preface" 109).

2. See, e.g., Todorov; Brooks, *Reading for the Plot*.

3. For instance, B. S. Johnson published *The Unfortunates* (1969) with all chapters but the first and the last unspecified, collected in a box and unbound, to be read in an order of the reader's choice; Julio Cortázar's *Hopscotch* (1963; in English, 1966) provided instructions of many possible orders in which the chapters might be read. More recently, the still-emerging form of hypertext fiction provides new ways for an author to refuse to dictate an order of experience.

4. The unsigned and generally positive reviewer wrote in the *New-York Daily Tribune* that "the rotten craft goes to the bottom like a shot, with all hands save a few members of the crew" (Simmons, Peters, and Stape 319).

5. For a fuller analysis of Conrad (and Faulkner) as making use of first-time readers' partial knowledge, see Bronstein, "On Not Re-reading Novels."

6. Watt 177ff. *Lord Jim* is certainly less full of such delayed decoding; a good example of the difference is the episode of the dog that causes Marlow to use the word "cur" in Jim's hearing and leads Jim to feel he has been insulted. In contrast to the instances in *Heart of Darkness*, Marlow carefully highlights the presence of the dog and refers to the "yellow-dog thing" (32) before the misunderstanding occurs, highlighting the retrospective understanding rather than the confusion of the moment. Watt says that "the term delayed decoding applies less well" (271) to this novel; but it is not merely because "the process . . . is so much more complex"; instead, it is that retrospection rather than the moment has become the primary source of meaning.

7. For instance, a recent postcolonial reading of *Lord Jim* claims that "Marlow is an obtuse man who does not understand the implications of the story he himself tells" (Henthorne 147); J. Hillis Miller comments that "a straightforward identification of Marlow and Conrad is an elementary reading mistake" ("Foreword" 7). A straightforward assumption of ironic distance is an equally elementary mistake, especially when Marlow's language and phrasing when making general statements so often echoes Conrad's.

8. This is a recurring theme of criticism; a particularly sensitive and less judgmental reading of these tensions is Peters. Erdinast-Vulcan has a similar argument.

9. For a venerable list of the classic Conradian "major inward conflicts," see Guerard 57–59. For a more recent analysis of Conrad as irremediably divided, see Daphna Erdinast-Vulcan: Conrad is a "modernist at war with modernity" (5).

10. Watt himself uses the term "thematic apposition" to describe Marlow's ordering of incidents according to his retrospective analysis in *Lord Jim* in order to force the reader to ask certain questions (*Conrad in the Nineteenth Century* 280–281). Even then, however, the thematic logic is framed as a production of *Marlow's* stages of understanding.

11. The second camp is far more numerous, though critics within it disagree about what exactly the political significance of Conrad's questioning habits is. Walkowitz, for instance, enlists Conrad as a producer of "critical cosmopolitanism": "By creating distrust for established reputations, Conrad creates a less natural conception of Englishness" (53). By contrast, other critics defend the political efficacy of realism. See, e.g., Gikandi "Realism"; Sorensen; and Andrade, "The Problem" and "Representing," discussed in the last section of this chapter.

12. For treatments of literary impressionism that discuss Conrad's relation to Ford, see Jesse Matz, *Literary Impressionism and Modernist Aesthetics*; and Todd K. Bender, *Literary Impressionism in Jean Rhys, Ford Madox Ford, Joseph Conrad, and Charlotte Brontë*.

13. "On le sente partout, mais qu'on ne le voie pas" (*Correspondence* II.681).

14. This structure has characteristics similar to Empson's "double irony"—the form of irony where it is no longer clear what would constitute an "unironic" misreading. Double irony can be corrosively skeptical, but it can also be protective of deeply held commitments (Empson 132–134).

15. See, for instance, Ares in the *Iliad*: "grim as murderous Ares, / his good son Panic stalking beside him" (Trans. Fagles 13.350–351). The epithets attached to the characters are throughout the novel as much in the style of mock-epic as they are mockery of newspaper copy; their vicious ironies carry a note of disappointment and regret from the start. Michael Greaney argues that "journalistic language infect[s] Conrad's prose, and mould[s] the most intimate fears of his characters into its own lexicon of cliché" (145); however, the irony cuts primarily against the world that fails in comparison to the language, rather than against language mockingly insufficient to the subtleties of the world.

16. For instance, all three feature a new figure invading established institutions with well-worn habits: the Assistant Commissioner, M. Vladimir, and the Professor seem to disdain Chief Inspector Heat, Verloc, and the older anarchists respectively.

17. Style as aesthetic effect is often neglected in Conrad criticism. For instance, although "*literary* style" is ostensibly what Rebecca Walkowitz's *Cosmopolitan Style* "focuses on" (2), it is unfortunately absent from the Conrad chapter in particular. The substance of Walkowitz's argument proceeds not from style but from content—what Conrad says, what characters think. Consequently her argument implies that Conrad's "literary tactic" is "purposeful imitation of what passes for nature" (37)—which is precisely the opposite of what the resolutely unnatural style of *The Secret Agent* does. In the one moment where she does discuss style, the analysis seems general, rather than appropriate to this specific novel: "By alternating between omniscient narrative and free indirect discourse, often several times in a single paragraph, Conrad conflates the practice of the novel with practices of social perception, such that the reader's knowledge is shaped by the way that characters read" (50). Conrad does alternate as she describes, but the effect is very different in *The Secret Agent* than it is in most other novels. The free indirect discourse is highly ironized, and his narrator equally alien and strange; the real ambiguity is in the reader's relation to the narrator's ironic commentary on the characters, and the characters' perspectives are never present without irony; see Armstrong, *Play* 89. For further discussion of gaps between narrator and character, see Lothe 185.

18. For other critics who have expressed skepticism of the second half, see Watt, *Conrad in the Nineteenth Century* 308; Esty, *Unseasonable* 88; Erdinast-Vulcan 35.

19. The shock of this twist may also be registered by the fact that when James has Marcher echo this passage in *The Beast in the Jungle* (see chapter 1 on the connection between these two works), he makes two contrasting possibilities: one involving death, the other a story of a life upended. Marcher describes having "to wait for—to have to meet, to face, to see suddenly break out in my life; possibly destroying all further consciousness, possibly annihilating me; possibly, on the other hand, only altering everything, striking at the root of all my world and leaving me to the consequences, however they shape themselves" (XVII.72). James reverses the order—death first, then the disruption of life—anticipating

the disillusionment Marcher will suffer at the end. Note the shared language: both have a tricolon of infinitives; both use *annihilate* and *destroy* as key verbs parallel to one another; Conrad's "whole precious world" and repeated "all" becomes James's "root of all my world."

20. Much later in the novel, there occurs a passage that has long been recognized as a kind of parody or echo of the confusing opening: Captain Mitchell's tour of the town for a visitor who doesn't know the history (473–489). Notably, Mitchell does offer explicit political commentary of the sort the narrator avoids in the opening pages. The reader, also, is in the opposite position—now knowing enough to put together the history in a way the visitor can't.

21. Jonathan Culler argues that the terminology of omniscience is at fault, in blurring the boundaries between "rather different phenomena"; as he points out, "It is the *idea* of omniscient narrative rather than the diverse practices to which the name applies that should sadden or outrage us" (201).

22. For a more characteristic example of critical distaste for Conrad's rhetoric, see Peter Nicholls's comments about his "inflated vocabulary" (171).

23. That this is characteristic of Nostromo can be seen in many examples; for instance, thinking of Captain Mitchell, "He had no discretion. He would betray the treasure. And Nostromo had made up his mind that the treasure should not be betrayed" (419).

24. Of course, he (again ambiguously) modifies it in the next sentence, "The brilliant Costaguanero of the boulevards had died from solitude and want of faith in himself and others" (496). Rather than requiring a change to the previous sentence, this makes more sense as a modulation of what might constitute saving simplicity: "faith in himself and others."

25. See, for instance, J. Hillis Miller, *Fiction and Repetition*.

26. Brown, *Utopian Generations*, is one of several studies that seek to approach influence-like relationships by moving beyond "influence" as the central trope. See, for instance, Mallios and Peterson. These critics apply to influence the trends of criticism more broadly in de-emphasizing authorship in favor of cultural surroundings: confluences of historical circumstances replace authors' reading history.

27. See also, most famously on this topic, Chakrabarty (discussed in the introduction).

28. A better analogy to Ngũgĩ's "preying on" is the model Pascale Casanova describes as the sixteenth-century "appropriation" of classical literature in France: "French poets were being counseled to seize, devour, and digest an ancient heritage in order to convert it into national literary 'assets'" (54). For a more complex analysis of the way Ngũgĩ negotiates the multiple traditions available for his use and the political implications of his choices, see Amoko. Gikandi, "Fantasy," is an impressionistic exploration of the different ways the literary past can connect to the politics of the present in postcolonial circumstances.

29. This attitude is visible, also, in the framing of a BBC program produced by an acquaintance of Ngũgĩ from Leeds, Edward Blishen, who praises early Ngũgĩ simultaneously for having "something original to offer" and for having "readiness to draw upon a serious study" of previous writers ("Modern African Writing").

30. There are a few allusions to *Heart of Darkness* in *Grain of Wheat*, all of them strongly associated with the perspective of the British officer Thompson; see 53–56, 134. Nothing from *Heart of Darkness* has the larger structural dimension that the *Under Western Eyes* and *Nostromo* connections do. See West-Pavlov for a comprehensive overview of *Heart of Darkness* and Ngũgĩ.

31. In a 1996 interview, Ngũgĩ makes a similar point: Conrad "does not actually have faith in those forces which can change imperialism" (Sander and Lindfors 374).

32. For other overviews of the similarities and differences, see Nazareth, "Teaching"; Gikandi, *Ngũgĩ*; Sewlall; and Sarvan. On *Petals of Blood* and *Nostromo*, see Ker.

33. Nazareth points out that *A Grain of Wheat* echoes *Nostromo* in content as well as form (*Literature* 132–133).

34. In 1964, Ngũgĩ was between writing *Weep Not Child* and *The River Between*; he had not yet begun *A Grain of Wheat*. West-Pavlov, Sewlall, and Sarvan, in discussing the later novel, cite the language about "requestioning things"; Ker applies this to *Petals of Blood* (76).

35. The audio is available at the British Library and is unambiguous. An early transcription ("Africa Abroad") also has a second "he questions" rather than "requestions."

36. See Sicherman's essays for a critique of the limited perspectives offered at Makerere and the beneficial effect of Leeds. The more "traditional" aesthetic criticism, like today's postcolonially informed critics, scorned the aspect of Conrad invested in the possibility of heroics; see, e.g., Leavis's dismissal of romance in *Lord Jim* (190).

37. Stephen Wall in *The Observer* commented, "To have a situation like the Kenya emergency written about from an African point of view should anyway extend European sympathies" (1967); the *TLS* said that Ngũgĩ "succeeds in distributing his dramatic sympathies with a finesse that really deserves the term 'negative capability'" ("African Anxieties" 1967).

38. Although full excavation and acknowledgment of British crimes during the state of emergency has been very slow to arrive, the 1960s saw the beginnings of mild revisionism in England in public discussion of Mau Mau, at least among the literary elite who might have been reading *A Grain of Wheat*; to take the *TLS* as an example, in 1962 a reviewer can take for granted that Mau Mau was "a cul-de-sac of tribal savagery and superstition" ("Terror in Kenya"); by 1967, two weeks after the review of *A Grain of Wheat*, another reviewer welcomes enthusiastically the argument that Mau Mau "was essentially a major element in the nationalist movement" ("Kikuyu"). The publication in 1963 of Josiah Mwangi Kariuki's memoir *"Mau Mau" Detainee* was a crucial turning point. By the time *A Grain of Wheat* arrived, in other words, the small subset of the British public attending to new African fiction had become willing to treat its depiction of events as plausible. See Elkins for a historian's much-belated account of events, which helped to precipitate a 2012 legal ruling in favor of surviving detainees.

39. Carol Sicherman points out that Ngũgĩ's tendency to mix anecdote, myth, and historical fact freely in his discussion of past events in his novels is in part a defense of the political force of such forms of knowledge: "Myths made things happen during the Emergency" ("Ngũgĩ wa Thiong'o and the Writing" 312).

40. The local echoes of *Nostromo* are myriad. The "tenacious gringo ghosts" take the form now of white Europeans slain by young men of the town: "The Foreigners were never seen again except that for years, late at night, you could see the whiteness of a ghost wailing to its kind for blood and vengeance" (147). Similarly a neighboring town is described as "famous only because it was originally the centre of hides and skins trade and also of trade in wattle barks" (103)—evoking Sulaco, which had "never been anything more important than a coasting port with a fairly large trade in ox-hides and indigo" in Conrad's novel.

41. For other critical approaches that seek to defend realism, see Sorensen, and Andrade ("The Problem"). Andrade elsewhere argues, as I do here, that modernist

techniques do not always foster alienated distance; but where she focuses on their representational capacity, I focus on what they do to readers' attitudes toward what they represent ("Representing").

42. Peter Nazareth reaches for a similar, though more paradoxical, metaphor: "The Conrad text becomes a door through which Ngũgĩ enters his own African world and thereby speaks to the world at large, the global world" ("Teaching" 170).

43. Gikandi's analysis of an alternation between allegory and irony in the text comes to a similar conclusion about questioning leading to certainty: "The purpose of irony in the novel is to secure the allegorical narrative of national independence at a time when its ideals are threatened at their foundations" (Ngũgĩ 112).

44. See the essays in Hamner for examples; many of these are the more common kind of reception study today—focusing on the uniqueness of particular reading communities.

45. See Nazareth, "Out of Darkness," "Teaching".

Chapter 4

1. David Wyatt, placing Faulkner in a line of twentieth-century American writers who offer "secret histories" that replace the platitudes of American myths, says that Faulkner seeks to "free his countrymen from unusable pasts" (90).

2. Faulkner studies has long been sensitive to the untimeliness of his novels—the way they required a decade or two to find an audience; the history of their postwar canonization as a context just as important as their Depression origins. On mid-century reception, see Schwartz, Barnhisel; on the Depression as a context of production, see Godden, and Atkinson, who—symptomatic of how large the postwar canonization looms—feels a need to justify his attention to prewar contexts: "Faulkner's unenthusiastic reception at the time should not be taken now as evidence of his detachment from the cultural milieu of the 1930s" (236).

3. Brian Glavey recuperates spatial form via its queer connections in Djuna Barnes's *Nightwood* as a technique of what he calls "dazzling estrangement": "a particular form of early-twentieth-century camouflage that works not by hiding its object but by confusing the spectator with bold and fantastic patterns of color" (752). A similar reading of Hightower would obviously be possible: his ambiguous queerness in the text, his strange and dramatic sermons in which "God and salvation and the galloping horses and his dead grandfather thundered" (446).

4. It should also be noted that Sartre, in condemning Faulkner for lacking faith in the future, relies on quotations that he takes to express Faulkner's views that I argue in chapter 1 are specifically placed as ideological antagonists, including the statement from the elder Compson, "The field only reveals to man . . ."

5. See Moreland for another analysis of Faulkner's writing as a process of development away from high modernism: "Faulkner attempted to exorcise the relatively unfocused ironic bitterness of cosmopolitan literary modernism" (27).

6. For a summary of the history of opposition to the appendix, see Cohen 249–252, 255–256. By contrast, the appendix made enough of an impression on Toni Morrison for her to cite it extensively in her MA thesis (Wofford 25).

7. Many of the "contradictions" in terms of character portrayal seem less stark when the appendix is viewed not as a competing version of the book but as merely one more part of it: for instance, Cohen's claim that the "sane" Jason of the appendix ill accords with

the neurotic and family-obsessed Jason of the novel is true; but this reads to me as a depiction of the same character at different points in time; I have no trouble believing that with Quentin IV, Benjy, and his parents gone, the novel's Jason could easily have competed with Snopeses. Seeking all of the young Jason in the appendix seems a curious proposition, as though the appendix could only be a replacement for the novel rather than an addition to it.

8. He uses the phrase *tour de force* twice in the same answer to an apparently irrelevant question; the phrase clearly pleased him (*Faulkner in the University* 87). The four parts of *The Sound and the Fury* were supposedly sequential attempts to capture Caddy (*Faulkner in the University* 1).

9. *Lion in the Garden* 58. Faulkner's other rubric for discussing this topic is *failure*: "In my opinion, my work has all failed, it ain't quite good enough, which is the only real reason to write another one" (*Faulkner in the University* 143). Where Conrad used the oscillation between skepticism and idealism to generate art, Faulkner uses the idea of continuing representational failure. Later asked about the ranking of novelists in which the comments on Hemingway occur, Faulkner said that Thomas Wolfe—whom he ranked first, "failed the best because he had tried the hardest, he had taken the longest gambles" (*Faulkner in the University* 206).

10. See, e.g., Weinstein, *Unknowing* 192. For Faulkner-specific readings along these lines, see Kartiganer, *The Fragile Thread* (1979), and Stephen M. Ross, *Fiction's Inexhaustible Voice* (1991).

11. For an example of recent close reading in this vein, see Godden, *The Economy of Complex Words*.

12. This kind of analysis accords well with Stanley Fish's call for attention to "the developing responses of the reader in relation to the words as they succeed one another in time" (387–388). My point is not to revive the debate over whether meaning resides with the author or the reader, but to examine the ways literary artifacts make use of readerly responses.

13. For a recent example of this sort of reading, see Weinstein 192.

14. Conrad's novels, for instance, as discussed in the previous chapter, historically have developed readerships that *do* see him as partaking in the pleasures of genre, rather than the critique of it.

15. Modernism as demystifying rupture from the past is an old critical narrative, but a live one. See, e.g., Mao and Walkowitz's re-enlivening of that narrative as "bad modernism" (3–5). Owens-Murphy, by contrast, points out modernism's continuing interest in romance as a genre.

16. See Wood for another example of different forms of reading changing a work's genre affiliation (585).

17. An allusion in *Absalom* suggests one of the great locales of this type of tragic structure: Charles Bon is described as having a "Scythian glitter" (77). The most famous of literary Scythians was Tamburlaine, the hero of Marlowe's tragedy. Faulkner liked and read Marlowe (*Faulkner in the University* 145); he also owned the *Complete Plays* (*Faulkner's Library* 70). The "Scythian glitter" remains something of a critical mystery (see Urgo and Polk 42). Tamburlaine promises "aspiring minds" and "the wondrous architecture of the world" but is ultimately really concerned with an "earthly crown," and cannot conceive of any better aim for his tremendous skill and will. Marlowe's tragedies often work by ironizing the limitations of their protagonists' dreams rather than their heights.

18. Sutpen has long been identified as "the South" writ large; see, e.g., Brivic 34–35.

19. Among other things, *The Hamlet*'s narrative structure is a superb demonstration of the ways in which a society can make it impossible for its poorest members to perceive the totality of the society that oppresses them.

20. For further readings in this vein, see Godden on how "economic structures may be read as the generative source of fictional forms" (2); and Urgo, discussed above. Godden's general reading of *The Hamlet* places it in the context of economic shifts at the time in order to make Flem stand in for the repressed sharecropper labor force.

21. The sheer excess of the simile suggests Michael Wood's argument about literary styles that invite "distracted reading": "not meaning but the effect of meaning in meaning's absence" (588).

22. In *The Town*, the sequel to *The Hamlet*, the Snopes family so perfectly follows their own orderly plot-line that Ratliff begins to think of them in terms of scientific laws: "that same sort of osmosis by which, according to Ratliff, they had covered Frenchman's Bend, the chain unbroken, every Snopes in Frenchman's Bend moving up one step, leaving that last slot at the bottom open for the next Snopes to appear from nowhere and fill" (8). The imagery combines the regularity of science with the hierarchical image of a chain of being.

23. This is perhaps why the few readings available of *Sometimes a Great Notion* tend to focus on psycho-biographical readings; e.g., with Hank and Lee Stamper, Kesey is "exploring the two predominant veins of his own personality" (McFarlane 53).

24. In conversation with Faulkner once, Cowley referred to "that class at Stanford which was so damned talented"—that is, the 1960 class that included Kesey (*Conversations with Malcolm Cowley* 205). Faulkner's response was sympathetic to the difficulties of running a classroom of "aggressive" young students, singling out "especially that combination of Kesey and [Larry] McMurtry, who seem to have been real brash characters" (205–206).

25. Though *Cuckoo's Nest* is famous these days primarily through the 1975 film, it was a bestseller when it appeared in 1962 and had a run as a Broadway play in 1963–1964.

26. Mark McGurl evokes an incongruity between Kesey's reputation and his institutional affiliation: "The fact that Kesey, of all people, was a creative writing graduate student tells us a lot" (*Program Era* 200). Kesey's career, up until the aftermath of the bus trip, might be described as a sequence of actions and affiliations in which the phrase "Kesey, of all people . . ." might appear.

27. See Aboul-Ela for a reading of multiple kinds of global use of Faulkner.

28. As with Conrad's postcolonial connections, critical treatment of these writers has often been marked by vague uncertainties that influence will inevitably privilege the earlier author over the later—see, e.g., Duvall.

29. *Conversations* 101. See a similar statement by Baldwin (*Conversations* 7). Ellison, who generally critiqued modernist American writers' unwillingness to confront America's racial history, carved out an exception for Faulkner (*Conversations* 19).

30. "The book I have been doing on the lane is a third person work, but something was lacking; I was not free to impose my perception and bizarre eye on the god-author who is supposed to be viewing the scene, so I tried something that will be extremely difficult to pull off, and to my knowledge, has never been tried before—the narrator is going to be a character" (*One Flew Over the Cuckoo's Nest* 338). Note that what he's talking about is not the simple fact of first-person narration, but the particular kind of character Bromden is, a narrative voice made flesh, silent to the characters yet present to them. Kesey conceived of

his writing during this period as a formal problem: schizophrenic pattern-discernment as a replacement for authorial commentary.

31. For an example of this extraordinary extension, see the hunting excursion of the hound Molly, who first enters the novel staring at the moon (228). Brief scenes of her punctuate human interactions and flashbacks for eighty pages, before a final intersection with the characters (308).

32. See Tanner 386; McGurl, *Program Era* 207–212.

Chapter 5

1. Coetzee is clearly of both camps, as his *The Master of Petersburg* is an early entry into the genre of fiction about real novelists. The reapproach to older material through its retelling or resetting in new time periods persists alongside the interest in novelizations of novelists' lives: Ozick, besides *Dictation*, also wrote *Foreign Bodies* (2010), discussed in the introduction, retelling *The Ambassadors* in 1952 Paris. The so-called Year of Henry James, which produced *The Master* and *Author, Author*, also saw Alan Hollinghurst's *The Line of Beauty*, featuring references to James amid Jamesian themes of homosexuality and the tension between art and life.

2. The stories of James's typist have another, more recent parallel: 2013 saw three novels centering on the difficult figure of Zelda Fitzgerald: *Z* by Anne Fowler; *Call Me Zelda* by Erika Robuck, and *Beautiful Fools* by R. Clifton Spargo. In 2015 there also appeared Stewart O'Nan's *West of Sunset*, primarily about F. Scott. The novels of modernists-as-characters seem to continue unabated.

3. Jameson describes modern pastiche as "speech through all the masks and voices stored up in the imaginary museum of a now global culture" (*Postmodernism* 18). This is perhaps how Ozick's novella starts, but not how its style ends.

4. For instance, this passage from *The Master* is derided as "oddly vague": "He was disturbed by the idea that he longed, now more than ever before, in this strange house in the country, for someone to hold him, not speak or move even, but to embrace him, stay with him" ("Pseudo-impressionism?" 114).

5. Kevin Ohi reads Jamesian style as offering a form of queer futurity that is the opposite of Lee Edelman's hegemonic reproductive futurism: rather than complacently reproducing the present, it looks to the future for change. Ohi glosses James: "The novel will prosper . . . as long as it *is* the future to which life aspires but with which it was does not coincide" (*Henry James and the Queerness of Style* 15).

6. Compare Ozick's "unchangeable yet altered" with, for instance, the Princess's statement in *The Golden Bowl*: "*Nothing* has passed between them—that's what has happened" (XXIV.213). James's novels are full of nothing being an event, and silences that contain dialogue.

7. Theodore Martin suggests, about Joyce Carol Oates's book *Wild Nights*—a series of impersonations of American modernists' styles in stories about them—that "imitation gives us access to the way that literature itself . . . inevitably exceeds the confines of its historical moment."

8. "'Typewriter' is ambiguous. The word meant both typing machine and female typist," says Kittler (183). For Heyns and Ozick, the more interesting problem is not in the elision of the space between woman and machine, but in the way the machine renders the woman's psyche open to invasion.

9. It's perilously easy to read these novels as yet another example of the ways individuals are trapped by the powerful voices and institutions around them: Jessica A. Kent, in one of the few scholarly treatments of Ozick's novella, suggests that "Ozick's fictional Theodora Bosanquet . . . can neither claim authorship herself nor escape from the power structures that surround her. And Cynthia Ozick is similarly trapped in a net of forces like ubiquitous technologies that shorten the attention span" (114). Of course Theodora and Ozick cannot "escape" societal forces around them; but Ozick's triumphant refashioning of older style and Theodora's break for independence are suggestions that the point is not to escape the net, but to become its weaver, to blur the boundary between spider and fly.

10. As discussed in the introduction, numerous critics have pointed out that aesthetic autonomy was actually a great deal more than that. See Siraganian; Goldstone.

Works Cited

Editions of Baldwin, Conrad, Faulkner, James, and Woolf
I have attempted to avoid cluttering up the text with unsightly acronyms for my major primary sources. I therefore lay out my practice with regard to primary editions here. Exceptions will be noted in the text.

James Baldwin
Collected Essays. Ed. Toni Morrison. New York: Library of America, 1998.
Conversations with James Baldwin. Jackson: University Press of Mississippi, 1989.
Giovanni's Room. New York: Delta, 1956.

Joseph Conrad
Citations to Joseph Conrad's works are primarily to the Dent collected editions and include volume titles and page numbers:
The Works of Joseph Conrad. London: J. M. Dent & Sons Ltd., 1923–1924.

The exceptions are those volumes where the *Cambridge Collected Works* edition is available. I have used the following:
Lord Jim: A Tale. Ed. J. H. Stape and Ernest W. SullivanII. Cambridge: Cambridge University Press, 2012.
Notes on Life and Letters. Ed. J. H. Stape. Cambridge: Cambridge University Press, 2004.
The Secret Agent. Ed. Bruce Harkness and S. W. Reid. Cambridge: Cambridge University Press, 1990.
Victory. Ed. J. H. Stape and Alexandre Fachard. Cambridge: Cambridge University Press, 2016.
Youth, Heart of Darkness, The End of the Tether. Ed. Owen Knowles. Cambridge: Cambridge University Press, 2010.

In the last part of chapter 1, I have used the Dent edition of the *Notes on Life and Letters* rather than Cambridge, as this is the edition Faulkner owned.

Citations to Conrad's letters are to the Cambridge edition, by volume and page number:

The Collected Letters of Joseph Conrad. 8 vols. Ed. Frederick R. Karl, Laurence Davies, and Owen Knowles. Cambridge: Cambridge University Press, 1983–2008.

Other sources:

The Secret Agent. Ridgway's, a Militant Weekly for God and Country. October 6, 1906: 12–15, 63. [New York Edition.]

William Faulkner

Citations to Faulkner's novels are to the Library of America texts. Other Faulkner works— primarily interviews, speeches, and letters—are mentioned in the text by title.

Essays, Speeches and Public Letters. Ed. James B. Meriwether. London: Chatto & Windus, 1967.

Faulkner in the University: Class Conferences at the University of Virginia 1957–1958. Ed. Frederick L. Gwynn and Joseph L. Blotner. Charlottesville: University of Virginia Press, 1959.

Lion in the Garden: Interviews with William Faulkner 1926–1962. Ed. James B. Meriwether and Michael Millgate. New York: Random House, 1968.

Novels 1926–1929: Soldier's Pay, Mosquitoes, Flags in the Dust, The Sound and the Fury. New York: Library of America, 2006.

Novels 1930–1935: As I Lay Dying; Sanctuary; Light in August; Pylon. New York: Library of America, 1985.

Novels 1936–1940: Absalom, Absalom!, The Unvanquished, If I Forget Thee, Jerusalem [The Wild Palms], The Hamlet. New York: Library of America, 1990.

Novels 1942–1954: Go Down, Moses; Intruder in the Dust; Requiem for a Nun; A Fable. New York: Library of America, 1994.

Novels 1957–1962: The Town; The Mansion; The Reivers. New York: Library of America, 1999.

Uncollected Stories. Ed. Joseph Blotner. New York: Vintage Books, 1979.

Henry James

Citations to James's novels and prefaces are primarily by volume and page number to the *New York Edition*:

The Novels and Tales of Henry James. 26 vols. New York: Charles Scribner's Sons, 1907–1917.

For *The Portrait of a Lady* and *The Ambassadors*, which are now available in the new Cambridge Edition of the *Complete Fiction*, I have used the relevant volumes:

The Ambassadors. Ed. Nicola Bradbury. Cambridge: Cambridge University Press, 2015.

The Portrait of a Lady. Ed. Michael Anesko. Cambridge: Cambridge University Press, 2016.

Essays beyond the prefaces are cited by volume and page number in the *Literary Criticism*:

Literary Criticism. Ed. Leon Edel. 2 vols. New York: Library of America, 1984.

The American Scene is cited from the following edition:

Collected Travel Writings: Great Britain and America. New York: Library of American, 1993. 351–736.

Other sources are listed here:

The Complete Notebooks of Henry James. Ed. Leon Edel and Lyall Harris Powers. Oxford: Oxford University Press, 1987.

Letters. Ed. Leon Edel. Volume IV. Cambridge, MA: Harvard University Press, 1984.

Novels 1901–1902: The Sacred Fount; The Wings of the Dove. New York: Library of America, 2006.

Virginia Woolf

Virginia Woolf's essays are cited by volume and page number:

The Essays of Virginia Woolf. 6 vols. Ed. Andrew McNeillie and Stuart N. Clark. San Diego: Harcourt, 1988–.

Other editions are as follows:

The Diary of Virginia Woolf. 5 vols. Ed. Anne Olivier Bell and Andrew McNeillie. New York: Harcourt Brace Jovanovich, 1979–1985.

Mrs. Dalloway. Ed. Morris Beja. Oxford: Shakespeare Head, 1996.

To the Lighthouse. Ed. Mark Hussey. New York: Harcourt, 2005.

The Waves. Harmondsworth: Penguin, 1964.

Other Works

Aboul-Ela, Hosam. *Other South: Faulkner, Coloniality, and the Mariátegui Tradition*. Pittsburgh: University of Pittsburgh Press, 2007.

Abrams, M. H. *The Mirror and the Lamp: Romantic Theory and the Critical Tradition*. Oxford: Oxford University Press, 1971.

Achebe, Chinua. *Hopes and Impediments: Selected Essays, 1965–1987*. London: Heinemann, 1988.

Adichie, Chimamanda Ngozi. *Americanah*. New York: Anchor Books, 2013.

———. *Half of a Yellow Sun*. London: Harper, 2007.

"Africa Abroad #81." April 15, 1964. Harry Ransom Centre. The Transcription Centre Collection. Box 5.5.

"African Anxieties." *Times Literary Supplement* (London), May 4, 1967: 373.

Amoko, Apollo Obonyo. *Postcolonialism in the Wake of the Nairobi Revolution*. New York: Palgrave Macmillan, 2010.

Anderson, Amanda. *The Powers of Distance: Cosmopolitanism and the Cultivation of Detachment*. Princeton, NJ: Princeton University Press, 2001.

Andrade, Susan Z. "The Problem of Realism and African Fiction." *Novel* 42.2 (Summer 2009): 183–189.

———. "Representing Slums and Home: Chris Abani's *GraceLand*." *Legacies of Modernism*. Ed. David James. Cambridge: Cambridge University Press, 2011. 225–242.

Appiah, Kwame Anthony. *The Ethics of Identity*. Princeton, NJ: Princeton University Press, 2005.

Armstrong, Paul. "In Defense of Reading: Or, Why Reading Still Matters in a Contextualist Age." *New Literary History* 42 (Spring 2011): 87–113.

———. *Play and the Politics of Reading: The Social Uses of Modernist Form*. Ithaca, NY: Cornell University Press, 2005.

Atkinson, Ted. *Faulkner and the Great Depression*. Athens: University of Georgia Press, 2006.

Austen, Jane. *Emma*. Ed. Fiona Stafford. London: Penguin, 2003.

Barnhisel, Greg. *Cold War Modernisms: Art, Literature, and American Cultural Diplomacy*. New York: Columbia University Press, 2015.

Bayley, John. *The Characters of Love: A Study in the Literature of Personality*. New York: Basic Books, 1960.

Belcher, Wendy Laura. *Abyssinia's Samuel Johnson: Ethiopian Thought in the Making of an English Author*. Oxford: Oxford University Press, 2012.

Bell, Millicent. *Meaning in Henry James*. Cambridge, MA: Harvard University Press, 1993.

Bender, Todd K. *Literary Impressionism in Jean Rhys, Ford Madox Ford, Joseph Conrad, and Charlotte Bronte*. New York: Garland, 1997.

Benedict, Clara, ed. *Constance Fenimore Woolson*. London: Ellis, n.d.

Berlant, Lauren. *Cruel Optimism*. Durham, NC: Duke University Press, 2011.

———. *The Female Complaint: The Unfinished Business of Sentimentality in American Culture*. Durham, NC: Duke University Press, 2008.

Berman, Jessica. *Modernist Commitments: Ethics, Politics, and Transnational Modernism*. New York: Columbia University Press, 2011.

Best, Stephen, and Sharon Marcus. "Surface Reading: An Introduction." *Representations* 108.1 (Fall 2009): 1–21.

Blair, Amy. *Reading Up: Middle-Class Readers and the Culture of Success in the Early Twentieth-Century United States*. Philadelphia: Temple University Press, 2012.

Blair, Sara. *Henry James and the Writing of Race and Nation*. Cambridge: Cambridge University Press, 1996.

Blishen, Edward. "Modern African Writing." African Writer's Club Audio Collection. Shelfmark C134/522 00:00′00″. Sound Archive, British Library, London, n.d.

Blotner, Joseph. *Selected Letters of William Faulkner*. New York: Random House, 1977,

———. *William Faulkner's Library: A Catalogue*. Charlottesville: University Press of Virginia, 1964.

Bloom, Harold. *The Anxiety of Influence: A Theory of Poetry*. 2nd ed. New York: Oxford University Press, 1997.

Booker, M. Keith. *The African Novel in English: An Introduction*. Portsmouth: Heinemann, 1998.

Booth, Wayne C. *The Rhetoric of Fiction*. 2nd ed. Harmondsworth: Penguin, 1983.

Bowman, David. "Read It Again, Sam." *New York Times*, December 4, 2011. Sunday Book Review: 75.

Branny, Grazyna. *A Conflict of Values: Alienation and Commitment in the Novels of Joseph Conrad and William Faulkner*. Kraków: Wydawnictwo Sponsor, 1997.

Brivic, Shelly. *Tears of Rage: The Racial Interface of Modern American Fiction*. Baton Rouge: Louisiana State University Press, 2008.

Bronstein, Michaela. "On Not Re-reading Novels: The Critical Value of First Reading." *Journal of Modern Literature* 39.3 (Spring 2016): 76–94.

———. "The Princess among the Polemicists: Aesthetics and Protest at Midcentury." *American Literary History* 29.1 (Spring 2017): 26–49.

Brooks, Peter. *Henry James Goes to Paris*. Princeton, NJ: Princeton University Press, 2007.

———. *The Melodramatic Imagination: Balzac, Henry James, Melodrama, and the Mode of Excess*. New Haven: Yale University Press, 1976.

———. *Reading for the Plot: Design and Intention in Narrative*. Cambridge, MA: Harvard University Press, 1984.

Brown, Nicholas. *Utopian Generations: The Political Horizon of Twentieth-Century Literature*. Princeton, NJ: Princeton University Press, 2005.

Browning, Robert. *The Ring and the Book*. Ed. Richard D. Altick. Harmondsworth: Penguin, 1971.

Butler, Christopher. *Early Modernism: Literature, Music, and Painting in Europe, 1900–1916*. Oxford: Clarendon Press, 1994.

Butler, Judith. *Bodies That Matter: On the Discursive Limits of "Sex"*. New York: Routledge, 1993.

———. *Giving an Account of Oneself*. New York: Fordham University Press, 2005.

Cameron, Sharon. *Thinking in Henry James*. Chicago: University of Chicago Press, 1989.

Caminero-Santangelo, Byron. *African Fiction and Joseph Conrad: Reading Postcolonial Intertextuality*. Albany: State University of New York Press, 2005.

Carothers, James B. "'In Conflict with Itself': The Nobel Prize Address in Faulknerian Contexts." *Faulkner and Formalism: Returns of the Text*. Ed. Annette Trefzer and Ann J. Abadie. Jackson: University Press of Mississippi, 2012. 20–40.

Casanova, Pascale. *The World Republic of Letters*. Trans. M. B. DeBevoise. Cambridge, MA: Harvard University Press, 2004.

Chakrabarty, Dipesh. *Provincializing Europe: Postcolonial Thought and Historical Difference*. Princeton, NJ: Princeton University Press, 2000.

Cleary, Joe. "Realism after Modernism and the Literary World-System." *Modern Language Quarterly* 73.3 (September 2012): 255–268.

Cohen, Philip. "'The Key to the Whole Book': Faulkner's *The Sound and the Fury*, the Compson Appendix, and Textual Instability." *Texts and Textuality: Textual Instability, Theory, and Interpretation*. Ed. Cohen. New York: Garland, 1997. 235–268.

Collits, Terry. "Anti-heroics and Epic Failures: The Case of *Nostromo*." *Conradian* 29.2 (Autumn 2004): 1–13.

Coates, Ta-Nehisi. *Between the World and Me*. New York: Spiegel & Grau, 2015.

———. "The Case for Reparations." *Atlantic* 313.5 (June 2014): 54–71.

———. "Is James Baldwin America's Greatest Essayist?" September 24, 2013. http://www.theatlantic.com/entertainment/archive/2013/09/is-james-baldwin-americas-greatest-essayist/279970/.

———. "Is James Baldwin America's Greatest Essayist?" September 26, 2013. http://www.theatlantic.com/entertainment/archive/2013/09/is-james-baldwin-americas-greatest-essayist/280041/.

Cook, Eleanor. *Against Coercion: Games Poets Play*. Stanford, CA: Stanford University Press, 1998.

Costello, Brannon W. "'Working' towards a Sense of Agency." *Twisted from the Ordinary: Essays on American Literary Naturalism*. Ed. Mary E. Papke. Knoxville: University of Tennessee Press, 2003. 169–187.

Cowley, Malcolm. *The Faulkner-Cowley File: Letters and Memories, 1944–1962*. New York: Viking, 1966.

Culler, Jonathan. *The Literary in Theory*. Stanford, CA: Stanford University Press, 2007.

Dames, Nicholas. *The Physiology of the Novel: Reading, Neural Science, and the Form of Victorian Fiction*. Oxford: Oxford University Press, 2007.

Davis, Todd F., and Kenneth Womack, eds. *Mapping the Ethical Turn: A Reader in Ethics, Culture, and Literary Theory*. Charlottesville: University Press of Virginia, 2001.

DeKoven, Marianne. *Rich and Strange: Gender, History, Modernism*. Princeton, NJ: Princeton University Press, 1991.

Derrida, Jacques. *Writing and Difference*. Trans. Alan Bass. Chicago: University of Chicago Press, 1978.

DiBattista, Maria. *Virginia Woolf's Major Novels: The Fables of Anon*. New Haven: Yale University Press, 1980.

Dickens, Charles. *Bleak House*. Ed. Nicola Bradbury. London: Penguin, 2003.

Dimock, Wai Chee. *Through Other Continents: American Literature across Deep Time*. Princeton, NJ: Princeton University Press, 2006.

———. "Weak Theory: Henry James, Colm Tóibín, and W. B. Yeats." *Critical Inquiry* 39 (Summer 2013): 732–753.

Duerden, Denis. Interview with Ngũgĩ wa Thiong'o. African Writer's Club Audio Collection. Shelfmark C134/401 00:22′05″. Sound Archive, British Library, London, 1964.

Duvall, John N. "Toni Morrison and the Anxiety of Faulknerian Influence." In Kolmerton, Ross, and Wittenberg: 3–16.

Eagleton, Terry. "Not Just Anybody." *London Review of Books* 39.1 (January 5, 2017): 35–37.

Eckman, Fern Marja. *The Furious Passage of James Baldwin*. New York: M. Evans, 1966.

Edel, Leon. *Henry James*. 5 vols. New York: Avon, 1953–1972.

Edelman, Lee. *No Future: Queer Theory and the Death Drive*. Durham, NC: Duke University Press, 2004.

Elfenbein, Andrew. "Defining Influence." *Modern Language Quarterly* 69.4 (December 2008): 433–436.

Eliot, George. *The Mill on the Floss*. Ed. A. S. Byatt. London: Penguin, 1985.

Eliot, T. S. "Kipling Redivivus." *Athanaeum*, May 9, 1919: 297–298.

———. *Selected Prose*. Ed. Frank Kermode. London: Faber and Faber, 1975.

———. *The Waste Land: A Facsimile and Transcript of the Original Drafts Including the Annotations of Ezra Pound*. New York: Harcourt Brace Jovanovich, 1971.

Elkins, Caroline. *Imperial Reckoning: The Untold Story of Britain's Gulag in Kenya*. New York: Henry Holt, 2005.

Ellison, Ralph. *The Collected Essays*. Ed. John F. Callahan. New York: Modern Library, 2003.

———. *Conversations with Ralph Ellison*. Jackson: University Press of Mississippi, 1995.

Ellmann, Richard. *James Joyce*. Rev. ed. Oxford: Oxford University Press, 1982.

Empson, William. *Using Biography*. Cambridge, MA: Harvard University Press, 1984.

Emre, Merve. "Jamesian Institutions." *American Literary History* 27.2 (2015): 226–255.

"English Department Faculty and Wives." *Faulkner at Virginia*. University of Virginia. May 13, 1957. Web. December 5, 2010. http://faulkner.lib.virginia.edu/display/wfaudio13.

Erdinast-Vulcan, Daphna. *Joseph Conrad and the Modern Temper*. Oxford: Clarendon Press, 1991.

Esty, Jed. *A Shrinking Island: Modernism and National Culture in England*. Princeton, NJ: Princeton University Press, 2004.

———. *Unseasonable Youth: Modernism, Colonialism, and the Fiction of Development*. Oxford: Oxford University Press, 2012.

Felman, Shoshana. "Turning the Screw of Interpretation." *Yale French Studies* 55–56 (1977): 94–207.

Felski, Rita. "After Suspicion." *Profession* 2009: 28–35.

———. "'Context Stinks!'" *New Literary History* 42.4 (Autumn 2011): 573–591.

———. "Introduction." *New Literary History* 42.2 (2011): v–ix.

———. *The Limits of Critique*. Chicago: University of Chicago Press, 2015.

———. *The Uses of Literature*. Malden: Blackwell, 2008.

Fielding, Henry. *The History of Tom Jones: A Foundling*. Ed. Martin C. Battestin and Fredson Bowers. Middletown, CT: Wesleyan University Press, 1975.

Fish, Stanley. *Self-Consuming Artifacts: The Experience of Seventeenth-Century Literature*. Berkeley: University of California Press, 1992.

Fitzgerald, F. Scott. *Tender Is the Night*. New York: Scribner, 1982.

Flaubert, Gustave. *Correspondence*. Volume II. Ed. Jean Bruneau. Paris: Gallimard, 1980.

Ford, Ford Madox. *The Good Soldier: A Tale of Passion*. New York: Vintage International, 1989.

———. *Joseph Conrad: A Personal Remembrance*. London: Duckworth, 1924.

Frank, Joseph. *The Idea of Spatial Form*. New Brunswick, NJ: Rutgers University Press, 1991.

———. "Spatial Form in Modern Literature: An Essay in Three Parts, Part III." *Sewanee Review* 53.4 (Autumn 1945): 643–653.

Freed-Thall, Hannah. *Spoiled Distinctions: Aesthetics and the Ordinary in French Modernism*. New York: Oxford, 2015.

Friedman, Susan Stanford. "Planetarity: Musing Modernist Studies." *Modernism/Modernity* 17.3 (September 2010): 471–499.

Gallagher, Catherine. "Formalism and Time." *Modern Language Quarterly* 61.1 (March 2000): 229–251.

———. *Nobody's Story: The Vanishing Acts of Women Writers in the Marketplace, 1670–1820*. Berkeley: University of California Press, 1994.

———. "The Rise of Fictionality." *The Novel*. Volume I: *History, Geography, and Culture*. Ed. Franco Moretti. Princeton, NJ: Princeton University Press, 2006. 336–363.

Freedman, Jonathan. *Professions of Taste: Henry James, British Aestheticism, and Commodity Culture*. Stanford, CA: Stanford University Press, 1990.

Garber, Marjorie, Beatrice Hanssen, and Rebecca L. Walkovitz, eds. *The Turn to Ethics*. New York: Routledge, 2000.

Genter, Robert. *Late Modernism: Art, Culture, and Politics in Cold War America*. Philadelphia: University of Pennsylvania Press, 2010.

Gikandi, Simon. "The Fantasy of the Library." *PMLA* 128.1 (January 2013): 9–20.

———. *Ngũgĩ wa Thiong'o*. Cambridge: Cambridge University Press, 2000.

———. "Realism, Romance, and the Problem of African Literary History." *Modern Language Quarterly* 73.3 (September 2012): 309–328.

Glassman, Steve. "The Influence of Conrad's *Chance* on *Absalom, Absalom!*" *Notes on Mississippi Writers* 15.1 (1983): 1–4.

Glavey, Brian. "Dazzling Estrangement: Modernism, Queer Ekphrasis, and the Spatial Form of *Nightwood*." *PMLA* 124.3 (May 2009): 749–763.

Godden, Richard. *William Faulkner: An Economy of Complex Words*. Princeton, NJ: Princeton University Press, 2007.

Goetz, William R. *Henry James and the Darkest Abyss of Romance*. Baton Rouge: Louisiana State University Press, 1986.

Goldstein, Rebecca. "The Ancient Quarrel: Philosophy and Literature, Part II." Tanner Lectures on Human Values. Whitney Humanities Center, New Haven. March 24, 2011.

Goldstone, Andrew. *Fictions of Autonomy: Modernism from Wilde to de Man*. Oxford: Oxford University Press, 2012.

Goode, Mike. "The Joy of Looking: What Blake's Pictures Want." *Representations* 119.1 (Summer 2012): 1–36.

Goodman, Paul. "Not Enough of a World to Grow In." *New York Times Book Review*, June 24, 1962: 5.

Gordon, Lyndall. *A Private Life of Henry James: Two Women and His Art*. New York: Norton, 1999.

Greaney, Michael. *Conrad, Language, and Narrative*. Cambridge: Cambridge University Press, 2002.

Guerard, Albert J. *Conrad the Novelist*. New York: Atheneum, 1970.

Guillory, John. "Genesis of the Media Concept." *Critical Inquiry* 36.2 (Winter 2010): 321–362.

Gwynn, Frederick L., and Joseph L. Blotner, eds. *Faulkner in the University*. Charlottesville: University Press of Virginia, 1959.

Hadley, Tessa. *Henry James and the Imagination of Pleasure*. Cambridge: Cambridge University Press, 2002.

Hamner, Robert D. *Joseph Conrad: Third World Perspectives*. Washington, DC: Three Continents Press, 1990.

Hayot, Eric. *On Literary Worlds*. New York: Oxford University Press, 2012.

Henthorne, Tom. *Conrad's Trojan Horses: Imperialism, Hybridity, and the Postcolonial Aesthetic*. Lubbock: Texas Tech University Press, 2008.

Herbert, Christopher. *Victorian Relativity: Radical Thought and Scientific Discovery*. Chicago: University of Chicago Press, 2001.

Hofmeyr, Isabel. *The Portable Bunyan: A Transnational History of "The Pilgrim's Progress"*. Princeton, NJ: Princeton University Press, 2004.

Homer. *The Iliad*. Trans. Robert Fagles. New York: Viking, 1990.

Horne, Philip. "The Lessons of Flaubert: James and *L'Éducation sentimentale*." *Yearbook of English Studies* 26 (1996): 154–162.

Huyssen, Andreas. *After the Great Divide: Modernism, Mass Culture, Postmodernism*. Bloomington: Indiana University Press, 1986.

Iser, Wolfgang. *The Implied Reader: Patterns of Communication in Prose Fiction from Bunyan to Beckett*. Baltimore: Johns Hopkins University Press, 1974.

James, David, ed. *The Legacies of Modernism: Historicising Postwar and Contemporary Fiction*. Cambridge: Cambridge University Press, 2012.

———. *Modernist Futures: Innovation and Inheritance in the Contemporary Novel*. Cambridge: Cambridge University Press, 2012.

James, David, and Urmila Seshagiri. "Metamodernism." *PMLA* 129.1 (2014): 87–100.

James Baldwin Collection. The Schomburg Center for Research in Black Culture. New York.

James Baldwin Papers. The Schomburg Center for Research in Black Culture. New York.

Jameson, Fredric. *The Antinomies of Realism*. London: Verso, 2015.

———. *The Political Unconscious: Narrative as a Socially Symbolic Act*. Ithaca, NY: Cornell University Press, 1981.

———. *Postmodernism: or, The Cultural Logic of Late Capitalism*. Durham, NC: Duke University Press, 1991.

Jauss, Hans Robert. *Toward an Aesthetic of Reception*. Trans. Timothy Bahti. Minneapolis: University of Minnesota Press, 1982.

Jean-Aubry, G. *Joseph Conrad: Life and Letters*. 2 vols. Garden City: Doubleday, 1927.

Jones, Edward P. *The Known World: A Novel*. New York: Amistad, 2003.

Joyce, James. *Ulysses: The Corrected Text*. Ed. Hans Walter Gabler. New York: Vintage, 1986.

Kalliney, Peter J. *Commonwealth of Letters: British Literary Culture and the Emergence of Postcolonial Aesthetics*. New York: Oxford University Press, 2013.

Kaplan, Carola M., Peter Mallios, and Andrea White, eds. *Conrad in the Twenty-First Century: Contemporary Approaches and Perspectives*. New York: Routledge, 2005.

Kartiganer, Donald M. *The Fragile Thread: The Meaning of Form in Faulkner's Novels*. Amherst: University of Massachusetts Press, 1979.

Kaye, Peter. *Dostoevsky and English Modernism, 1900–1930*. New York: Cambridge University Press, 1999.

Kent, Jessica A. "Speaking in James: Cynthia Ozick's 'Dictation' and 'The Jolly Corner.'" *Henry James Review* 26 (2015): 101–116.

Ker, David I. *The African Novel and the Modernist Tradition*. New York: Peter Lang, 1997.

Kesey, Ken. *One Flew Over the Cuckoo's Nest*. Ed. John Clark Pratt. New York: Viking Press, 1973.

———. *Sometimes a Great Notion*. New York: Penguin, 2006.

"Kikuyu." *Times Literary Supplement* (London), May 18, 1967: 417.

Kittler, Friedrich A. *Gramophone, Film, Typewriter*. Trans. Geoffrey Winthrop-Young and Michael Wutz. Stanford, CA: Stanford University Press, 1999.

Koc, Barbara. "Joseph Conrad's Inspirations in Faulkner." *American Studies* 16 (1998): 49–56.

Kolmerton, Carol A., Stephen M. Ross, and Judith Bryant Wittenberg, eds. *Unflinching Gaze: Morrison and Faulkner Re-envisioned*. Oxford: University Press of Mississippi, 1997.

Krook-Gilead, Dorothea. *The Ordeal of Consciousness in Henry James*. Cambridge: Cambridge University Press, 1967.

Kurnick, David. *Empty Houses: Theatrical Failure and the Novel*. Princeton, NJ: Princeton University Press, 2012.

Kventsel, Anna. *Decadence in the Late Novels of Henry James*. New York: Palgrave Macmillan, 2007.

Landy, Joshua. *How to Do Things with Fictions*. Oxford: Oxford University Press, 2012.

Larson, Jil. *Ethics and Narrative in the English Novel, 1880–1914*. Cambridge: Cambridge University Press, 2001.

Latour, Bruno. "Why Has Critique Run Out of Steam? From Matters of Fact to Matters of Concern." *Critical Inquiry* 30.2 (Winter 2004): 225–248.

Lazarus, Neil. *The Postcolonial Unconscious*. Cambridge: Cambridge University Press, 2011.

Leavis, F. R. *The Great Tradition*. New York: New York University Press, 1973.

Lecourt, Sebastian. "Idylls of the Buddh': Buddhist Modernism and Victorian Poetics in Colonial Ceylon." *PMLA* 131.3 (2016): 668–685.

Leeming, David Adams. "An Interview with James Baldwin on Henry James." *Henry James Review* 8.1 (Fall 1986): 47–56.

———. *James Baldwin: A Biography*. New York: Knopf, 1994.

Levenson, Michael H. *A Genealogy of Modernism: A Study of English Literary Doctrine 1908–1922*. Cambridge: Cambridge University Press, 1984.

———. *Modernism and the Fate of Individuality: Character and Novelistic Form from Conrad to Woolf*. Cambridge: Cambridge University Press, 1991.

Levine, Caroline. *Forms: Whole, Rhythm, Hierarchy, Network*. Princeton, NJ: Princeton University Press, 2015.

Lothe, Jakob. *Conrad's Narrative Method*. Oxford: Clarendon Press, 1989.

Lubbock, Percy. *The Craft of Fiction*. New York: Jonathan Cape and Harrison Smith, 1929.

Lukács, Georg. "Realism in the Balance." *Aesthetics and Politics*. London: Verso, 2007. 28–59.

———. *The Theory of the Novel*. Trans. Anna Bostock. Cambridge, MA: MIT Press, 1971.

———. *Writer and Critic and Other Essays*. Ed. and trans. Arthur D. Kahn. New York: Grosset & Dunlap, 1970.

Lynch, Deidre Shauna. *The Economy of Character: Novels, Market Culture, and the Business of Inner Meaning*. Chicago: University of Chicago Press, 1998.

———. *Loving Literature: A Cultural History*. Chicago: University of Chicago Press, 2015.

Mabanckou, Alain. *Letter to Jimmy*. Trans. Sara Meli Ansari. Berkeley, CA: Soft Skull Press, 2014.

———. *Lettre à Jimmy*. Paris: Fayard, 2007.

MacFarlane, Robert. *Original Copy: Plagiarism and Originality in Nineteenth-Century Literature*. Oxford: Oxford University Press, 2007.

Mallios, Peter Lancelot. *Our Conrad: Constituting American Modernity*. Stanford, CA: Stanford University Press, 2010.

Mantel, Hilary. *Wolf Hall*. New York: Picador, 2009.

Mao, Douglas, and Rebecca L. Walkowitz, eds. *Bad Modernisms*. Durham, NC: Duke University Press, 2006.

———. "The New Modernist Studies." *PMLA* 123.3 (May 2008): 737–748.

Marlowe, Christopher. *The Complete Plays*. Ed. Mark Thornton Burnett. London: Dent, 1999.

Martin, Theodore. "Repetition with Indifference: Impersonation, Anachronism, and Literary History." Paper presented at Modernist Studies Association Conference, Buffalo, NY, 2011.

Matthiessen, F. O. *Henry James: The Major Phase*. London: Oxford University Press, 1944.

Matz, Jesse. *Lasting Impressions: The Legacies of Modernism*. New York: Columbia, 2016.

———. *Literary Impressionism and Modernist Aesthetics*. Cambridge: Cambridge University Press, 2001.

———. "Pseudo-impressionism?" *The Legacies of Modernism: Historicising Postwar and Contemporary Fiction*. Ed. David James. Cambridge: Cambridge University Press, 2012. 114–132.

McFarlane, Scott. *The Hippie Narrative: A Literary Perspective on the Counterculture*. Jefferson: McFarland, 2007.

McGann, Jerome J. *The Romantic Ideology: A Critical Investigation*. Chicago: University of Chicago Press, 1985.

McGurl, Mark. *The Novel Art: Elevations of American Fiction after Henry James*. Princeton, NJ: Princeton University Press, 2001.

———. *The Program Era: Postwar Fiction and the Rise of Creative Writing*. Cambridge, MA: Harvard University Press, 2009.

McKeon, Michael. *The Origins of the English Novel, 1600–1740*. Baltimore: Johns Hopkins University Press, 1987.

McWhirter, David. *Desire and Love in Henry James: A Study of the Late Novels*. Cambridge: Cambridge University Press, 1989.

Mead, Rebecca. "*Middlemarch* and Me: What George Eliot Teaches Us." *New Yorker*, February 14, 2011: 76–83.

Meisel, Perry. *The Myth of the Modern: A Study in British Literature and Criticism after 1850.* New Haven: Yale University Press, 1987.

Meissner, Collin. *Henry James and the Language of Experience.* Cambridge: Cambridge University Press, 1999.

Mengiste, Maaza. Interview with Aaron Bady. *Post45.* Web. October 17, 2014. http://post45. research.yale.edu/2014/10/interview-maaza-mengiste/.

Meriwether, James B. "A Prefatory Note by Faulkner for the Compson Appendix." *American Literature* 43.2 (May 1971): 281–284.

Meyers, Jeffrey. "Conrad's Influence on Modern Writers." *Twentieth Century Literature* 26.2 (Summer 1990): 186–206.

Miller, J. Hillis. *Fiction and Repetition: Seven English Novels.* Cambridge, MA: Harvard University Press, 1982.

———. "Foreword." In Kaplan, Carola M., Peter Mallios, and Andrea White, eds. *Conrad in the Twenty-First Century: Contemporary Approaches and Perspectives.* New York: Routledge, 2005. 1–14.

Miller, Tyrus. *Late Modernism: Politics, Fiction, and the Arts between the World Wars.* Berkeley: University of California Press, 1999.

Milton, John. *Paradise Lost.* Ed. Alastair Fowler. 2nd ed. Harlow: Longman, 1998.

Minter, David. *Faulkner's Questioning Narratives: Fiction of His Major Phase, 1929–42.* Urbana: University of Illinois Press, 2001.

Moreland, Richard C. *Faulkner and Modernism: Rereading and Rewriting.* Madison: University of Wisconsin Press, 1990.

Morrison, Toni. *Jazz.* New York: Viking, 2004.

———. *Playing in the Dark: Whiteness and the Literary Imagination.* New York: Vintage, 1993.

———. *Toni Morrison: Conversations.* Ed. Carolyn C. Denard. Jackson: University Press of Mississippi, 2008.

Moses, Omri. *Out of Character: Modernism, Vitalism, Psychic Life.* Stanford, CA: Stanford University Press, 2014.

Murphet, Julian. "The Mole and the Multiple: A Chiasmus of Character." *New Literary History* 42.2 (Spring 2011): 255–276.

Murray, Gilbert. *Five Stages of Greek Religion.* New York: Columbia University Press, 1925.

Mwangi, Evan Maina. *Africa Writes Back to Self: Metafiction, Gender, Sexuality.* Albany: SUNY Press, 2009.

Nazareth, Peter. *Literature and Society in Modern Africa.* Nairobi: Kenya Literature Bureau, 1972.

———. "Out of Darkness: Conrad and Other Third World Writers." In Hamner, 217–231.

———. "Teaching *A Grain of Wheat* as a Dialogue with Conrad." *Approaches to Teaching the Works of Ngũgĩ wa Thiong'o.* Ed. Oliver Lovesey. New York: Modern Language Association, 2012. 165–170.

Nettels, Elsa. *James and Conrad.* Athens: University of Georgia Press, 1977.

Neuman, Shirley. "*Heart of Darkness*, Virginia Woolf, and the Specter of Domination." *Virginia Woolf: New Critical Essays.* Ed. Patricia Clements and Isobel Grundy. Totowa, NJ: Barnes, 1983. 57–76.

Ngũgĩ wa Thiong'o. *Birth of a Dream Weaver: A Writer's Awakening.* New York: New Press, 2016.

———. *Decolonising the Mind: The Politics of Language in African Literature*. London: Heinemann, 1986.

———. *Devil on the Cross*. Trans. Ngũgĩ. Oxford: Heinemann, 1982.

———. *Globalectics: Theory and the Politics of Knowing*. New York: Columbia University Press, 2012.

———. *A Grain of Wheat*. Rev. ed. Oxford: Heinemann, 1986.

———. *Homecoming: Essays on African and Caribbean Literature, Culture and Politics*. New York: Lawrence Hill, 1973.

———. *Moving the Centre: The Struggle for Cultural Freedoms*. Oxford: Heinemann, 1993.

———. *Petals of Blood*. New York: Penguin, 2005.

———. *Wizard of the Crow*. Trans. Ngũgĩ. New York: Pantheon Books, 2006.

———. *Writers in Politics*. London: Heinemann, 1981.

Nicholls, Peter. *Modernisms: A Literary Guide*. London: Macmillan, 1995.

Nietzsche, Friedrich. *The Will to Power*. Trans. Walter Kaufman and R. J. Hollingdale. Ed. Walter Kaufman. New York: Random House, 1967.

North, Joseph. *Literary Criticism: A Concise Political History*. Cambridge, MA: Harvard University Press, 2017.

Nussbaum, Martha. *Love's Knowledge: Essays on Philosophy and Literature*. Oxford: Oxford University Press, 1992.

Ohi, Kevin. "The Beast's Storied End." *Henry James Review* 33.1 (Winter 2012): 1–16.

———. *Henry James and the Queerness of Style*. Minneapolis: University of Minnesota Press, 2011.

Olson, Liesl. *Modernism and the Ordinary*. Oxford: Oxford University Press, 2009.

Osundare, Niyi. *The Word Is an Egg*. Ibadan, Nigeria: Kraft Books, 2000.

Ozick, Cynthia. *Dictation: A Quartet*. Boston: Houghton Mifflin, 2008.

———. *Foreign Bodies*. Boston: Houghton Mifflin, 2011.

———. "An (Unfortunate) Interview with Henry James." *Threepenny Review* 100 (Winter 2005): 16–17.

Perry, Paul. *On the Bus: The Complete Guide to the Legendary Trip of Ken Kesey and the Merry Pranksters and the Birth of the Counterculture*. New York: Thunder's Mouth Press, 1990.

Peters, John G. *Conrad and Impressionism*. Cambridge: Cambridge University Press, 2001.

Peterson, Dale. *Up from Bondage: The Literatures of Russian and African American Soul*. Durham, NC: Duke University Press, 2000.

Phillips, Siobhan. *The Poetics of the Everyday: Creative Repetition in Modern American Verse*. New York: Columbia University Press, 2010.

Pippin, Robert B. *Henry James and Modern Moral Life*. Cambridge: Cambridge University Press, 2000.

Plimpton, George, ed. *Beat Writers at Work*. New York: Random House, 1999.

Poirier, Richard. *The Comic Sense of Henry James: A Study of the Early Novels*. New York: Oxford University Press, 1960.

———. *Poetry and Pragmatism*. Cambridge, MA: Harvard University Press, 1992.

Posnock, Ross. *Color and Culture: Black Writers and the Making of the Modern Intellectual*. Cambridge, MA: Harvard University Press, 1998.

Puchner, Martin. "The Aftershocks of *Blast*: Manifestos, Satire, and the Rear-Guard of Modernism." In Mao and Walkowitz, 44–67.

Reed, Anthony. *Freedom Time: The Poetics and Politics of Black Experimental Writing.* Baltimore: Johns Hopkins University Press, 2014.

Reesman, Jeanne Campbell. *American Designs: The Late Novels of James and Faulkner.* Philadelphia: University of Pennsylvania Press, 1991.

Richardson, Brian. "Conrad and Posthumanist Narration: Fabricating Class and Consciousness Onboard the *Narcissus.*" In Kaplan et al., 213–222.

Richardson, Samuel. *Clarissa, or, The History of a Young Lady.* Ed. Angus Ross. London: Penguin, 1985.

Ricks, Christopher. *Allusion to the Poets.* Oxford: Oxford University Press, 2002.

———. *Tennyson.* 2nd ed. Berkeley: University of California Press, 1989.

Rivkin, Julie. *False Positions: The Representational Logics of Henry James's Fiction.* Stanford, CA: Stanford University Press, 1996.

Roach, Joseph. *Cities of the Dead: Circum-Atlantic Performance.* New York: Columbia University Press, 1996.

Robert Park Mills Papers. Harry Ransom Center, Austin, TX.

Rosen, Jeremy. *Minor Characters Have Their Day: Genre and the Contemporary Literary Marketplace.* New York: Columbia University Press, 2016.

Rosenquist, Rod. *Modernism, the Market and the Institution of the New.* Cambridge: Cambridge University Press, 2009.

Ross, Stephen M. "Conrad's Influence on Faulkner's *Absalom, Absalom!*" *Studies in American Fiction* 2:2 (Autumn 1974): 199–209.

———. *Fiction's Inexhaustible Voice: Speech and Writing in Faulkner.* Athens: University of Georgia Press, 1989.

Rowe, John Carlos. *The Other Henry James.* Durham, NC: Duke University Press, 1998.

Said, Edward W. *Culture and Imperialism.* New York: Vintage, 1994.

———. *Orientalism.* New York: Vintage Books, 1979; repr. 1994.

Saint-Amour, Paul K. *Tense Future: Modernism, Total War, Encyclopedic Form.* Oxford: Oxford University Press, 2015.

Saldívar, Ramón. "Faulkner and the World Culture of the Global South." *Fifty Years after Faulkner.* Ed. Jay Watson and Ann J. Abadie. Jackson: University Press of Mississippi, 2016. 3–19.

Salmon, Richard. *Henry James and the Culture of Publicity.* Cambridge: Cambridge University Press, 1997.

Sander, Reinhard, and Bernth Lindfors, eds. *Ngũgĩ wa Thiong'o Speaks: Interviews with the Kenyan Writer.* Trenton, NJ: Africa World Press, 2006.

Sartre, Jean-Paul. "Time in Faulkner: *The Sound and the Fury.*" *William Faulkner: Three Decades of Criticism.* Ed. Frederick J. Hoffman and Olga W. Vickery. New York: Harcourt, Brace & World, 1963. 225–232.

Sarvan, C. Ponnuthurai. "Under African Eyes." In Hamner, 153–160.

Scarry, Elaine. *Dreaming by the Book.* Princeton, NJ: Princeton University Press, 1999.

Schoenbach, Lisi. *Pragmatic Modernism.* Oxford: Oxford University Press, 2012.

Schwartz, Lawrence H. *Creating Faulkner's Reputation: The Politics of Modern Literary Criticism.* Knoxville: University of Tennessee Press, 1988.

Sedgwick, Eve Kosofsky. *Tendencies*. Durham: Duke University Press, 1993.

———. *Touching Feeling: Affect, Pedagogy, Performativity*. Durham, NC: Duke University Press, 2003.

Seltzer, Mark. *Henry James and the Art of Power*. Ithaca, NY: Cornell University Press, 1984.

Sewlall, Harry. "Writing from the Periphery: The Case of Ngugi and Conrad." *English in Africa* 30.1 (May 2003): 55–69.

Sicherman, Carol. "Ngũgĩ's British Education." *Ngũgĩ wa Thiong'o: Texts and Contexts*. Ed. Charles Cantalupo. Trenton, NJ: Africa World Press, 1995.

———. "Ngũgĩ's Colonial Education: 'The Subversion . . . of the African *Mind*.'" *Critical Essays on Ngũgĩ wa Thiong'o*. Ed. Peter Nazarath. New York: Twayne, 2000. 17–47.

———. "Ngũgĩ wa Thiong'o and the Writing of Kenyan History." *Critical Essays on Ngũgĩ wa Thiong'o*. Ed. Peter Nazarath. New York: Twayne, 2000. 299–320.

Sidney, Sir Philip. *The Oxford Authors: Sir Philip Sidney*. Ed. Katherine Duncan-Jones. Oxford: Oxford University Press, 1989.

Simmons, Allan H., John G. Peters, and J. H. Stape, eds. *Joseph Conrad: Contemporary Reviews*. Volume I. Cambridge: Cambridge University Press, 2012.

Sinclair, May. "The Novels of Dorothy Richardson." *The Gender of Modernism: A Critical Anthology*. Ed. Bonnie Kime Scott. Bloomington: Indiana University Press, 1990. 442–448.

Siraganian, Lisa. *Modernism's Other Work: The Art Object's Political Life*. Oxford: Oxford University Press, 2012.

Smith, Zadie. *Changing My Mind: Occasional Essays*. New York: Penguin, 2009.

Solomon, Eric. "Joseph Conrad, William Faulkner, and the Nobel Prize Speech." *Notes and Queries* 14.7 (July 1967): 247–248.

Sontag, Susan. *Against Interpretation: And Other Essays*. New York: Picador, 2001.

Sorensen, Eli Park. *Postcolonial Studies and the Literary: Theory, Interpretation and the Novel*. Houndmills: Palgrave Macmillan, 2010.

Spivak, Gayatri Chakravorty. *Other Asias*. Oxford: Blackwell, 2008.

———. *The Post-colonial Critic: Interviews, Strategies, Dialogues*. Ed. Sarah Harasym. New York: Routledge, 1990.

Stallworthy, Jon. *Wilfred Owen*. London: Oxford University Press and Chatto and Windus, 1974.

Stone, Robert. "The Prince of Possibility." *New Yorker*, June 14, 2004: 70–89.

Strauss, Harold. "Mr. Faulkner Is Ambushed in Words." *New York Times Book Review*, November 1, 1936: 7.

Tanner, Tony. *City of Words: American Fiction, 1950–1970*. London: Jonathan Cape, 1971.

"The Strength of One." *Time*, July 24, 1964.

"Terror in Kenya." *Times Literary Supplement* (London), October 26, 1962: 819.

Thucydides. *History of the Peloponnesian War*. Trans. Rex Warner. Harmondsworth: Penguin,1954.

———. *The Landmark Thucydides: A Comprehensive Guide to "The Peloponnesian War"*. Ed. Robert B. Strassler. New York: Simon & Schuster, 1998.

Todorov, Tzvetan. *The Poetics of Prose*. Trans. Richard Howard. Ithaca, NY: Cornell University Press, 1977.

Tóibín, Colm. "The Henry James of Harlem: James Baldwin's Struggles." *The Guardian* (London), September 14, 2001.

———. *The Master: A Novel*. New York: Scribner, 2004.

Turner, Jack. *Awakening to Race: Individualism and Social Consciousness in America*. Chicago: University of Chicago Press, 2012.

Urgo, Joseph R. and Noel Polk. *Reading Faulkner: "Absalom, Absalom!"*. Jackson: University Press of Mississippi, 2010.

Vásquez, Juan Gabriel. *The Secret History of Costaguana*. Trans. Anne McLean. London: Bloomsbury, 2010.

Vermeule, Blakey. *Why Do We Care about Literary Characters?* Baltimore: Johns Hopkins University Press, 2010.

Walkowitz, Rebecca L. *Cosmopolitan Style: Modernism beyond the Nation*. New York: Columbia University Press, 2007.

Wall, Stephen. "True to the National Life." *The Observer* (London), March 26, 1967: 22.

Warner, Michael. "Uncritical Reading." *Polemic: Critical or Uncritical*. Ed. Jane Gallop. New York: Routledge, 2004. 13–38.

Warren, Kenneth L. *Black and White Strangers: Race and American Literary Realism*. Chicago: University of Chicago Press, 1993.

Watt, Ian. *Conrad in the Nineteenth Century*. Berkeley: University of California Press, 1979.

———. "Conrad's Preface to *The Nigger of the 'Narcissus.'*" *Novel: A Forum on Fiction* 7.2 (Winter 1974): 101–115.

———. *Essays on Conrad*. Cambridge: Cambridge University Press, 2000.

———. *The Rise of the Novel: Studies in Defoe, Richardson, and Fielding*. London: Chatto & Windus, 1960.

Wegelin, Christof. "'Endure' and 'Prevail': Faulkner's Modification of Conrad." *Notes and Queries* 14.7 (July 1967): 375–376.

Weinstein, Philip M. *Henry James and the Requirements of the Imagination*. Cambridge, MA: Harvard University Press, 1971.

———. *Unknowing: The Work of Modernist Fiction*. Ithaca, NY: Cornell University Press, 2005.

———. *What Else but Love? The Ordeal of Race in Faulkner and Morrison*. New York: Columbia University Press, 1996.

Williams, Jeffrey J. "The New Modesty in Literary Criticism." *Chronicle of Higher Education*, January 5, 2015. Web.

Wofford, Chloe Ardelia. *Virginia Woolf's and William Faulkner's Treatment of the Alienated*. Diss., Cornell University, 1955.

Wolfe, Tom. *The Electric Kool-Aid Acid Test*. New York: Bantam Books, 1969.

Wollaeger, Mark A. *Joseph Conrad and the Fictions of Skepticism*. Stanford, CA: Stanford University Press, 1990.

———. "The Woolfs in the Jungle: Intertextuality, Sexuality, and the Emergence of Female Modernism in *The Voyage Out, The Village in the Jungle*, and *Heart of Darkness*." *MLQ: Modern Language Quarterly* 63.1 (2003): 33–69.

Woloch, Alex. *The One vs. the Many: Minor Characters and the Space of the Protagonist in the Novel*. Princeton, NJ: Princeton University, 2003.

Wood, Michael. "Distraction Theory: How to Read While Thinking of Something Else." *Michigan Quarterly Review* 48.4 (Fall 2009): 577–588.

Wyatt, David. *Secret Histories: Reading Twentieth-Century American Literature.* Baltimore: Johns Hopkins University Press, 2010.

Yardley, Jonathan. "Joseph Conrad's Dark 'Victory.'" *Washington Post,* May 9, 2005. Web. March 1, 2011. http://www.washingtonpost.com/wp-dyn/content/article/2005/05/08/AR2005050800989.html.

Yeazell, Ruth Bernard. *Language and Knowledge in the Late Novels of Henry James.* Chicago: University of Chicago Press, 1976.

Young, Thomas Daniel, ed. *Conversations with Malcolm Cowley.* Oxford: University Press of Mississippi, 1986.

Index

Made in the USA
Coppell, TX
09 November 2021

65446611R00160